The Journal of Charlotte Forten
A Free Negro in the Slave Era

The Journal of Charlotte Forten

A Free Negro in the Slave Era

*Edited, with an Introduction and Notes,
by Ray Allen Billington*

W · W · NORTON & COMPANY

New York · London

Printed in the United States of America

All Rights Reserved

First published as a Norton paperback 1981

Library of Congress Cataloging in Publication Data
Forten, Charlotte L
  The journal of Charlotte Forten.
  Includes bibliographical references and index.
  1. Forten, Charlotte L. 2. Afro-American
teachers—United States—Biography. I. Billington,
Ray Allen, 1903–
LA2317.F67A33   1981   371.1′0092′4 [B]   80–20834

ISBN 0-393-00046-X

W. W. Norton & Company, Inc., 500 Fifth Avenue, New York, N.Y. 10110
W. W. Norton & Company Ltd 10 Coptic Street, London, WC1A 1PU

4 5 6 7 8 9 0

Contents

Introduction

The Journal of Charlotte L. Forten

Introduction

1. Charlotte L. Forten: *Philadelphia and Salem*

CHARLOTTE L. FORTEN was a delicate young woman of sixteen when in 1854 she left her native Philadelphia to launch the educational and teaching career described in the following *Journal*. Her interests were those of other intelligent girls reared in that calm Quaker city during its antebellum days; she read widely and with a catholic taste that embraced everything from the classics to sentimental poetry, attended lectures avidly, listened rapturously to the musical recitals of wandering artists, gazed worshipfully on the steel engravings that passed for art among unsophisticated Americans, and took mild pleasure in the ailments that were the stock in trade of all well-bred females during the Victorian era. Yet one thing distinguished Charlotte Forten from other Philadelphia belles. She was a Negro, destined to endure the constant insults that were the lot of persons of color in pre-Civil-War America.

That no other influence was so strong in shaping Charlotte Forten's thoughts is amply revealed in the *Journal* that follows. When she began keeping that record, on a warm May morning in 1854, she had just arrived in Salem, Massachusetts, from Philadelphia. She was then, if we may believe her contemporaries, a handsome girl, delicate, slender, and with a finely chiseled countenance which revealed in the lightness of the skin a trace of white blood among her ancestors. All who knew her commented on the alert intelligence of her face and on the frailty of her graceful body. Indeed, as the pages of her *Journal* disclose, she was destined to long periods when "lung fever" forced her to forsake her studies and teaching. But on that May morning illness was furthest from her thoughts. Ahead lay the adventure of learning, and that was exciting enough to justify the diary she was beginning.

Miss Forten could not know, as she traced the opening words in a fine, bold hand, that she was starting a uniquely human document. Nor did her first entry reveal the unusual nature of the entries to follow: "A wish to record the passing events of my life, which, even if quite unimportant to others, naturally possess great interest to myself, and of which it will be pleasant to have some remembrance, has induced me to commence this journal." This, even in its stilted phrases, might have launched any one of the thousands of diaries kept by young women of that era. Yet the *Journal* that unfolded during the next decade bore no resemblance to any other. Instead it served as a moving record of the reactions of a sensitive young Negro to the white world about her.

For her race was always uppermost in Charlotte Forten's thoughts. The color of her skin determined her attitude toward her fellow humans, toward her country, and toward her God. From the accident of pigmentation stemmed even her driving ambition. She *must* excel among the students of the Salem grammar school in which she first enrolled or the normal school where she completed her education. She *must* read constantly; tucked among the pages of her manuscript *Journal* was a yellowed paper listing more than one hundred books completed in one year. She *must* master French, German, and Latin in addition to her regular school work. Every lesson learned well was a triumph not only for herself but for the oppressed Negro people of mid-century America. By excelling in all things she could help convince a hostile world that Negroes were as capable of self-improvement as whites.

That this was the source of her ambition was abundantly revealed in Miss Forten's *Journal*. "Would that there were far more intelligent colored people!" she wrote at one time. "And yet we could hardly expect more of those, who have so many unsurmountable difficulties to contend with. But despite them all let our motto still be 'Excelsior' and we cannot fail to make some improvement. At times I feel it almost impossible not to despond entirely of there ever being a better, brighter day for us. None but those who experience it can know what it is—this constant, galling sense of cruel injustice and wrong. I cannot help feeling it very often,—it intrudes upon my happiest moments, and spreads a dark, deep gloom over everything." Miss Forten was plunged into equal despair whenever a Negro failed to excel in competition with whites. On one occasion she attended a "reading" by Mary F. Webb, who enjoyed a minor reputation for her rendition of Shakespeare's plays and verse. "I was not very much pleased," Charlotte Forten wrote sadly. "I wish colored persons would not attempt to do anything of the kind unless they can compare favorably with others.—But I know that I should not assume to criticize; and most sincerely hope if she has talent, it may be cultivated, —and that she may succeed in her vocation—reflecting credit upon herself and her race."

Every page of Charlotte Forten's *Journal* reflected her determination to excel in all things. She was vexed, on the morning she began her diary, that the sun had risen before her, even though she had awakened before five o'clock. A few months later, as she looked back over her first seventeen years on the occasion of a birthday, she asked herself: "Have I improved them as I should have done?" Overcritical as always, she felt that she had not. "I feel grieved and ashamed to think how very little I know to what I should know of what is really good and useful. May this knowledge of my *want* of knowledge be to me a fresh incentive to more earnest, thoughtful action, more persevering study." Little wonder, in view of this attitude, that progress seemed alarmingly slow. Charlotte Forten might impress others with the catholicity of her literary tastes or with her rich knowledge of the past, but she was always more conscious of the tasks remaining than of those accomplished. Once more in a reflective mood, on her twentieth birthday, she wrote: "Very, very fast the years are passing away,—and I,— Oh! how little am I improving them. . . . Twenty years I have lived. I shall *not* live twenty years more,—I feel it. I believe I have but few years to live.—Then I *must,* I *will* improve.—I will pray for strength to keep this resolution;—I have broken so many. *This* I *must* keep."

If ambition was one of Miss Forten's virtues, modesty was another. "When I read of the great and gifted ones of the earth," she confided in her *Journal,* "I feel more deeply my own ignorance and inefficiency.—How very little after the most diligent and persevering study can I hope to resemble them." Later triumphs did not decrease her humility. Thus she could not believe that her poetic efforts were worthy of the name, despite the publication of her verses in magazines and newspapers. "How often," she complained, "have I invoked in vain the 'spirit of song'; the muse is always most unyielding, despite my assurances, that should she deign to bless me, my first offering would be upon the shrine of Liberty." Even her friendships were marred by the fear that her presence was distasteful to others. Once, on leaving Salem briefly, she said her good-bys to a favorite teacher who "gently reproved me when we were parting, for not returning her embrace. I fear she thought me cold, but it was not so. I know not why it is that when I think and feel the most, I say the least. I suppose it is my nature, not to express by word or action how much I really feel."

Charlotte Forten's conflicts—between modesty and talent, ambition and apparent lack of realization, affection and shyness—all stemmed from her constant awareness that she was a Negro. A product of generations of discrimination, she could never hope to establish bonds of perfect friendship with whites, no matter how unprejudiced those whites might be. Between the two races, in that day of slavery, was a barrier that neither could completely remove. Miss Forten did her best, just as did her many friends in Salem; yet a consciousness of difference remained. She noted this on rejoining her classmates after a vacation: "Most of them greeted me cordially, and were it not for the thought that *will* intrude, of the want of *entire sympathy* even of those I know and like the best, I should greatly enjoy their society."

This racial consciousness endows Miss Forten's *Journal* with an importance in the twentieth century that it scarcely enjoyed in the nineteenth. Enlightened individuals today have dedicated themselves to a crusade for equality and human decency. Yet how few among them—how few among the non-persecuted, that is—can know the effect of prejudice on its victims. Miss Forten's *Journal* makes this effect terrifyingly clear. Whenever she was barred from the railroad cars or an "ice cream saloon" or a museum or a school because of the color of her skin she returned home, sick at heart, to pour out her resentment on the pages of her diary. No believer in the golden rule can read that record today without reawakening to the need for decency among men.

"I wonder," she wrote after rejoining her classmates at the close of a vacation, "that every colored person is not a misanthrope. Surely we have something to make us hate mankind. I have met girls in the schoolroom—they have been thoroughly kind and cordial to me,—perhaps the next day met them on the street—they feared to recognize me; these I can but regard now with scorn and contempt,—once I liked them, believing them incapable of such meanness. Others give the most distant recognition possible.—I, of course, acknowledge no such recognitions, and they soon cease entirely. These are but trifles, certainly, to the great, public wrongs which we as a people are obliged to endure. But to those who experience them, these apparent trifles are most wearing and discouraging; even to the child's mind they reveal volumes of deceit and heartlessness, and early teach a lesson of suspicion and distrust. Oh! it is hard to go through life meeting contempt with contempt, hatred with hatred, fearing, with too good reason to love and trust hardly anyone whose skin is white,—however lovable, attractive, and congenial in seeming. In the bitter, passionate feelings of my soul again and again there rises the questions? 'When, oh! when shall this cease?' 'Is there no help?' 'How long oh! how long must we continue to suffer—to endure?'

10

Conscience answers it is wrong, it is ignoble to despair; let us labor earnestly and faithfully to acquire knowledge, to break down the barriers of prejudice and oppression. Let us take courage; never ceasing to work,—hoping and believing that if not for us, for another generation there is a brighter day in store,—when slavery and prejudice shall vanish before the glorious light of Liberty and Truth; when the rights of every colored man shall everywhere be acknowledged and respected, and he shall be treated as a *man* and a *brother!*"

Try as she did to counsel patience to the oppressed, Charlotte Forten found the practice more difficult than the preaching—and little wonder. Each new insult drove her to more outspoken rebellion. In the end prejudice drove this sensitive girl, who was an ardent patriot and a zealous Christian, to the point where she could denounce her country and almost deny her God.

That she should denounce the United States for sanctioning the institution of slavery was almost inevitable. Every Fourth of July celebration allowed her to contrast, in her *Journal,* the boast of liberty made by orators with the grim reality of the slave system. "The *patriots,* poor fools, were celebrating the anniversary of their vaunted *independence,*" she wrote on one occasion. "Strange! that they cannot feel their *own* degradation—the weight of the chains which they have imposed upon *themselves.*" Again she wrote: "The celebration of this day! What a mockery it is! My soul sickens of it. Am glad to see that the people are much less demonstrative in their mock patriotism than of old." A year later she reverted to the same theme: "Spent the afternoon and eve in *trying* to rest; but in vain. *Patriotic* young America kept up [such] a din in celebrating their glorious *Fourth,* that rest was impossible."

To Miss Forten life in England seemed vastly preferable to life in a land where her countrymen were held in bondage. "Oh! England," she confided in her *Journal,* "my heart yearns towards thee as to a loved and loving friend! I long to behold thee, to dwell in one of thy quiet homes, far from the scenes of my early childhood; far from the land, my native land—where I am hated and oppressed because God has given me a *dark skin.* How did this cruel, this absurd prejudice ever exist? When I think of it a feeling of indignation rises in my soul too deep for utterance. . . . When, Oh, when will these dark clouds clear away? When will the glorious light of Liberty and Justice appear?" So intense was Miss Forten's love for England that she feared for that country's future when the first transatlantic cable linked the two continents. "The Queen's message arrived

11

safely through the wonderful submarine telegraph," she wrote in her *Journal;* "the bells are pealing forth merrily. But *I cannot* rejoice that England, my beloved England should be brought so very near this wicked land. I tremble for the consequences, but I will *hope* for the best. Thank God for *Hope!*"

The hatred of discrimination that drove Charlotte Forten to the point where she denied her national heritage almost forced her on one gloomy day, to renounce her God. "Hatred of oppression," she confessed, "seems to me so blended with hatred of the oppressor that I cannot separate them. I feel that no other injury could be so hard to bear, so very hard to forgive, as that inflicted by cruel oppression and prejudice. How *can* I be a Christian when so many in common with myself, for no crime suffer so cruelly, so unjustly? It seems in vain to try, even to hope."

That the racial question should constantly intrude on Charlotte Forten's consciousness as she wrote her *Journal* was not surprising; for sixteen years she had been regularly reminded that her dark skin doomed her to an inferior social station. When she was still a child, she and her parents had been barred from stores and denied service in restaurants. They had been forced to sit in segregated sections of omnibuses and railroad cars. They had been turned away from lectures and theaters. They had heard thoughtless white men refer to them as "niggers" without even realizing the insulting sting of that word. From behind drawn curtains in her grandfather's spacious Philadelphia home on Lombard Street the youthful Charlotte had watched terror-stricken as runaway slaves were hounded by mobs or returned in shackles to their masters. The continual recurrence of these incidents was enough to convince any young woman of her sensitivity that nothing else in the world was so important as the battle against prejudice.

The environment in which she lived was not the only factor that led Miss Forten to dedicate her life to the cause of decency. Equally influential was her immediate background. From the time that she lisped her first words she heard talk of Negro rights about the family table; from the time she could first comprehend she listened to abolitionists as they plotted freedom for the slaves while gathered in the Forten living room. Reared in an atmosphere of crusading zeal, she was predestined to play a minor yet significant role in the contest that ended with Abraham Lincoln's Emancipation Proclamation. Most influential among those who turned her youthful mind in that direction was her grandfather, James Forten. A man of wealth, idealism, and determination, he cast his shadow over the two generation of Fortens who followed in his footsteps.

James Forten's attention was directed toward the plight of the slaves virtually from the day of his birth. Born in 1766 of free Negro parents, he received a fragmentary education in the school of Anthony Benezet, famed Quaker abolitionist, before volunteering as powder boy aboard a Philadelphia privateer during the Revolution. No sooner was the war over than he displayed the rebellious spirit that marked his later career. Why, he asked himself, should he stay in a land that proclaimed all men equal yet condemned those of darker skins to second-class citizenship? Why not escape to England, where men were judged by character rather than by color? These were the motives that drove him abroad for an important twelve-month period. In Britain he met more abolitionists—earnest young men, such as Granville Sharpe, who were lifting their voices against the slave trade and forced labor in the colonies. Young Forten listened entranced to their pleas; here indeed was a cause worth fighting—and dying—for. During that year he became an avowed abolitionist, ready to dedicate his life to the crusade against slavery.[1]

Back in his native land, Forten soon established himself as a leader of the Philadelphia Negro community. Apprenticed to a sailmaker, he displayed such skill that he was made foreman when only twenty and became proprietor of the establishment twelve years later. According to contemporary records, his invention of a device to handle sails earned him a fortune of $100,000. While amassing this sum he found time for innumerable civil activities, ranging from helping to defend Philadelphia during the War of 1812 to serving as a pioneer member of one of the city's first Negro churches.[2] A wealthy and respected citizen, he might well have settled into a life of affluent indolence, with never a thought for the less fortunate members of his race.

But James Forten was of different stamp. As he climbed upward on the economic ladder, he gave increasing attention to the nation's most unpopular crusade—that of abolitionism. His religious connections first directed his attention to the need for reform; in 1800 he signed a petition circulated by two Philadelphia ministers asking Congress to modify the Fugitive Slave Act of 1793 and to adopt "such measures as shall in due course emancipate the whole of their brethren from their present situation."[3] As a petitioner, Forten watched with disgust while congressmen rejected the request, then ruled that such petitions had a "tendency to create disquiet and jealousy, and ought therefore to receive no encouragement or countenance from this House." When this resolution was passed by a thumping vote of eighty-five to one, Forten consoled himself by writing the lone champion of the Negroes' cause;[4] but from that date he was determined to do everything in his power to change the attitude of his unsympathetic countrymen.

Forten's first opportunity came in 1813, when the Pennsylvania legislature was debating a bill to ban the entrance of free Negroes into the state. James Forten's attack on this measure was voiced through five letters published in pamphlet form. "Has the God," he asked, "who made the white man and the black, left any record declaring us a different species. Are we not sustained by the same power, supported by the same food, hurt by the same wounds, wounded by the same wrongs, pleased with the same delights, and propagated by the same means. And should we not then enjoy the same liberty, and be protected by the same laws." The legislators, he hoped, "who have hitherto guarded their fellow creatures, without regard to the colour of their skin, will still stretch forth the wings of protection to that race, whose persons have been the scorn, and whose calamities have been the jest of the world for ages."[5]

The importance of Forten's views cannot be overestimated. Unlike most reformers of that day, he was convinced that no biological difference distinguished Negroes from whites. In this conviction he not only anticipated the basic concept of abolitionism but challenged the contentions of every antislavery leader of his own day. To these humanitarians, whose philosophy was voiced through the American Colonization Society, the Negro was fit only for the barbarism of Africa or the servile life of an American slave. Knowing that slavery was wrong, they planned to win freedom for the Negroes, who would then be sent to Liberia at the Society's expense. Many liberal Northerners embraced colonization, but James Forten refused to be misled. Believing unalterably in the equality of the races, he clung tenaciously to the stand later popularized by William Lloyd Garrison and Theodore Dwight Weld; the slaves should be freed, he held, then educated to take their place in American society. These views stamp Forten as one of the first true abolitionists in the United States.

Forten's opposition to the principles of the American Colonization Society was first voiced in 1817, when its leaders, recognizing his influence among Philadelphia Negroes, asked him to endorse their program. They dangled a tempting bait before him; a man of his prestige, they said, would doubtless become
14

the ruler of Liberia if he cast his lot with them. Forten refused to be tempted. He would, he reputedly told them, "rather remain as James Forten, sail-maker, in Philadelphia, than enjoy the highest offices in the gift of their society."[6] But mere refusal was not enough; his countrymen must be warned of this insidious plot that would eventually drive all Negroes from their adopted land. With this in mind, Forten sought the support of the Reverend Richard Allen, Absolom Jones, Robert Douglass, and others prominent in Philadelphia's Negro society, and with them planned a protest meeting at the Bethel Church. When the group assembled in January, 1817, with Forten in the chair, stirring resolutions were unanimously adopted:[7]

Whereas, our ancestors (not of choice) were the first successful cultivators of the wilds of America, we, their descendants, feel ourselves entitled to participate in the blessings of her luxuriant soil, which their blood and sweat enriched; and that any measure or system of measures, having a tendency to banish us from her bosom, would not only be cruel, but in direct violation of those principles which have been the boast of this republic.

Resolved, That we view with deep abhorrence the unmerited stigma attempted to be cast upon the reputation of the free people of color by the prompters of this measure, 'that they are a dangerous and useless part of the community,' when, in the state of disfranchisement in which they live, in the hour of danger they ceased to remember their wrongs, and rallied around the standard of their country.

Resolved, That we will never separate ourselves voluntarily from the slave population of this country; they are our brethren by the ties of consanguinity, suffering, and wrong; and we feel there is more virtue in suffering privations with them, than fancied advantages for a season.

Resolved, That without arts, without science, or a proper knowledge of government, to cast into the savage wilds of Africa the free people of color, seems to us the circuitous route by which they must return to perpetual bondage.

Resolved, That, having the strongest confidence in the justice of God and the philanthropy of the free states, we cheerfully submit our destinies to the guidance of Him who suffers not a sparrow to fall without His special providence.

When the colonizers, undeterred by these protests, prepared

to launch a Philadelphia auxiliary of the American Colonization Society during the summer of 1817, Forten was again responsible for a protest meeting, which assembled three thousand strong at the Green Court schoolhouse on August 10. After the usual parade of speakers, an "Address to the humane and benevolent Inhabitants of the city and county of Philadelphia" was unanimously adopted. Arguing that colonization would deprive the freed slaves of the benefits of civilization and religious instruction, this able document from Forten's pen insisted that Liberia would soon be "the abode of every vice, and the home of every misery." Moreover, it would raise the price of slaves still in bondage until masters would be unwilling to grant them freedom. "Let not a purpose be assisted which will stay the cause of the entire abolition of slavery," the address concluded, "and which may defeat it altogether; which proffers to those who do not ask for them *benefits,* but which they consider *injuries,* and which must insure to the multitudes, whose prayers can only reach through us, *misery, sufferings, and perpetual slavery.*"[8]

From that time until his death Forten spared no efforts to reveal the true nature of colonization to his countrymen, both white and Negro. Two years later, in November, 1819, he again presided over a large meeting, which resolved "That the people of color of Philadelphia now enter and proclaim their most solemn protest against the proposition to send their people to Africa, and against every measure which may have a tendency to convey the idea that they give the project a single particle of countenance or encouragement."[9] Forten was also primarily responsible for a national convention of Negroes which met at Philadelphia on September 15, 1830, to oppose colonization. Similar gatherings were held yearly thereafter, always with James Forten in a leading role.[10] His influence, as much as any other, was responsible for the opposition of Northern Negroes to the American Colonization Society.

The mellowing influence of age did not modify Forten's views on colonization. In 1833, when nearly sixty years of age, he still spoke with the fire of youth when a visitor asked his views on the subject: "My great-grandfather was brought to this country a slave from Africa. My grandfather obtained his own freedom. My father never wore the yoke. He rendered valuable service to his country in the war of our Revolution; and I, though then a boy, was a drummer in that war. I was taken prisoner, and was made to suffer not a little on board the Jersey prison-ship. I have since lived and labored in a useful employment, have acquired property, and have paid taxes in this city. Here I have dwelt until I am nearly sixty years of age, and have brought up and educated a family, as you see, thus far. Yet some ingenious gentlemen have recently discovered that I am still an African; that a continent, three thousand miles, and more, from the place where I was born, is my native country. And I am advised to go home. Well, it may be so. Perhaps if I should only be set on the shore of that distant land, I should recognize all I might see there, and run at once to the old hut where my forefathers lived a hundred years ago."[11]

James Forten's opposition to the American Colonization Society had important results for both himself and his country. His stout advocacy of racial equality helped convince William Lloyd Garrison that colonization was an evil, thus laying the basis for the rise of abolitionism.[12] This, in turn, gave Forten an outlet for his reforming zeal; he threw himself into the Garrisonian crusade with an energy that belied both his advancing years and his social position.

For by the 1830's, when the antislavery movement hit its stride, Forten was a man of substance. His prosperous sailmaking shop, where he presided over a force of forty workers, both white and Negro, had allowed him to amass a fortune of over $100,000 by 1832. This he used to "live in as handsome a style as anyone could wish to live."[13] Gathered in his spacious home on Lombard Street were his wife, his eight children, and other relatives; at times no less than twenty-two persons assembled about the family board.[14] A man of "commanding mind and well informed," he was respected by whites and Negroes alike, largely because of the high moral principles to which he dedicated his life. He never drank, and he was a steadfast supporter of temperance societies as well as of organizations advocating universal peace and women's rights.[15] Forten was also the guiding spirit behind the American Moral Reform Society, an agency of Negro men dedicated to the "promotion of Education, Temperance, Economy, and Universal Liberty."[16] As founder and perennial president of the society, he labored effectively to better the standards of free Negroes throughout the nation.

All this comfort Forten was willing to sacrifice. Knowing that mobs might damage his property or threaten his aged limbs, he still showed no hesitation when the banner of abolitionism was unfurled by William Lloyd Garrison. To him the Boston reformer was "a chosen instrument, in the Divine hand, to accomplish the great work of the abolition of American slavery,"[17] and he must be aided no matter what the cost. Even before the first issue of *The Liberator* appeared, Forten was soliciting subscriptions among Philadelphia Negroes; by December 31, 1830, he could forward money from twenty-seven subscribers, together with a word of encouragement. "I hope your efforts may not be in vain," he wrote; "and that 'The Liberator' be the means of exposing more and more of the odious system of Slavery, and of raising up friends to the oppressed and degraded People of Colour, throughout the Union. Whilst so much is doing in the world, to ameliorate the condition of mankind, and the spirit of Freedom is marching with rapid strides, and causing tryants to tremble; may America wake from the apathy in which she has long slumbered. She must sooner or later, fall in with the irresistable current!"[18]

Forten's enthusiasm mounted with the actual appearance of *The Liberator,* on January 1, 1831. A month later he sent Garrison twenty more subscriptions; two months later he staged a mass meeting to arouse interest in the cause.[19] But he did not solicit support from others alone; his own coffers were so generously opened that only the wealthy New York merchants, Arthur and Lewis Tappan, contributed more to abolitionism than he did.[20] His only reward was to observe the spreading support for Garrisonianism. "It has," he wrote jubilantly during the spring of 1831, "roused up a spirit in our young people, that has been slumbering for years, and we shall produce writers able to vindicate our cause."[21] Garrison, in turn, developed a warm affection for "the greatly esteemed and venerated sailmaker of Philadelphia," as he called Forten. Seldom did he visit Philadelphia without making his headquarters in the Lombard Street house. "Such visits," wrote the elderly Forten on one occasion, "are cheering, they are as green spots in the journey of life."[22]

His contacts with Garrison allowed Forten to play a significant role in the American Anti-Slavery Society. His house was a regular meeting place for those who gathered to launch the society in the winter of 1833, and he himself served frequently on the Board of Managers, solicited subscriptions for *The Liberator,* and occasionally provided funds when the paper was in financial difficulties.[23] Little wonder that the Society's members in 1840 lauded him with a heart-warming verse that noted his opposition to colonization:

> *James Forten, right well*
> *I love to hear tell*

Of thy aid in our much boasted war;
And mark with what scorn
Does thy noble heart spurn
The friends of Liberia's shore
James Forten!
The friends of Liberia's shore.[24]

National acclaim did not dim Forten's interest in the local aspects of abolitionism. Time and again he arranged mass meetings to press for emancipation or to demand equality for the races;[25] time and again he circulated petitions to the state or national legislatures asking protection for runaway slaves or the abolition of bonded servitude. "Let our motto be," he advised the state lawmakers in 1836, "the Law Knows No Distinction."[26] His prominent local position allowed him to serve as delegate to numerous state gatherings, such as that held in Harrisburg[27] in 1837 to urge the end of slavery and colonization.

Only death ended James Forten's crusade. In the fall of 1841 he was forced to write Garrison that ill health would keep him from active labor in the future, but that his interest in abolitionism was as firm, as ardent, and as undiminished as ever; a year later he died, at the ripe age of seventy-six. His funeral, on February 24, 1842, was one of the largest in the history of Philadelphia. Marching in the procession that escorted his body to the grave were several thousand Negroes and several hundred whites; and men and women of both races paid tribute to his memory in a public gathering that followed.[28] James Forten passed from the scene while the cause that he advocated was still in its infancy, but he left behind him five sons and daughters ready to carry the standard that he had unfurled.

They were children[29] of whom he could be proud—those sons and daughters of James Forten. As rich in idealism as in worldly goods, they threw themselves into the cause of abolitionism with an enthusiasm that rivaled their father's zeal. Margaretta Forten divided her time between a Philadelphia schoolroom and the secretaryship of the Philadelphia Female Anti-Slavery Society; Sarah Forten was a leader in a national convention of Negro women that met in 1837 to press for abolition; Harriet Forten was prominent in the Philadelphia society; James Forten, Jr., appeared frequently at antislavery meetings as speaker or vocalist. For a generation the Fortens' Philadelphia home was a mecca for abolitionists.[30] So warm was their hospitality and so persuasive their charm that the great poet of abolitionism, John

Greenleaf Whittier, immortalized them in a poem, "To the Daughters of James Forten":[31]

> Sisters!—the proud and vain may pass ye by
> With the rude taunt and cold malicious eye;
> Point the pale hand deridingly and slow,
> In scorn's vile gesture at the darker brow;
> Curl the pressed lip with sneers which might befit
> Some mocking spirit from the nether pit;
> Yet, from a heart whence Truth and Love have borne
> The last remains of Prejudice and Scorn,
> From a warm heart, which, thanks to God, hath felt
> Pride's charm to loosen and its iron melt,
> Fervent and pure let this frail tribute bear
> A Brother's blessing with a Brother's prayer.
>
> And what, my sisters, though upon your brows
> The deeper coloring of your kindred glows
> Shall I less love the workmanship of Him
> Before whose wisdom all our own is dim?
> Shall my heart learn to graduate its thrill?
> But for the White, and for the Black be still?
> Let the thought perish, while the heart can feel
> The blessed memory of your grateful zeal,
> While it can prize the excellence of mind
> The chaste demeanor and the state refined,
> Still are ye all my sisters, meet to share
> A Brother's blessing and a Brother's prayer.

Two among the children of James Forten were especially influential in shaping the character of his granddaughter, Charlotte Forten. One was her father. A sailmaker by trade, Robert Bridges Forten shared the interest in abolition that was the family's heritage. As a young man he frequently addressed antislavery meetings;[32] as a father he kept his daughter at home rather than allow her to attend the segregated schools of Philadelphia. So deeply did he hate intolerance that he frequently considered leaving the United States for the less bigoted atmosphere of Canada or England.[33] He did flee to Britain just before the outbreak of the Civil War, only to return when he recognized that educated colored men should join Lincoln's holy crusade. Enlisting as a private in the Forty-Third United States Colored Regiment on March 14, 1864, he was immediately assigned to recruiting service in Maryland.[34] There he succumbed to erysipelas, dying late in April, 1864. His body was taken to Philadelphia, where, for the first time in America, a Negro was buried with full military honors.[35]

If Robert Forten's idealism inspired his daughter, so also did the humanitarianism of her uncle, Robert Purvis, the husband of Harriet Forten. A striking figure of a man, so light in color that he could easily have denied his race, Purvis was the free-born son of a Moorish-Negro mother and an English father. He early determined to dedicate his life and his inherited fortune to the cause of the slaves. As a young man he served as the coworker of Benjamin Lundy, an early abolitionist; when only twenty-three he was one of the sixty selected in 1833 to sign the original declaration of the American Anti-Slavery Society. Whittier, after listening to him speak on that occasion, felt that he had "never seen a finer face and figure, and his manners, words, and bearing are in keeping."[36]

Important as was his early contribution, Purvis only stood on the threshold of his abolitionist career in 1833. From that date until the Civil War he was one of Garrison's staunchest supporters, serving on the executive committee, as vice president, and finally as president of the American Anti-Slavery Society.[37] His enthusiasm helped carry the crusade into lethargic Pennsylvania, where he was an early member of the Pennsylvania Anti-Slavery Society and one of its guiding spirits.[38] His refusal to pay a local school tax helped end racial discrimination in one of Philadelphia's suburbs,[39] and his advocacy of the American Moral Reform Society was rivaled only by that of his father-in-law, James Forten.[40] Even more memorable was his service to runaway slaves bound for Canada. In 1852 he founded the Vigilance Committee of Philadelphia, which during the next eight years spirited hundreds of fugitives through the city, hiding them when federal officials were near and financing the last stages of their perilous journey. His contributions of time and money to this dangerous cause won him the popular title of "Father of the Underground Railroad."[41]

Purvis' support of abolitionism was the more remarkable because of his great wealth and secure social position. He and his family lived in princely style in an "elegant country home" at Byberry, a suburb fifteen miles from Philadelphia. His champion livestock, raised on two large farms, frequently captured premium ribbons at the annual Philadelphia fairs. Amid these luxurious surroundings, abolitionists gathered regularly to bask in the genial hospitality for which Purvis was famous. His home, one remarked, "may be called 'Saints' Rest,' for here all the abolitionists find that 'the wicked cease from troubling and the weary are at rest.' The house and extensive grounds are in tasteful English style."[42] Harriet Purvis contributed her share to the fame of her home; she was described as "very lady-like in manners and conversation; something of the ease and blandness of a southern lady. The style of living here is quite uncommonly rich and elegant."[43]

In these pleasant surroundings Charlotte Forten spent much of her early life, for after the death of her mother, when she was still a young girl, she made Byberry her second home. There she went when worn with the labors of study or teaching, to recapture lost strength or to listen enchanted to the abolitionists who were usually present. Even when she was away from Philadelphia she saw Purvis more than she saw her other relatives, as he traveled widely in the cause of abolition. His children, too, were Miss Forten's intimates; every visit to Byberry was enlivened by cheerful times with her cousins Robert, Jr., Harriet, and Charles.[44] Their principal concern, like their father's, was antislavery; from them Charlotte Forten heard the doctrines of radical abolitionism from morning until night.

Little wonder that when Miss Forten was ready to launch her own career she was so steeped in the cause that the plight of the slave transcended all other interests in her life. She was sixteen then, "in blood . . . between the Anglo-Saxon and the African, with . . . countenance beaming with intelligence, and a mind richly stored with recollections of the best authors."[45] A lonely girl who had spent her life in her grandfather's house,[46] she had been educated by tutors when denied admission to the white schools of Philadelphia. Her father, sensing her need for companionsehip, decided in 1854 that she should continue her education in Massachusetts. He selected Salem as her future home, partly because there was no discrimination in the schools there, partly because she could live with a family friend, Charles Lenox Remond.

The atmosphere in that peaceful New England town was remarkably akin to that in which Miss Forten had been reared. Remond, the proprietor of her foster home, was even better known than Robert Purvis as a Negro abolitionist. Salem born, he had joined the crusade in 1838, when he was appointed lecturing agent for the Massachusetts Anti-Slavery Society, a post that he occupied almost continuously until the Civil War. His fame as a speaker had won him a position as delegate to the World's Anti-Slavery Convention at London in 1840, where his remarkable success as an orator and fund raiser aroused international acclaim. Returning to the United States as the nation's most prominent Negro, he had enjoyed a brief period in the limelight before Frederick Douglass supplanted him as the idol of Negro Americans. Remond was never able to adjust to this secondary role. Increasingly bitter and irascible, he offended friend and foe alike, although he continued to speak for anti-slavery.[47]

This was the master of the Salem household where Miss Forten found herself in the spring of 1854. Remond was, at that time, forty-four years old, "small in stature, of spare make, neat wiry build, genteel appearance, and pleasant voice." Carefully dressed and a skilled horseman, he was known to his associates as the "Count D'Orsay of the Anti-slavery movement."[48] The family, which lived on Dean Street, included Mr. Remond's wife, Amy Matilda Remond, a brother, and Mr. Remond's sister, Sarah Parker Remond.[49] All were interested in abolition; both Charles Lenox Remond and his sister were lecturing agents for the Massachusetts Anti-Slavery Society during the 1850's, and when they were at home they talked of little else.[50] Remond, moreover, was "sensitive to a fault, and feeling sorely the prejudice against color" never tired of dwelling upon the wrongs done his people.[51] In Salem as in Philadelphia Miss Forten's attention was focused on the racial question.

Remond's home served as a headquarters for all anti-slavery lecturers passing through the city. There William Lloyd Garrison stopped on his frequent visits to Salem. There William Wells Brown stayed on his return from a triumphant European tour. There Wendell Phillips, the orator of abolitionism, made his headquarters, and there the beloved John Greenleaf Whittier paid his respects on the rare occasions when he could be lured from his Amesbury retreat. Little wonder that Miss Forten, constantly rubbing elbows with the great and near-great of the anti-slavery crusade, could think of little else, or that her principal enjoyment was found in attending abolitionist lectures and sewing circles, fairs, and other activities sponsored by the Salem Female Anti-Slavery Society.[52]

Yet, avid as her interest was in improving the lot of her people, she was greatly concerned too with her own intellectual development. There was no selfishness in this attitude; Miss Forten was soberly aware that every Negro who gained cultural pre-eminence was living proof of the equality of the races. She *must* prove that a dark skin could conceal a mind second to none. This was her ambition when, on her arrival in Salem, she enrolled at the Higginson Grammar School to study under Mary L. Shepard, the principal.[53] The two became fast friends, particularly after Charlotte Forten found that Miss Shepard shared her feelings on abolition. Doubly inspired now, the youthful Charlotte mastered her studies with an enthusiasm that won the respect of both teachers and pupils, who looked upon her as an "attentive and progressive student."[54]

Her graduation from grammar school, in February, 1855, was the occasion for a tribute that both pleased and embarrassed Miss Forten. She, with a few other students, had composed hymns to be sung at the annual examination. The prize-winning poem, "A Parting Hymn," was printed and distributed to the audience, but its author was unknown. A contemporary, who probably relied more on imagination than on observation, has reconstructed the scene that followed: "After the singing of the hymn the principal said: 'Ladies and gentlemen, the beautiful hymn just sung is the composition of one of the students of this school, but who the talented person is I am unaware. Will the author step forward?' A moment's silence, and every eye was turned in the direction of the principal, who seeing no one stir, looked around with a degree of amazement. Again he [sic] repeated, 'Will the author of the hymn step forward?' A movement among the female pupils showed that the last call had been successful. The buzzing and whispering throughout the large hall indicated the intense interest felt by all. 'Sit down; keep your seats,' exclaimed the principal, as the crowd rose to their feet, or bent forward to catch a glimpse of the young lady, who had now reached the front of the platform. Thunders of applause greeted the announcement that the distinguished authoress then before them was Charlotte L. Forten. Her finely-chiseled features, well-developed forehead, countenance beaming with intelligence, and her dark complexion, showing her identity with an oppressed and injured race, all conspired to make the scene an exciting one. The audience was made up of some of the most aristocratic people in one of the most aristocratic towns in America. The impression left upon their minds was great in behalf of the race thus so nobly represented."[55]

Having decided on a career as a teacher, Miss Forten enrolled in the Salem Normal School, from which she was graduated, in the language of the Salem Register, "with decided éclat" in July, 1856.[56] Through the intercession of the principal of the normal school, Richard Edwards, and with the hearty support of her grammar-school teachers, she immediately became a teacher in the Epes Grammar School of Salem.[57] Despite the prejudice that existed among the less enlightened townsmen, her appointment was accepted by both school board and pupils without even a flurry of excitement, and Miss Forten soon found herself immersed in the routine of classes, lecture-going, and study that was the lot of village teachers a century ago.

The next two years were among the happiest in Charlotte Forten's life. Although she never enjoyed teaching, Salem offered plentiful opportunity for her to pursue her real interests: abolitionism and learning. Her life was a round of anti-slavery lectures at Salem, Boston, Framingham, and Danvers, as she won the friendship of Garrison, Phillips, Whittier, and other stars who sparkled in the firmament of radical abolitionism. Equally avid was her pursuit in learning. She read constantly, sometimes as many as a hundred books a year. Such spare time as was left she devoted to learning French and trying unsuccessfully to master German. Little wonder that one of her friends could write of her: "An excellent student and a lover of books, she has a finely-cultivated mind, well stored with incidents drawn from the classics."[58]

Such an interest in literature in that Victorian day predestined Miss Forten to try her hand at writing. From the time her "Parting Hymn" was acclaimed at the grammar-school graduation she produced a succession of sentimental poems and essays which ranged from a hymn sung at the semiannual normal-school examination in 1856[59] through such poetic effusions as "The Two Voices," "The Wind Among the Poplars," "The Angel's Visit," and "The Slave-Girl's Prayer."[60] Perhaps her literary style was best portrayed in an essay, "Glimpses of New England," which was published in the *National Anti-Slavery Standard*.[61]

The beach, which is at some distance from the town, is delightful. It was here that I first saw the sea, and stood 'entranced in silent awe,' gazing upon the waves as they marched, in one mass of the richest green, to the shore, then suddenly broke into foam, white and beautiful as the winter snow. I remember one pleasant afternoon which I spent with a friend, gathering shells and seaweed on the beach, or sitting on the rocks, listening to the wild music of the waves, and watching the clouds of spray as they sprang high up in the air, then fell again in snowy wreaths at our feet. We lingered there until the sun had sunk into his ocean bed. On our homeward walk we passed Forest River, a winding, picturesque little stream, dotted with rocky islands. Over the river, and along our quiet way, the moon shed her soft and silvery light. And as we approached Salem, the lights, gleaming from every window of the large factory, gave us a cheerful welcome.

Perhaps wishful thinking occasioned a contemporary to remark that her writing, "for style and true poetical diction, is not surpassed by anything in the English language."[62]

Only one unpleasant occurrence marred Miss Forten's years in Salem. The death of Amy Matilda Remond, wife of Charles Lenox Remond, on August 15, 1856, was a sad blow; equally upsetting was Mr. Remond's growing irritability during the next year. After enduring his disagreeable ways as long as possible, she moved, in December, 1857, to the home of another friend, Mrs. Caroline E. Putnam, a cultured Salem Negro whose husband, Israel Putnam, operated a grocery store.[63] There the atmosphere was more congenial. But a new problem soon arose to plague Miss Forten. Never strong, she found teaching and study so trying that her health began to fail. When a rest at the Byberry home of her uncle, Robert Purvis, failed to revive her, she reluctantly concluded that she must stop teaching. In March, 1858, she resigned from the Salem schools and returned to Philadelphia.[64]

No finer tribute could be paid to this cultured woman than the notice of her resignation in the *Salem Register:*[65]

We are sorry to hear that Miss Charlotte L. Forten has been compelled by ill health to resign her position as assistant in the Epes Grammar School in this city, which she has occupied with great credit to herself and usefulness to the school, for a year or two past. Miss Forten is a young lady of color, identified with that hated race whose maltreatment by our own people is a living reproach to us as a professedly Christian nation. She is a native of Philadelphia, but was educated in the public schools in Salem. She passed through the Higgins [sic] Grammar School for girls with decided éclat, and subsequently entered the State Normal School, and graduated with success. In both these schools, she had secured, in no common degree, the respect and interest of her teachers, and of her fellow pupils. She was subsequently appointed by the school committee to be an assistant in the Epes Grammar School. She was warmly recommended by her former teachers. She was graciously received by the parents of the district, and soon endeared herself to the pupils (white) under her charge. From the beginning, her connection with the school has been of the happiest and most useful character, disturbed, we believe, by no unpleasant circumstance. Her services have given entire satisfaction to the Principal of the school, and to the school committee, and have received their free approbation. We are happy to record this instance of the success of this lady as teacher in our public schools. We do not mention it so much to praise Miss Forten as to give credit to the community and to the school committee that sanctioned this experiment. It is honorable to our city, and to the school committee which appointed her. Miss Forten is hereafter to reside in Philadelphia.

To this the *National Anti-Slavery Standard* added: "The reader will not fully appreciate the value of this testimony to the literary ability and moral worth of a coloured lady unless he is reminded of the fact that Salem is the most conservative of all the cities of Massachusetts. Who will say, after this, that the prejudice against colour is invincible."[66]

The next four years were uneventful. For a time Miss Forten languished in Philadelphia and Byberry, slowly recovering her health and strength. When able to work once more she taught briefly at the school of her aunt, Margaretta Forten, in Philadelphia. During the winter of 1860 and again in the summer of 1861 she returned to her Salem school. During most of this time she neglected her *Journal;* occasionally a year or more elapsed without a single entry. But with the outbreak of the Civil War her interest reawakened. Once more she saw a chance to serve her own people, this time as a teacher of freed slaves in the South. Thus began the most interesting phase of Miss Forten's life.

2. A Social Experiment: *Port Royal, South Carolina*

The chain of events that plunged Charlotte Forten into her exciting Civil War role began in April, 1861, when President Lincoln proclaimed the Confederate coast between Virginia and Texas under blockade. To order the Southern ports closed was one thing; to guard a coast line three thousand miles long was quite another, the Union navy soon discovered. Ships were brought from abroad, purchased, or reconverted; but after six months of expensive effort only a few principal harbors were closed to Confederate shipping. Clearly the task of building up a navy large enough to hem in the entire seaboard was too staggering to undertake; some other type of blockade was necessary. By the fall of 1861 Northern strategists had the answer: they would capture harbors along the Southern coast as a base for ships that could sally forth against Confederate merchantmen. Port Royal harbor, they decided, must be taken first. Broad and well protected, this fine port commanded the vital

27

seaports at Charleston and Savannah, which must be bottled up if the Southerners were to be starved into submission.[1]

Preparations for the attack were begun in Ocotber, 1861, when the steam frigate *Wabash* was relieved of blockade duty, fitted out as a flagship, and sent to a rendezvous point at Hampton Roads, Virginia. There it was joined by the *Susquehanna* and fourteen transports carrying twelve thousand soldiers under the command of General Thomas W. Sherman. This was the formidable force that sailed from Hampton Roads on October 29, 1861, dropping anchor off Hilton Head Island on November 6. The Confederates were caught napping by this maneuver, largely because they could not believe that so imposing a fleet would be sent against the isolated harbor at Port Royal. To the last they clung to the belief that well-defended Charleston was the Union objective; only when the Northerners were at their very gates did they fall belatedly to their defenses. Two dirt forts that guarded the entrance to Port Royal Sound —Fort Beauregard on Phillips Island and Fort Walker on Hilton Head—were hurriedly strengthened, and earthworks were thrown up about Beaufort, the principal city on Port Royal Island.[2]

These efforts were in vain. On the morning of November 7, 1861, the Union fleet steamed slowly into attacking position, with the sixty-gun *Wabash* in the lead. Sailing back and forth through the entrance to the Sound, the giant force raked the Confederate positions with a deadly fire all through the morning and part of the afternoon. By mid-afternoon even the staunchest Southerners realized that their cause was lost. The order to retreat was issued; by nightfall the Sea Islands and the whole Port Royal district were in Northern hands.[3] To assure adequate control of the conquered territory, as well as efficient cooperation between the army and navy there, the War Department, on March 16, 1862, established the Military Department of the South, comprising the states of South Carolina, Georgia, and Florida. Major General David Hunter, a soldier of long standing whose abolitionist views made him acceptable to the captured slaves, was placed in command, with headquarters at Hilton Head at the entrance to the Sound.[4]

With the Port Royal area safe in Union hands, the stage was set for an interesting social experiment. Some ten thousand slaves remained in the region, left there by masters who had fled inland at the approach of the attacking squadron. What was the legal status of these "contrabands of war"[5] How could they be used by the Northern armies? How could they be persuaded to harvest crops of cotton and grain left standing in the fields?[6]

These problems must be solved before life at Port Royal could return to anything approaching normal. Their solution was complicated by the backwardness of the former slaves. Isolated from the mainland and even from near-by Negroes by the tidal inlets that interlaced all the Sea Islands, they had lived for generations virtually without contact with the outside world. Moreover, the density of the slave population—there were ten Negroes for every one white man in the St. Helena region—had doomed them to a life in which opportunities for education or progress were few. This was shown even in their speech; they spoke a garbled mixture of imperfect words and expressions that their ancestors had learned from the few whites whom they had known. The soldiers who tried to converse with them were utterly mystified by their strange talk and stranger customs.[7]

General Sherman, the commander of the twelve thousand soldiers at Port Royal, was particularly interested in supervising and training these unfortunate people. Accordingly he wrote the War Department, on January 15, 1862, urging "that suitable instructors be sent to the Negroes, to teach them all the necessary rudiments of civilization, and . . . that agents properly qualified, be employed and sent here to take charge of the plantations and superintend the work of the blacks until they be sufficiently enlightened to think and provide for themselves."[8] The request was referred to the Treasury Department, which had just been granted control of all captured plantations; fortunately, Secretary of the Treasury Salmon P. Chase was one of the few men in Washington able to grasp the full implications of Sherman's suggestion. Of humane disposition and visionary foresight, he realized that more was involved than the fate of a few thousand former slaves. Here was a chance to demonstrate the capabilities of the Negroes! If they could be trained by skilled supervisors, educated by experienced teachers, and given a helping hand by the government, the freedmen would forever refute the argument of those who held that Negroes were fit only for a life of bondage. Port Royal, in Chase's eyes, would become the scene of a social experiment of importance to the entire South.[9]

Edward L. Pierce, a young Harvard Law School graduate who had worked in Chase's Cincinnati law office and as his secretary in Washington, was chosen to administer the program. Pierce was ideally suited for the post. His long record as an abolitionist assured the Negroes sympathetic treatment. Moreover, he brought a wealth of practical experience to the task. When serving as a private in the Third Massachusetts Regiment at the beginning of the war he had been detailed to supervise a detachment of "contrabands" at Fort Monroe, Virginia. In both theory and practice he was well equipped to undertake the difficult mission.

Pierce set out for the scene of his experiment on January 13, 1862, armed with a commission as Special Agent of the Treasury Department.[10] The situation awaiting him was far from encouraging. The Negroes were sullen and suspicious of all whites after a taste of discipline from the regular army officers. Yet a brief survey of the situation was enough to convince Pierce that proper training would soon convert them into a "happy, industrious, law-abiding, free and Christian people." This could be accomplished, he reported to the Treasury Department, by appointing carefully selected men as superintendents of the plantations. He recommended that these superintendents be paid a sufficient salary—$1,000 a year—to assure ability and honesty. Each would have complete authority over the plantation assigned him, subject only to the supervision of a director-general, who "should be a man of the best ability and character." The superintendents would direct the Negro workers on each plantation, paying them according to a graduated scale that would be determined by their wants, the government's resources, and profits. Pierce also proposed that missionaries and teachers be sent to work among the former slaves, and he suggested that Northern philanthropists would be willing to pay their salaries.[11]

Secretary Chase lost no time in translating Pierce's report into reality. On February 19, 1862, Pierce was named superintendent-general of the Port Royal Negroes, with orders to "prevent the deterioration of the estates, secure their best cultivation, and promote the welfare of the laborers." At the same time General Sherman was urged to cooperate fully in the experiment.[12] There remained the task of recruiting superintendents, teachers, and missionaries. This proved difficult at first, largely because the Treasury Department made no provision for the agents' salaries; but private benevolence soon came to Pierce's aid. When abolitionists learned that men and money were needed to train the former slaves, they hurriedly formed societies to collect funds, enlist teachers, and see to it that the experiment was successfully launched. During February and early March, 1862, the Educational Commission was organized in Boston, the Freedmen's Relief Association in New York, and the Port Royal Relief Association in Philadelphia. These three organizations paid all salaries until July 1, 1862, when the Treasury Department, having collected $200,000 from the sale of confiscated cotton, assumed the expense of supporting the superintendents. Compensation for teachers and missionaries, however, was still provided by the societies.[13]

While money was being raised, the task of enlisting superintendents began. Volunteers were so plentiful that by March 3, 1862, forty-one men and twelve women, all whites, sailed from New York, reaching Beaufort on March 9. Within two weeks all were assigned to posts, with each superintendent having charge of five or six plantations and as many as five hundred Negroes. The teachers were assigned the deserted homes of planters; they taught the former slaves to read, distributed clothing, visited the sick, and sought in other ways to improve the lot of the Negroes.[14]

The first results were far from encouraging. Some of the superintendents and teachers proved unsatisfactory; although most sincerely wished to aid the downtrodden freedmen, a few were governed by baser motives. Those who had come south "hoping the climate would be good for their health, or from a spirit of romance, or to see a semi-tropical country with its peculiar production, or in a spirit of sectarian zeal," did the cause more harm than good.[15] A more serious handicap was the attitude of the Negroes. Suspicious of whites, they viewed with alarm the discipline imposed by overzealous superintendents to bring plantations into production. The freedmen would gladly plant corn, and did so, but rebelled when called upon to labor in cotton fields as they had in slavery days.[16] Many a harassed superintendent longed for the comparative quiet of a Northern battlefield before the first Sea Island crop was harvested.

To make matters worse, the experiment had scarcely been launched when an incident occurred that threatened to alienate the former slaves entirely. For this the mistaken zeal of Major General David Hunter, commander of the Department of the South, was responsible. Abolitionist in sentiment, this outspoken old soldier had little sympathy with the slow workings of a Union government that kept Negroes in technical bondage even though they were actually free. Hence on May 11, 1862, he announced his willingness to enlist former slaves in the army, at the same time ordering all able-bodied young Negro men to Hilton Head for military training.[17] This, Hunter reasoned, would convince the freedmen that they were on equal terms with their white brethren. Unfortunaely, the Negroes did not look on the order in that light. To them military training seemed uncommonly like slavery. Many of them had been told by fleeing masters that the Yankees would send them to

31

Cuba; was this, they asked themselves, a step that would lead to a wholesale deportation? As unrest spread among them, Edward Pierce hurriedly protested to both General Hunter and the Secretary of the Treasury.[18]

Pierce's complaint led to a complete reorganization of the Port Royal administration. Washington officials believed that an impossible situation had been created by the division of authority between agents of the army and agents of the Treasury Department; one or the other should be in complete command. As Port Royal was principally of strategic importance, military control was indicated. Hence in June, 1862, jurisdiction over the region was transferred to Edward M. Stanton, the Secretary of War. He selected as his agent at Port Royal Brigadier General Rufus Saxton, who on June 16, 1862, was ordered south to "take such measures, make such rules and regulatrons for the cultivation of the land and protection, employment, and government of the inhabitants as circumstances might seem to require." He was told that his actions were to be "independent of that of other military authorities of the department," and that he was responsible only to General Hunter.[19]

General Saxton was well fitted for his post. A native of Massachusetts, he was a man of sensitivity and humanitarian instincts. Although not an abolitionist, he shared Garrison's belief that Negroes should be granted complete social equality after being educated to their new responsibilities. Under his sympathetic direction the experiment at Port Royal continued until 1864, when all government plantations were leased to white superintendents. He stayed on one more year, supervising "freedmen's affairs" and helping the teachers, until the Freedmen's Bureau Act of 1865 relieved him of further responsibility.[20] General Saxton, as much as Edward Pierce, was responsible for the success of the Port Royal social experiment.

This was the situation when Charlotte Forten, bearing a letter from John Greenleaf Whittier, went before the Boston Educational Commission in August, 1862, asking to be sent to Port Royal as a teacher. When the members of that body gave her no satisfaction, she turned to the Philadelphia Port Royal Relief Association. This time she was welcomed eagerly, for the secretary of the Philadelphia organization was J. Miller McKim, an abolitionist who had long been one of Miss Forten's friends. In October, 1862, she sailed from New York as an accredited agent of the Association, accompanied by an elderly Quaker, John A. Hunn, who was bound for Port Royal to open a store.[21]

Miss Forten found much to interest her when she reached her new home on St. Helena Island. She was fascinated by the tropical vegetation, the warm winter days, and the great plantation houses. She was entranced by the childern who flocked to her school. She was captivated by the older Negroes and never tired of recording their quaint speech or their religious songs. But most of all she was intrigued with the social experiment that had brought her to Port Royal. She and her fellow teachers were destined to prove that Negroes were as capable of self-improvement as whites! Here was a cause worth any sacrifice, when the future of a whole race depended on the outcome. Little wonder that no other subject was treated in such detail in the pages of her *Journal.*

The experiment was just being launched when Charlotte Forten arrived at Port Royal. The teachers and officials hoped to demonstrate two things. One was the ability of the former slaves to learn; Miss Forten and her fellow workers labored mightily to instruct their charges in the three R's and exhibited unrestrained delight whenever success crowned their efforts. The other was the bravery of the Negro men; General Saxton wanted to show that they fought as fearlessly as their white-skinned brethren. Miss Forten was as interested in the Negro troops as she was in the youngsters who crowded her schoolroom. Intimately acquainted with both the soldiers and their officers, she recorded their experiences with an enthusiasm that she had formerly reserved for abolition meetings.

The experiment with Negro troops that Miss Forten described began shortly before she reached Port Royal. General Saxton, lacking sufficient white troops to guard the district, naturally hit upon the idea of forming a "black regiment" from the husky young freedmen who were everywhere about. Knowing that his plan must have official blessing, he journeyed northward in August, 1862, to lay the proposal before Secretary of War Edward M. Stanton. The Secretary, who had recently been authorized by Congress to utilize "contrabands,"[22] empowered Saxton "to raise a colored regiment not to exceed 3,000 men and to detail officers to command it."[23] When the commander returned to Port Royal, in October, 1862, he threw himself at once into the task of creating the First South Carolina Volunteers.

His first necessity was a suitable commanding officer. For this post he chose Colonel Thomas Wentworth Higginson, a Unitarian clergyman from Worcester, Masschusetts, who was then a captain in the Fifty-First Massachusetts Regiment. In all

33

the land he could have found no one better fitted for this assignment. An active abolitionist for years before he entered military service, Higginson was thoroughly sympathetic with the Negro troops under his command. He was, moreover, a forceful administrator, an able strategist, and an inspiring leader.[24] Firm yet kind, he won the confidence of the Port Royal Negroes so thoroughly that the recruiting agents were swamped with applications. By the beginning of 1863 his regiment was at full strength and ready to engage in the fighting inevitable at so important a base.[25]

The Negro troops did not have to wait long before showing their mettle, for during the summer of 1863 the long-awaited attack on Charleston plunged them into one of the war's bloodiest battles. This important Southern city was better defended than most Confederate ports. Vessels approaching its harbor must pass through a narrow inlet between two sandy islands: Sullivan's Island, which bristled with the guns of Forts Beauregard and Moultrie, and Morris Island, which was guarded by the imposing Fort Wagner. Each island was separated from the mainland by a morass that was virtually impassable for troops. Within the harbor Fort Sumter barred the approaches to the city, and smaller batteries on the mainland could rake an attacker with a heavy cross fire.[26] Little wonder that these imposing defenses doomed a sea attack on Charleston made in April, 1863[27] Union officers were not ready to admit defeat, however. Naval strategists argued that the blockade could never be effective until the city was occupied; statesmen insisted that its capture was needed to bolster Northern morale. They would never rest until the cradle of the Confederacy was in Union hands.

The next attack, all agreed, must be from both land and sea. Leadership was entrusted to two new commanders, Brigadier General Q. A. Gillmore, who was placed in charge of the army's Department of the South, and Admiral John H. Dahlgren, who was given control of the navy's South Atlantic Squadron. Together they worked out a bold plan. They would seize Folly Island, erect batteries near Lighthouse Inlet, and send troops storming across the narrow inlet to Morris Island. A land assault on Fort Wagner would then open the inner harbor to the Union fleet.

The attack was launched on July 3, 1863, when General Gillmore's troops landed on the south shore of Folly Island. Seven days of feverish labor were needed to erect batteries, but on July 10 the force swept across Lighthouse Inlet. After a day of bitter fighting the Union soldiers held the southern half of

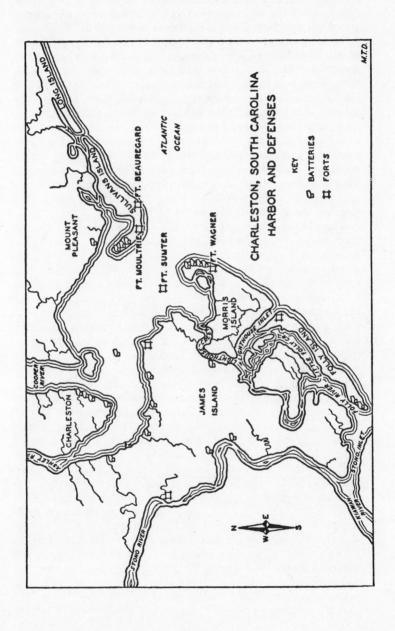

CHARLESTON, SOUTH CAROLINA
HARBOR AND DEFENSES

KEY

    BATTERIES

    FORTS

FT. BEAUREGARD

FT. MOULTRIE

FT. SUMTER

FT. WAGNER

ATLANTIC OCEAN

SULLIVANS ISLAND

LONG ISLAND

MOUNT PLEASANT

COOPER RIVER

CHARLESTON

ASHLEY R.

JAMES ISLAND

MORRIS ISLAND

LIGHTHOUSE CREEK

LIGHTHOUSE INLET

LITTLE FOLLY R.

FOLLY ISLAND

FOLLY RIVER

STONO RIVER

STONO INLET

KIWAH RIVER

N W E S

M.T.D.

Morris Island and were within six hundred yards of Fort Wagner. Seven days later the Northern forces made their all-out attack on the fort. General Gillmore arranged his men carefully. In the van was the Fifty-Fourth Massachusetts Regiment of Negro volunteers, whose commander, Colonel Robert Shaw, insisted on this place of honor and danger for his men. Behind them were two brigades of white troops. When darkness fell the soldiers started forward at double-quick time, keeping absolutely silent until within two hundred yards of the fort. Then they burst into a yell and dashed forward into the Confederate fire. Their initial rush carried the Negro troops over the parapets, where they engaged in bitter hand-to-hand fighting before the enemy rallied to drive them back. The night ended with Fort Wagner still safe in Southern hands, and with the bodies of scores of the Fifty-Fourth Massachusetts troops—including Colonel Shaw—scattered over the battlefield.[28]

This defeat convinced General Gillmore that his depleted force could never take the Confederate position by assault. Instead he ordered batteries erected on Morris Island to bombard Forts Wagner and Sumter into submission. By the end of August Fort Sumter was in ruins, and on September 5 battered Fort Wagner succumbed to a joint army-navy attack. Although the Union troops held their position until the close of the war, they made no further attempt to capture Charleston. That city remained in Southern hands until it fell before General Sherman's land force, in February, 1865.[29]

Charlotte Forten witnessed these stirring events from the comparative safety of Port Royal. She cheered the Negro troops as they sallied out to raid the enemy coast, rejoiced when they returned triumphant, and tearfully recorded the loss of their dead. She thrilled as the fleet sailed away to attack Charleston, suffered while awaiting news of the assault, and mourned when she learned the Fifty-Fourth Massachusetts Regiment had been cut to pieces and its brave leader, Colonel Shaw, had been killed. Yet Miss Forten never forgot the principal task before her. Even in the midst of battle she found time to care for her school, initiate former slaves into the mysteries of reading and writing, and comfort the Negro troops stationed at Port Royal. Her only reward was the knowledge that the social experiment was successful. Dispatches indicated that more and more freedmen were buying land on the Sea Islands, that two thousand children were enrolled in schools, that thousands of adults were receiving instruction in the churches before the Sunday-morning services.[30] Charlotte Forten could return north in May, 1864, knowing that Negroes were as capable of progress as whites.

For the next dozen years Miss Forten lived quietly in Philadelphia, doubtless reading widely, and certainly teaching on occasion. During this period of her life she gained a modest reputation as a writer. Two of her articles about the Port Royal experiment were published in the *Atlantic Monthly*,[31] and less ambitious pieces from her pen appeared in the *Christian Register,* the *Boston Commonwealth,* and the *New England Magazine.*[32] Her linguistic skill was shown in 1869, when Charles Scribner and Company published her translation of M. M. Erckmann-Chatrian's *Madame Therese; or, the Volunteers of '92.*[33] Some years later she paid gracious tribute to her close friend, John Greenleaf Whittier, in the *New England Magazine.*[34]

Amid these intellectual pursuits, Miss Forten was able to find time for affairs of the heart. On December 19, 1878, she was married to a man as remarkable as herself, the Reverend Francis J. Grimké.

Francis Grimké's father was Henry Grimké, a South Carolina planter, whose two sisters, Sarah and Angelina, were prominent abolitionists. Through one of his slaves, Nancy Weston, Henry Grimké sired three sons, John, Archibald, and Francis, who was born near Charleston on November 4, 1850. On his death in 1852 Grimké willed his slaves to his eldest son, E. Montague Grimké, specifying only that his three slave children—the half-brothers of their new owner—should be freed. For a time this injunction was followed, but when Francis was only ten years old his half-brother threatened to sell him into slavery once more. Unwilling to accept this fate, the youth escaped and found work as a valet of a Confederate officer. Taken ill after two years of service, he returned to his Charleston home, only to be clapped into prison by his brother-owner, then sold to another officer. Through the remainder of the Civil War Francis Grimké toiled as a servant, but with the collapse of the Confederacy he attracted the attention of agents of the United States Sanitary Commission. Impressed by the youngster's intelligence and good behavior, they sent him to Massachusetts with his brother, Archibald. There the two boys worked until a vacancy at Lincoln University, in Oxford, Pennsylvania, allowed them to continue their education. In 1866 both enrolled at this college.[35]

Four years of study at Lincoln demonstrated the remarkable

abilities of the Grimké brothers. Never did either fall below the third position in his class; when they were graduated, in 1870, Francis Grimké led the class and served as valedictorian, and Archibald stood third among the graduating seniors.[36] After graduation both stayed on at Lincoln University for a short time, Francis studying law and serving as "agent" of the university, Archibald working as instructor and librarian.[37]

While the two young men were in college an incident occurred that attracted nation-wide attention among reformers. In February, 1868, Angelina Grimké Weld, sister of the boy's father and wife of the abolitionist Theodore Dwight Weld, read in the *National Anti-Slavery Standard* that a literary society at Lincoln University was to be addressed by Francis Grimké. Knowing that the Grimké name was confined to the Charleston family, she concluded that this must be a former slave of her brother's who had adopted the name. Still, she was troubled; perhaps there was a more intimate connection with the family! After a month of worrying she wrote the young man only to learn the truth—that he and his brother were truly her nephews. Her horror on receiving this information was occasioned not by prejudice but by disgust with her own brother. The family honor could be redeemed only by publicly accepting the Grimké boys as her blood relatives.

Having reached this decision, Angelina Weld wrote Francis and Archibald a long letter in the tone of one addressing newly found legitimate nephews. "I am glad," she told them, "you have taken the name of Grimké. It was once one of the noblest names of Carolina. You, my young friends, now bear this *once* honored name. I charge you most solemnly, by your upright conduct and your life-long devotion to the eternal principles of justice and humanity and religion, to lift this name out of the dust where it now lies, and set it once more among the princes of our land." This kindly advice was followed by other letters; in June Mrs. Weld visited Lincoln University to observe the commencement ceremonies and publicly proclaim her relationship to the boys. From that time she and her husband not only aided them financially but considered them members of the family.[38]

Well they might, for a few young men could have done more to restore the Grimké name to a position "among the princes" than Archibald and Francis. The former was graduated from Harvard Law School with distinction, developed a thriving law practice, edited a Boston newspaper between 1883 and 1895,

38

acted as United States consul to the Republic of Santo Domingo between 1894 and 1898, served as president of the American Negro Academy in Washington during the early twentieth century, organized one of Boston's leading Negro literary societies, and found time to write a dozen books and pamphlets, ranging from biographies of Garrison and Sumner to defenses of Negro rights.[39]

Francis J. Grimké's career was no less distinguished. After studying law for a time at Lincoln and Howard universities, he entered the Princeton Theological Seminary in 1875 and was graduated in June, 1878, only a few months after his marriage to Charlotte L. Forten. Until 1885 he served as minister of the Fifteenth Street Presbyterian Church in Washington; then ill health drove him to Florida, where he became pastor of the Laura Street Presbyterian Church in Jacksonville. By 1889, his health restored, he was able to resume his Washington pastorate, which he held until his death, in October, 1937. During those years his sermons attracted nation-wide attention among white and Negro people alike. His primary concern, like his wife's, was the racial question; he was a never-tiring champion of Negro rights and an unswerving foe of prejudice. Little wonder that the editor of his collected works has called him "one of the most distinguished clergymen of his time," or that he was known as the "Black Puritan" because of his uncompromising righteousness.[40]

In the Reverend Francis Grimké, Charlotte Forten found the ideal husband. With social views and literary interests in common, they lived an idyllic life, marred only by the death of their one child in 1880.[41] Charlotte Forten Grimké died on July 23, 1914, after a lingering illness that had kept her bedridden for thirteen months. Her bequest to humanity was a journal which could reveal to a later generation her undying belief in human decency and equality.

3. A Note on The Journal of Charlotte Forten

Charlotte Forten began writing the following *Journal* at Salem on May 24, 1854, and made her last entry at Port Royal on May 15, 1864. In addition she kept a fragmentary diary between November, 1885, and July, 1892, after her marriage to the Reverend Francis Grimké. She kept her journal in ordinary board-covered notebooks, writing in ink in a cultivated and legible hand.

On Mrs. Grimké's death, her husband entrusted her writings to one of her closest personal friends, Dr. Anna J. Cooper, of

Washington. Dr. Cooper was good enough to lend me both the original manuscript diaries and the typewritten copy of them that she had laboriously made, together with other biographical data collected over the course of years during which she knew Mrs. Grimké.

In preparing Miss Forten's *Journal* for publication I have taken certain liberties with the text. Large sections in the period between 1854 and 1862 have been deleted. These describe the weather, family affairs, the landscape, and other matters of purely local interest. Space limitations have also forced me to omit many of her comments on the books that she read. In each case, however, I have tried to retain enough of the original to impart the flavor of the *Journal*. All items dealing with public figures, abolitionism, and Miss Forten's intellectual development have been fully reproduced. The portions describing her experiences in South Carolina are printed in their entirety, with only a few lines on family affairs omitted. Wherever omissions have been made the fact has been indicated in the usual manner, and in no case has the sense or meaning been distorted. I have, however, taken the liberty of dividing the South Carolina portions of the *Journal* into paragraphs and the whole work into parts; the part divisions and the titles are my own additions and do not appear in the manuscript *Journal*. Miss Forten's spelling and punctuation have, of course, been reproduced without change.

Of those who have cooperated to make possible the publication of Miss Forten's diaries, none has been more helpful than Dr. Anna J. Cooper. It is my earnest hope that this book will contribute in some small way to that better racial understanding to which both Miss Forten and Dr. Cooper dedicated their lives. I am deeply indebted also to Professor Dwight L. Dumond, of the University of Michigan, and to Professor John Hope Franklin, of Howard University, who have read portions of the manuscript at various stages of its preparation and have given invaluable advice. Two former students of mine at Northwestern University, Thelma Saxon Lewis and Howard Bell, have given generously of their time and knowledge in helping me prepare the *Journal* for the printer. This task was aided by a generous financial grant from the Committee on Research of the Graduate School of Northwestern University. My gratitude extends also to the staffs of the libraries where the research on the diaries was done: the Newberry Library and the Crerar Library, of Chicago; the Deering Library, of Northwestern University; the Widener Library, of Harvard

University; and the Massachusetts State House Library, of Boston. The manuscript diaries have been deposited at the library of Howard University by Dr. Cooper.

RAY ALLEN BILLINGTON

A WISH to record the passing events of my life, which, even if quite unimportant to others, naturally possess great interest to myself, and of which it will be pleasant to have some remembrance, has induced me to commence this journal. I feel that keeping a diary will be a pleasant and profitable employment of my leisure hours, and will afford me much pleasure in after years, by recalling to my mind the memories of other days, thoughts of much-loved friends from whom I may then be separated, with whom I now pass many happy hours, in taking delightful walks, and holding 'sweet converse'; the interesting books that I read; and the different people, places, and things that I am permitted to see.

Besides this, it will doubtless enable me to judge correctly of the growth and improvement of my mind from year to year.

C. L. F.

Salem, May, 1854

Part 1

Salem Schooldays

May 24, 1854 - December 31, 1854

Wednesday, May 24, 1854. Rose at five. The sun was shining brightly through my window, and I felt vexed with myself that he should have risen before me; I shall not let him have that advantage again very soon. How bright and beautiful are these May mornings!—The air is so pure and balmy, the trees are in full blossom, and the little birds sing sweetly. I stand by the window listening to their music, but suddenly remember that I have an Arithmetic lesson which employs me until breakfast; then to school;[1] recited my lessons, and commenced my journal. After dinner practiced a music lesson, did some sewing, and then took a pleasant walk by the water. I stood for some time, admiring the waves as they rose and fell, sparkling in the sun, and could not help envying a party of boys who were enjoying themselves in a sailing-boat. On my way home, I stopped at Mrs. Putnam's[2] and commenced reading "Hard Times," a new story by Dickens. . . .[3]

Thursday, May 25, 1854. Did not intend to write this evening, but have just heard of something which is worth recording;—something which must ever rouse in the mind of every true friend of liberty and humanity, feelings of the deepest indignation and sorrow.[4] Another fugitive from bondage has been arrested; a poor man, who for two short months has trod the soil and breathed the air of the "Old Bay State," was arrested like a criminal in the streets of her capital, and is now kept strictly guarded,—a double police force is required, the military are in readiness; and all this done to prevent a man, whom God has created in his own image, from regaining that freedom with which, he, in common with every other human being, is endowed. I can only hope and pray most earnestly that Boston will not again disgrace herself by sending him back to a bondage worse than death; or rather that she will redeem herself from the disgrace which his arrest alone has brought upon her. . . .

Friday, May 26, 1854. Had a conversation with Miss [Mary] Shepard[5] about slavery; she is, as I thought, thoroughly opposed to it, but does not agree with me in thinking that the churches and ministers are generally supporters of the infamous system; I believe it firmly. Mr. Barnes,[6] one of the most prominent of the Philadelphia clergy, who does not profess to be an abolitionist, has declared his belief that 'the American church is the bulwark of slavery.' Words cannot express all that I feel; all that is felt by the friends of Freedom, when thinking of this great obstacle to the removal of slavery from our land. Alas! that it should be so.—I was much disappointed in not seeing the eclipse,[7] which, it was expected would be the most entire that has taken place for years; but the weather was rainy, and the sky obscured by clouds; so after spending half the afternoon on the roof of the house in eager expectation, I saw nothing, heard since that the sun made his appearance for a minute or two, but I was not fortunate enough to catch even that momentary glimpse of him. . . .

Saturday, May 27. . . . Returned home, read the Anti-Slavery papers, and then went down to the depot to meet father;[8] he had arrived in Boston early in the morning, regretted very much that he had not reached there the evening before to attend the great meeting at Faneuil Hall.[9] He says that the excitement in Boston is very great; the trial of the poor man takes place on Monday.[10] We scarcely dare to think of what may be the result; there seems to be nothing too bad for these Northern tools of slavery to do.

Sunday, May 28. A lovely day; in the morning I read in the Bible and wrote letters; in the afternoon took a quiet walk in Harmony Grove,[11] and as I passed by many an 'unknown grave,' the question of 'who sleeps below?' rose often to my mind, and led to a long train of thoughts, of whose those departed ones might have been, how much beloved, how deeply regretted and how worthy of such love and such regret. I love to walk on the Sabbath, for all is so peaceful; the noise and labor of everyday life has ceased; and in perfect silence we can commune with Nature and with Nature's God. . . .

Tuesday, May 30. Rose very early and was busy until nine o'clock; then, at Mrs. Putnam's urgent request, went to keep store for her while she went to Boston to attend the Anti-Slavery Convention.[12] I was very anxious to go, and will certainly do so to-morrow; the arrest of the alleged fugitive will give additional interest to the meetings, I should think. His trial is still going on and I can scarcely think of anything else; read again to-day as most suitable to my feelings and to the times, "The Run-away Slave at Pilgrim's Point," by Elizabeth B. Browning; how powerfully it is written! how earnestly and touchingly does the writer portray the bitter anguish of the poor fugitive as she thinks over all the wrongs and sufferings that she has endured, and of the sin to which tryants have driven her but which they alone must answer for! It seems as if no one could read this poem without having his sympathies roused to the utmost in behalf of the oppressed.—After a long conversation with my friends on their return, on this all-absorbing subject, we separated for the night, and I went to bed, weary and sad.

Wednesday, May 31. . . . Sarah [Remond][13] and I went to Boston in the morning. Everything was much quieter—outwardly than we expected, but still much real indignation and excitement prevail. We walked past the Court-House, which is now lawlessly converted into a prison, and filled with soldiers, some of whom were looking from the windows, with an air of insolent authority which made my blood boil, while I felt the strongest contempt for their cowardice and servility. We went to the meeting, but the best speakers were absent, engaged in the most arduous and untiring efforts in behalf of the poor fugitive; but though we missed the glowing eloquence of Phillips,[14] Garrison,[15] and Parker,[16] still there were excellent speeches made, and our hearts responded to the exalted sentiments of Truth and Liberty which were uttered. The exciting intelligence which occasionally came in relation to the trial, added fresh zeal to the speakers, of whom Stephen Foster and his wife were the principal.[17] The latter addressed, in the most eloquent language, the women present, entreating them to urge their husbands and brothers to action, and also to give their aid on all occasions in our just and holy cause.—I did not see father the whole day; he, of course, was deeply interested in the trial.—Dined at Mr. Garrison's; his wife is one of the loveliest persons I have ever seen, worthy of such a husband. At the table, I watched earnestly the expression of that noble face, as he spoke beautifully in support of the non-resistant principles to which he has kept firm; his is indeed the very highest Christian spirit, to which I cannot hope to reach, however, for I believe in 'resistance to tyrants,' and would fight for liberty until death. We came home in the evening, and felt sick at heart as we passed through the streets of Boston on our way to the depot, seeing the military as they rode along, ready at any time to prove themselves the minions of the south.

Thursday, June 1st. . . . The trial is over at last; the commissioner's decision will be given to-morrow. We are all in the greatest suspense; what will that decision be? Alas! that any one should have the power to decide the right of a fellow being to himself! It is thought by many that he will be acquitted of the *great crime* of leaving a life of bondage, as the legal evidence is not thought sufficient to convict him. But it is only too probable that they will sacrifice him to propitiate the South, since so many at the North dared oppose the passage of the infamous Nebraska Bill.—Miss Putnam was married this evening. Mr. Frothingham performed the ceremony, and in his prayer alluded touchingly to the events of this week; he afterwards in conversation with the bridegroom, (Mr. Gilliard), spoke in the most feeling manner about this case;—his sympathies are all on the right side.[18] The wedding was a pleasant one; the bride looked very lovely; and we enjoyed ourselves as much as is possible in these exciting times. It is impossible to be happy now.

Friday, June 2. Our worst fears are realized; the decision was against poor Burns, and he has been sent back to a bondage worse, a thousand times worse than death. Even an attempt at rescue was utterly impossible; the prisoner was completely surrounded by soldiers with bayonets fixed, a cannon loaded, ready to be fired at the slightest sign.[19] To-day Massachusetts has again been disgraced; again has she shewed her submission to the Slave Power; and Oh! with what deep sorrow do we think of what will doubtless be the fate of that poor man, when he is again consigned to the horrors of Slavery. With what scorn must that government be regarded, which cowardly assembles thousands of soldiers to satisfy the demands of slaveholders; to deprive of his freedom a man, created in God's own image, whose sole offense is the color of his skin! And if resistance is offered to this outrage, these soldiers are to shoot down American citizens without mercy; and this by the express orders of a government which proudly boasts of being the freeest [*sic*] in the world; this on the very soil where the Revolution of 1776 began; in sight of the battle-field, were thousands of brave men fought and died in opposing British tyranny, which was nothing compared with the American oppression of to-day. In looking over my diary, I perceive that I did not mention that there was on the Friday night after the man's arrest, an attempt made to rescue him, but although it failed, on account of there not being men enough engaged in it, all honor should be given to those who bravely made the attempt. I can write no more. A cloud seems hanging over me, over all our persecuted race, which nothing can dispel.

Sunday, June 4. A beautiful day. The sky is cloudless, the sun shines warm and bright, and a delicious breeze fans my cheek as I sit by the window writing. How strange it is that in a world so beautiful, there can be so much wickedness; on this delightful day, while many are enjoying themselves in their happy homes, not poor Burns only, but millions beside are suffering in chains; and how many Christian ministers to-day will mention him, or those who suffer with him? How many will speak from the pulpit against the cruel outrage on humanity which has just been committed; or against the many, even worse ones, which are committed in this country every day? Too well do we know that there are but very few, and these few alone deserve to be called the ministers of Christ, whose doctrine was 'Break every yoke, and let the oppressed go free.'—During the past week, we have had a vacation, which I had expected to enjoy very much, but it was of course impossible for me to do so. To-morrow school commences, and although the pleasure I shall feel in again seeing by beloved teacher, and in resuming my studies will be much saddened by recent events, yet they shall be a fresh incentive to more earnest study, to aid me in fitting myself for laboring in a holy cause, for enabling me to do much towards changing the condition of my oppressed and suffering people. Would that those with whom I shall recite to-morrow could sympathize with me in this; would that they could look upon all God's creatures without respect to color, feeling that it is character alone which makes the true man or woman! I earnestly hope that the time will come when they will feel thus. . . .

Monday, June 5. Rose very early, after passing a sleepless night.—Studied my lessons, and then went to school. Miss [Elizabeth] Church[20] and I counted the merits of the first and second classes for Miss Shepard; after school, had an hour's conversation with her about slavery and prejudice. I fully appreciate her kindness, and sympathy with me; she wishes me to cultivate a Christian spirit in thinking of my enemies; I know it is right, and will endeavor to do so, but it does seem very difficult. . . .

Wednesday, June 7. After school returned home and did some ironing; then practiced a music lesson. In the afternoon, read Mr. Parker's sermon on "The New Crime Against Humanity," written with his usual truthful eloquence.[21] I wish that I could have heard him deliver it. The subject naturally possesses the greatest interest for me. . . .

Saturday, June 10. Received two letters, one from father. . . . To my great disappointment, father has decided not to remove to N[ew] England. He is, as I feared he would be, much prejudiced against it on account of the recent slave case, or, he says, he is so against Boston, and I think he extends that feeling to the whole state at least. I shall write to-morrow, and use every argument I can think of, to induce him to change his opinion. I do not wish to have my long-cherished plan of our having together a pleasant N[ew] England home, defeated. In the afternoon went to impart the unwelcome tidings to Miss [Sarah] Remond, who assured me that she had been quite certain of it before. She had a volume of Mrs. Browning's poems, from which I read "Prometheus Bound" and "Casa Guidi Windows". . . .

Monday, June 12. Did not feel very well this morning, but was much better after taking a walk. . . . I enjoyed the novelty of wandering over the hills, and ascending some of the highest of them, had a fine view of the town and harbor. It seemed like a beautiful landscape; and I wished for the artist's power or the poet's still richer gift to immortalize it. I stood and watched the last rays of the glorious sun as it slowly disappeared behind the hills, lending a beautiful tinge to the water of a winding, romantic little stream that flowed at our feet; and felt so much delighted that it was with reluctance that I left the spot, and turned my steps homeward. . . .

Tuesday, June 13. One of the loveliest days of this lovely month; regretted that I had not time to take a long walk, which gives me the truest enjoyment of this delightful weather. After school, stayed with Miss [Mary] Shepard, who was writing some sentiments for a fair; I wondered how she could write them so easily and rapidly; they were all excellent, and one so very amusing that I wish I dared insert it here. How often have I invoked in vain the 'spirit of song'; the muse is always most unyielding, despite my assurances, that should she deign to bless me, my first offering should be upon the shrine of Liberty. . . .

Friday, June 16. Another delightful morning; the sky is cloudless, the sun is shining brightly; and, as I sit by the window, studying, a robin redbreast perched on the large apple tree in the garden, warbles his morning salutation in my ear;—music far sweeter to me than the clearer tones of the Canary birds in their cages, for they are captives, while he is free! I would not keep even a bird in bondage. . . .

Saturday, June 17. A bad headache has prevented my enjoying the fine weather to-day, or taking as much exercise as I generally do. Did some sewing on my return from school.— Read the Liberator, then practiced a music lesson. . . . In the evening Miss [Sarah] Remond read aloud Mr. Frothingham's[22] Sermon, whose stern truths shocked so many of his congregation. We, of course, were deeply interested in it, and felt grate-

48

ful to this truly Christian minister for his eloquent defence of oppressed humanity. While Miss R[emond] was reading, Miss Osborne came in, and said she believed that we never talked or read anything but Anti-Slavery; she was quite tired of it. We assured her that she could never hear anything better; and said it was natural that we should speak and read much, on a subject so interesting to us. . . .

Sunday, June 18. . . . In the afternoon went to Lynn to hear a lecture from Wendell Phillips.—The ride was very delightful. We passed the bay—how calm and beautiful the water looked; a light haze was over it, which made it look like a cloud in the distance. I longed to enjoy a sail on its bosom. I love the water, and sometimes think I could live 'on the ocean wave.' A delicious breeze was stirring, laden with the fragrance of locust and sweetbriar. It was indeed one of the loveliest days of summer. Mr. Phillips spoke eloquently and beautifully, as he always does, spoke earnestly of the recent slave case, and showed the position of Slavery and Freedom in this country, and the great strength and wickedness of the former. I wish I could transfer a few of those glowing words and noble sentiments to paper; but that is quite impossible. The Hutchinsons were at the lecture, and sang very beautifully.[23]—Mr. Phillips has promised to stay with us, the next time he comes to Salem. . . .

Tuesday, June 20. Rose very early and took a pleasant walk in Danvers. I noticed that nearly every house we passed, however humble in other respects, was adorned with beautiful flowers. The sun has just risen and was shedding his bright rays over hills and trees, lending an additional charm to the beauty of the scene. . . . Went to school. The weather was oppressively hot; one could scarcely study.—In the afternoon wrote a composition; subject, "A Day In June," which was very appropriate.—On my return home, commenced reading Macaulay's History of England. I know that I shall like it, as I do everything that relates to England; there is charm for me even in its very name. . . .

Wednesday, June 21. Had anticipated much pleasure in taking a morning walk with Miss [Mary] Shepard, but the weather was too chilly and disagreeable. What a change from yesterday! Bright smiling June seems to have given place to cloudy, gloomy November; but it will not be for a long time; she is too lovely to give us many frowns.—After school went home with Miss Shepard and stayed there for some time; she was talking to me of a lovely friend, who in the midst of health had been suddenly taken away; it seemed very sad. I felt as if I

49

had known her,—so good and so gifted, so very lovable as she must have been. I felt deeply interested, as I always do when conversing with Miss Shepard, and was surprised when I got home to find how late it was. . . .

Thursday, June 22. Copied my composition; then studied until breakfast. Went to school.—At recess read another number of "Martin Merrivale."—After morning school read "Moll Pitcher," to Mrs. [Charles L.] Remond.[24] How very beautifully it is written! One can almost see the old witch and hear those frightful incantations, which so powerfully affected the young and beautiful girl, who sought her dismal abode. The poet's description of Nahant is exquisite, and has made me more desirous than ever of visiting that beautiful spot. . . .

Friday, June 23. Saw some engravings of castles and mountains in Wales. The scenery was wild and beautiful. How very grand those mountains appear, towering to the very clouds! I should love to see them, and those old, ruined castles, now overgrown with ivy, whose stately rooms, once filled with the gay and the beautiful, are now desolate, and mouldering to decay.—After school, read in the History of England.—Then did some sewing, while Sarah [Remond] read aloud Mr. [Charles L.] Remond's speech in the Convention,[25] which I like very much. . . .

Sunday, June 25. Have been writing nearly all day.—This afternoon went to an Anti-Slavery meeting in Danvers, from which I have just returned. Mr. Foss spoke eloquently, and with that warmth and sincerity which evidently come from the heart.[26] He said he was rejoiced that the people at the North were beginning to feel that slavery is no longer confined to the black man alone, but that they too must wear the yoke; and they are becoming roused on the subject at last. He spoke of the objections made by many to the Abolitionists, on the plea of their using too violent language; they say that the slaveholders are driven by it to worse measures; what they need is mild entreaty, etc., etc. But the petition against the Nebraska Bill, couched in the very mildest terms by the clergymen of the North, was received even less favorably by the South, than the hardest sayings of the Abolitionists; and they were abused and denounced more severely than the latter have ever been.— As we walked home, Miss [Sarah] Remond and I were wishing that we could have an anti-slavery meeting in the neighborhood every Sunday, and as well attended as this was. . . .

Monday, June 26. Went to the Essex Institute and saw many curiosities. Mr. King showed us some specimens from his botanical garden; they were highly magnified; the first we saw was a very small portion of the green slime found in impure water; when seen through the microscope, it appeared like a large piece of seaweed and looked very beautiful.—Then we saw the first growth of a pear tree; every fibre and the many little cells of which it is composed were plainly visible; it resembled another, and still smaller portion of green slime when magnified. Mr. King told us that in the beginning every vegetable substance is composed of the same kind of cells and fibres; so that the largest elm-tree in its first growth resembles this slimy substance. He showed us a very small water-flea so highly magnified that we could see the heart and every palpitation very plainly.

Among the curiosities were Gov. Bradford's christening blanket, mittens and shirt, which had a very odd and antique appearance. Dr. Wheatland showed us a miniature canoe, and a Chinese hammock, composed of net silk with a border of beautiful feather-work; a very elegant and pleasant conveyance for those Chinese ladies who cannot walk on account of the smallness of their feet. Their ideas of beauty and comfort are certainly very strange. I was much interested in the collection of shells and stones, and in the beautiful coral which always brings to my mind thoughts of the sea. The gentlemen kindly gave us much useful information, and we spent two hours there very pleasantly. . . .[27]

Sunday, July 2. A delightful day—In the morning read several chapters in the New Testament. The third verse of the last chapter of Hebrews—"Remember them that are in bonds as bound with them" suggested many thoughts to my mind: *Remember the poor slave as bound with him.* How few even of those who are opposed to slavery realize this! If they felt thus so ardent, so untiring, would be their efforts that they would soon accomplish the overthrow of this iniquitous system. All honor for the noble few who do feel for the suffering bondman *as bound with him,* and act accordingly! . . .

Friday, July 17. This afternoon heard a very interesting lecture on Ecuador, and received much useful information concerning that beautiful country; the variety of its climate, soil and productions; the grandeur of its mountain scenery; the splendor of its capital, and the character, dress and manners of its inhabitants.—On my return home, found that Mrs. [C. L.] Remond, with her usual kindness, had arranged that I should take her place in the carriage. I had a delightful ride on the sea shore. The waves looked very beautiful as they rose and fell sparkling in the sunlight. And in the distance, a steamboat which to us appeared to be standing perfectly still, though perhaps in reality it was gliding rapidly over the calm, and deep blue water of the bay, seemed like a single white cloud in the azure sky. We passed "High Rock," at the foot of which stood the residence of the far-famed "Moll Pitcher," the weird heroine of Whittier's beautiful poem. On the summit of this bold eminence stands the tasteful cottage of the Hutchinson family. It seems a fit abode for those gifted and warm hearted children of song. I enjoyed the ride the more because Mr. [C. L.] Remond allowed me to drive nearly all the way.

Saturday, July 8. This morning took a very pleasant walk with Miss [Mary] Shepard. We walked through Harmony Grove; the air was pure and balmy, and the trees and flowers looked very beautiful as they waved over the last resting-place of many a loved and lost one. Miss Shepard read several exquisite poems written by the sister of Mrs. Hemans; they are full of deep, tender feeling, and one, a lament for the loss of her loved and highly gifted sister, was particularly touching and beautiful. We talked of many things, and I felt pleased and happy as I always do in the society of my beloved teacher.—In the afternoon did some sewing.—Then read in Macaulay's "History of England." His account of the Norman Conquest is very interesting.—In the evening went to the Anti-Slavery meeting at Lyceum Hall. There were but very few present. Mr. Foss spoke eloquently for an hour, and then the meeting adjourned until to-morrow.[28]

Sunday, July 9. Attended the meetings during the day and evening. I felt sorry and disappointed to see such a small number of persons present. The intense heat of the weather perhaps accounted for this. Though for such a cause I thought much more than that might have been endured. Very eloquent and interesting speeches were made by Mr. Garrison and Mr. Foss in the afternoon and evening. After tea I went to Miss [Sarah] Remond's where Mr. Garrison had taken tea, and felt happier and better after listening to the conversation of that truly good and great man.

Monday, July 10. I have seen to-day a portrait of Hawthorne, one of the finest that has ever been taken of him. He has a splendid head. That noble, expansive brow bears the unmistakable impress of genius and superior intellect. And in the depths of those dark, expressive eyes there is a strange, mysterious influence which one feels in reading his works, and which I felt most forcibly when reading that thrilling story "The Scarlet Letter." Yet there is in his countenance no trace of that gloom which pervades some of his writings; particularly that strange tale "The Unpardonable Sin," and many of the "Twice

Told Tales." After reading them, I had pictured the author to myself as very dark and gloomy-looking. But I was agreeably disappointed. Grave, earnest, thoughtful, he appears, but not gloomy. His sister, who, with much kindness showed me his portrait, is very singular-looking.[29] She has an eerie, spectral look which instantly brought to my mind the poem of "The Ancient Mariner," and for a moment gave me the strange, undefined feeling of dread and yet of fascination which I so powerfully experienced while reading that ghostly tale. But her cordial, pleasant manner quickly dispelled this feeling. And I soon realized that however peculiar she might appear, or be in reality, she was no "shadowy visitant from another world," as at first I could almost have fancied. She showed me another portrait of Hawthorne taken when he was very young. His countenance, though glowing with genius, has more of the careless, sanguine expression of youth than the profound, elevated thought which distinguishes his maturer years, and gives to his fine face and to his deeply interesting writings that mysterious charm which is felt and acknowledged by all. Miss Hawthorne showed me a piece of the English yew, the "sepulchral yew," whose dark branches are seen in every country churchyard of England and seems there the emblem of mourning as the "weeping willow" here. . . .

Saturday, July 15. Have been very busy to-day.—On my return from school did some sewing, and made some gingerbread.—Afterwards adopted "Bloomer" costume and ascended the highest cherry tree, which being the first feat of the kind ever performed by me, I deem worthy of note.—Obtained some fine fruit, and felt for the time "monarch of all I surveyed," and then descended from my elevated position.—In the evening spent some time very delightfully with Miss [Mary] Shepard looking over her beautiful books and many elegant little curiosities.

Monday, July 17. This afternoon Miss Shepard allowed Lizzie [Church] and me to read a few pages of her journal which interested us very much; but we dared not appropriate any more of its precious contents.—I have seen to-day a picture of a dear old English church. How beautiful and picturesque it was with its ivy-wreathed spire and moss-covered walls! There could not be a lovelier spot than this consecrated to the worship of God. How delightful it would be to sit on the banks of the sparkling stream which winds so prettily among the ancient trees, and listen to the sweet music of the village bells as they chime the hour of prayer. Oh! England my heart yearns towards thee as to a loved and loving friend! I long to behold thee, to dwell in one of thy quiet homes, far from the scenes of my early childhood; far from the land, my native land—where I am hated and oppressed because God has given me a *dark skin*. How did this cruel, thus absurd prejudice ever exist? how can it exist? When I think of it a feeling of indignation rises in my soul too deep for utterance. This evening I have been thinking of it very much. When, Oh, when will these dark clouds clear away? When will the glorious light of Liberty and Justice appear? The prospect seems very gloomy. But I will try not to despond. . . .

Wednesday, July 19. This afternoon went with our dear teacher and some of the scholars to Marblehead Beach. Miss Hawthorne, the sister of the author, and Miss Anderson, our teacher's very dear friend, were of the party. . . . We ensconced ourselves among them in a delightful recess shaded by a huge rock, and watched the waves as they dashed against the rocks, and rising high in the air at times almost enveloped us in a cloud of spray. We wandered on the beach for some time gathering a variety of beautiful stones and sea-weed, and Miss Hawthorne gave me a singular stone, "to remember the place by," she said. After watching the glorious sunset, we rode home very pleasantly in the deepening twilight. . . .

Monday, July 24. To-day Lizzie [Church] and I finished reading "The Genius of Scotland,"[30] and I return reluctantly from delightful imaginary wanderings "among the braes o' Yarrow," and over many a "heathery dell" and "bonnie burn" of dear "auld Scotia," through the splendid halls of Abbotsford, and the humbler, but not less consecrated home of Burns, and from many a quiet home upon the hill-side where the poor shepherd boy, neglected and unknown has caught from his solitary communings with Nature the true spirit of poetry, and breathed it forth in strains the most touching and beautiful. How many of Scotland's sons have been thus gifted! Again I have imagined myself standing on the banks of "Loch leven" and gazing on the stately old castle once the prison of the beautiful and unfortunate Mary Stuart, or wandering by the "classic Esk" or the "silver Tweed" near which so many gifted bards have dwelt. I was much interested in the life of the lovely young poetess, Mary Lundie Duncan, "Sweet bird of Scotia's tuneful clime" as one of our own most gifted poetesses designates her. It seems very sad that one so richly endowed with genius and goodness should pass away so soon. Beautiful, happy Scotland! Well may her sons be proud of her. . . .

Friday, July 28. This morning Miss Creamer, a friend of our teacher, came into the school. She is a very learned lady; a

Latin teacher in Troy Seminary, and an authoress. I certainly did feel some alarm, when I saw her entering the room. But she was so very kind and pleasant that I soon felt more at ease. She asked us a few questions and told an amusing anecdote of one of her pupils. She seems to be a very nervous and excitable person, and I found myself frequently contrasting her appearance with that of our dear teacher, who looked so perfectly calm and composed, that I began to flatter myself that she was not experiencing any uneasiness about our acquitting ourselves creditably. I rather think that I was mistaken in this. But we felt very happy to hear her say afterwards that she was much pleased, and thought we did very well. I do think reading one's compositions before strangers is a trying task. If I were to tell Mrs. R[emond] this, I know she would ask how I could expect to become what I often say I should like to be—an Anti-Slavery lecturer. But I think that I should then trust to the inspiration of the subject.—This evening read "Poems of Phillis Wheatly [sic]," an African slave, who lived in Boston at the time of the Revolution.[31] She was a wonderfully gifted woman, and many of her poems are very beautiful. Her character and genius afford a striking proof of the falseness of the assertion made by some that hers is an inferior race. . . .

Tuesday, August 1. To-day is the twentieth anniversary of British emancipation. The joy that we feel at an event so just and so glorious is greatly saddened by thoughts of the bitter and cruel oppression which still exists in our own land, so proudly claiming to be "the land of the free." And how very distant seems the day when she will follow the example of "the mother country," and liberate her millions of suffering slaves! This morning I went with Mr. and Mrs. R[emond] to the celebration at Abington.[32] The weather was delightful, and a very large number of persons was assembled in the beautiful grove. Mr. Garrison, Wendell Phillips and many other distinguished friends of freedom were present, and spoke eloquently. Mr. Garrison gave an interesting account of the rise and progress of the anti-slavery movement in Great Britain. I had not seen Mr. Higginson[33] before. He is very fine looking, and has one of the deepest, richest voices that I have ever heard. I was much pleased with Mr. M'Cluer, a genial, warm-hearted Scotchman who was arrested in Boston during the trial of Burns.[34] He has a broad, Scotch accent which I was particularly delighted to hear as I have been reading very much about Scotland lately. The sadness that I had felt was almost entirely dissipated by the hopeful feelings expressed by the principal speakers. And when they sang the beautiful songs for the occasion, there was something very pleasant in the blending of so many voices in the open air. And still more pleasant to think that it was for a cause so holy that they had assembled then and there. Sarah [Remond] and I had a sail in one of those charming little row-boats which are my particular favorites. It was very delightful to me to feel that I was so near the water; and I could not resist the temptation to cool my hands in the sparkling waves. I greatly enjoyed sitting under the shade of the noble pine trees and listening to the eloquent speeches in behalf of the slaves; every sentiment of which met a warm response in my heart. On returning home we stopped in Boston and passed some time very pleasantly in the Common listening to the music which enlivened the stillness of the sultry night. It was quite late when we reached home. And I retired to rest feeling that this had been one of the happiest days of my life, and thinking hopefully of the happy glorious day when every fetter shall be broken, and throughout this land there shall no longer be a single slave!

Saturday, August 5. To-day vacation commenced.—How busy we have been this morning in school! Lizzie [Church] and I cleared desks and drawers, arranged books and papers, and put everything in order, rejoicing that we could be of the slightest assistance to our dear teacher [Miss Mary Shepard]. I felt very sad to part with that kind friend, even for a few weeks. She gently reproved me when we were parting, for not returning her embrace. I fear she thought me cold, but it was not so. I know not why it is that when I think and feel the most, I say the least. I suppose it is my nature, not to express by word or action how much I really feel. But it was with real sorrow that I parted from the beloved teacher to whom I owe so much, so much more than I can ever repay, for the kindness which has made this last few months so happy and useful to me. She has supplied me with several excellent books to read during vacation. . . .

Tuesday, August 8. Miss [Mary] Shepard has not gone away yet, and this morning I took a delightful walk with her in Harmony Grove. Never did it look so beautiful as on this very loveliest of summer mornings, so happy, so peaceful one almost felt like resting in that quiet spot, beneath the soft, green grass. My teacher talked to me of a beloved sister who is sleeping here. As she spoke, it almost seemed to me as if I had known her; one of those noble, gentle, warm-hearted spiritual beings, too pure and heavenly for this world. Oh! how lovely it was this morning; all was so bright and beautiful, and yet so calm. Again I parted with my dear teacher, feeling how much

56

I should miss her society, in which I always find so much enjoyment. . . .

Friday, August 11. I have been thinking lately very much about death,—that strange, mysterious, awful reality, that is constantly around and among us, that power which takes away from us so many of those whom we love and honor, or those who have persecuted and oppressed us, our bitter enemies whom we vainly endeavor not to hate. Oh! I long to be good, to be able to meet death calmly and fearlessly, strong in faith and holiness. But this I know can only be through the One who died for us, through the pure and perfect love of Him, who was all holiness and love. But how can I hope to be worthy of His love while I still cherish this feeling towards my enemies, this unforgiving spirit? This is a question which I ask myself very often. Other things in comparison with this seem easy to overcome. But hatred of oppression seems to me so blended with hatred of the oppressor I cannot separate them. I feel that no other injury could be so hard to bear, so very hard to forgive, as that inflicted by cruel oppression and prejudice. How *can* I be a Christian when so many in common with myself, for no crime suffer so cruelly, so unjustly? It seems in vain to try, even to hope. And yet I still long to resemble Him in the last degree, for I know that it must be so ere that I can accomplish anything that is really good and useful in life.

Wednesday, August 16. . . . This evening I had a conversation with Mr. N[ell?][35] about the "spiritual rappings."—He is a firm believer in their "spiritual" origin. He spoke of the different manner in which the different "spirits" manifested their presence,—some merely *touching* the mediums, others thoroughly *shaking* them, etc. I told him that I thought I required a very "thorough shaking" to make me a believer. Yet I must not presume to say that I entirely disbelieve that which the wisest cannot understand.

Thursday, August 17. My birthday.[36]—How much I feel to-day my own utter insignificance! It is true the years of my life are but few. But have I improved them as I should have done? No! I feel grieved and ashamed to think how very little I know to what I should know of what is really good and useful. May this knowledge of my *want* of knowledge be to me a fresh incentive to more earnest, thoughtful action, more persevering study! I trust, I believe it will. . . .

Friday, August 25. Our usually quiet city has been quite noisy for the last two days with the drums and other accompaniments of the military.—I shall be thankful when their "muster" is over. I never liked soldiers, and since the disgraceful

57

capture of poor Burns, they are more hateful to me than ever. . . .

Tuesday, August 29. To-day we have an agreeable visitor; quite a distinguished daguerrotypist and artist—Mr. B[all][37] from Cincinnati, whose genius and perseverance have triumphed even over prejudice so far as to make his elegant establishment one of the most profitable and fashionable in the country. . . .

Tuesday, Sept. 5. . . . I have suffered much to-day,—my friends Mrs. P[utnam] and her daughters were refused admission to the Museum, after having tickets given them, solely on account of their complexion. Insulting language was used to them—Of course they felt and exhibited deep, bitter indignation; but of what avail was it? none, but to excite the ridicule of those contemptible creatures, miserable doughfaces who do not deserve the name of men. I will not attempt to write more. —No words can express my feelings. But these cruel wrongs cannot be much longer endured. A day of retribution must come. God grant that it may come very soon! . . .

Monday, Sept. 11. This evening I went . . . to see representations of Niagara Falls, the Mammoth Cave, and those beautiful combinations of nature and art—Fairmount Water Works and Boston Common.[38] The picture of the Mammoth Cave is beautiful. We could almost imagine that we were gazing on some region of fairy-land. The numberless crystals with which the rocky walls and ceilings are studded, glitter like diamonds in the torchlight. In our progress through the cave we see dark, fearful abysses, which are in striking contrast with the charming grottos. I should not think it possible any representation could give one a just conception of the sublimity of Niagara. The picture of Fairmount is excellent. The noble basin, the miniature waterfalls, suspension bridge, and the beautiful gardens on the banks of the Schuylkill looked exactly as I saw them last; and recalled to my mind many pleasing memories of delightful rambles there, with beloved friends, some of whom I shall see no more. But the Mammoth Cave was the most attractive feature of the exhibition, and it was truly magnificent. I said to Ada "When the slaves are set free we shall certainly visit this beautiful, enchanted cavern."—Most despondingly she replied "Then I fear we shall never behold it." . . .

Thursday, Sept. 14. Spent the evening at Mrs. Putnam's.— We had quite a spirited discussion on Mr. Sumner and his party.[39]—One or two recited poetry—Mrs. P[utnam] wishes each of us to learn something, to recite when we meet again.

Sunday, Sept. 17. Spent the afternoon at Mrs. Putnam's.

. . . I was much interested in a conversation between Mrs. P[utnam] and her grandson—little Eddie, about slavery and prejudice.—I saw how hard she struggled to repress those deep, bitter emotions, which, I think she feels more strongly than many do, and to speak calmly to the child who listened with eager interest.—He is uncommonly intelligent and observing for one so young. . . .

Friday, Sept. 22. Read Lowell's "Fable for Critics."[40] It is an extremely amusing criticism on critics, and the leading American poets, including the author himself.—Studied a history lesson.—In the evening went to the Horticultural Exhibition, and saw some very fine fruit and some beautiful flowers.

Tuesday, Sept. 26. To-day Mr. and Mrs. R[emond] left for Syracuse.—I know that we shall miss Mrs. Remond very much—S[arah] is appointed principal housekeeper, and I assistant during her absence.—Read a beautiful eulogium on Pascal.—His character interested me greatly—such a noble nature, —so brilliant, so profound, yet so perfectly simple and childlike. He was one to be loved and venerated.—When I read of the great and gifted ones of earth, I feel more deeply my own ignorance and insufficiency.—How very little after the most diligent and persevering study can I hope to resemble them!

Wednesday, Sept. 27. Have just received a letter from father, which contains a very unexpected summons.—I must return home next month.—It would give me much pleasure to see the loved ones there. But I cannot bear to think of leaving Salem, now that I have just begun to learn.—Most earnestly do I wish to possess what is most invaluable,—a thorough education. I will write immediately and use every argument to induce father to permit me to remain a little longer.—I feel as if I *cannot* go now. Oh! I do hope that father will consent to my staying.

Saturday, Sept. 30. My dear, kind teacher [Mary Shepard] has written to father; I cannot but hope that *her* letter will have some effect.—My friends are very unwilling to have me go; they all sympathize with me in my desire to acquire all the knowledge that I possibly can. . . .

Tuesday, Oct. 3. This afternoon I had a lesson in teaching —I heard the recitations of the third and fourth classes—we got along very pleasantly, and one pretty, rosy-cheeked girl told me afterwards that she liked me *very* much for a teacher. —In the evening did some sewing; and read in Macaulay's "History of England." . . .

Saturday, Oct. 7. This evening Mr. and Mrs. Remond arrived from Syracuse. W[illiam] Wells Brown accompanied them.[41] He has improved greatly both in appearance and conversation during his residence in England.

Sunday, Oct. 8. This morning I had a delightful ride to Lawrence with Mr. and Miss R[emond] and Mr. B[rown]. The country now looks very beautiful. The trees are tinted with the brilliant and gorgeous hues of autumn. We went to the anti-slavery meetings,[42]—which were extremely interesting and well-attended. I had the great pleasure of conversing with Mr. Garrison and Mr. Phillips. We were looking at some fine pictures of the Queens of England, and afterwards at some grand old Italian and German cathedrals, and Mr. Phillips told me about some of them which he had visited. To me it was a great enjoyment and privilege to listen to the conversation of one so highly gifted.

There are some very picturesque little waterfalls formed by the great dam in Lawrence; the town itself is new—a busy manufacturing place, quite unlike quiet, old-fashioned Salem. I prefer the latter. . . .

Saturday, Oct. 14. Last night I attended a concert by the "Luca Family."[43] The youngest of the brothers, a boy of sixteen, as a pianist is really wonderful. I regretted that they had not a larger audience, which they well deserved. They are staying with us.

Thursday, Oct. 19. The "Luca Family" are with us again; so that we have delightful music continually. The young pianist has composed a very beautiful schottish. We are trying to find a name for it, when Mrs. Remond proposed that it should be called the "Liberty Schottish," and dedicated to Mr. Garrison; and this was agreed upon. Of course Ada[laide] thoroughly appreciates our musical life, and is with us frequently.

This evening Sarah, Ada, and myself passed very pleasantly at Mrs. Ives;[44]—There I saw a very fine picture representing a scene in Napoleon's Russian campaign, during which the soldiers suffered so horribly.—A soldier is dying, almost buried beneath the snow; one arm is drawn closely around the dead body of a companion, perhaps a beloved son or brother,—while the hand which convulsively grasps his musket has every muscle strained to the utmost. The expression of his face I shall never forget. Anguish and despair are blended with inflexible courage and determination in his compressed lips and flashing eyes. I almost felt as if he could speak; but words could not have told more than did that painfully expressive face.

A Mr. D[?] was present, with whose fiery enthusiastic nature

I was pleased.—We talked much about Napoleon, and Washington. Some one said that many persons refused to believe that the latter used profane language. I could not help saying that I believed that a person who *would hold slaves* would swear. Of course the "Father of his Country" was eloquently defended from the charge of *willingly* holding slaves. For the rest of the evening our conversation was upon slavery. . . .

Monday, Oct. 23. At last I have received the long expected letter which to my great joy, contains the eagerly desired permission to remain. I thank father very much for his kindness, and am determined that so far as I am concerned, he shall never have cause to regret it. I will spare no effort to become what he desires that I should be; to prepare myself for the responsible duties of a teacher, and to live for the good that I can do my oppressed and suffering fellow-creatures. . . .

Sunday, Oct. 29. Went to the first of the course of anti-slavery lectures, which was given by Mr. Prince of Essex.[45] It was excellent, and very well-attended. The lecturer had not *quite* so much enthusiasm as I like, but he is interesting and warm-hearted. Miss Shepard was there—she said that she was pleased with the lecture. I hope that she will be persuaded to attend the whole course. If she were better acquainted with the sentiments of the abolitionists, I do not think that she could regard any of them as unchristian; but she would see them as they are—truly christian, noble-hearted, devoted to the Right. . . .

Thursday, Nov. 2. This morning our kind teacher, who is always doing something for our enjoyment and instruction, planned for some of us a visit to the Essex Institute. We saw some very old portraits. Among them were those of Dr. Holyoke, an eminent physician of Salem, who lived to be a hundred years old—John Higginson, the son of the first minister of Salem from whom our school received its name—Gov. Bradstreet, Gov. Endicott, and the wife of Mr. Holyoke, the first president of Harvard College, a stately lady of the olden time. We saw the likeness of Oliver Cromwell; and the dark, severe countenance, I thought an index to the character of the stern Lord Protector.

Dr. Wheatland showed us the first newspaper printed in Salem, and another also very old edited by a lady. Lizzie [Church] and I remarked that while the other paper contained no miscellaneous stories, the first article in the ladies' paper was a tragic story, with a most romantic title. Whether this would be ascribed to the *finer taste*, or to the weaker mind of our sex, I know not. I do know, however that *my* appreciation of the generality of newspaper stories has greatly diminished of late.

We saw through a microscope, some infusoria—very minute insects which were found in fossil slate in Europe, and other specimens taken from ditches in this country—some of them so exceedingly small that it is said to require one hundred and eighty-seven millions of them to weigh a single grain. Those we saw were highly magnified. We saw also through the microscope several other very small insects, and minute portions of leaves and of the root of a plant which appeared very singular. We examined the eye of a common fly, which, when magnified resembled a piece of lace.

Dr. Wheatland showed us some pictures of African huts near Cape Palma—and told us that one of them was the residence of a priest or doctor, from whom the natives, when about to take a journey, procure charms, which, they believe will effectually guard them from danger. When passing this place, they scatter a portion of food to the chickens, believing that the spirits of their deceased friends exist in them!

We saw a beautiful birch basket, made by some of the Tuscorora Indians, which showed great taste in the arrangement of colors; and some vessels made by them for containing water, exactly similar to those used by the East Indians. Dr Wheatland said that this was a proof that men, as well as animals possess instinct—causing them to manufacture articles similar to those made by other nations, of whose existence they were ignorant. I thought that it might also be probable, if, as is supposed the American Indians are descended from some of the inhabitants of Asia, that their ancestors in emigrating to this continent brought some of these vessels with them, and taught their children how to make them. We were much indebted to the kindness of Capt. King and Dr. Wheatland for many interesting microscopic views, and much useful information about the old publications and the early settlers of Salem.

Sunday, Nov. 5. This evening attended Mr. Remond's lecture at Lyceum Hall.[46] It was excellent—on the never-failing topic which to us is all-important. Would it were so to every one! Not long should we have to mourn the existence of the terrible sin of slavery in our land. Read some of Mrs. Browning's beautiful poems, and Dr. Cheever's Lectures on Bunyan. They are earnestly, beautifully written. Sometimes I feel that their deep, religious thought is beyond my comprehension. Yet I cannot but acknowledge its truth, and admire its beauty and fervor.

Wednesday, Nov. 8. This evening attended a lecture on

Jerusalem and Damascus.[47] It was very interesting, but as I have read so much about the Holy Land I should have preferred hearing a lecture on some subject with which I was less familiar. The lecturer—Rev. Mr. Thompson of New York, is evidently a very enthusiastic person, and he is certainly a fine lecturer. I was much interested in his account of the ruins of Baalbec—of that ancient city, situated in a fertile plain, near the large and beautiful city of Damascus, nothing is known—not even by whom it was founded, or when, and by what means destroyed. What a contrast must these desolate ruins present to the busy, flourishing city so near them! And how strange it seems that its history should be involved in such entire obscurity. . . .

Sunday, Nov. 12. A rainy day. Read and wrote nearly all day. This evening attended an anti-slavery lecture by the Rev. Mr. Stone.[48] He spoke with deep feeling. He is an earnest, true hearted man, who has suffered for the good cause. . . .

Wednesday, Nov. 15. Have just returned from a lecture by Mr. Quincy.[49] The lecturer contrasted the prosperity and customs of the North with that of the South, showing the great superiority of the former in all that contributes to the true enjoyment of life. Many of his remarks were extremely interesting—others very amusing. He spoke much of the two most distinguished men of Virginia—Capt. John Smith, the brave, heroic settler; and Randolph of Roanoke, the celebrated orator and statesman whose dying act of justice at least entitles his memory to respect. I can see but little merit in knowing and openly acknowledging the sin of slavery and even rebuking it as he did, and yet persisting in doing the wrong. Mr. Quincy, though evidently a man of somewhat liberal views is widely different from his truly liberty-loving brother.—To divert my thoughts from American wickedness read Macaulay's character of Charles the Second—turned from republican despotism of to-day to the monarchical tyranny of two centuries ago. The contrast is by no means very striking, as far as actual tyranny is concerned.

Saturday, Nov. 18. Rose before four—it was very dark and cold. Studied Philosophy. . . . Afterwards Mr. B[rown] arrived, and we talked about England. He talks continually about his daughters.[50] They must be prodigies. I feel extremely curious to see them, and hope they are as finely educated and accomplished as he evidently thinks they are. Would that there were far more intelligent colored people! And yet we could hardly expect more of those, who have so many unsurmountable difficulties to contend with. But despite them all let our motto still be "Excelsior", and we cannot fail to make some improvement. At times I feel it almost impossible not to despond entirely of there ever being a better, brighter day for us. None but those who experience it can know what it is—this constant, galling sense of cruel injustice and wrong. I cannot help feeling it very often,—it intrudes upon my happiest moments, and spreads a dark, deep gloom over everything.

Sunday, Nov. 19. . . . This evening went to Mr. Brown's lecture. I thought that he spoke much better than he usually does. His manner was more animated. But although in private conversation he has greatly improved, I do not think he is a very good lecturer. As a writer he is very highly spoken of by some of the leading English journals.

Tuesday, Nov. 21. Attended a lecture by Rev. Mr. Higginson of Worcester—subject "The Puritan Clergyman."[51] It was very interesting and amusing, giving one an excellent idea of the manners and customs of the old Puritans. For some time he spoke sarcastically and severely about them; but afterwards paid a tribute of admiration and respect to their stern virtues and thorough consistency of action. I wished that my dear teacher had been there to hear the lecture, for she had a most enthusiastic love for the old Puritan fathers, and I knew she would appreciate it. . . .

Thursday, Nov. 23. This evening accompanied Miss Shepard on a visit to one of her friends—Miss Upton. They are very agreeable people, and I passed the evening pleasantly.—I told my dear teacher that if I could in the very least degree help to lessen the cruel, unjust prejudice which exists against us, I would go willingly. I think it hardly probable that I was so fortunate, but enjoyed the evening far more than I had anticipated. My beloved teacher and I walked home in the quiet starlight—star*shine* she said it might be called—and why not? we have sunshine and moonshine, and surely it is delightful—the light of those fair stars "which are the poetry of heaven." And more delightful it seemed to me with that dear friend, the remembrance of whose kind words and loving sympathy will remain, even after I have parted from her, one of the happiest of my life. . . .

Sunday, Nov. 26. Finished reading "Ida May."[52] It is extremely interesting but I do not think it compares with "Uncle Tom's Cabin." Still it shows plainly the evils of slavery, and may do much good. I read it with pleasure, as I do everything which is written in opposition to this iniquitous system. This evening listened to one of the most eloquent and radical anti-slavery lectures that I have ever heard. It was given by Rev.

Mr. Hodges of Watertown, one of the few ministers who dare speak and act as freemen, obeying the Higher Law, and scorning all lower laws which are opposed to Justice and Humanity.[53] His subject was the final issue of slavery, and he showed in the most conclusive manner how utterly impossible it is for liberty and slavery to exist in union; one of them must eventually triumph. He thinks that the latter will do so, 'and the country sink into inevitable ruin. And then on the ruins of the old republic, will be founded a new and glorious one, whose people will take warning from the fate of this, and form a union which shall be free from the curse of slavery. . . .

Sunday, Dec. 3. . . . Evening.—Have just returned from an interesting lecture by Mr. Garrison.[54] I had the pleasure of shaking hands with the great and good man. He could scarcely have had a more disagreeable night. It is extremely windy and stormy. While I write the rain pours, and the wind blows a perfect hurricane. What a contrast to the quiet beauty of last night! . . .

Wednesday, Dec. 6. Studied arithmetic and philosophy, and in the afternoon went to a sewing party, or "bee" as the New Englanders call it.—Such parties possess not the slightest attraction for me, unless they are for the anti-slavery fair. Then I always feel it both a duty and a pleasure to go. My teacher, with her usual kindness, gave me her Lyceum ticket. Dr. Solger was expected to lecture, but having another engagement Prof. Agassiz supplied his place.[55] The subject was the formation of animals, and though interesting and instructive I felt somewhat disappointed, as I heard him deliver a lecture nearly similar, and it did not quite compensate for what I had expected to hear about Europe.

Monday, Dec. 4. Wrote letters, read poetry, and studied history.—This evening went to the anti-slavery sewing circle at Mrs. Ives.'[56]—Nellie and I established ourselves at a pretty little table, and sewed and talked very pleasantly. She is one of those intelligent, affectionate children whom it is impossible not to love. She was quite enthusiastic in her admiration of Mr. Garrison who had been staying with them, and we fully agreed with regard to his uncommon excellence.

Sunday, Dec. 10. . . . This evening attended Rev. Mr. Appleton's lecture.[57] I had expected to hear the most radical anti-slavery, nor was I disappointed. The lecturer forcibly and eloquently advocated the principles of moral action against slavery, denouncing all political action as being necessarily based on the Constitution, the very root of the evil; declared that the "timid good" were no accession to the anti-slavery ranks, but

rather a hindrance to work of freedom, which would be benefitted by their leaving it; and that nothing but an open and
manly denunciation of slavery, and those who support and
apologize for it, or fear to speak against it, would ever be of
the slightest avail. All of which, of course had my entire sympathy and approbation. . . .

Sunday, Dec. 17. This evening Sarah's husband [J. D. Gil-
liard] arrived from California; Mr. Nell[58] accompanied him
from Boston. We were very much surprised to see him. Of
course Sarah is very happy. There was so much to be said, so
many questions to be asked and answered, that we had nearly
forgotten Lucy Stone's lecture.[59] We found the hall so much
crowded that it was almost impossible to procure a seat. The
lecture was earnest and impressive, and some parts of it very
beautiful. It was an appeal to the noblest and warmest sympathies of our nature, in behalf of the oppressed. I saw many
among her large and attentive audience, who had probably
never attended an anti-slavery lecture before. I hope her touching appeal may not have been made in vain—that they may
think rightly on this subject. And from noble *thoughts* spring
noble *words* and *deeds*.

Monday, Dec. 25. Christmas Day. The return of this season brings to my mind many recollections both sad and pleasing, thoughts of home, and the happy family meetings we have
had on this delightful day. I imagine that I can see grandmother's loved countenance as she listens to the happy voices
of the little ones around her wishing her a "Merry Christmas."
The busy preparations for the grand dinner, the display of
Christmas gifts, the pleasant salutations—I think of them all,
and cannot help wishing that I could make one of the happy
group assembled there. . . .

This morning Sarah [Remond] and I went to Boston to the
Anti-Slavery Fair,[60] in which I was somewhat disappointed, as
many of the most beautiful articles had been sold, and they had
but very few books, mostly French and German. The rooms
were tastefully decorated with evergreens, and looked quite
Christmas-like. In the afternoon the boys accompanied me to
the Museum. We saw a play entitled "The Dream," which I did
not think particularly interesting. I want very much to see
"Othello" or "Macbeth" or some other of Shakespeare's grand
tragedies. These lighter dramas possess very little interest for
me. In the evening returned to the fair, and saw Mr. Phillips
for a few moments. . . .

Sunday, Dec. 31. The last day of the old year. I can scarcely
realize that I have spent the whole of it away from home.

Yet, although separated from many of my dearest friends, this year has been to me a very happy one. Happy, because the field of knowledge, for the first time has seemed widely open to me; because I have studied more, and, I trust, learned more than during any other year of my life. I have been taught how very little I really know, and, with the knowledge of my ignorance, I feel an earnest desire to become very much wiser. . . .

Part 2

Student and Abolitionist

January 1, 1855 - May 29, 1856

Friday, Jan. 12. · This evening attended a lecture by Rev. Henry Ward Beecher of Brooklyn. The subject was "Patriotism."[1] I thought the lecture extremely interesting, and many parts of it very touching and beautiful. His manner is not at all polished or elegant, but he says so many excellent things with such forcible earnestness or irresistible humor, that we quite forget it. As I had hoped he bore his testimony against the wicked and unjust laws of our land, which it is not *patriotism* to make or to obey. He also eloquently advocated the right of woman to vote; and paid a beautiful tribute to the lovely and noble-minded Lucretia Mott. In listening to Mr. Beecher one feels convinced of his *sincerity;* and we would always rather know that a person *means* what he says, even if we differ from him. . . .

Tuesday, Jan. 23. Read a report of one of Lowell's lectures on English Poetry. They are very interesting and contain many beautiful thoughts which only a true poet could have. In the evening took a pleasant walk with my dear teacher, as far as the entrance of Harmony Grove. The moon was shedding a soft light over the beautiful spot, and the perfect quiet was only broken by the music of a tiny waterfall which the dark evergreens concealed from our sight. It was a lovely night. We stopped at Mrs. Putnam's and spent some time there in very animated conversation about slavery and prejudice. On my return home found a "surprise party" assembled there. Finished the evening very pleasantly with music, singing and conversation.

Wednesday, Jan. 24. . . . This evening attended a lecture by Mr. Pierpont. His subject was, "The Effects of Physical Science upon the Moral World."[2] He lacked animation, and his lecture was extremely uninteresting to me. I was much disappointed in it.

Thursday, Jan. 25. Miss Shepard read to me some exquisite lines, "Canst Thou not Watch One Hour?" They are so very beautiful that I would not forget them, although I cannot even hope to possess the spirit of Christian forebearance and patience which they breathe. We think that Whittier must have written them.[3] I hope that he did, for I can enjoy good and beautiful things so much more when I know that those who write them are themselves *good*, and devoted to the Right. . . .

Monday, Jan. 29. This evening took a delightful ride by moonlight with Mr. and Mrs. Remond and Mr. Brown.— Attended a meeting which was addressed by Mr. B[rown].[4]

Tuesday, Jan. 30. Attended a lecture by Rev. Theodore Parker. I have long wished very much to see and hear this remarkable man, and my pleasant anticipations were fully realized. His subject was "The Anglo Saxon Race."[5] He gave an extremely interesting and instructive sketch of their origin and peculiar traits of character. And while he acknowledged their superiority in the sciences and in what is *practical* in life, he also showed how inferior they are generally to other races in imagination, love and appreciation of the beautiful, and true moral worth. He spoke of their aggressive spirit, which continually prompted them to make war upon and exterminate other races, and to take possession of their country, and of their strong love of *individual* liberty; but described them as too selfish to be fond of *equality*. One of their greatest failings is a lack of conscientiousness—they are *downright* before *men* but *not upright* before God. This is somewhat exemplified by pauperism in England and slavery in America. Every eighth man in England is a pauper; every eighth man in America is *worse* than a pauper—he does not own the hands with which he works—the feet upon which he stands. Every eighth woman in America does not own herself nor the child upon her bosom.

Wednesday, Jan. 31. Again I have had the pleasure of hearing Mr. Parker. The lecture of this evening was even more interesting than the other; it was on the "character, condition and propspects of America." I will not attempt an account of it as I could not do it justice. I can only say that it was impressive and true—full of earnest thought and the warmest zeal for truth. Both this evening and last when he spoke of slavery it seemed to me as if I could *feel* the half suppressed sensation which it occasioned. It is *some* encouragement that nearly all the finest orators now are anti-slavery. . . .

Wednesday, Feb. 7. Attended a lecture by Mr. Curtis on "Success."[6] He is a very fine orator, his voice rich and musical, and his manner polished and elegant. The aim of the lecture was to show how often mere wordly prosperity is confounded with *true success* and how widely dissimilar they are. He expressed many true and noble sentiments; and in conclusion

69

spoke of America as more *prosperous* than *successful*. Success he declared to be a nobler and higher aim than earthly prosperity. . . .

Wednesday, Feb. 14. This afternoon had a sleigh ride—the first I had this season. The hills and evergreens look very beautifully in their snowy mantle. Wet met the Hutchinsons[7] who seemed heartily glad to see Mr. Remond. They have promised to visit Salem again, and I hope it will be soon. I admire those warm-hearted minstrels of the "Old Granite State."

Thursday, Feb. 15. The day before examination, and a very busy day it is. The old school-room has been undergoing a thorough process of renovation, and looks really very bright and respectable. We had quite a dinner-party at the school-house, with Miss Shepard for the presiding genius, and a merry, delightful party it was.

Friday, Feb. 16. Evening—The dreaded examination day is over at last, and we feel very much relieved. The school-room was densely crowded. The girls did very well, and our teacher expressed herself much pleased. Everything passed off pleasantly, and everybody seemed very much delighted. I am extremely tired, but our dear teacher must be more so. I can scarcely bear to think how very soon I shall have to leave her. To me no one can ever supply her place. . . .

Wednesday, Feb. 28. This evening attended a very interesting and eloquent lecture on Switzerland, by Rev. Mr. Waterson.[8]

Tuesday, March 6. Our class spent the evening at Miss Shepard's. We took the daguerreotypes which were handsomely finished in separate cases, arranged in one frame,—and a small work-box. Our teacher was much pleased with the presents.—We spent the evening very pleasantly. Lizzie [Church] and I remained long after the others had gone, sitting before the cheerful grate-fire and conversing with our beloved friend, our teacher no longer.

Wednesday, Mar. 7. This evening attended one of Lowell's lectures on English Poetry.[9] The subject of this was particularly "the imaginative faculty." I thought it very beautiful, and although I had previously read it, enjoyed it greatly. The poet's personal appearance is extremely unpretending. His figure is slight and rather short and his face, were it not for the whiskers and *moustache* which completely cover the lower part, would, I think look almost feminine. His voice is rich and musical, but scarcely loud enough for a lecturer. But the great beauty of his thoughts and language causes the listener to for-

70

get any minor deficiency. I have always admired him as one of the great Poets of Humanity.

Friday, Mar. 9. Passed the evening quite pleasantly with most of our former class at Miss Dalton's. The girls were in high spirits, nearly all of them having triumphantly entered the High School. I hope very earnestly that father will consent to my entering the Normal School,[10] or rather to my applying for admission. . . .

Tuesday, Mar. 13. Went through the examination and entered the Normal School.[11] I have not yet heard from father; but as I had to give no pledge to remain a certain length of time, and this is the only opportunity I should have until another term, I thought it best to enter the school. It was with a very delightful sensation of relief that I received the welcome intelligence of my being admitted; for greatly had I feared it might be otherwise.

Wednesday, Mar. 14. Heard Ralph Waldo Emerson lecture on France.[12] The lecture was very interesting and entertaining though not particularly flattering does *his* estimate seem to be of the gay and fickle inhabitants of "la belle France." I had felt quite eager to hear the gifted man who, Wendell Phillips says, is thought in England to stand at the head of American literature. He is a fine lecturer, and a very peculiar-looking man.

Friday, Mar. 16. To my great surprise, received a letter from father summoning me to return home as soon as possible. I feel deeply grieved; it seems harder than ever to leave now that I have just entered upon a course of study which I so earnestly hoped would thoroughly qualify me for the duties of a teacher. The few days I have spent at the Normal School have been very pleasant although I have felt a little strange and lonely. But the teachers are kind, and the teaching so thorough and earnest that it increases the love of knowledge and the desire to acquire it. Mr. Edwards[13] kindly assured me that he very much regretted my being obliged to leave. Although it would give me much pleasure to see my kind friends at home, I cannot but regret that I must go now, feeling as I do that a year longer at school would be of great benefit to me. This evening went to Miss Shepard who earnestly declared that I *must not* go, and who made me a *very* kind offer, which I do not think *can* be accepted with the little hope I now possess of being able to repay it.

Saturday, March 17. This morning Mr. Edwards came to see me, and told me that he had no doubt of my being able to

71

obtain a situation as teacher here if I went through the Normal School. He wishes me to write to father and assure him of this. Miss Shepard urged me to consent to her writing to him about what she proposes. I do indeed feel deeply obliged to her for her very great kindness to me; whether it be as she wishes it or not. I shall continue at school until I hear from home again, as Mr. Edwards said he would like to have me do so.

Sunday, Mar. 18. Wrote a long letter to father, which I shall send . . . tomorrow. . . .

Wednesday, Mar. 28. Received a few lines from father. To my very great joy he consents to my remaining in the Normal School. Aunt M[argaretta][14] also writes and asks if I wrote the lines to "W.L.G." in the Liberator.[15] If ever I write doggerel again I shall be careful not to sign my own initials. This evening attended a lecture on Hayti by Mr. Clark of Boston.[16] The lecturer spoke eloquently of the Haytians, from whom he had received much kindness,—and paid a well-deserved tribute to the brave and unfortunate Toussaint. I was beginning to think him an earnest friend of freedom when he proved to be a colonizationist and then a very decided and unpleasant "change came o'er the spirit of my dream." . . .

Thursday, Apr. 5. Fast Day, and we have no school. Mr. Nell spent the afternoon and evening with us. . . .[17]

Tuesday, May 1. May-day; but tears instead of smiles are ushering in "the delicate-footed May." More and more pleasant becomes my Normal School life. Yet I have made but very few acquaintances, and cannot but feel that among all my school companions there is not a single one who gives me her full and entire sympathy. My studies are my truest friends. . . .

Wednesday, May 30. Ellen and I went to Boston. Went in to the anti-slavery convention for a short time; was not able to stay long.[18] Mr. Phillips introduced Anthony Burns in the most beautiful manner.[19] In the afternoon went to see the Panorama,[20] which I liked very much. In the evening went to the meetings again. Mr. Higginson[21] gave a very interesting lecture; he is a particular favorite of mine. Mrs. Ernestine Rose spoke well but too long.[22] Then Mr. Phillips spoke beautifully, eulogizing the former speaker—her consistency—her devotion to truth and right everywhere.

Thursday, May 31. Attended the meetings all day. Several very interesting speeches were made; in the afternoon an animated discussion on the Constitution was carried on between Mr. Garrison, Mr. Pierpont,[23] Mr. Burleigh[24] and others.[25] In the evening Mr. Phillips made one of the most eloquent speeches I have ever heard even from his eloquent lips.[26] Theodore Parker spoke; I was somewhat disappointed in him. The Hall was crowded; and while Wendell Phillips was speaking, I gazed on the hundreds of earnest faces, and thought that those glowing words so full of eloquence and truth could not be lost upon *all* of those to whom they were addressed.

Friday, June 1. Summer, the wayward loiterer has come at last. The song of the birds, melodious and sweet ushers her in. This morning returned to Salem; grateful indeed is its quietness and coolness after the noise and heat of Boston; the Common is the one bright beautiful spot of that crowded city which to my mind redeems it somewhat. As to its inhabitants, they are redeemed only by the few noble spirits—the best and noblest that the world has ever seen.

Wednesday, July 4. . . . All our household save S[arah][27] and myself have gone to the Framingham celebration.[28] . . . Here all is cool, quiet and pleasant; and gratefully refreshing is coolness and quiet after the heat and noise of last night.—The *patriots*, poor fools, were celebrating the anniversary of their vaunted *independence*. Strange! that they cannot feel their *own* degradation—the weight of the chains which they have imposed upon *themselves*. . . .

Monday, July 16, 1855. Examination day.—No further comment is needed.

Tuesday, July 17. I breathe freely,—our trial is over, and happy are we to escape from the hot, crowded school-room;—for it has been densely crowded all day. This evening the scholars had a pleasant meeting in the school house and the last farewells were said. . . .

Wednesday, Aug. 1. Went with Aunt M[argaretta][29] and a party of friends to the celebration at Abington.[30] Our much-loved Garrison was not there,—His absence could not fail to be felt. But Mr. Phillips and other able speakers were there and many eloquent speeches were made. We had a plasant sail on the beautiful pond attached to the Grove;—and passed altogether a delightful day.

Sunday, Aug. 12. Had a delightful ride to Reading, to an anti-slavery meeting. The road is beautiful and our Penn[sylvania] friends warmly admired scenery which the eastern part of the Keystone State cannot boast of. Mr. Garrison and Mr. Phillips spoke very beautifully. To our great regret we were obliged to leave while Mr. P[hillips] was speaking.[31] Our ride home was extremely pleasant. . . .

Friday, Aug. 17. My eighteenth birthday.—Spent the afternoon and evening very pleasantly at Mrs. Putnam's. Miss

73

Brown was there,[32] I think I shall like her. Her father's fondness for her is rather too demonstrative. I guess she is a sensible girl. I enjoy talking with her about her European life.—She is pleasant and communicative, and though coming lastly from England, has, I think, lived in France too much to acquire a great deal of that reserve which characterizes the manners of the English.

Sunday, Aug. 26. Spent the evening at Mrs. Putnam's. Mr. Nell was there.[33] We amused ourselves with making conundrums, reading and reciting poetry. . . .

Wednesday, Sept. 12. To-day school commenced.—Most happy am I to return to the companionship of my studies,— ever my most valued friends. It is pleasant to meet the scholars again; most of them greeted me cordially, and were it not for the thought that *will* intrude, of the want of *entire sympathy* even of those I know and like best, I should greatly enjoy their society. There is one young girl and only one—Miss [Sarah] B[rown] who I believe thoroughly and heartily appreciates anti-slavery,—*radical* anti-slavery, and has no prejudice against color. I wonder that every colored person is not a misanthrope. Surely we have everything to make us hate mankind. I have met girls in the schoolroom[—] they have been thoroughly kind and cordial to me,—perhaps the next day met them in the street—they feared to recognize me; these I can but regard now with scorn and contempt,—once I liked them, believing them incapable of such meanness. Others give the most distant recognition possible.—I, of course, acknowledge no such recognitions, and they soon cease entirely. These are but trifles, certainly, to the great, public wrongs which we as a people are obliged to endure. But to those who experience them, these apparent trifles are most wearing and discouraging; even to the child's mind they reveal volumes of deceit and heartlessness, and early teach a lesson of suspicion and distrust. Oh! it is hard to go through life meeting contempt with contempt, hatred with hatred, fearing, with too good reason, to love and trust hardly any one whose skin is white,—however lovable, attractive and congenial in seeming. In the bitter, passionate feelings of my soul again and again there rises the questions "When, oh! when shall this cease?" "Is there no help?" "How long oh! how long must we continue to suffer—to endure?" Conscience answers it is wrong, it is ignoble to despair; let us labor earnestly and faithfully to acquire knowledge, to break down the barriers of prejudice and oppression. Let us take courage; never ceasing to work,—hoping and believing that if not for us, for another generation there is a better, brighter day in store,—when slavery and prejudice shall vanish before the glorious light of Liberty and Truth; when the rights of every colored man shall everywhere be acknowledged and respected, and he shall be treated as a *man* and a *brother!*

September. This evening Miss B[rown] and I joined the Female Anti-Slavery Society.[34] I am glad to have persuaded her to do so. She seems an earnest hearted girl, in whom I cannot help having some confidence. I can only hope and pray that she will be true, and courageous enough to meet the opposition which every friend of freedom must encounter. . . .

Friday, October 19. Walked to Marblehead with some of the girls to attend the teachers' meeting. . . . In the evening . . . listened to a very beautiful lecture from Rev. Mr. Huntingdon, —his subject was "Unconscious Tuition." But I felt a want, for among the many true and beautiful sentiments which he uttered not the faintest indication that he was even aware of the existence of that cruel and disgraceful system which refuses all teachings—all that can elevate and improve to millions of the inhabitants of this *glorious* (?) republic. Had a pleasant walk to Salem in the moonlight. . . .

Sunday, Oct. 21. The twentieth anniversary of the day on which beloved Garrison was mobbed and insulted in the streets of Boston.[35] To-day on the very spot where that little band of noble-hearted women so heroically maintained the right, the dauntless Pioneer of our glorious cause stands with many true-hearted co-workers, surrounded by hundreds of eager, sympathizing listeners. The men who dragged him with a rope around his neck through the streets of Boston,—to their own shame—not his—would blush to confess it to-day. And even his bitter enemies are forced, despite themselves, to respect his self-sacrificing unfaltering devotion to Liberty and Truth. Dear, honored friends, I cannot be with you in your gathering to-day, but the light of your loved countenances,—the tones of your eloquent voices fall upon my grateful heart. This evening my necessary absence from the meeting in Boston,[36] upon which my thoughts have dwelt all day, was somewhat compensated for by listening to an excellent and very interesting lecture from Rev. S. Johnson of Lynn. *The first of our course.*—[37]

Sunday, Oct. 28. This has indeed been one of the happiest days of my life.—Wendell Phillips, Mr. Hovey,[38] and Miss Holley[39] and Miss P[hillips] have spent it with us,—could it fail to be a happy one? Mr. Phillips is the most fascinating person I ever saw. That graceful affability which characterizes the truly great, he embodies, with all that is truly good and noble. Mrs. Hovey is exceedingly entertaining. He has travelled much;

and presented Mrs. R[emond] with a precious relic—a piece of mosaic pavement from the Baths of Caracalla, Rome, built sixteen hundred years ago. How strange it seems that sixteen centuries ago this stone was laid—almost incredible! While gazing on such relics a strange influence from the mighty, mysterious Past comes over us—conjuring up visions of that olden time, long past, but never to be forgotten; for the soul of man rests not in the *Present,* nor soars only in the great *Future,* which imagination paints for it, but also does it love to dwell in the deep, soul-stirring memories of the Past. Mr. Phillips' lecture was worthy of himself[40]—I can bestow no higher praise upon it. Oh! it is a source of some consolation to feel—to know that some of the noblest minds—the greatest intellects of the age are enlisted in our behalf.—

Friday, Nov. 1. This evening heard Charles Sumner for the first time.[41] He said many excellent things, but I cannot agree with very many of his views—particularly with his reverence for the Constitution and the Union. I believe, though greatly mistaken he yet has a warm, true heart, and certainly he is an elegant and eloquent orator. Though very different from, and inferior to Mr. Phillips, in my opinion.—

Sunday, Nov. 4. Mr. Swasey of Newburyport lectured.[42] He is a new convert and a most zealous one. His lecture though rather long was on the whole a very good one. . . .

Monday, Nov. 19. Prof. Guiot commenced his lectures on Physical Geography before our school to-day.[43] They promise to be extremely interesting. This evening attended Mrs. Webb's readings; they were principally from Shakespeare.[44] I was not very much pleased. I wish colored persons would not attempt to do anything of the kind unless they can compare favorably with others.—But I know that I should not presume to criticize; and most sincerely hope if she has talent, it may be cultivated,—and that she may succeed in her vocation—reflecting credit upon herself and her race.—

Wednesday, Nov. 21. To-day Prof. Guiot finished his lectures.—Those of to-day were on the Creation.—His theory is the geological one. Many parts of the lectures were too abstruse and profound to be easily understood. But the grandeur of the subject, and the earnest eloquence of the orator failed not to make them deeply interesting.

Friday, Nov. 23. We are to have vacation next week—Thanksgiving week. The happy voices of the girls as they spoke of "going home" made me feel rather home-sick. But as I cannot go to either of my homes,—to Canada (where father has recently moved) or to Phil[adelphia], I must try not to think of them. This evening took a pleasant walk with Maria B.—the most intimate of my school-companions. She is an agreeable, intelligent girl, whom I wish very earnestly to interest in anti-slavery.

Sunday, Nov. 25. ... This evening Rev. J. F. Clarke gave us an excellent lecture—one of the best we have had.[45] His subject was the "Demoralization of the North by Slavery." ...

Sunday, Dec. 16. ... This evening listened to a tolerably good lecture on slavery by Rev. Antoinette Brown.[46] Her manner is too passive, and although she said some excellent things it was plain to be seen that she did not know as much on this subject as on that of Woman's Rights.

Tuesday, Dec. 18. A dear, good man has spent the day at our school—Mr. May of Syracuse—one of the most delightful persons I have ever met.[47] Mr. Russell introduced me to him, and he inquired with the greatest kindness after our family.

Wednesday, Dec. 19. This afternoon Mr. M[ay] gave us an interesting lecture on the Idiot Schools. He eloquently portrayed the good and noble qualities necessary for the faithful teacher of an idiot school,—the untiring devotion, the self-sacrificing spirit, possessed in an eminent degree by every truly successful teacher in these schools especially. Other teachers have only to *train* the minds of their pupils;—the teacher of an idiot may be said to *make* the mind before training it—he may almost be said to *create* the materials which he is to work upon. He has trials to encounter far beyond what the most severely tried of other teachers has to endure, and far greater, if he is successful, should be the credit awarded to him. Mr. May also delivered before the Lyceum a lecture—extremely interesting and useful, on Magna Charta and the New Constitution of New York.[48]

Sunday, Dec. 23. This evening had the very great pleasure of hearing dear Mr. May speak on anti-slavery.[49] It was one of the best lectures I have ever heard. And I thanked him with my whole heart for the beautiful and well deserved tribute which he paid Mr. Garrison, who is so very greatly unappreciated and misrepresented. He compared him to the fountain in the Black Forest of Germany where the mighty Danube—the great "anti-slavery stream" has its source; and failed not to mention the numerous valuable tributaries who have contributed to its mass of waters—ever receiving a new impulse from the great Fountain Head. He had a large, and extremely attentive audience.—

Christmas Day, 1855. Alone; I do not know when I have been alone before on Christmas—never, I think.—Wrote a long letter to Aunt M[argaretta] while I was writing, Mrs. Gilliard[50] came in and insisted on my accompanying her home. I spent part of the day and took dinner there. . . . Went to hear Ralph Waldo Emerson, who lectured on Beauty.[51] I liked his originality, though his manner is not particularly interesting. Altogether we were much pleased with the lecture.

Sunday, Dec. 30. Yesterday, Mrs. Remond,[52] who has been attending the Boston Bazaar,[53] came home. . . . Heard read, and read partly myself—"Caste" which is an interesting anti-slavery, anti-prejudice story.[54]

This evening listened to an excellent lecture before our Society, from Mr. Frothingham. . . .[55]

Sunday, Jan. 27 [1856]. (Wrote a hymn for examination.[56]) The last few weeks have been but successions of constant study, with but little variation. I have heard but one lecture—that of Mr. Parker,—which was, of course, excellent.[57] His subject was the "Productive Industry of the Age" and he contrasted it with the military achievements of the "olden time"; and strikingly showed the beneficial effects of the industry of our age. Every time I listen to this wonderful man, I become more deeply impressed with the magnificence of his intellect and the sincere goodness and nobleness of his heart. This evening Mr. Hodges gave us a very good anti-slavery lecture.[58] For the first time Mrs. Remond was obliged to introduce the lecturer it was a great trial to her, but she did well ne'ertheless. . . .

Saturday, Feb. 2. This evening our beloved Mr. Garrison and his wife arrived.[59]—Most gladly did we welcome them. The Remonds and Putnams spent the evening with us, and we had a delightful time. Mr. Garrison was very genial as he always is, and sang delightfully.

Sunday, Feb. 3. This has been one of the happiest days of my life. More and more do I love and admire that great and good man. His wife is a lovely woman; it is indeed delightful to see so happy and noble a couple. This evening Mr. Garrison gave us one of the best lectures I ever heard him deliver. Always interesting to me, to-night he was unusually entertaining. Just before the lecture Mr. Innis announced the fact of Mr. Banks' election, which was received with tumultuous applause.[60] Mr. G[arrison] spoke beautifully of the "*Banks* of Massachusetts impeding the onward progress of the waves of southern despotism."—

Monday, Feb. 4. This morning Mr. and Mrs. G[arrison] left. They kindly invited me to pay them a visit, which I will be glad to do. This was the first time they have stayed with us since I have been here. And the pleasure, the very great pleasure which I experienced from their visit, will prevent me from soon forgetting it.—

Friday, Feb. 8. Next week we shall have our examination. I dread it, and do most heartily wish it was over!

Tuesday, Feb. 12. The last day of our examination. Thank Heaven it is over at last! I am completely tired out, and need rest, both in body and mind. We have got along very well—I could say pleasantly on the last afternoon, were it not for a few unpleasant remarks of Mr. Russell.[61] The best way is to forget them as soon as possible. The exercises of the graduating class, on this afternoon were very interesting.

Wednesday, Feb. 13. I should be sorry that we have vacation were it not that I need rest. This morning Mr. R[emond] left for Phila[delphia]. I felt very anxious to go, but it was impossible. We met at the school house, and formed a Normal Association. . . .

Saturday, Mar. 1. . . . I would gladly go out and enjoy to the full the clear, bracing air and the bright sunlight; but I was *wise* enough to take a severe cold and must pay the penalty by keeping a close prisoner on this delightful day. I have just heard that my beloved friend Miss Shepard is much better, and I feel better and happier for knowing it.[62] A few evenings since attended a pleasant surprise party at Mrs. P[utnam]'s. Several of the company were dressed as ladies of the olden time, and very comical they looked in short skirts, high-heeled shoes, huge collars, and combs which are miniature steeples. I was persuaded to dress in full Bloomer costume, which I have since had good cause to regret, however. . . .

Thursday, March 6. Received a long and pleasant letter from Sarah Brown.[63] I was very glad to hear from her, and shall send her some anti-slavery tracts when I write. She is a most agreeable and good-hearted girl, interested in anti-slavery; but I do most earnestly hope to see her more so.—

Monday, Mar. 10. This evening went to see 'Hamlet.' It is the first play of Shakespeare's that I [have] ever seen and I enjoyed it very much. I suppose if I had ever seen any better acting than Mr. Marshall's I should not have been so much pleased. The tragedy I have always liked very much; and many parts of it are as familiar as household words.—

Tuesday, Mar. 11. Went to hear the Misses Hall—the 'Singing Sisters.'[64] They sang very sweetly. One of them has a particularly fine voice.—On returning home found a very old friend of our family,—Mr. Coffin,—the former teacher of my father and uncles. I have seldom met any one who possessed such extensive and varied knowledge, and yet from his perfectly unassuming, and perhaps unrefined manner, a stranger would never suspect it. He is exceedingly entertaining, and, as I know him to be a radical abolitionist I like him very much. His daughter has just entered our Normal School. . . .

Sunday, March 16. . . . To-day we had our election for those who are to write our poem, valedictory, and dissertation. Miss Pitman was chosen to write the dissertation; Lizzie Church the valedictory, and my unworthy self to write the poem;[65] I most respectfully declined, but every one insists upon my doing it; so I suppose I must make the attempt. But it is a most formidable undertaking for me, and one which, I greatly fear, is quite beyond my powers. . . .

Wednesday, April 2. This afternoon I had a long conversation with Mr. Edwards.[66] He spoke very kindly to me, far more so than I deserve, and urged me to come back next term. When I very earnestly assured him that it was quite impossible, he asked me why in such a manner that I could not avoid telling him frankly. He said he would see if something could not be done. I said nothing, but I know too well that nothing *can* be done. Indeed though I very much wish to spend another term here, I desire nothing so much as some employment which shall enable me to pay my debts.—I hope I shall be fortunate enough to obtain some situation as a teacher. . . .

Saturday, May 11. All day I have been worrying about that poem. That troublesome poem which has yet to be commenced. Oh! that I could become suddenly inspired and write as only great poets can write. Or that I might write a beautiful poem of two hundred lines in my sleep as Coleridge did. Alas! in vain are all such longings. I must depend upon *myself* alone. And what can that self produce? Nothing, nothing but *doggerel!* This evening read Plutarch's Lycurgus.—

Friday, May 2. To-day Mr. Purvis arrived.[67] I think he looks poorly. Felt glad to see him. We have vacation this week instead of next, for which I am sorry, because next week the Boston meetings take place.

Wednesday, May 29. Went up to Boston this afternoon with Mr. Purvis, Mrs. P[urvis] and Miss L[ucy] Remond. We went to the Pillsbury Festival,[68] which was a very brilliant and successful one. . . . Excellent speeches were made by our best speakers. Mr. P[hillips] was as usual eloquent as fascinating. Mr. Pillsbury spoke for a little while with deep feeling; his health is not entirely restored. I like him much. Had the happiness of seeing Mrs. Chapman[69] for the first time. I think her the most beautiful women I ever saw. Also the very great pleasure of seeing Mrs. Chase of R[hode] I[sland][70] to whom I wrote applying for the situation of governess. Her reply was a *very* kind letter. I love her for it. She is a lovely looking woman, I shall be glad to have such a friend. . . .

Part 3

Teacher and Invalid

June 18, 1856 - June 11, 1857

Wednesday, June 18.   Amazing, wonderful news I have heard to-day! It has completely astounded me. I cannot realize it.— Mr. Edwards[1] called me into his room with a face full of such grave mystery, that I at once commenced reviewing my past conduct, and wondering what terrible misdeed I,—a very model of deportment" had committed within the precincts of our Normal world. The mystery was most pleasantly solved. I have received the offer of a situation as teacher in one of the public schools of this city,—of this conservative, aristocratic old city of Salem!!! Wonderful indeed it is! I know that it is principally through the exertions of my kind teacher, although he will not acknowledge it.—I thank him with all my heart. I had a long talk with the Principal of the school, whom I like much.[2] Again and again I ask myself—'*Can* it be true?' It seems impossible. I shall commence to-morrow.—

Thursday, June 19.   To-day, a rainy and gloomy one I have devoted to my new duties. Of course I cannot decide how I like them yet.—I thought it best to commence immediately, although the term has not quite closed. I could not write about it yesterday, the last day of my school-life. Yet I cannot think it quite over until after the examination, in which Mr. Edwards has kindly arranged that I shall take part.

Saturday, June 21.   I find the children rather boisterous and unmanageable; but Mr. Warren[3] thinks there is a slight improvement in them. That is some comfort. . . .

Saturday, June 28.   The weather is hot; the children restless, and I find a teacher's life not nearly as pleasant as a scholar's. But I do not despair. Oh! no! I have faith. Ever shall my motto be, *"Labor omnia vincit."*—I found my scholars very pleasant and obliging. They bring me beautiful flowers every day. Many of them interesting children. Others very far from being so.—May I be granted strength to do my duty in the great field of labor upon which I have entered!

Thursday, July 3.   My dear friend Mrs. Remond has been

slightly unwell for some time. I am truly sorry that she will not be well enough to attend the celebration to-morrow. . . .

Friday, July 4. To-day a large party of us . . . went to the Anti-Slavery celebration at Framingham.[4] It was clear when we started, but before we reached Boston, the rain poured in torrents. However we went on to F[ramingham] the meeting was held in the Hall in the morning, and was very interesting. In the afternoon adjourned to the grove, but it was too rainy to remain there long. . . .

Friday, July 18. . . . This evening was spent at Mr. Edwards' with our class. We had a very pleasant evening. Talked anti-slavery most of the time. Had a long talk with Mr. Clark [?], who accompanied me home. He is a 'Liberty Party' man, and I vainly tried to persuade him that all political action was wrong. I like to hear him talk. He is so earnest and such a close reasoner.—Stood talking outside the gate until after eleven. My dear Mrs. R[emond] does not seem to improve. I fear she gets worse. This terribly oppressive heat is very unfavorable to her. . . .

Tuesday, July 22. This afternoon we were examined in "School and Schoolmaster." Essays were read.[5] Miss Pitman's D[issertation], My poor poem,[6] and Lizzie's V[aledictory]— which is a beautiful production; charming as dear Lizzie's self. Crowds of people were there. Our diplomas were awarded. I was lucky enough to get one. This evening we had a delightful meeting at the school house,—our last. It was one of the pleasantest meetings we have had. And now I realize that my school days are indeed over. And many sad regrets I feel that it is indeed so. The days of my N[ew] England school life, though spent far from home and early friends, have still been among the happiest of my life. I have been fortunate enough to receive the instruction of the best and kindest teachers; and the few friends I have made are warm and true.—New England! I love to tread thy soil,—trod by the few noble spirits,—Garrison, Phillips and others,—the truest and noblest in the land; to breathe the pure air of thy hills, which is breathed by them; to gaze upon thy grand old rocks, "lashed by the fury of the ocean wave," upon thy granite hills, thy noble trees, and winding, sparkling streams, to all of which a greater charm is added by the thought that *they* the good and gifted ones, have gazed upon them also.

Friday, July 25. At Dr. Wheatland's[7] request took him that poor, miserable poem. I wish he would not have it published.

83

It is *not worth* it. I think this will be the last of my attempts at poetizing. I am heartily ashamed of it.

Sunday, July 27. Our beloved patient grows worse.[8] She cannot endure this terribly oppressive heat. Oh! how much these weeks of illness have changed her. As I gaze upon her, lying on her bed of suffering, I can scarcely realize that it is indeed she, who a few, short months ago, seemed in such perfect health and spirits. Dear, dear friend, I earnestly, fondly hope that she will recover.—

Friday, Aug. 1. Intended to go to the Celebration,[9] . . . but our dear Mrs. R[emond] is so much worse that none of us can leave. I very much fear that she will not be spared to us. But I cannot bear to think of it. God grant that it may not be so! . . .

Friday, Aug. 15. All is over! this morning between four and five, the dearly loved one passed away from us, to join the dwellers in the "Silent Land." The nurse and I sat up with her during the night,—

> *"We watched her breathing through the night,*
> *Her breathing soft and low*
> *As in the breast the wave of life*
> *Kept heaving to and fro."*

She is gone! Peacefully, without a murmur she passed away. The loveliest of women, the best and kindest of friends to me, —*her* place can never, never be filled.[10]—

Saturday, Aug. 16. The funeral takes place to-day.

Sunday, Aug. 17. My nineteenth birthday—the saddest I have ever known.—Yesterday the remains of our dear friend were laid in the grave. Mr. and Mrs. Garrison, Mr. Phillips and many other friends who knew and loved her well were present. Truly might it be said of her,

> *"None knew her but to love her,*
> *None named her but to praise."*

I do not think there is in the world a more amiable or lovable person.—Poor dear Sarah [Remond], I pity her; she has had many trials for one so young.—

Monday, Aug. 18. Our house is *very* lonely now, without the dearly loved mother and friend. *She* is indeed happy. We grieve for *ourselves* alone.—No one can ever supply her place to us,—Never! . . .

Sunday, Sept. 7. This evening walked to Danvers, and heard an anti-slavery lecture from Mr. Brown.[11] Liked it pretty well. Commenced "English Traits," which I shall like very much, I think. . . .

Wednesday, Oct. 15. To-day Sarah Pitman and I went into our dear Normal School. We have been there pretty often of late. It is very pleasant to see our loved teachers and the *few* pleasant companions who are left of our broken band.—This evening our sewing circle met at Mrs. Putman's.[12] Had a pleasand chat with Mr. P[utnam] and Mr. Nell before it commenced and afterwards. Mr. N[ell] lent me an oid book of very interesting sketches of some old Greek poets. . . .

Sunday, Oct. 19. Heard an excellent lecture from Mr. Appleton.[13] One of the best I ever listened to. He spoke particularly of disunion. . . .

Sunday, Oct. 26. Mr. R[emond] lectured for us this evening. His lecture was very good.[14] I particularly liked what he said about Kansas.[15] Everybody has so much sympathy for the sufferers there, and so little for the poor slave, who for centuries has suffered tenfold worse miseries.—Still I am glad that *something* has roused the people of the North at last.—

Oct. Went with Mr. Putnam to hear Mr. Dana,[16] who taught me more about Kansas than I ever knew before. A very great political excitement prevails.

Monday, Nov. 3. Summer came to-day.[17] I read eagerly the account of his reception. Coming as it did from the *heart* of the people it must have [been] exceedingly gratifying to the noble man. I long to see him.—

Saturday, Nov. 8. Alas! for the hope of the people! Again has Might triumphed over Right; Falsehood over Truth; Slavery over Freedom. But these things cannot last much longer. Surely a just God will not permit them. . . .[18]

Sunday, Nov. 16. Mr. and Miss R[emond] went to the Essex Co[unty] meeting at Georgetown.[19] I could not go but wanted to badly. Mr. Ellis lectured.[20] Very good lecture.— Some parts of it surprisingly radical for him. . . .

Monday, Dec. 8. Went to the A[nti] S[lavery] sewing circle at Miss Chase's.[21] Only three or four were present. We had a very pleasant evening. Miss Chase shewed us an inkstand which she had purchased at a children's Fair, held for the benefit of the Kansas sufferers. It's prettily carved out of a knot of oak,— and was sent to the Fair by Mrs. Child, who had received it from a boy, who had read with great pleasure her "Letters from New York."[22] How pleasant it must have been to the gifted lady to receive such a token! It is not strange that it was sent to her. No. one could read *her* writings without the most enthusiastic admiration of the high-souled writer. I am sure that *I* cannot. "*Philothea*" is a book never to be forgotten.[23] I always think of it with a feeling of grateful pleasure that it was written, and that I have had the delightful privilege of reading it. . . .

Wednesday, Dec. 10. Went to my dear Normal School and had some pleasant conversation with my friends. Took tea with Mrs. P[utnam] and Mrs. G(illiard). Attended the Lyceum lecture. It was given by Prof. Hoyt of Exeter.[24] Subject—some of our popular fallacies.—One of the best lectures I ever listened to; thoroughly liberal in spirit, and abounding in passages of great truth and beauty. The popular fallacies he mentioned particularly were—The eager pursuit of material riches rather than worth. The confounding of *wealth* with *material riches;* of *law* with *legislative enactments;* of *reverence* with *servility;* of true *religion* with a mere *religious creed.* Such lectures are truly *mental* and *moral* feasts, and cannot fail to accomplish a great good. . . .

Sunday, Dec. 14. One of the "dark days." Rains incessantly. Went to hear Mr. Woodbridge of Lowell lecture before our society. Excellent lecture.—Principally an examination of the character of slavery.—Very few were present;—not more than two dozen. . . .

Monday, Dec. 15. Our society met at Mrs. Ives'.[25] Came home and read Hawthorne's 'Tanglewood Tales'. . . .

Friday, Dec 19. Came home from school, weary and cold, but found something which refreshed and inspirited me,—filled me with joy and astonishment,—a letter from Whittier,—the 'Great Poet of Humanity'![26] It was an answer to one which I wrote to him—because—*I could not help it;* the Spirit moved me. *His* letter, most unexpected by me, is *very* kind and beautiful, most worthy of his noble self. I thank him for it with all my heart. A letter in *his own* handwriting!—He can never know the happiness—the delight it gives me. But oh, it grieves me deeply to know that he is ill,—that his health has failed fearfully of late. How *could* we bear to lose him? I *will not* think that it is possible.—

Saturday, Dec. 20. Spent the afternoon very delightfully with my dear friend Miss S[hepard]. Showed her my precious letter, which I would show to no one else in Salem. She appreciates it thoroughly; and kindly pardons my presumption in writing to him,—the noblest poet, the noblest *man* of the age, with *very* few exceptions.—

Sunday, Dec. 21. Have just returned from Parker Pillsbury's lecture.[27] One of the best Anti-Slavery lectures I ever heard. While listening to him I could not help thinking of

Luther of old.—Indeed as it has been said of Luther, I believe, "his words were half battles." Glorious indeed they were—those battles for suffering humanity. They excited me to such a degree of enthusiasm, that I could have risen risen and thanked and blessed him for them, then and there. As Sidney says of the Ballad of Chevy Chase, "they stir the soul like the sound of the trumpet," but to a higher, nobler impulse than that of *physical* resistance; to a stern *moral* resolve of sternest *moral* warfare against the terrible curse of our country and of the age.—Such a lecture renews one's strength; makes one feel equal to any labor, for the ennobling of mankind.—

Monday, Dec. 22. Went to hear Dr. Elder at the Lyceum.[28]—Subject "Natural History of Civilization." Lecture was not particularly interesting; though he is a very peculiar and comical person. . . .

Christmas Day, Dec. [1856]. Spent the day very delightfully at the Fair.[29]—Saw many beautiful things and interesting people. Had the good fortune to be made known to three of the noblest and best of women;—Mesdames Chapman,[30] Follen,[31] and Child;[32] who were very kind and pleasant to me. Saw all the most distinguished champions of our cause. Mr. Phillips' kind pressure of the hand and beaming smile, I shall not soon forget, nor the cordial greetings of our dauntless pioneer, and his lovely wife. Mrs. Drake of Leominster I found a very social and pleasant person.[33] She was anxious to have me go with her to Fitchburg, and attend the Fair. Mrs. Follen has a real *motherly* kindness of manner.[34] She is a lovely looking, silver haired old lady; Mrs. Chapman's irresistible sweetness and grace of manner, I have no words to describe. Mrs. Child smilingly told me that she visited our house once,—when *I* must have been a "wee toddling." She is not quite so spiritual looking as one would expect to see the author of "Philothea," but is a very charming person nevertheless. I attended our Salem table part of the time, and then assisted Mrs. Follen. One of the most interesting people whom I met was Charles R. Whipple, who came up, and commenced talking to me.[35] We had a long and very delightful conversation. He is a fine conversationist (as well as an excellent writer) and a very social and attractive person. Mr. Hovey was as genial as usual.[36] Altogether this has been a most delightful day to me; and I am *very* sorry that I cannot accept the numerous invitations that I have received to remain here during the Fair.—Had the very great *honor* and pleasure of walking through the Fair, *arm-in-arm* with Mrs. Chapman. . . .

Wednesday, Dec. 31. The last day of the Old Year! Many

and sad have been the changes since first we greeted thee, old friend! Wednesday, 12 o'clock.—The clock strikes twelve! The year has gone! And with it I bid farewell, a last farewell to thee, my Journal! The year has gone! Gone, with its sorrows and its joys—Gone to join its brethren in the shadowy regions of the Past! Dear, dear friend, who hast gone before us to the Spirit Land! In that bright land thou sayest not 'farewell' to the *Old* nor welcomest in the *New*. *There* all is joy and peace forever more. But for us! Oh! how sadly we say 'farewell' to the closing year,—the year in which thy dear and precious existence closed on earth forever. May I ever remember thy beautiful example. Have I improved the past year as I might have done? Alas! I have not.—Too many hours have been spent in fruit*less* dreamings;—golden anticipations of the Future. They are over now; and I commence the New Year, a little wiser, I hope, from the experience of the Old.—Dear friends at home;—I think of you to-night. You cannot hear me; but in my heart I wish you a happy, *very* happy New Year; —with the earnest, longing hope that ere *it* passes away, I may be with you once again!

Have received one New Year's gift;—a beautiful and most acceptable one—"Tennyson's Poems,"—from my dear friend Miss Shepard.—In it I have just read "The Death of the Old Year."—Once more, my beloved Journal, who art become a part of myself,—I say to thee, and to the Old Year,—Farewell!

Salem, Jan. 1. 1857. Welcome in, New Year! with thy many changes; thy fullness of joy or sorrow, unknown, undreamed of now.—Have formed many good resolutions for the opening year, but think it wisest to commit none of them to paper. . . .

Friday, Jan. 2. Felt much disappointed and grieved at not being able to attend the Festival at Faneuil Hall, celebrating the twenty-fifth anniversary of the formation of the Mass[achusetts] A[nti] S[lavery] Society.[37]—*Dared* to compose a letter to Mr. Phillips—'The Spirit moved me.'—I really could not help it.—Felt as if I *must* say something, something to express my heartfelt gratitude and admiration for the noble friends of the oppressed, who meet in the "Old Cradle of Liberty" tonight.

Friday, Jan. 9. Went to Thalberg's Concert, for which Mr. Shearman very kindly sent me a ticket.[38] Such glorious strains I never heard before from the piano. They were most inspiring. The singing was very fine;—all in Italian, but, although I understood not a word, I could not wish it changed, so exquisitely rich and musical are the tones of that beautiful language. The singers were a true son and daughter of fair Italy, with the rich glowing complexion and the splendid dark hair and eyes peculiar to that sunny clime.—It was a rare and most delightful treat for me.—Read with great pleasure a very interesting accoun[t] of the Festival (in Lib[erator]) and some of the very beautiful and appropriate letters read there. Those of Rev. Mr. Frothingham and Mrs. Foster, liked particularly. . . .[39]

Sunday, Jan. 11. Wrote to——Miss Martineau![40] Am astonished and shocked at my own presumption.—but felt *impelled* to write by one of those 'Spirit movings' which *will* not be resisted. Have always greatly admired and loved Miss Martineau, and have thought of her much since seeing her exquisite work at the Fair. Felt that I must say *something* to show the admiration and gratitude with which I regard her. It may give her some pleasure to hear in this way from a young colored girl in a distant land. . . .

Tuesday, Jan. 13. This evening Mr. Frothingham[41] lectured on 'The Relation of the Bible to Slavery.' One of the most beautiful, earnest and convincing lectures I have ever heard. It made me feel *very happy.* Do not know Mr. F[rothingham] personally, but after the lecture, longed to shake hands with him. Should not have had the courage to do so, had not my kind friend, Mrs. P[utnam] presented me to him. His kind pressure of my hand and beaming gracious smile I shall always remember. Of course *he* does not believe that the Bible sanctions slavery, and most clearly and convincingly did he *prove* that it does not. A man with such a heart and mind as his is truly a host in himself,—one of the noblest of all mankind.—

Wednesday, Jan. 14. Attended Mr. Frothingham's lecture on 'Epicurus.'[42] It was very interesting and instructive but did not compare with the admirable lecture of last evening. Greek scholars would enjoy it.—

Thursday, Jan. 15. As usual read and studied all the evening. Feel a little lonesome at times.—Still no news from Canada. It grieves me deeply that father should act so strangely. It seems as if my only parent has quite forsaken me. I lay awake all last night, thinking about it, and could not help crying. I wish he *would* write to me.—

Friday, Jan. 16. . . . Miss S[hepard] lent me two of Hillard's new Readers.[43] They contain excellent selections from the best writers; but with sorrow—with contempt for the author's cowardice, I notice that he most carefully avoided the *mention* of slavery. Even in quoting from *Whittier,* the true poet of Humanity, and giving a beautiful sketch of him, not one word is said of his noble devotion to the cause of the slave, —not one line of the many glorious ones he has written for

89

freedom, does Mr. H[illard] *dare* to quote! Such moral pusilla-
nimity is degrading, most pitiable. . . .

Sunday, Jan. 18. Dined with Mr. and Mrs. P[utnam]. We
talked of the wrongs and sufferings of our race. Mr. P[utnam]
thought me too sensitive.—But oh, how inexpressibly bitter and
agonizing it is to feel oneself an outcast from the rest of mankind, as we are in this country! To me it is *dreadful, dreadful.*
Were I to indulge in the thought I fear I should become insane.
But I do not *despair.* I will not *despair;* though *very* often I can
hardly help doing so. God help us! We are indeed a wretched
people. Oh, that I could do *much* towards bettering our condition. I will do *all,* all the *very little* that lies in my power, while
life and strength last! . . .

Thursday, Jan. 22. Came from school cold and weary.—
Found to my joyful surprise, a letter from Mr. Phillips.[44]—
How *very* kind he was to *write.* I feel *very* grateful to him. He
is indeed a noble-hearted man. I can never, never express all
the reverence and admiration which I feel for him. How delightful it would be to be admitted to his society; Alas I can
never hope to be fitted for that great privilege. But I *can* love
and admire him, and shall ever do so, with all my heart.—
Looked over many old letters, which gave me rather a sad and
lonesome feeling. . . .

Monday, May 26. Attended school.—This evening heard
Rev. T. Parker's lecture on Franklin.[45] It was admirable. He
spoke beautifully of Franklin's anti-slavery views. 'He, the
most famous man of America, almost of the age, was not
ashamed to be known as the President of an Abolition Society.'
—Noticed in Mr. P[arker] as I do in all our great liberal men,
how much more eloquent they become in speaking of slavery.
This ever exciting subject kindles in them a noble enthusiasm,
which always finds expression in the most beautiful and elevated language. . . .

Friday, Jan. 30. Went to the meetings with Mrs. P[utnam]
and her daughter.[46] First person whom I met on entering the
Meionian was Mr. Phillips. He spoke to me *very* kindly. Asked
me if I received 'his note,' and thanked me warmly for writing
him so kind a letter. My heart was too full to say much. Mrs.
Foster, that most excellent of women, gave me so warm and
kind a greeting that I was quite touched.[47] She pressed my
hand with great fervor, and said most earnestly, 'God bless
you, my dear, I am most happy to meet you.' The speeches
were nearly all excellent. Those of Messrs, Garrison, Phillips,
Parker and Pillsbury especially so. Mr. Phillips made the clos-

ing speech—a noble one;—one of the most eloquent I have ever heard even from his eloquent lips. The meetings were held in the Tremont Temple, which is very beautiful. The gas lights are arranged in the ceiling like groups of stars. The effect of the light falling in this way on the rich carving and gilding of the room, is enchantingly beautiful.—Like a scene of fairyland.—

Saturday, Jan. 31. A terribly stormy day. Felt much disappointed, as there were many places of interest which I had intended to visit. Went, in the midst of the storm to several book-stores, trying to replace Miss Upton's book; but was unsuccessful. Shall leave Mr. N[ell] to prosecute the search.[48] The store of Phillips, Sampson and Co. is very splendid. Went with Mr. Nell to Rev. T. Parker's library. The great man gave me a cordial greeting, which rather surprised me for I had heard that he was cold to strangers. But he happened to be in a genial mood to-day. Went first to his principal library, which is also his study. It contains *ten thousand* volumes, in almost every language. Mr. Parker showed me the works of the Christian Fathers—one hundred vols. It was delightful to see so many books. I wanted to spend weeks there. Thought of that exquisite little poem by Anne C. Lynch, 'Thoughts in a Library' commencing—

'*Speak low, tread softly through these halls,*
Here genius reigns sublime,
Here dwell in silent majesty,
The monarchs of the mind.'—

The great man showed us a little chest of drawers in which his mother kept his clothes when he was a child. He opened one drawer and said there was where she used to keep his buttons, and he keeps them there now. Another drawer is filled with toys which he keeps for the amusement of children who come to visit him. These things revealed to me a beautiful trait of character. In a window of this favorite apartment stands an orange tree filled with fine fruit. The table was covered with his writing materials. Some sheets of written paper I thought were probably part of his sermon for to-morrow. Before the table stood his plain, cane-bottomed arm-chair. He accompanied me around the room talking very delightfully. On leaving he presented me with two of his finest sermons, and cordially invited me to come again.

After leaving the library, which occupies the third story of his house, we descended to the parlor. Parts of *its* walls are also covered with books. It contains some of the finest engravings I have ever seen. One of them—'The Angel bearing St. Catharine to Heaven,' is exquisitely beautiful. An exquisite wreath of the leaves and berries of the laurel and myrtle appropriately encircles a fine picture of the noble Sumner. From the parlor we descended to another room also filled with books. The entire library contains *fifteen thousand* vols.[49] I shall always remember my visit to it, and my very pleasant interview with its great and learned, yet most genial-hearted owner. Was very desirous of hearing him preach to-morrow, but did not dare to remain lest the road should become blockaded with snow. Came home this afternoon with Mrs. P[utnam]. . . .

Wednesday, Feb. 4. . . . Finished 'Eleven Weeks in Europe' and commenced 'The Autobiography of a Female Slave.'[50] The authoress is a gifted young southern lady;— a cousin of Sir E. L. Bulwer. . . .

Thursday, Feb. 5. . . . Studied Latin this evening, and again looked over 'Madeline' by Julia Kavanagh, a tale founded on fact.[51] The character of the heroine, a poor peasant girl of Auvergne, is *very* noble. Her pure, heroic, self-sacrificing spirit affected me much.—Strenghtened my own aspirations for something high and holy,—my earnest longings to do *something* for the good of others. I know that I am very selfish. Always the thought of *self-culture* presents itself *first*. With that, I think I can accomplish something more—nobler, more enduring. I will try not to forget, that, while striving to improve myself, I may at least *commence* to work for others. . . .

Saturday, Feb. 7. . . . The 'Autobiography' is very thrilling. Some parts of it almost too horrible to be believed;—did we not know that they *cannot* exceed the terrible reality.—It is *dreadful, dreadful* that *such* scenes can be daily and hourly enacted in this enlightened age, and *most* enlightened republic. How long, Oh Lord, how long, wilt thou delay thy vengeance? . . .

Sunday, Feb. 8. Finished 'The Autobiography of a Female Slave.' To me it is deeply interesting. The writer's style has not, perhaps, that perfect elegance and simplicity, which distinguishes the *best* writers, but she evidently *feels* deeply on the subject, and her book is calculated to awaken our deepest sympathies. I thank her for writing it. Hers must be a brave, true soul thus to surmount all obstacles, to soar above all the prejudices, which, from childhood must have been instilled into her mind, and take upon herself the defence of a down-trodden and degraded race!

Re-commenced 'Rollin's Ancient History'[52] which I intend to read regularly, and read several papers of the Spectator. Committed some poetry to memory. . . .

Wednesday, Feb. 11. . . . Have just returned from hearing R. W. Emerson.—Subject 'Works and Days' from Hesiod's poem.[53]—One of the most beautiful and eloquent lectures I ever heard. The lecturer spoke particularly of the *preciousness* of time, the too often unappreciated worth of a *day*. We *must live* in the *Present* rather than in the past and Future, for the *present hour* alone is ours. *Now* we must *act*—*now* we must *enjoy*. Eternity is boundless,—yet the *present hour* is worth the whole of it. He spoke of the great superiority of *character* over *talent,* and illustrated by an old Grecian fable so beautiful that I must remember it. "Apollo challenged Jove to shoot at a great distance. Mars shook the lots together in his helmet, and it fell to Phoebus to have the first shot. He drew his bow, and his arrow flew into the far West, Jove, at a single stride, cleared the whole distance, and asked, 'Where shall I shoot, I see no space over which the arrow may fly.' The victory was given to Jove who had not shot a single arrow."—Most beautifully did the 'poet-philosopher' speak of the earth and sky in many figures, the most beautiful of which, was, I think, this—'The earth is a cup, of which the sky is the cover, in which is contained the glorious bounty of Nature.' Very many other eloquent and beautiful expressions I heard from those eloquent lips, but I vainly try to recall them. But the impression made on my mind will be a lasting one. I have felt strengthened in all earnest and noble purposes since hearing that lecture. Never, never before have I so forcibly felt the *preciousness* of time. And Oh, how deeply do the words and the presence of such a man as Emerson, make us feel the utter insignificance, the great inferiority of *ourselves.* 'Tis a sad lesson, but a most salutary one; for who, while earnestly feeling that *he is* nothing, *knows* nothing, comparatively, will not strive with all his might to *know* and to *be something*? Poets and philosophers! the great, the gifted of the earth.—I thank you for teaching me this lesson—so sad, so humbling, yet so truly useful and ennobling! . . .

Friday, Feb. 13. Studied Latin and French.—This evening went to a spiritual meeting.[54] A rapping medium was present. Many very satisfactory answers were given—satisfactory because they showed almost conclusively that there was no imposture. But I cannot think there is a *spiritual* agency. Still I am open to conviction. . . .

Thursday, Feb. 19. . . . On returning home, found a ticket for Mr. Alger's lecture.[55] It was "A Parallel between the *Ancient* and *Modern* Chivalry,"—one of the finest lectures I have ever heard. The lecturer spoke in high terms of the many noble qualities which adorned the knighthood of the ancient times;—was most eloquent and enthusiastic in his praise of those brave old chevaliers, more than one of which was *"sans peur et sans reproche."* Then he spoke earnestly and beautifully of the chivalry of the modern time, of whom such philantropists as Elizabeth Fry, and Howard and Miss Nightingale, are the worthy representatives; and paid an exquisitely beautiful tribute to Mrs. Stowe. He concluded most eloquently, by urging all to cultivate those high and noble qualities,—to strengthen those lofty aims which should make them as pure, as high-souled and blameless in the *moral* chivalry of our nineteenth century as were the ancient knights in their *martial* chivalry of five hundred years ago. This lecture, next to Emerson's, I place in my list of rich and rare "mental feasts." . . .

Monday, Feb. 23. Studied French in the morning. Attended school as usual. In the evening went to a Promenade Concert by the Germania Band.[56] The hall was beautifully decorated with flags and flowers, and the music was most inspiring. Had never attended such a concert before, and thought it a beautiful sight. Found on my return home, that Mr. R[emond] has arrived.[57] We were not surprised. . . .

Wednesday, Feb. 25. . . . Heard Lowell's lecture on "Dante."[58] It is *very* beautiful. Enjoyed it perfectly. *Must* read the *"Inferno"* now. He says that, when he opens it, the gates of earth close behind him, and he communes with saints and angels. I liked particularly his saying that "all great poets are necessarily somewhat *provincial;*—nothing, that has not had a *living experience,* can have a *living expression."* For Dante he has an enthusiastic admiration; and most beautifully, as only a true *poet can* speak, did he speak of the nobility of his life—a life which great suffering continued to purify and ennoble;—sustained by a contant faith in God,—a sublime trust in His power and goodness. Then he spoke of the high and noble influence which the *human* love of Beatrice, exerted upon him; leading him ever higher and higher to a fuller appreciation of the *Divine* love. Dante, he says, was a *true* poet; and a highly imaginative one. Not only, may it be said of him that he represents Italy, but almost that he *is* Italy.—This beautiful lecture I cannot place below Emerson's. It is almost *too much* happiness to have heard *both.*

Thursday, Feb. 26. Studied French. Spent the evening at Miss R[emond's], listening with much pleasure to her animated and interesting account of her lecturing tour; her visit to Niagara,—now in all its glorious winter beauty; to Montreal and other interesting places. . . .[59]

Friday, Feb. 27. Went with Lizzie C[hurch] to return Miss Manning's books. This is a *very* pleasant home; with beautiful books, plants, and fine engravings;—one,—"Milton at the Age of Twelve," is exquisitely beautiful. I never saw so perfectly angelic a face. I can never forget it,—*never;* and *wish* I had it, —I *can't help* wishing so. Lizzie and I had a pleasant talk about about our favorite books. Pre-eminent, of course, is our beloved Mrs. Browning. L[izzie] thoroughly appreciates the beautiful. She is a lovely girl.—Read a most ridiculous slaveholder's letter, which Mr. R[emond] has. I wonder if this blundering epistle is a fair sample of the productions of the Southern *chivalry*. Am inclined to think it is. 'Tis horrible, horrible to think that such as *these* have uncontrolled dominion over hundreds of their fellow men! When, oh when, will these things cease? Will they *ever* cease? I sometimes ask myself. They *will;* —I do not, *cannot* doubt that God is just, therefore *know* they will. . . .

Friday, March 6. Last night Miss R[emond] entertained me with an account of her tour, and of the delightful day she spent with Mr. Phillips. . . . I listened with most unwearied attention until the "small hours of the morn" stole upon us.

Well can I appreciate the glorious privilege (though I've never enjoyed it,) of being on terms of intimacy with such a man. Am afraid much of envy stole into the pleasure with which I listened to Miss R[emond's] animated accounts;—for the friendship of a great, a truly noble *genius* has, since childhood, been one of the most fondly cherished of my many dreams. It can never be realized. 'Tis folly to cherish it;—for *he* could give everything, while *I* can give nothing.—"Princes must mate with princes." . . .

Sunday, March 8. Finished "Aurora." Think it one of the most beautiful books I've ever read. So full of earnest, powerful beautiful thought. 'Tis a book that I shall want to read often, as one does all Mrs. Browning's poems.[60] Beautiful as they all are, this, which she calls "her most mature work, and the one into which her highest convictions of Life and Art have entered," far exceeds them all. . . .

Tuesday, March 17. On my return from school, was delighted and surprised to find a *very* kind and characteristic letter from Miss Martineau. I thank her *very* much for it. 'Twas forwarded by Mrs. Chapman.[61] Of course I shall always prize it very highly. . . .

Sunday, March 29. Went very early this morning to Boston. . . . Before we left Salem, our conveyance broke down; —but we soon obtained a better one, and had quite a pleasant ride. Mr. Phillips, who preached for Mr. Parker (who is ill) was . . . like Herodes of old, the *tongue of our* Athens.[62] Every time I hear him, I like him better, admire him more. This *sermon* was truly *very* beautiful. The music and singing I thought very fine. Went to Mrs. Lockley's. Mary and I took a walk on the Common, and saw some beautiful flowers in the greenhouses. How delightful it is to see flowers now, when there are around us only the "bare woods with outstretched hands," and the bleak, brown hills. In the evening our party, except myself, went to the Concert—"Thalberg's." . . .

Monday, March 30. Started from Boston at six.—Lost our road, and, after leaving Lynn, and riding for miles along a beautiful road, completely skirted with fine evergreens, with occasional glimpses of the sea between,—found ourselves near Lynnfield on the road to Lowell. 'Twas provoking, for I wanted to reach home in time for school. But, finding it impossible, made myself as comfortable as possible. Breakfasted at Lynnfield, and after spending some time there to rest our *cheval,* rode leisurely home to Salem. The ride would have been delightful,—I should have enjoyed it perfectly; had not the thought of school disturbed me. . . .

Thursday, Apr. 9. Attended Mr. Stone's lecture on the "Drama."[63] It was very interesting. The lecturer considered the drama principally in its connection with religion. He read some passages from Shakespeare. After the lecture, studied a French lesson, and gave Sarah[64] one. . . .

Sunday, Apr. 12. Another *rare* day. How delightful it is to hear the song of the robins when one wakes in the morning. I *love* these spring mornings. The air is so pure, sky and earth are so beautiful. I could *live* out of doors. This is Easter; and my thoughts go back to my childish days, when Annie and I joyfully welcomed in the "feast of eggs." When we used to go [to] the Catholic Church, and admire and enjoy, as children *do,* the beauty of its decorations,—the singing,—the incense, and the grand tones of the organ. And with these memories comes that of the dear, motherly face, whose kind, loving smile beamed on us day by day, making our lives better and happier. Beloved mother! *more* than mother to me;—I *long* to see thee again; thee and my *own* mother,—the darling brother, *all* the loved ones who have gone before.[65] Some time I feel that it will not be long,—not *very* long, ere we all meet again. How often it comes over me! this longing for a mother's love,—a mother's care. I *know* there is none other like it. 'Tis a selfish feeling, but I *cannot* control it. . . .

Sunday, Apr. 19. The robins' song awoke me this morning. Lay awake a great while, musing, as usual.—Spent the day at home. Read "Philip the Second."[66] Commenced writing a story—subject "prejudice against color." . . . 'Tis not probable that it will ever be finished—or if finished, worth publishing. I'm quite sure it will not. Still am determined to write on; and trust to Fate for its success.—

Monday, Apr. 20. Attended Mrs. Kemble's reading;— "Merchant of Venice."[67] Was perfectly enchanted. Her power of voice is *very* wonderful;—her power of expression scarcely less so. Rarely have I felt so excited. Wish I *could* attend her other readings, but 'tis impossible. *This* I shall never forget. . . .

Thursday, Apr. 23. Had unusually bad lessons, and felt rather dispirited till this evening, when I went to Mr. Stone's lecture on the "Song." It was *very* beautiful—the noblest sentiments, finely expressed. It is delightful to hear such, when, as in this case, we know they come from the *heart* of the speaker, —that his *practice* ever accords with his *teachings*. He spoke of all the great poets from Chaucer to Tennyson; his idea was that the true "song" is an inspiration; this is particularly true of the *sonnet;*—and after alluding to the sonnets of Shakespeare, of Wordsworth, and other great poets, he concluded by paying a beautiful tribute to the sonnets of Jones Very,[68] and quoted that really exquisite one—"Wilt thou not visit me?"—The poet was present; and must have felt gratified at *such* a tribute from *such* a man. I hope these lectures will be published. I want to *study* them. . . .

Saturday, Apr. 25. After school assisted . . . [in the] store. Am going to try to earn three dollars in four weeks, that I may go with my dear Miss R[emond] to Bridgewater. . . .

Thursday, Apr. 30. Played ball at recess with the children. 'Tis fine exercise. This evening—Mr. Stone's lecture—"The Essay." 'Twas excellent, but not so interesting to me as the "Song." He spoke particularly of Bacon and Montaigne, with whom I am not familiar. I best appreciated and liked his allusion to Emerson the "poet philosopher," to whom he paid a beautiful and well-deserved tribute. . . .

Friday, May 1. A beautiful May-day. Went "Maying" in the "Pastures." Met several parties of girls with wreaths on their heads. They looked quite picturesque. Found few flowers; but had, as usual, a most delightful walk. Came home, thoroughly tired; and finished "Neighbor Jackwood."[69] Its radical anti-slavery I like very much. But in the book, generally, I am rather disappointed. . . .

Saturday, May 2. . . . Spent most of the afternoon at home, alone, sewing—and day-dreaming. Paid a short visit to Miss S[hepard] who told me that I came very near getting a situation in her school; but it was found that I was "very popular in my district" and thought best not to remove me.[70] I am glad if I do give general satisfaction, but I cannot help feeling grieved that I cannot be with Miss S[hepard]. 'Twould make me very happy.—This evening received some Edinburgh Reviews from Mr. N[ell]. I shall enjoy reading them. . . .

Monday, May 4. A miserable day; came from school *very* weary, and found to my joyful surprise, a letter from father, —at last. He says he had written several times, and has not heard from me. 'Tis very strange. He thinks of going to England or Scotland; if so, I shall go. But I must not anticipate. It would be too delightful. . . .

Wednesday, May 6. After school went on the hills with some of my scholars, and found some violets;—the first I've seen this season. Beautiful violets!—Very joyfully do I welcome them, and the delicate and fairy-like anemone. Gathered quite a bouquet of both, and took them to Miss S[hepard]. I like to give flowers to one who so truly loves and appreciates them. Had a long talk with her about Anti-slavery. . . .

Thursday, May 7. . . . Never, since I've been teaching, have my scholars done so miserably as they have this week. I feel almost utterly discouraged and miserable. I will not indulge the feeling. I *must* not. Sometimes I'm fairly desperate. Went to Mr. Stone's last lecture on the "Sermon."—It was very fine; and made me feel better and happier. After he had concluded, a gentleman moved that the thanks of the audience be offered to Mr. Stone, for a series of lectures,—so beautiful and so instructive. It was unanimously adopted, and Mr. Stone's reply was most beautiful and touching.

Friday, May 8. School prospects do not brighten. I cannot fully enjoy even this delightful May weather. I am disappointed about Bridgewater, as Mr. Edwards gives vacation a week sooner. . . .

Sunday, May 24. A lovely day, just as a *May*-day ought to be. Am not strong enough to walk out. . . . Read "Philip," and finished "Charlotte Brontë." (1st. vol.)[71] What a noble life was hers. Poverty, illness; many other difficulties which would have seemed insurmountable to a less courageous spirit were nobly overcome by one; who was yet as gentle and loving as she was firm. *Such* a life inspires one with faith and hope and courage "to *do* and to *endure*." Read some excellent criticisms on different books, in some of the old "Edinburgh Reviews." . . .

Wednesday, May 27.   Went to Boston with S[arah] and Mr. P[utnam]. Attended the Anti-slavery meetings all the day and evening.[72] Many of the speeches were excellent. Our noble Garrison and Phillips spoke, as usual most eloquently. Mr. P[hillip]'s eve[ning] speech was particularly fine, I thought. The Common is perfectly beautiful now. The young grass is a fresh bright green; the birds are singing among the delicate leaves, and the delicious music, the coolness, and the beauty of the fountain are the crowning glory of all. I enjoy them all perfectly, perfectly.—

Thursday, May 28.   Again attended the meetings most of the day and evening. In the afternoon visited some stores, and saw several fine pictures. Two of them are particularly beautiful,—"Shakespeare and his Contemporaries," and "Walter Scott and his Friends at Abbotsford." All the names are written out, and it is delightful to see grouped around the two great master minds, so many others among the noblest and most gifted of that age. Among the many fine faces around "The Wizard of the North" that of "Christopher North" was particularly striking and noble, and Lockhart's by far the most classically beautiful. It reminded me of Byron's.—Mr. Phillips, Mr. Garrison, and Mr. Pillsbury were, of course, the most deeply interesting speakers. Was very glad to meet Miss Anthony[73] Like Mr. Powell very much indeed.[74] . . . Now that the pleasant excitement of the meetings is over, feel *very, very* tired.

Friday, May 29.   Despite the rain, went with a large party to Mount Auburn.[75] The ride through Cambridge was most delightful. How often I have longed to see the venerable old town. We saw Longfellow's house, once the head-quarters of Washington. It has not the antiquated appearance which I had hoped and expected to see. How *could* the poet have had it renewed. How *could* he allow the traces of the honored hand of Time to be effaced. We could not see Lowell's house, only the noble old trees among which it is completely concealed. It must be truly a fitting home for a poet.—

I have no words to describe the beauty of Mt. Auburn; and the glorious view from the Observatory, I shall ever remember.

It was a splendid picture, a blending of Nature and Art, in which, as ever, the hand of the Great Artist is by far the most visible and skilful. Deeply it is impressed upon my mind, and often it will come to me from the treasure house of Memory, to soothe and gladden me in the sorrowful hours of which I have too many, far too many for my own good, I fear. . . . In the pleasant and luxurious horse-cars—(a great improvement on omnibuses) we rode from Mt. Auburn to Watertown to visit the L's [?]. Dined there, and went afterwards to Cushing's Garden, but just as we were entering it, a thunderstorm commenced, and we were obliged to return without seeing the beautiful flowers. Spent the evening at Watertown looking over some finely illustrated vols. of Shakespeare, and playing whist. . . .

Saturday, May 30. Returned home very weary. . . .

Sunday, May 31. My friend Miss S[hepard] brought me the second volume of "Charlotte Brontë." Commenced it, and read some of Mrs. Stowe's "Mayflower." . . .[76]

Thursday, June 4. As usual, after the least exertion, feel perfectly exhausted. . . . Did little else but sleep all day. This evening my too kind friend Miss S[hepard] came in, bringing some exquisite flowers and spent some time with me. It was *so* delightful to have her here. We talked about our noble, our beloved Whittier. She, with her usual self-sacrificing kindness and generosity wishes me to spend a few weeks in the country at her expense. But I feel as if I *ought* not to do it. I know how *she* feels about it. But it would not be *just* to her. I *know* that it would not be. We are going to talk it over again. I—so unworthy—am blest indeed, in having so *very* kind a friend. . . .

Sunday, June 7. Dr. . . . came, and examined my lungs. Advises me not to enter school again this summer. Shall be glad to rest if it can only be arranged so that I may have my school again in the Fall. If it cannot be so, I know not what I *shall* do. . . .

Tuesday, June 9. Mr. E[dwards][77] came to see me this morning, and greatly relieved my mind. Think the arrangement I desire can be made. How much I owe to Mr. E's kindness! . . .

Thursday, June 11. To my great joy Lizzie and S[arah] came this morning. Am very, *very* tired packing, and bidding people good-bye. If it be clear to-morrow, this is the last day that I shall spend, (for some time) in New England, dear, beautiful New England.—Even to go home I shall leave it, not without regret. I shall miss the pure air of the hills, the long, pleasant walks; but I shall see the dear faces, hear the kind voices of home! sweet home!—

Part 4

Philadelphia and Salem

June 12, 1857 - January 1, 1860

Friday, June 12. Left Salem this morning. It is beautiful now; I cannot leave it without regret. Went to Boston with a large party. . . . Got into the invalid car, and had a pleasant ride to Fall River; sometimes reading, sometimes looking out of the window, as I lay on the soft cushions. But there is little worth seeing. We took the boat before dark, and had a delightful sail down the bay until we reached Newport; after that it became rough, and we hastened to get in our berths. I was not sick, but did not dare to move a finger or even open my eyes lest I should be so. It was a peculiar feeling. Poor Mrs. P[utnam][1] was very sick and did not close her eyes all night. . . .

Saturday, June 13. Rose before five and went on deck. The sail past Long Island was beautiful. There was a glorious sunrise. Was much interested in looking at the prisons and the shipping. . . . The ride from N[ew] Y[ork] to Phila[delphia] was very tedious; the only thing that made it tolerable to me was that we rode for miles past a canal. As I had never seen one before, I was rather interested in watching the lazy boats. They seemed to me a hundred years behind the age.—Reached home this evening. They were perfectly astonished to see us. It is pleasant to be home again. *Bon nuit,*—my journal!

Phila. Sunday, June 14. Yes it *is* pleasant to be home; but how very, very different it is from my dear N[ew] England. The air is almost suffocating here. I miss the pure air of our dear old hills. . . .

Wednesday, June 17. Went to Byberry.[2] On the boat met Miss Peabody,[3] and Mattie Griffiths, the author of "Autobiography of a Female Slave."[4] Miss P[eabody] read to us an account of her last visit to Washington Allston. It was beautifully written and deeply interesting. Miss P[eabody] is certainly a highly cultivated and intellectual woman. She converses finely —We spent the day very pleasantly at Byberry. . . . Our conversation was almost entirely about prejudice. The ladies expressed themselves very warmly against it. On reaching the city, Mrs. P[utnam] and I were *refused* at *two* ice cream saloons, successively. Oh, how terribly I felt! Could say but few words. Mrs. P[utnam] told one of the people some wholesome truths, which cannot be soon forgotten. It is dreadful! dreadful! I cannot stay in such a place. I long for N[ew] E[ngland].

Thursday, June 18. Mrs. P[utnam] had a letter from Salem. They are all well. . . . Went to Independence Hall.— The old bell with its famous inscription, the mottoes, the relics, the pictures of the heroes of the Revolution—the *saviours* of their country,—what a *mockery* they all seemed,—*here* where there breathes not a freeman, black or white. . . .

Monday, June 22. A delightful day. Jumped into the hay wagon—drawn by two really handsome grey mules, and took a pleasant ride with Charley. The air, so pure and refreshing did me much good. . . . Mr. Purvis is most entertaining.[5] We had a long talk with him to-day about the colored people and their wicked folly. It is really deplorable. They do nothing themselves, yet continually abuse their only friends. I am perfectly sick of them. . . .

Tuesday, June 23. Came to town this morning. Refused again in a saloon. This place is thoroughly *hateful* to me. Spent most of the day lying down, reading "Barnaby Rudge."[6]

Wednesday, June 24. Visited Girard College.[7] It is a very fine building, after the model of the Madeleine in Paris, it is said. The columns by which it is supported, are very grand, and were imported from Italy at an immense cost. The lofty marble staircases in the interior, impressed me particularly. The view from the top of the College is very fine and extensive. But, on contrasting it with the view of the Observatory at Mt. Auburn, I greatly missed the noble hills and the picturesque winding river which give to the latter so much beauty and character.

Thursday, June 25. This morning, Mrs. P[utnam] left.— Her *attempt* at departure was a fitting *finale* to our pleasant adventures in this delectable city. She was refused admission to the car in which she wished to go, on the C. and A. Railroad, and was *ordered* to go in the "colored car," which she, of course indignantly refused to do; and was obliged to return home and wait for the ten o'clock "Way Line," in which she met with no difficulty. I longed to return with her. I shall be better able to appreciate than ever the blessings we enjoy in N[ew] England. . . .

Saturday, July 4. The celebration of this day! What a mockery it is! My soul sickens of it. Am glad to see that the people are much less demonstrative in their mock patriotism than of old. . . .

Sunday, July 5. At last, at last after hiding for a whole

week the sun deigns to show us his face again. Right glad are we to see him. This is truly a *perfect* day. Mr. C[hew][8] came, and insisted upon taking me to Broadbent's where I had an excellent likeness taken. Miss J[?] was there, and showed me a daguerreotype of a young slave girl who escaped in a box. . . . My heart was full as I gazed at it; full of admiration for the heroic girl, who risked *all* for freedom; full of bitter indignation that in this boasted land of liberty such a thing *could occur.* Were she of any other nation her heroism would receive all due honor from these Americans, but *as it is,* there is not even a single spot in this broad land, where her rights can be protected,—not one. Only in the dominions of a *queen* is she free. How long, Oh! how long will this continue! . . .

Wednesday, July 8. Another lovely day. Aunt M[argaretta] and I took a long walk. Stopped at the A[nti] S[lavery] Office. Mr. McK[im][9] was very gracious and pleasant. Mr. S[till] with his most fascinating smile amazed me by asking, "Have you written any poetry lately?" I paused a moment, at a loss what to say;—then replied, "No sir, I *never* wrote any," and turned away rather abruptly, to speak to some one else. I fear I must have appeared rude, but I couldn't help it. 'Twas such a queer question for him, a perfect stranger, to ask me. . . .

Friday, July 24. . . . This eve went to Parkinson's Garden. It was like fairy-land. Brilliant lights were gleaming among the trees, fountains were playing—the coolness was delicious. —Under a graceful canopy was seated a full orchestra who played finely.—The audience had seats canopied only by the dark blue sky. A Scotch "lassie" sang "Macgregor's gathering" with great spirit. After the concert came splendid fire works. At one of these representing the "cross of the legion of honor" the band played the national air of France. It was most beautiful and inspiring. Altogether the scene was a most delightful and novel one to me. . . .

Tuesday, July 28. Left Byberry this morning.—Almost immediately on my return, bade everybody a last farewell. . . . A long and tedious ride to New York. . . .

Friday, July 31. Left this afternoon in the boat with a very large party, . . . The day is lovely; the scenery on Long Island perfectly beautiful, and, with so *very* pleasant a party, I spent a delightful evening. The sunset was grand;—and long after it we sat on deck in the gathering darkness, through which gleamed the lights of the shore and gazed at the water. I *felt a strange happiness.*—

Newport, Saturday, Aug. 1. After a good rocking "in the cradle of the deep,"—reached Newport after three this morning. It was very dark but we were soon established in a nice boarding house, and slept soundly till daylight.

This part of Newport is certainly not very prepossessing; but I like its old-fashioned appearance. . . . I walked out on an exploring expedition, and discovered a very beautiful Catholic Church,—received permission to go in, and stood overwhelmed by the beauty, the splendor which burst upon us. The painted glass windows were the most splendid I ever saw; the stone arches,—the organ so grand and imposing. It is very splendid. We stood a great while admiring it. There is something so impressive in such a building.

The girls and I walked to the Beach; it was not so fine, nor were there so many people there as I expected,—but we were much amused seeing the bathers as they plunged with such hearty zest among the waves; of course I envied them, and longed for one, if only one nice bath in those clear bright waves. Then we walked to the rocks which are far less imposing, in this part, at least, than those at Marblehead,—seated ourselves and looked out over the deep blue waters; the little bathing houses with their white roofs looked very prettily in the distance. The Beach presented a very gay appearance enlivened by splendid carriages and horses, equestrians, and bathers in every variety of costume.—

Came home *very* tired and spent the afternoon in bed. . . .

Sunday, Aug. 2. Perfectly delightful morn. . . . Took a nice walk. The streets and houses in this part are not at all remarkable for their beauty.—Returned home, read and wrote busily. This afternoon went to the "Sea Girt House" and saw the magnificent view from its summit—the view of the ocean. It was grand,—finer even than my favorite view from Mt. Auburn Obs[ervatory]. We went to vespers in the Catholic Church. The organ is a splendid one, but the singing was poor. The effect of the rich solemn music stealing through that beautiful building, was singularly impressive; in perfect keeping with the grand stone arches, beautiful altars and statues, and exquisite stained windows.—After tea, took a long walk on "The Island," past some beautiful houses, and finely kept grounds. . . . Our walk was perfectly delightful. We passed the famous "Ocean House,"[10] brilliantly lighted up, and looking *very* bright and cheerful. This sea air is delightful; it greatly strengthens me.—

Monday, Aug. 3. Another walk this morn, to the "Forty Steps"—a beautiful place.[11] We sat upon the rocks which are very fine, but do not compare with those of Marblehead. Had a delightful time climbing the rocks, and wading in the water. . . . This afternoon a delightful sail to the Fort.[12] We walked around it on the top, enjoying the fine view. It is a noble building. When we first entered we contrasted the perfect quiet which reigned around with the din and confusion which must have existed there in time of war, and almost fancied we could hear the thunder of the cannon and the sharp crack of the rifle resounding through the "Fort Adams" of the Revolution. Soon the stillness was broken by the noise of carriage wheels, and in a little time the area enclosed within the walls was filled with splendid carriages of every description, each bearing, of course, its burden of elegant ladies. I never saw such fine horses.—In the green in the center the Germania Band took their station, and played beautifully. The grand appearance of the Fort, the splendor and brilliancy of the vehicles and their occupants, the beauty of the music—altogether formed one of the most beautiful and picturesque scenes I ever enjoyed. I shall never forget it—nor the charming sail back to Newport. Just as the sun was setting; the water was so beautifully transparent. . . .

Salem, Tuesday, Aug. 4. Left N[ewport] with regret; had a *very* pleasant sail up the Bay to Prov[idence]. Felt sorry we could see no more of the city; took the cars to Boston. Very, very pleasant it is to be in the dear Old Bay State again. Told the girls I felt brighter and better the moment I crossed the boundary line, they laughed at me, and wished to know *when* the moment was, which I couldn't exactly tell.—I am glad to be in Salem again. We slept nearly all the afternoon. This evening visited some of my friends and was warmly welcomed.—

Wednesday, Aug. 5. Terrible day for our Convention;[13]— rain pouring. Sorry my friends cannot attend. Rode to the school-house;—after the exercises there walked to . . . Church and listened to the oration by Prof. Felton. Most of it was excellent; but there was one part,—a *tirade* against Spiritualism, which I disliked exceedingly;—it seemed to me very inappropriate and uncharitable. The dinner at the Bowditch School Room was excellent. Very good and amusing speeches were made, and everybody evidently enjoyed themselves greatly. . . . The room was beautifully decorated with blue and white hangings, with evergreens woven into the names of Mann, Bowditch, Sears and other distinguished friends of education, with portraits of S. C. Phillips[,] J. Q. Adams, Sumner and others, and with exquisite bouquets of flowers. The effect was very beautiful indeed. In the evening the girls accompanied me to the Normal Lecture Room, to which the floral decorations had been removed. A large party was assembled; we had toasts and many amusing *impromptu* speeches, and enjoyed the evening very much.—There were fewer familiar faces than I had hoped; but it is *very* pleasant to see *them* again. . . .

Sunday, Aug. 9. Longed to spend the day in quiet, but as usual, visitors came.—Did some reading and writing—more *sleeping,* not feeling well;—and in the eve. walked to D[anvers] to hear my dear Mr. Garrison.[14] 'Twas delightful to see his loved face, to hear his familiar voice again;—to feel the warm pressure of his hand, and the sudden strength and hopefulness which *his* presence always inspires, even in our weakest and most desponding moods. He spoke as usual, nobly and well, and to-night my heart is filled with thankfulness that God has given us so glorious a Pioneer.—

Monday, Aug. 10. I scarcely know myself tonight;—a great and sudden joy has completely dazzled—overpowered me. This evening Miss R[emond][15] sent for me in haste saying a gentleman wished to see me. I went wondering who it *could* be, and found——Whittier! one of the few men whom I truly reverence for their great minds and greater hearts. I cannot *say* all that I *felt*—even to *thee,* my Journal! I stood like one bewildered before the noble poet, whose kindly, earnest greeting *could* not increase my love and admiration for him;—my heart was full, but I *could* not speak, though constantly tormented by the thought that *he* would think me very stupid, very foolish;—but after a few simple words from him I felt more at ease, and though I still could say but very little, and left the talking part to Miss R[emond] who can *always talk,* it was such a pleasure to listen to *him,* to have *him* before me, to watch that noble, spiritual face, those glorious eyes—there are no eyes like them—that I felt *very, very* happy.—The memory of this interview will be a life-long happiness to me.— Shall I try to tell thee, my Journal, *something* of what he said? First we spoke of my old home and my present home. He asked me if I liked N[ew] E[ngland]—it was *such* a pleasure to tell him that I loved it well,—to see the approving smile, the sudden lighting of those earnest eyes! In comparing P[ennsyl]vani[a] and N[ew] E[ngland] he spoke of the superior richness of the soil of the former, but said that here, though there were fewer and smaller farms, larger crops were raised on the same extent of ground, because vastly more labor and pains were bestowed upon its cultivation. Then I remembered that the poet was also a *farmer.* By some strange transition we got from *agriculture* to *spiritualism*. Whittier said that he too (having read them) thought that Prof. F[elton's] views were most uncharitable. Though *he* cannot believe in it; he thinks it wrong and unjust to condemn all interested in it.—The transition from this subject to that of the "future life" was easy. I shall never forget how earnestly, how beautifully the poet expressed his *perfect faith*, that faith so evident in his writings, in his holy and consistent life.—

At his request I took him to see Miss S[hepard]. The joy and surprise were almost more than she could bear. I stayed but a little while, then left them together. The poet gave me a cordial invitation to visit him and his sister at their home. God Bless him! This is a day to be marked with a white stone. . . .

Friday, Aug. 14. Hottest day of the season. Glad enough to stay quietly at home, though strongly persuaded to take a jaunt. Did a little writing and sewing, but devoted most of the day to reading the "Old Curiosity Shop," and finished it. Tis very, very beautiful. There could not be a lovelier, a nobler conception than Little Nell; and most of the other characters are, in their way, inimitable. Quilp is most unnatural; but there is a strange and frightful interest attached to the monster, throughout the book;—and his horrible wickedness only shows forth in brilliant and beautiful contrast the true nobility of such characters as Rit, and Garlands, etc., and the angelic goodness of darling Little Nell. I believe I think of Dickens' writings as of Mr. Phillips' speeches;—the last which I read, always seems to me the best;—at any rate, I give now to the Old Curiosity Shop the highest place in my admiration of the great author's works; of which, however, I have still many more to read.—Rec'd a letter from the noble Whittier; who requests me to obtain a letter he wrote to grandfather. What treasures *his* letters are! In the evening heard the *Miserere* and other good music, by the band. . . .

Monday, Aug. 17.—My twentieth birthday.—Very, very fast the years are passing away,—and I,—Ah! how little am I improving them. I thought so to-day after I had finished "Jane Eyre,"[16] which has so powerfully interested and excited me. The excitement was not a healthy one, I know—and reason told me I *ought* to have been better employed.—But we have so much company now that it is impossible to accomplish anything.—This afternoon was regularly bored, victimized by two dull people.—I do wish they would leave us to the enjoyment of our own family circle, which is such a pleasant one now.— Twenty years! I have lived. I shall *not* live twenty years more, —I feel it. I believe I have but few years to live.—Them I

must, I *will* improve.—I will pray for strength to keep *thi*[
resolution;—I have broken so many. *This* I *must* keep. . . .

Thursday, Aug. 20. . . . Went to see Miss S[hepard], and
had a long talk with her about our noble Whittier. He has been
pleased to speak most approvingly of my poor attempts at letter writing. I thank him, with all my heart. Miss S[hepard],
with her usual great kindness, has made several plans for our
mutual enjoyment, during vacation. . . .

Sunday, Aug. 23. Finished "Dombey and Son."—Like it
even better than The Old Curiosity Shop.—The death of little Paul is as touching and beautiful as that of Little Nell. . . .

Monday, Aug. 24. . . . This eve[ning], to our great surprise, who should come in but Mr. R[emond] and Mr. Hovey.[17]
—The former as morose and disagreeable, the latter as
pleasant, as usual.[18] The sooner I leave this house and Mr.
R[emond]'s presence, the better, I think. I *cannot* stay much
longer. . . .

Friday, Sept. 4. Very hot morning. . . . I have been exam-
ining myself, to-night,—trying to fathom my own thoughts
and feelings; and I find, alas! too much, too much of *selfishness!* And yet I know that, in this world of care and sorrow,
however weary and sad the heart may be, true *un*selfishness
must ever be a source of the purest and highest happiness.
Every kindly word, every gentle and generous deed we bestow
upon others,—every ray of sunshine which penetrates the darkness of another's life, through the opening which *our* hands
have made, *must* give to us a truer, nobler pleasure than any
self-indulgence can impart. Knowing this, feeling it with my
whole heart,—I ask thee, Oh! Heavenly Father! to make me
truly *unselfish*, to give to me a heart-felt interest in the welfare
of others;—a spirit willing to sacrifice *my own;*—to live "for
the *good* that I can do! . . .

Monday, Sept. 7. First day of school. 'Tis pleasant to see
the bright young faces again;—but it *isn't* pleasant to go to
work. I hope it *will* be soon. . . .

Friday, Sept. 18. A hard day at school. This constant *warfare* is *crushing*, killing me. I am *desperate* to-night. Even the
pleasing variety of my French lesson has not relieved me. I am
desperate, and shall write no more to-night. . . .

Sunday, Oct. 11. . . . This eve. attended the first lecture of
our course by Mr. Stone.[19] 'Twas *very* good. To-night I have
been reading old letters;—they have made me feel rather sad
and homesick. I have constantly a longing for something higher
and nobler, than I have known. Constantly I ask myself
Cowley's question "what shall I do to be forever known?" This

is ambition, I know. It is selfish, it is wrong. But, oh! how very hard it is to do and feel what is right. . . .

Saturday, Oct. 17. Spent the day in Boston. Ascended Bunker Hill Monument from which the view is fine. Salem and the White Mts. can be seen. The view of the bay is extensive. The wind rushed through the monument sounding like the wail of departed spirits.—The statue of Warren seems to me *wonderfully* beautiful.[20] In the afternoon had an interesting visit to the Navy Yard. At the Museum saw a beautiful and thrilling "The Sea of Ice" written to illustrate Dr. Kane's perils and adventures.[21] . . .

Sunday, Oct. 18. Another lovely day. Spent the morning at home writing. This afternoon read with Miss S[hepard]. Walked to the Grove. Very beautifully the mellow autumnal light fell on the changing foliage. To-night heard one of the most beautiful and excellent Anti-Slavery lectures, by Rev. Mr. F[urness].[22] It did my very soul good. Most earnestly and truly did he speak of the terrible prejudice against color. He particularly dwelt on the dreadful effects produced by slavery on the morals of the people; how some of the greatest minds had utterly debased themselves at the bidding of the Slave Power. I have rarely heard anything more eloquent than were many passages of his lecture. My heart was so full of gratitude, of deep and earnest appreciation, I could not help writing a few lines to express to him *something* of what I felt. Thank God for such brave, earnest hearts as these! . . .

Wednesday, Oct. 28. Spent the afternoon at home, busily sewing. Miss S[hepard] brought me some beautiful flowers. Took a French lesson, and read "The Atlantic Monthly," just published.[23] It ought to be excellent for the most gifted minds on both sides of the Atlantic are among its contributors. Read aloud a sad but finely written story, "The Mourning Veil;" and a beautiful poetic tribute to Florence Nightingale—"Santa Filomena," by Longfellow. . . .

Wed. Nov. 11. Heard an excellent lecture on education by Rev. Dr. Bellows.[24] The real theme of the lecture was the importance of the highest possible education. He quite scourged the Americans for their supreme self-conceit—for the little gratitude and reverence which they felt towards the Mother Land for the treasures of Art, Science and Literature in which she so immeasurably surpasses them. I liked his remarks, as a whole, exceedingly, though he *did* call the Brownings and Tennyson "beautiful corrupters of the English language" for their many unheard-of and obscure words and expressions. As Miss S[hepard] says, it made us wince because we could not, enthusiastic admirers of these poets as we are, help acknowledging to ourselves that it was all too true. . . .

Sunday, Nov. 15. Another wintry day. . . . Read in the "Atlantic Monthly" a very interesting description of the Manchester Exhibition, evidently written by one well versed in Art.—Also a poem "Brahma" by R. W. Emerson, remarkable only for its utter obscurity.[25] Can't understand a word of it. Evidently poetry is not the philosopher's forte. . . .

Saturday, Nov. 21. Close of the term. All the scholars met together, and sang most sweetly; it was very pleasant to hear them, and to see so many beaming, happy little faces. . . . Sewed and read some interesting articles in "Harper's Monthly." Read a very interesting article on "Brahma," and a paraphase of it, which renders it much clearer, and more comprehensible. . . .

Friday, Nov. 27. Spent most of the day busily sewing. This eve. took my last French lesson. I am very, very sorry to discontinue them. But I can't afford to keep on. . . .

Sunday, Nov. 29. Visitors as usual in the morn. interrupting my writing and reading. This afternoon walked to S[outh] Danvers, to hear Parker Pillsbury.[26] As usual the speech of "My Luther" was full of fiery, earnest eloquence; and I enjoyed it greatly. This eve heard our beloved Garrison, and had the very, very great pleasure of shaking hands with him.[27]—

Monday, Nov. 30. School again. Children wild and unmangeable, as usual after vacation. . . .

Friday, Dec. 4. Translated "Corinne,"[28] . . . wrote to the noble W[hittier] and read my beloved Liberator. . . .

Tuesday, Dec. 8. Heard Mr. J. F. Clarke's lecture on the "Yankee."[29] An excellent lecture very amusing and interesting. The true-hearted man was not *afraid* to speak of slavery, and that most truthfully and beautifully. Afterwards, wrote considerably.—

Wednesday, Dec. 9. A rainy day; we are positively going to move this week. So nothing have I done but pack, pack all the afternoon. A little reading to-night. . . .

Saturday, Dec. 12. Packing, packing most busily all day. This eve. thoroughly tired bade the old house good-bye. . . . S[arah] and I are established at Mrs. P[utnam's].[30] Could not leave the house which has been my home ever since I have been in Salem, without regret—a *little*. Have thought much of *her* who was its guardian genius, without whom it seems so changed—so changed! Dear, lost friend *I* shall never forget thee,—never! . . .

Wednesday, Dec. 16. Find it delightful to rise so early.

Can accomplish so much more. Sent my story to the "Home Journal."[31] Shall have little peace of mind till I know its fate. . . . This eve. heard a splendid lecture on Toussaint by our noble Mr. Phillips.[32] It was a glorious and well deserved tribute to the "First of the Blacks." My enthusiastic enjoyment knew no bounds. What heightened it was that a large part of the audience was composed of people who would not go to an avowedly Anti-Slavery lecture. But they had a grand dose of Anti-slavery and anti-prejudice to-night. It was enough for them to hear him say, as *he* alone *could* say it—"I *hate* prejudice against color; I *despise* it!" In concluding he said, as nearly as I can remember "I would compare Toussaint to Cromwell, but Cromwell shed much blood in clutching at a throne. But Toussaint walked by natural gravitation into the leadership of his people, without a crime. I would compare him to Napoleon, but Napoleon's whole career was *covered* with cheatery.—This black chief *"never broke his word."* I would compare him to Washington—but Washington *held slaves.*— This man's hands were clean. There are none worthy to compare with him, in *purity* of character, save Tell and Jay."—

Thursday, Dec. 17. S[arah] and others of the family gone to the Boston Fair,[33] to which I *long* to go, but cannot, so there's no use of repining. My sad heart was gladdened, even more than a visit to the Fair would have gladdened it, by a letter from father,—at last! It is as I thought. He is *utterly unable* to assist me. Ah! if he had only confided this to me long ago, I would *never, never* have asked his assistance. The letter was full of affection. Dear father! he is sorely tried. I wish *I* could be of some assistance to him. I will write and tell him how much I feel with him. . . .

Monday, Dec. 21. Went to an Amateur Concert for the benefit of the poor. Some beautiful singing. The "Mass" I liked especially. The music of the Catholic Church is so rich and impressive. Mrs. Norton's exquisite song—"The Outward Bound" was given by a quartette,—a sister and three brothers, —with fine effect. Rather too much operatic music for me. . . .

Thursday, Dec. 24. Christmas eve. Busy preparing to go to Boston, when my kind friend Miss S[hepard] came in, bringing me a Christmas present from her father;—a complete and most ingenious set of Jack Straws. She spent some time with us.

Friday, Christmas Day. Went to Boston at seven, 'twas bitter cold. Visited several bookstores, and saw many magnificent books among which was Mrs. Clarke's "World-Noted Women," splendidly illustrated with engravings of the most distinguished women from Sappho to Florence Nightingale. Then went to the Fair, and saw many beautiful articles; the most beautiful was a set of photographs of the different ruins of Rome executed by Mrs. Jameson's son-in-law and sent by her from Rome to the Bazaar. The explanations were written by her, and accompanied by her autograph. Photographing seems to me the best way of representing columns. One could hardly realize that these were on paper, they seemed to stand out from it in such fine relief. On Mrs. Stowe's table[34] was a statuette of Uncle Tiff executed by a colored French artist; exquisite statuettes of the Venus de Medici and Canova's Venus of the Bath; —a model of the famous Warwick Vase, *very* beautifully carved. Saw Sumner, Emerson, Wendell Phillips, all in the Fair at once. It was *glorious* to see such a trio. I feasted my eyes. Sumner looks pale and weak but still bears the unmistakeable stamp of "nature's nobleman[.]"[35] To-night went to the Boston Theatre. The play—"Satan in Paris," was nothing but I enjoyed seeing the Theatre. It is so beautiful. The chandelier especially attracted my attention. Its lights were arranged like groups of stars, and produced a fine effect on the beautifully painted ceiling. I had never seen a *bona-fide* Theatre before.

Saturday, Dec. 26. Spent the day at the Fair. Looked over those exquisite photographs again, with Mr. and Mrs. May and was much pleased and benefitted by their interesting comments.[36] Mrs. M[ay] is one of the most refined and truly elegant women I've ever seen. Saw some very old French books— more than two hundred years old; and exquisite illustrations of "Tam O'Shanter." Heard my queenly Mrs. C[hapman][37] speak French "like a stream of silver" with some interesting French emigrants. Saw Sumner again, and Giles. Last night of the Fair. Was introduced to the gifted Mrs. Dall.[38] . . . Left with regret, and reached home at midnight. It is a *glorious* night;— a pure white robe of spotless snow beautifies the earth. . . .

Friday, New Year's morn. 1858. Welcome in, New Year! A *perfect day* ushers thee in. I greet thee with mingled tears of joy and sorrow. I will record no *vows,* no good resolutions *this* year,—to shed, at the beginning of the *next,* bitter, repentant tears over their graves. In the secret depths of my own heart I make some vows. Oh! may God give me strength to keep them!

New Year's Night. Made some calls. . . . At Miss S[arah] R[emond's] saw an exquisite old picture of Sappho, a most inspired face. Saw Miss S[hepard's] beautiful gifts. Heard that the mother of our noble Whittier is dead.[39] Ah! this will be a sad New Year to him. With all my heart I feel for him and his sister in this sad loss. . . .

Saturday, Jan. 2. . . . I wonder why it is that I have this strange feeling of not *living out myself.* My existence seems not *full* not expansive enough. I must need some great emotion to rouse the dormant energies of my nature. What means this constant restlessness, this longing for—something,—I know not what? . . . Alas! I shall never, never be able to say— "My minde to me a *kingdome,* is
　　　　Such perfecte *peace* therein dothe dwelle." . . .

Saturday, Jan. 16. . . . This afternoon a little girl professing to be a medium, came in. Some raps were produced, but nothing more satisfactory. I grow more and more skeptical about Spiritualism. . . .

Wednesday, Jan. 20. A lecture from Emerson—really on the true beauty of Nature, and the pleasure and benefit to be derived from walking amid this beauty.[40] I have rarely enjoyed so rich a mental feast. I am really *grieved* that my mind is in such a stupid state, so "care laden," that I cannot treasure up, as I once could, the golden words which fell from the poet-philosopher's lips. A walk with Emerson would be intensely yet *silently* delightful. I cannot but believe that he is one of the truest of Nature's interpreters. . . .

Monday, Jan. 25. Public examination.—Horrid nuisance! Went off very well. *Dreadfully* tired. Heard an interesting lecture by Dr. Gusdorff (Which I was almost too stupid to appreciate) on the "Transformation of Matter."[41] . . .

Wednesday, Jan. 27. . . . Heard the lion-like Dr. Cheever to-night. He was grand and fearless.[42] Miss S[hepard] and I enjoyed him together.—And now farewell, farewell to thee! my dear old friend, my *only confidant!*—my journal!

Monday, Feb. 1 [1858]. Read and wrote. Spent the afternoon with Miss R[emond] and had a long talk about lecturing. Rec'd a letter and papers from Mr. N[ell] who is *very* kind. Read a very fine Essay on Milton by Macaulay. It is written with even more brilliancy than his History.—Went to the society at Mrs. I[ve]s'.[43] . . .

Sunday, Feb. 7. Mr. P[utnam] and I spent the morning in writing a Parody for Mr. N[ell] on the "Red, White and Blue." *His* share of it is very good,—mine—miserable.[44] Went this afternoon to the new Catholic Church.[45] The stained windows and the exquisitely painted ceiling are very beautiful, but I was disappointed in the rest of the buildings. There are no pictures in it. The music was fine, but the singing rather poor. This eve. read some poetry aloud, and the "Confessions." They are *very* interesting. Mr. P[utnam] read to us some splendid passages from Macaulay's Biographical Essays. His description of the Italian of Machiavelli's time, and another—of "Johnson's Boswell" impressed me as being the finest pen-and-ink portraits that I have ever known of. . . .

Thursday, Feb. 11. *Au desespoir* to-day. . . . I think I *must* go home. I am weary! I am weary! And oh, so unsettled and troubled! I know not what to do. I *ought* not to go. I *cannot* stay. I am *heart sick,* and my physical strength is giving way fast; I feel it. If I could go right on and *die, soon,* how gladly would I do so. But oh, to *drag* on so from day to day. I have no longer the *heart* to do it. And if it be possible for me to feel secure of another situation on my return, I will go home *now.* And *write,* if *I* can.—

Monday, Feb. 15. After school read Emerson and played chess. In the "Eclectic" read a very searching criticism on "Aurora;" another finely-written one on A. Smith's "City Poems", a beautiful and most appreciative sketch of Mrs. Browning; and the most deeply interesting accounts I have yet seen from India;—all from foreign periodicals.[46]—

Tuesday, Feb. 16. Read Emerson and Mrs. Browning (my favorite "Lady Geraldine"). Studied a little German. . . . The pronunciation seems hard, and most unmusical to me, after the sweeter, softer *francaise.* But I wish very much to acquire it. Afterwards,—French. . . .

Friday, Feb. 19. Wrote to dear noble Mr. G[arrison] requesting his autograph. Had a letter and some papers from Mr. N[ell]. That poor Ms!, its fate is not decided yet. Finished the first volume of Emerson's "Essays." I cannot *quite* understand *everything* that he says; but I understand enough to admire and enjoy, and be benefitted by. He has taught me many a good and noble lesson, for which I thank him with all my heart. Studied French.—Read Corinne. . . .

Monday, Feb. 22. Wrote to Aunt M[argaretta] and, with considerable trepidation, to the noble Sumner, for his autograph. . . .

Saturday, Feb. 27. A day to be marked with a *white stone.* Returning from school, weary and sad, as usual, found *two* parcels from Sumner. One containing an extract from one of his speeches, and bearing his signature;—the other filled with other valuable autographs,—of the Duchess of Sutherland, the Duchess of Argyle, the Earl of Shaftsbury, Longfellow, W. H. Furness, Sen. Blair, Jared Sparks, and Lady Napier, the lady of the British Minister at Washington. The first three particularly surprised and delighted me. How very, very kind it was in Mr. Sumner! To an entire stranger, too. I suppose I have to thank my color for it. I can hardly conceive of any worse handwriting than the Duchess of Sutherland's. Her daughter and the Earl of S[haftesbury] write much better. Lady Napier, very prettily. Longfellow writes a little like Mr. Nell. I am full of the most joyful surprise. . . .

Monday, March 1st. Had a very kind note from . . . Mr. A[?] in which he very kindly assures me that he will do all in his power to get me another situation when I shall want one. Now I shall *certainly* resign. . . . I feel that my health demands it. L[ucy] tells me that Mr. F[rank] Webb has received an appointment as postmaster in Jamaica. Probably Annie [Webb] will accompany them.[47] If she *wants* me, I shall be delighted to go. Next week, for home, sweet home! A pleasant day for the first of spring. . . .

Wednesday, March 3. Announced my determination of leaving; to everybody's astonishment.[48] I am sorely disturbed in mind. Constantly I ask myself—"Am I doing right?" Yet I *believe* that I am. If I entirely lose my health *now* of what use will my life be to me? None. I shall only be dependent, miserably dependent on others. I would ten thousand times rather die than that. . . .

Friday, Mar. 5. Went to Boston, to Mr. N[ell's]. "Attucks Celebration."[49] For me the greatest attraction was hearing Phillips and Garrison once more, perhaps for the last time. Old Faneuil Hall presented quite a gay scene after the meeting. There was a large crowd of finely dressed dancers, of whose movements, I was, for some time an amused spectator. But after awhile I grew terribly tired, and was glad to leave.

Saturday, Mar. 6. Came home in the earliest train. . . . Spent the eve. as usual in the rocking chair,—feeling dismal enough because my aching head and side prevented my doing anything. . . .

Wednesday, Mar. 10. The last day in beautiful N[ew] England. Had several visitors this afternoon, and all the "Good Byes" were said. . . .

Thursday, Mar. 11. Philadelphia. Left Salem at six. Spent the whole day in the cars. The ride from Boston to N[ew] Y[ork] is rather tedious,—especially when one is not well. The succession of snow-crowned hills, contrasting with dark, glossy evergreens, and interspersed with villages and towns between is at first, pleasing to the eye, but after awhile one wearies of it. Longfellow's sweet and musical rhymes beguiled much of the time. We approached the "Armory," and then I read the poet's beautiful "Arsenal at Springfield." Arrived here after eleven, thoroughly worn out. . . .

Friday, Mar. 19. Went to Earle's Gallery, and saw some beautiful paintings. The statue of Beatrice was gone; but there is an exquisite picture of her here. What a sweet, lovely face is hers. How terrible must have been the wrongs which could have driven that gentle, lovely girl to so dark a crime! There is a beautiful little picture of Red Riding Hood;—the sweetest little face I ever saw. The soft, violet eyes, the tinted cheeks, the rosebud lips, and the bright scarlet hood drawn so cunningly over her sunny head,—all are charming.—Saw also a striking picture which must, I think, represent the murder of Virginia by her father. To my unpractised eyes this picture is very fine. It is the moment after the fatal blow is received, and the lovely Virginia falls back into the arms of one who is standing near. Her form and features are *perfect*. An expression of horror, not unmingled with awe and admiration rests on the faces of the spectators. The countenance of Virginius, as he raises on high the bloody dagger, is lighted up with the loftiest enthusiasm. Saw also a picture of West's,—a scene from Hamlet,—where Ophelia comes in mad, and singing as she offers her flowers. Every lover of Hamlet knows how touching this scene is. The artist has represented it finely. Saw "Christus Consolator," with the manacled slave, which the *pious* people of our land are so careful as to leave out of their prayer books. Saw a picture of "St. Catherine Borne by the Angels," exactly like the one I saw at Mr. Parker's. The legend of St. Catherine is beautiful. . . .

Thursday, April 1. Sewed; read Bulwer's fine tragedy of "Richelieu."[50] It is beautiful. Went to Independence Square, and sat there a long time, watching the graceful little squirrels as they bounded so lightly over the green grass—as green now —almost—as if it were summer, and tried to imagine that I was in dear Old Salem, far away from the crowd and tumult of a great city. But it needed only to turn from the trees, the grass, and the squirrels, and look out upon the busy street, to dispel the illusion. What a crowd went hurrying past; and among them all, how few pleasant and happy faces! how many sad and careworn ones! . . .

Sunday, Apr. 4. This morning looked over some of dear grandfather's old letters. There was a very interesting letter from a gentleman, travelling in France and Italy, and another of equal interest to me because of the writer—N. P. Rogers. And what an insight these letters are into dear grandfather's own character. With how much veneration and respect to himself are they all expressed! And it makes me proud and happy to think how worthy of it he was! Would that some of his family resembled. I grieve to say they *do not;* far, far from it. Looked over a book of painted flowers. Very, very beautiful they are. The graceful lily, the brilliant carnation, the sweet, modest violet, and my own darling mignonette with many others, were so beautifully and faithfully represented that I felt a thrill of delight when looking at them. "Stars of earth"! how dear to my heart ye are! . . .

Byberry, Saturday, Apr. 10. Had a delightful sail up the river. . . . Our ride home was very pleasant. Already the country is beginning to look quite summer-like. What a relief it is to escape from the close and crowded city, from the sight of glaring brick walls, with only *patches* of the sky between to the pure, fresh air of the country, to feel God's green and beautiful carpet beneath one's feet, to see His blue and boundless canopy above. Rec'd a warm welcome from my Byberry cousins. In the eve. Hattie sang and played for me. Robert [Purvis, Jr.] came.[51]

Sunday, Apr. 11. A rainy day. Feel very miserable. Tried to enter into the pleasant conversation which was going on around me. Hattie has a friend here who reminds me very much of Lizzie Church.[52] She is about her size, and has just such long, light hair, and beautiful blue eyes. She is a little poetess,—a sweet, gentle creature. I have fallen quite in love with her. We had quite an animated discussion about Shakespere's plays, with Aunt H[arriet],[53] who pretends that she agrees with Miss [sic] Bacon. We are quite sure it can only be pretense. I *know* that *Shakespere,* and *he* only wrote those immortal Plays. To look at that noble unrivalled head alone, would convince me of that. Robert left. . . .

Thursday, Apr. 15. Aunt H[arriet] was sick. Spent most of the day in her room. Read in her album two beautiful poems by Mrs. Child and by Whittier, addressed "To the Daughters of James Forten."[54] Finished the delightful "Letters." I love and thank Mrs. Child for writing such a book.[55] This eve. Mr. P[urvis] talked with me about my dear lost mother; I love to hear of her. What a pleasure it would be to me if I had a portrait of her, my own dear mother! . . .

Tuesday, April 20. Worked busily all day. In the afternoon . . . read . . . Mr. Helper's book "The Impending Crisis."[56] It is *excellent.* One of the best arguments against slavery I've ever heard. . . .

Saturday, Apr. 24. Went to the A[nti] S[lavery] office. Was glad to meet Mr. P[urvi]s there. The noble Sumner is in town.[57] Oh! if I could only have a *glimpse* of him. It makes my heart ache to think of the wide, wide gulf between us. I shall never meet him, even to hear him converse with others, myself a passive listener; yet how I *long* to do so. But even a sight of him would do my soul good. I stayed at the Office as long as I could, hoping that he might chance to come in. But I waited in vain. . . .

Sunday, 25. Wrote some letters. While writing the bell rang. I, not feeling very well, was still *en deshabille,* and made my escape. Afterwards came in and found lovely Mrs. Mott[58] and some friends, among whom was an English lady; a most delightful and interesting person. She is the wife of an eminent French writer, whose name I can't remember. He has written a book on the Unity of the Races.[59] She is very social and talked with me about N[ew] E[ngland] and seemed to appreciate my enthusiasm for it. She resides in Algeria; likes it very much; and thinks the natives—Arabs and Africans are the finest people in the world. Thinks the mixed races superior to any other. *I* think she is truly a "Jewel of a woman." Am perfectly charmed; felt sorry that I could not have seen more of her. . . .

Tuesday, Apr. 27. Morn. passed as usual. This afternoon went to the A[nti] S[lavery] Office, hoping, I confess, to obtain a glimpse of Sumner, but of course, I had not that great pleasure. Paid several visits. Saw in Chestnut St. some beautiful pictures. Two splendid portraits of Victoria and Albert in their robes of state. How magnificently they *look.* . . .

Wednesday, Apr. 28. Wrote, studied and practised. Aunt H[arriet] came in, and she and I went to see Rosa Bonheur's famous picture of "The Horse-Fair."—What a *marvellous* picture it is! There are numbers of horses in all positions,—splendid-looking and wonderfully life-like. Some of the most prominent ones particularly impressed me. There were two powerful white horses near the center of the picture. One cannot realize that they are *painted,* they or the rider who sits on one of them,—his head bare, his shirt-sleeves rolled up, every sinew of his brawny arms plainly visible as he strains every nerve, uses his utmost strength to hold his horse. These are *real* horses, this is a *real* man. Again, on the left, is a magnificent black horse, his fore feet rearing up in the air, his nostrils distended. How proud, how conscious he is of his own beauty and power! I think *he* is my favorite. On his left is a beautiful sorrel, very graceful, yet gentle looking. *His* head is not raised so loftily as my favorite's. I think he must be a lady's horse. Still farther to the left is a very fine roan a "strawberry roan."
—Aunt H[arriet],—who knows more about horses than I,—

says. He is a very grand looking horse. All these, and many others are perfect *marvels* to me. Every one *stands out* from the canvas; has a wonderful *individuality*. Aunt H[arriet] thought the trees almost as marvelous as the horses. They are certainly very beautiful. But no description could do justice to this mighty masterpiece of Art. We saw also a smaller picture by the same artist,—representing cattle ploughing in Flanders; and hard work it seems, for there are six oxen yoked to one plough, and yet they are toiling on very slowly and heavily.—Returning home we saw in the window of a picture store, two paintings, the same, or copies of the same, that we had previously seen at the Crystal Palace. They both represent market-places at night; probably in Italy or some other country of southern Europe. Groups of people are standing around a fruit stall. The fruit is perfectly natural. The light from a candle on the table falls on the faces of the woman [sic] standing near, with very fine effect. But the mournful beauty of *one* picture I shall never forget. It represents Lady Jane Grey at the moment before her execution. Her eyes are bandaged, and she kneels by the fatal block. Her confessor bends over her, whispering to her the last words of hope and consolation. Her face is white as marble; its expression perfectly resigned, angelic. The beautiful, long hair falls over the uncovered neck and shoulders. One of her ladies-in-waiting has fainted. The other turns shudderingly away. The executioner stands near leaning on the axe. Even on *his* face there is an expression of compassion. This is a most touching picture; and impressed me deeply. I think of it often. . . .

Sunday, May 16. Commenced writing some "Glimpses of New England." . . .

Tuesday, May 18. Had a great surprise in the arrival of Mr. Putnam and Mr. Nell.[60] Stood almost transfixed with astonishment. Was delighted to see them, and took them to Mrs. C[hew]'s.

Wednesday, May 19. Read my "Glimpses" to Mr. P[utnam] and N[ell] who were pleased to commend them much more highly than they deserve. Then paid a round of visits with them, and spent most of the eve. at Mrs. C[hew]'s. Returning home found a note from my dear Miss L[arcom] awaiting me[61]—enclosing a sprig of arbutus gathered by Whittier and his sister. He writes her word that they crossed the Mass[achusetts] line into N[ew] H[ampshire] to gather it. For the poet-hands that gathered it, for the loving heart that gave, as well as for its own sweetness and beauty, what a precious treasure it will be to me. . . .

120

Friday, May 21. Had to finish the "Glimpses" th
for Mr. P[utnam] insisted on taking them with him to
lished. His kind intentions will be defeated, for he'll
one willing to publish such stuff. He and Mr. N[ell]
this morn. . . .

Monday, May 31. The last day of spring. A most ⟨....⟩ay-
like May this has been. Commenced teaching to-day, and found
it quite pleasant. The children are well-behaved and eager to
learn. Studied French and wrote. . . .

Tuesday, June 15. Have been under-going a thorough self-
examination. The result is a mingled feeling of sorrow, shame
and self-contempt. Have realized more deeply and bitterly
than ever in my life my own ignorance and folly. Not only am
I without the gifts of Nature,—wit, beauty and talent; without
the accomplishments which nearly every one of my age, whom
I know, possesses; but I am not even *intelligent*. And for *this*
there is not the *shadow* of an excuse. Have had many advantages of late years; and it is entirely owing to my own want of
energy, perseverance and application, that I have not improved
them. It grieves me deeply to think of this. I have read an immense quantity, and it has all amounted to nothing,—because
I have been too indolent and foolish to take the trouble of
reflecting. Have wasted more time than I dare think of, in idle
day-dreams, one of which was, how much I should *know* and
do before I was twenty-one. And here I am nearly twenty-one,
and only a *wasted life* to look back upon.—Add to intellectual
defects a disposition whose despondency and fretfulness have
constantly led me to look on the dark side of things, and effectually prevented me from contributing to the happiness of
others; whose contrariness has often induced me to "do those
things which I ought *not* to have done, and to leave undone
those which I *ought* to have done," and *wanted* to do,—and
we have as dismal a picture as one could look upon; and yet
hardly dismal enough to be faithful. Of course, I want to *try*
to reform. But how to begin! Havn't the least spark of order or
method in my composition, and fear I'm wholly incapable of
forming any regular plan of improvement. Wish I had some of
the superabundant energy and perseverance which some whom
I know possess, just to enable me to *keep* the good resolutions
which are so easily made and so very easily broken. . . .

Thursday, June 17. After school had a delightful ride to
a garden. Saw a large variety of beautiful plants. Quantities of
my darling heliotropes. The leaf of the begonia I thought very
singular and beautiful, and also the flower of the clematis. The
country through which we rode was quite hilly, and much

ₐore picturesque than I'd supposed any part of B[yberry] to be. Returning we saw an old slave who had bought himself. He was hoeing corn very industriously, near a "little hut among the bushes" and quite a respectable one, too,—which he has built for himself. A little farther on was a woman seated by the road-side, her bonnet thrown off, and evidently bent on enjoying the cool of the day. Aunt H[arriet] was actually wicked enough to call her "Jane Eyre." A bundle through which cakes and oranges were conspicuous, lay on the ground beside her. Altogether she formed quite a picture of ease and comfort. Still farther on was another picture which would have gladdened *Mrs. Child's* heart;—a little sun-burned, barefooted boy, evidently not more than two or three years old; with the brightest pair of eyes, the most *speaking* face that I ever saw. We could not admire him sufficiently. He had such an arch, bright, spirited expression. A little rustic gate of white pilings against which he was leaning formed a framework for this charming picture, which will long "hang on Memory's wall." . . .

Friday, June 18. To my great astonishment see that my poor "Glimpses" are published in the Standard.[62] They are not worth it. Have been reading Browning's "Paracelsus." Some of it is very beautiful, I think. . . .

Monday, July 5. Saw Mrs. C[hew] start for N[ew] E[ngland]. Ah! how I longed to go with her! My own, my beloved N[ew] E[ngland]! When shall I see thee again!

Spent the afternoon and eve in *trying* to rest; but in vain. *Patriotic* young America kept up [such] a din in celebrating their glorious *Fourth*, that *rest* was impossible. My very soul is sick of such a mockery. All the day my thoughts reverted to that delightful Grove at Framingham where the noblest and best and most eloquent of our land uttered *their* testimony against hypocrisy. And I *yearned* to be there. . . .

Monday, Aug. 2. A rainy and dull day. Hope it does not rain in N[ew] E[ngland] and prevent the Celebration in that beautiful Abington Grove.[63] Noble, untiring, eloquent friends of the slave! I am with you in spirit to-day. . . .

Tuesday, Aug. 17. My birthday. Twenty-one to-day! it grieves me to think of it;—to think that I have wasted so many years. I dare not dwell upon the thought! Saw to-day a book of leaves from Rome, and all the "hallowed shrines" of Italy. They were beautiful; and ah what a passionate longing— as ever—did such names as the Coliseum, The Forum, the Tomb of Juliet, Venice, St. Peter's, Florence, awake in this too restless,—eager soul of mine. Sacred, sacred spots! Sacred to genius and beauty and deathless fame, ah little did I think, years ago, that twenty-one summers should pass over me without my realizing the cherished all-absorbing dream of my heart —the dream of beholding ye! And now when all hope of such happiness should have flown, the dream still lingers on. Foolish, foolish girl! When will you be strong and sensible!

I suppose I *ought* to rejoice to-day for all the city seems to be rejoicing. The Queen's message arrived safely through the wonderful submarine telegraph, the bells are pealing forth merrily.[64] But *I cannot* rejoice that England, my beloved England should be brought so very near this wicked land. I tremble for the consequences, but I will *hope* for the best. Thank God for Hope! . . .

Saturday, Sept. 11. Heard from Mr. P[utnam]. Miss S[arah] P. R[emond] I hear, has burst out most *venomously* upon my poor "Glimpses"—accusing them of being pro-slavery, and heaven knows what all. I *pity* her. . . .

Sunday, Sept. 19. Heard the lovely and excellent Mrs. Mott preach at "Friend's Meeting."—The sermon was, of course, beautiful and radical. She said many good things about Peace, Temperance, and Anti-Slavery. She and Mr. M[ott],[65] the P[urvises],[66] and quite a large party dined with us. Howard Gilbert was here. He is quite a literary character,—a hard student and good writer; . . . and I quite like him. He explained some passages in Pic[ciola][67] for us, and talked about the modern languages, in which he is a proficient. He is a thorough Garrisonian, but rather bitter in his denunciations; and he and Mr. P[urvis] had some very spicy discussions. Though he *is* rather too egotistical, I can't help admiring his earnestness and enthusiasm. . . .

Thursday, Oct. 14. Went to the city. Did some shopping with Aunt H[arriet]. Saw some beautiful pictures, and some silks that were really magnificent—as a work of art. Attended the meeting of the A[nti] S[lavery] Society. Mary Grew[68] and lovely Mrs. Mott gave very interesting accounts of the West Chester meetings.[69] . . .

Saturday, Oct. 23. Read "Picciola" and sewed. This eve. Mr. G[rew] came in very unexpectedly, and accompanied us to the Lyceum. Had a sharp discussion on the question "Is a citizen of the United States ever justifiable in breaking the laws of his country if he believes them to be morally wrong?" Some of the debaters were unusually rude and there was a greater display of ignorance than I have ever before seen, for the especial benefit of the fastidious Mr. G[rew]. He was terribly shocked, I know. . . .

Saturday, Oct. 30. . . . Rode to the sewing circle at the Jameses. The largest and pleasantest we've ever had. . . . Enjoyed myself very much. Driving home met with quite an adventure. There was the thickest fog I have ever seen, and although we had lamps to the carriage it was impossible to see more than a few yards ahead. I was sitting on the front seat with Mr. P[urvis], and should have enjoyed the novelty of finding our way through the darkness had not Aunt H[arriet] been so much alarmed. Suddenly the light from the lamps fell on the face and figure of a man who was walking leisurely along the roadside. He seemed to gaze at us very intently, and had just passed when suddenly the snapping of a pistol near us startled our horse, and frightened us not a little. The man had doubtlessly done it, but whether to frighten us or really fire at us we know not. At any rate he entirely succeeded in doing the former, and I think we shall not soon venture out again on such a dark night.—Finished some sewing. . . .

Monday, Nov. 15. A gloomy, chilly, and, to me, most depressing day. We have our first snow. It is an earnest of Winter, which I dread more than I have words to express. I am *sick*, today, sick, sick at heart;—and though I had *almost* resolved to forbear committing sad thoughts and gloomy feelings to my pages, dear Journal, and have very rarely done so, yet, to-night I long for a confidant—and *thou* art my only one. In the twilight—I sat by the fire and watched the bright, usually so cheering blaze. But it cheered me not. Thoughts of the past came thronging upon me;—thoughts of the loved faces on which I used to look so fondly;—of the loved voices which were music to my ear, and ever sent a thrill of joy to my heart—voices now silent forever. I am *lonely* to-night. I long for one earnest sympathizing soul to be in close communion with my own. I long for the pressure of a loving hand in mine, the touch of loving lips upon my aching brow. I long to lay my weary head upon an earnest heart, which beats for me,—to which *I* am dearer far than all the world beside. There is none, for me, and never will be. I could only love one whom I could look up to, and reverence, and that *one* would never think of such a poor little ignoramus as I. But what a selfish creature I am. This is a forlorn old maid's reverie, and yet I am only twenty-one. But I am weary of life, and would gladly lay me down and rest in the quiet grave. There, alone, is peace, peace! . . .

Friday, Nov. 19. Went to town with Aunt H[arriet]. . . . his eve. went to hear Mr. Curtis. I have rarely been so delighted with any lecture as I have been to-night with "Fair Play for Women."[70] It is as much Anti-Slavery as Woman's Rights. The magnificent voice of the orator—the finest voice I have ever heard, his youth, beauty and eloquence, and the fearlessness with which he avowed his noble and radical sentiments before that immense, fashionable, and doubtless mostly proslavery audience,—all these impressed me greatly, and awakened all my enthusiasm. I *will not* despair when such noble souls as he devote the glory of their genius and their youth to the holy cause of Truth and Freedom. . . .

Sunday, Nov. 21. Rain poured in torrents. Had a visit from "Dimmock Charlton," an interesting old African, whose story I read some time ago in the Standard. Wrote to Mr. Curtis— *dared* to write to him—(anonymously, of course) informing him of the exclusion of colored persons from the Musical Fund, (at which he is to lecture.) and trying to express my grateful admiration of his lecture. Returned to B[yberry] in the pouring rain. . . .

Monday, Nov. 29. This eve. learned "Sandalphon," which I like best of all the poems in the new volume. Have hardly had time to glance at the Atlantic. Read "Anis" by Holmes.[71] The story is a touching one that of a poor forsaken colored child in one of the hospitals (I believe) of Mass[achusetts] who had a disease so disgusting and malignant that no one could be found to nurse her, until a fair and noble young girl of high position, offered her services, and went and kindly and carefully nursed the poor child until she recovered. All honor to the brave, warm heart of that young girl! The poem is really beautiful, and I was particularly pleased with it as it is probably the first really liberal thing that Holmes has ever written. Indeed I am altogether pleasantly disappointed in him since reading some of the really exquisite poems appended to the "Autocrat." I had always supposed that his forte lay entirely in the humorous, and that he would not *dare* to attempt the sentimental. "The Minister's Wooing" is a veritable N[ew] England story, attributed to Mrs. Stowe. There is but little poetry, and that, it seems to me, not nearly so good as usual. . . .

Tuesday, Dec. 14. Too unwell to go to the Fair,[72] and very low spirited. . . . Wrote some stanzas which express what I've *felt*. They are the "Two Voices." . . .

Christmas Day, 1858. A pleasant day. . . . What did I do? Occupied myself part of the day in making evergreen wreaths to adorn the picture frames, so as to give the rooms as Christmas like an appearance as possible. Then looked over my old journals till my heart ached. In the eve. acted charades and read "Lady Geraldine." . . . I like the way it is written in the old edition better than in this—some things in it. But both are very beautiful. Rec'd Andromeda (Kingsley's) from Tacie, The Autocrat from Mr. Brown, and an exquisite pearl-handled pen-knife from R[obert Purvis, Jr.]. This week sent my "Two Voices" to the Standard.[73] But have no idea that they will publish it. 'Tis not worth publishing. . . .

Friday, Dec. 31. All the eve. read the "Odyssey" (Pope) and finished it. Sat up to see the old year out with Aunt H[arriet] and Mr. P[urvis] and read Tennyson's "Death of the Old Year." I am charmed with the "Odyssey."—How terrible and exciting are the dangers through which Ulysses passed, how spirited the scene of the bending of the bow, and how beautiful many other passages—particularly the meeting of the hero with his sire the old Laertes. But the slaughter of the suitors is too horrible and revolting. It made me shudder.—

'Tis twelve! Farewell, old year! And welcome, welcome in the New! one year ago to-night I was in dear old Salem, and little did I imagine that the next New Year would find me here. But so it is! How little do we know. How little *can* we dream of what the future has in store for us.—But I must retire, and spend the first few hours of the New Year in the land of dreams.—

New Year's Day 1859. How strange the date looks to me! Ah! how the years are slipping and sliding away from us. Again T. is here, and *her* presence opens the year pleasantly for me.— New Year! may'st thou be a year of *triumphs* for me. Of triumphs over all sorrows and trials. A year of brave endurance, and of *earnest* labor. If I live until this day one year, may I feel that I have *done* something, for *others* as well as for myself.— Recommenced Latin. I *will* persevere! . . .

Thursday, Feb. 10. Went to town. Attended the Annual Meeting.[74] Miss Grew's Report was excellent. Read an excellent and most interesting article in The Westminster Review on "The Capabilities of Woman." It was a criticism on several books written written [sic] by ladies who were assistant nurses at the Crimea, and the thoroughly liberal and appreciative spirit in which it is written pleased me greatly. . . .

Saturday, Feb. 12. Read the excellent speeches made at the Boston meetings. Mr. Phillips was especially fine.[75] The A[nti] S[lavery] Festival was a complete success;—far more profitable than the Bazaar. I am so glad of it. Tis all owing to Mrs. Chapman. She is indeed a host in herself.[76] This eve. our Lyceum met. Had a very spirited debate on the question "Do the signs of the times indicate the downfall [*sic*] of this Repub-lic?" Of course we took the affirmative, and after a long and animated discussion, thanks to Mr. P[urvis] it was decided in our favor.[77] . . .

Monday, Apr. 4. Heard to-day that there has been another fugitive arrested. There is to be a trial.[78] God grant that the poor man may be released from the clutches of the slave-hunters. Mr. P[urvis] has gone down. We wait anxiously to hear the result of the trial. How long, oh, how long shall such a state of things as this—last?

Wednesday, April 6. Good news! After waiting with in-tense and painful anxiety for the result of the three days' trial we are at last gladdened by the news that the alleged fugitive, Daniel Dangerfield, has been released.—The Commissioner *said* that he released him because he was not satisfied of his identity. Others are inclined to believe that the pressure of pub-lic sentiment—which was, strange to say, almost universally on the right side—was too overwhelming for the Com[missioner] to resist, particularly as his own family—even his wife, it is said, declared that they could only discard him if he sent the man into slavery. It is encouraging to know that there was so much right and just feeling about the matter. It gives one some hope even for Philadelphia. Last night the court sat for *four-teen hours,* the longest session that has ever been held in this city. Many ladies stayed during the entire night, among whom was the noble and venerable Lucretia Mott, untiring and de-voted to the last.[79] She is truly lovely—saintly in look as in spirit, for a beautiful soul shines through her beautiful face. She is indeed one of the "blest of earth," one of those whose "very presence is a benediction!"

Friday, Apr. 8. Long, long to be remembered. This eve. attended a very large Anti-Slavery meeting at Sansom Hall celebrating Daniel's release. A crowd of Southerners was pres-ent, and ere the meeting had progressed far they created a great disturbance, stamping, hallooing, groaning etc. so that it was impossible to hear a word that the speakers were saying. In vain did the President strive to preserve order,—the tumult in-creased every moment, and at one time there was a precipitate rush forward. We thought we should be crushed, but I did not feel at all frightened; I was too excited to think of fear. The veterans in the cause said that it reminded them of the time when the new and beautiful Pennsylvania Hall, which was af-terward burned to the ground—was mobbed. But at last the

127

police arrived. Many of the disturbers were arrested, and order restored. Mr. P[urvis'] speech was fine; decidedly the most effective. A young Englishman spoke fearlessly and well.—The meeting was one of deep interest. I shall long remember it.[80]

Saturday, Apr. 9. The hero of the last few days came here to-night. He is a sturdy, sensible seeming man. It makes my heart beat quickly to see one who has just had so narrow an escape from a doom far darker and more terrible than death. Nor is he quite safe yet, for we hear that there are warrants out for his re-arrest. Poor man! there can be no rest for his weary feet nearer than the free soil of Canada. We shall be obliged to keep him very close.

Saturday, Apr. 23. D[aniel] has left us and we hear with joy that he is safe in Canada. Oh, stars and stripes, that wave so proudly over our *mockery* of freedom, what is your protection. Hear that the noble Whittier is in town, wish, hope that I may have the pleasure of seeing his face again. It would be *too* delightful if he would only come up here and see us. But I dare not hope that. . . .

Phila. Sunday, April 24. Paid several visits, and in the eve. went . . . to hear Dr. Furness.[81] Most beautifully he spoke. And his sermon was full of the love of *man* and therefore of the love of God. Heard the most exquisite singing there, by a lady, of the Lord's Prayer. Dr. F[urness] is a perfect Christian. How much good it does one to listen to words of truth from the lips of those true ministers—too few, alas! who *practise* what they preach,—whose lives are a beautiful exemplification of their teachings. I *cannot* listen to those who do not live up to their preaching.

Saturday, Apr. 30. Went to town with Mr. P[urvis] . . . to see Whittier. Had a delightful visit. He was in one of his most genial moods, and laughed and talked most charmingly. He looks much better than I feared to see him, and says that he feels better. I am so glad. It was a real happiness to see him again, and in such excellent spirits. Grand, noble man that he is! Another great happiness is in store for me. Thanks to the kindness of my good friends Prof. Crosby and Mary S[hepard] I am offered a situation in the school of the latter.[82] *That* is indeed a pleasure, and I shall have time to study some at the dear old Normal. I have had a truly kind and happy home here, and have become much attached to it. But the great advantage of attending school, the pleasure of being with Mary S[hepard] and, above all, my conviction that it is my *duty* to go (some of my friends think it is *not*) prevent me from hesitating a moment about going. Prof. C[rosby] and indeed all my N[ew] E[ngland] friends are very, very kind and good. At the Office I was introduced to Dr. Furness, and had a very pleasant conversation with him. He is as genial and affable as he is noble and fearless. I have a high reverence for him. . . .

Saturday, May 7. Went to town, and saw Aunt M[argaretta] who has just returned from N[ew] E[ngland]. Had a talk about the friends in old S[alem]. Am grieved to hear that Mrs. P[utnam]'s little girl is dangerously ill. Poor Mrs. P[utnam]! I pity her sincerely. But oh, how greatly it grieves and saddens me to think of the death of Mr. Hovey.[83] He was so truly good and noble. The cause of light and Truth, cannot afford to lose such a friend. Why must such noble, true-hearted men leave us?

Salem, Jan. 1, 1860.[84] Can it be possible that so many months have elapsed since my pen last touched thy pages, old friend! Carelessly enough we say "time flies." Do we, after all, realize *how* it flies? How the months, days and hours *rush* along, bearing us on—on upon their swift, unwearying wings! To me there is something deeply impressive in this strange flight of Time. Standing now upon the threshold of another year, how solemn, how strangely solemn seem the Past and the Future; the *dead* and the *newly born* year;—memories, gladdening and sorrowing of the one, eager hopes, desires, resolves for the other;—how they crowd upon us now! Do they avail aught? I ask myself. Alas! too often, I fear they do not. Too often past experiences, and high resolves for the Future, are forgotten, swallowed up in the excitement of the Present moment. Have been reading to-day Arnold's History of Rome. How it thrills one to know of those heroic deeds done "in the brave days of old." And how blessed it is that all the wealth of the ages can be ours, if we choose to grasp it! That we can live, not in this century, this corner of the world, alone, but in every century, and every age, and every clime! That we can listen to the words of orators, poets and sages; that we can enter into every conflict, share every joy, thrill with every noble deed, known since the world began. And hence are *books* to us a treasure and a blessing unspeakable. And they are doubly this when one is shut out from society as I am, and has not opportunities of studying those living, breathing, *human* books, which are, I doubt not, after all, the most profoundly interesting and useful study. From that kind of pleasure, that kind of improvement I am barred; but, thank God! none can deprive me of the other kind. And I will strive to be resigned during the little while we have to stay here.—and in that higher sphere do I not *know* the cruelty the injustice of man ceases? *There* do Right, and Justice and Love abide.

Part 5

From Salem to St. Helena Island

June 22, 1862 - November 29, 1862

Salem, June 22, 1862. More penitent than ever I come to
thee again, old Journal, long neglected friend. More than two
years have elapsed since I last talked to thee.—two years full
of changes. A little while ago a friend read to me Miss Mul-
lock's "Life for a Life."[1] The Journal letters, which I liked so
much,—were at first addressed to an unknown friend. So shall
mine be. What name shall I give to thee, oh *ami inconnu*? It
will be safer to give merely an initial—A. And so, dear A. I
will tell you a little of my life for the past two years. When I
wrote to you last,—on a bright, lovely New Year's Day, I was
here in old Salem, and in this very house. What a busy winter
that was for me, I was assisting my dear Miss S[hepard] with
one of her classes,[2] and at the same time studying, and reciting
at the Normal, Latin, French and a little Algebra. Besides I
was taking German lessons. Now was I not busy, dear A? Yet
it seems to me I was never so happy. I enjoyed life perfectly,
and all the winter was strong and well. But when Spring came
my health gave way. First my eyesight failed me, and the German which I liked better than anything else, which it was a real
luxury to study had to be given up, and then all my other studies. My health continuing to fail, I was obliged to stop teaching,
and go away. Went to Bridgewater, and in the Kingmans' delightful home grew gradually stronger. Then went to the Water
Cure at Worcester, where the excellent Dr. R[ogers] did me a
world of good[3]—spiritually as well as physically. To me he
seems one of the best and noblest types of manhood I ever saw.
In my heart I shall thank him always. Early in September, came
back from W[orcester] and recommenced teaching, feeling
quite well. But late in October had a violent attack of lung
fever, which brought me very, very near the grave, and entirely
unfitted me for further work. My physician's commands were
positive that I sh'ld not attempt spending the winter in S[alem],
and I was obliged to return to P[hiladelphia]. A weary winter I
had there, unable to work, and having but little congenial society, and suffering the many deprivations which all of our un-

happy race must suffer in the so-called "City of Brotherly Love." What a mockery that name is! But over those weary months it is better to draw the veil, and forget. In May I went to Byberry to see poor R[obert Purvis, Jr.] . . . ill with lung disease. And all the beautiful summer I stayed there trying to nurse and amuse him as well as I cl'd. It was so sad to see one so young, so full of energy and ambition, doomed to lead a life of inaction, and the weariness which ill health brings. R[obert] seemed to improve as the summer advanced, and in the Fall I left him, to take charge of Aunt M[argaretta]'s school in the city.[4] A small school—but the children were mostly bright and interesting; and I was thankful to have anything to do. . . .

In March, poor R[obert] died.[5] When I saw him lying so cold and still, and witnessed the agony of the loving hearts around him, I wished, dear A., that I cl'd have been taken instead of him. He had everything to live for, and I so very little. It seems hard; yet we *know* it must be right. . . . Week before last I had a letter form Mary S[hepard] asking me to come on and take charge of S. C.'s [?] classes during the summer, as she was obliged to go away. How gladly I accepted, you, dear A., may imagine. I had been *longing* so for a breath of N[ew] E[ngland] air; for a glimpse of the sea, for a walk over our good old hills. . . . We left P[hiladelphia] on Tuesday, the 10th; stopped a little while in N[ew] Y[ork]. . . . Then took the evening boat, and reached here Wed[nesday] morn. Mrs. I[ves][6] gave us a most cordial welcome; and we immediately felt quite at home. . . .

Sunday, July 6.   Let me see? How did I spend last week? In teaching, as usual, until Friday, on which, being the "glorious Fourth," we had no school, and I went to Framingham to the Grove Meeting.[7] The day was lovely, and I had a delightful time. Greatly to my disappointment Mr. Phillips was not there. But is was better that he sh'ld not attempt speaking in the open air.—His throat was troubling him so much. Mr. G[arrison] and all his children were there looking as well and happy as possible. He and Mr. Heywood[8] and Miss Anthony[9] made the best speeches. One cannot listen to Mr. H[eywood] without feeling that he is a "born orator." . . . Met some old friends at Framingham. Dr. and Mrs. Rogers were there from W[orcester]. How glad I was to see the Dr. again. But it grieved me to see him looking so far from well. He has been quite ill since Feb[ruary], with pleurisy. He is certainly one of the most thoroughly good men in the world. . . . After the meeting spent a day or two in Boston. Had a lovely walk on the Common, Saturday morning. How fresh and beautiful the grass and trees looked. . . . On my way home, stopped at Williams and Everett's and saw a magnificent bust of Milton in marble. Saw a picture of "Rahl of the Rhine," which was really startling in its *lifelikeness.* The legend runs this wise.—Rahl and two wild companions were in the habit of meeting to drink together. And one night they took a vow that they w'ld continue to meet on that same night of every year, even although two of them sh'ld be dead. And the vow was kept. The painting, which is a large and very fine one, represents Rahl as raising a glass of wine, and at the same moment the four ghostly hands of his two dead companions are stretched out and clutch the other two glasses, while Rahl stands transfixed with fear and horror. There is something very life-like and striking about this picture. One cannot look at it without a shudder.—In the afternoon . . . spent a little time at the Atheneum.[10] My attention was particularly attracted by a magnificent bust of John Brown, (in marble,) and by a landscape—I think it must have been a part of the German Alps—by a German artist. I thought it one of the most beautiful pictures I ever saw, but you know, dear A., that there never was a greater ignoramus than I about matters of Art. Still I do believe no one could have helped liking this picture. It was so lovely—Grand mountains, *real* mountains, rising above the clouds in the background, a lovely valley with a clear stream flowing through it at the foot of the mts. Near the stream was a party of gipsies in bright, picturesque costumes, preparing their meal. Over all bent a sky, blue and beautiful as an Italian sky. It was a most *enjoyable* picture, and one to be easily recalled. Had but little time to devote to others. . . . To-day—Sunday—had the great happiness of hearing Mr. Phillips. . . . Music Hall was crowded.[11] The heat was so intense that I c'ld scarcely breathe. I thought, before the lecture commenced, that I sh'ld certainly have to go out. But after Mr. P[hillips] commenced speaking I forgot everything else. It was a grand, glorious speech, such as he alone can make. I wish the poor, miserable President whom he so justly criticized c'ld have heard it. It grieved me to see him looking so pale and weary. And his throat troubles him much. I cannot bear to think of his health failing. Yet something I fear it is. Oh dear A. let us pray to the good All-Father to spare this noble soul to see the result of his life-long labors—the freedom of the slave. . . . Ah, friend of mine, I must not forget to tell you about a little adventure I met with to-day. I was boarding with Mrs. R[?] a very good anti-slavery woman, and kind and pleasant as can be. Well, when I appeared at the dinner-table to-day, it seems that a *gentleman* took umbrage at sitting at the same table with one whose skin chanced to be "not colored like his own," and rose and left the table. Poor man! he feared contamination. But the charming part of the affair is that I, with eyes intent upon my dinner, and mind entirely engrossed (by Mr. Phillips' glorious words, which were still sounding in my soul), did not notice this person's presence nor disappearance. So his proceedings were quite lost upon me, and I sh'ld have been in a state of blissful ignorance as to his very existence had not the hostess afterward spoken to me about it, expressing the wish, good woman—that my "feelings were not hurt." I told her the truth, and begged her to set her mind perfectly at ease, for even had I have noticed the simpleton's behavior it w'ld not have troubled me. I felt too thorough a contempt for such people to allow myself to be wounded by them. This wise gentleman was an *officer in the navy*, I understand. An honor to his country's service— isn't he? But he is not alone, I know full well. The name of his kindred is Legion,—but I defy and despise them all. I hope as I grow older I get a little more philosophy. Such things do not wound me so deeply as of yore. But they create a bitterness of feeling, which is far from desirable. "When, when will these outrages cease?" often my soul cries out—"How long, oh Lord, how long?"—You w'ld have pitied me during the last part of my ride back to S[alem] this afternoon. The first part of the ride—from B[oston] to L[ynn] in the horse cars, w'ld have been quite pleasant but for the heat. One has a good opportunity of seeing the surrounding country—traveling in this way. At L[ynn] we met the stage, or rather omnibus. We packed in;— thirty outside; the inside crowded to suffocation with odorous Irish and their screaming babies;—the heat intense. Altogether it was quite unbearable. The driver refused to move with such a load. Nobody was willing to get off. And I think we must have been detained at L[ynn] an hour, till at last an open wagon drove up, and taking off part of the load, we started for S[alem]. We were altogether about three hours going from B[oston] to S[alem]. . . .

Wednesday, Aug. 6. Spent the day at Nahant. Had a glorious time. . . . Returning, how much we enjoyed the beautiful drive from N[ahant] to L[ynn] a narrow strip of land with the sea on either hand, and sea glowing in the sunset. It was very beautiful. Soon after I reached home . . . came . . . the kindest note from Whittier, in answer to one I had written asking what day we sh'ld come. (His sister had urgently invited us to come before I left N[ew] E[ngland].) We are to go on Saturday. My mind is filled with pleasant anticipations. Good night.—

Saturday, Aug. 9. Another "day to be marked with a
134

white stone. Mary [Shepard] and I started early. . . . We changed cars at L[ynn] then proceeded to Amesbury. Did not see Whittier at the station. Drove to the house; met with a warm welcome from his sister. She looks very frail. Just as we entered the door of the house a lady came in behind us, whom we found afterward to be Lucy Larcom[12]—a pleasant, mother-ly, unassuming kind of person, really quite lovable. W[hittier] was in one of his most delightful genial moods. His sister as lovely, childlike—I had almost said as Angelic as ever. The day was showery, and we c'ld not take any walks, but I enjoyed my-self perfectly in the house. W[hittier] told us some amusing anecdotes of how he was pestered by people coming to see him —people who were utter strangers. Sometimes, he said they brought their carpet-bags. "Oh, Mr. W[hittier], not their car-pet-bags!" we exclaimed. "Yes, actually" he replied, smiling quite grimly, "and they all have the same speeches to make 'Mr. W[hittier] we have read y[ou]r writings and admired them very much, and had such a great desire to see you'." He said he was thankful to live in such a quiet little place as Amesbury, where nobody said anything to him about his writings, and where he was not thought of as a writer. He said sometimes he had tracked these lion-hunters, and found that the same people went to Emerson and Longfellow and others. Emerson did not care so much for them. He rather enjoyed studying character in all its different phases. He (W[hittier]) and his sister told us a comical story about a "Mrs. Hanaford's husband," this Mrs. H[anaford] it seems, being one of the most persistent lion-hunters. The conversation turned on many topics, and was most enjoyable throughout. Miss W[hittier] showed us photo-graphs of her friends. Among them was one of a Mrs. Howell of Phila[delphia] (whom gossip once said W[hittier] w'ld mar-ry) a face faultless in outline and coloring—exquisitely beauti-ful, yet lacking a little in depth of expression. Miss W[hittier] says it does not do her justice. That she is more beautiful than her picture. Then she must look like an angel. The picture of Helen W[hittier] the lovely, gifted girl who died in Italy, charmed me. A face at once most gentle and yet most spirited, beautiful, noble, and lighted up by the soul within. A cherished and only child, she died at seventeen. Miss W[hittier] showed us the picture of an Italian girl, in which she found a striking likeness to me. Everybody else agreed that there was a resem-blance. But I utterly failed to see it: I thought the Italian girl very pretty, and I know myself to be the very opposite. We left the poet's home with regret. Such a quiet lovely home. It made my heart ache to see his sister looking so frail, knowing what these two are to each other. I was glad to find that she was going away for a while with Lucy Larcom, she is such a motherly person—one by whom it must be a real happiness to be taken care of. W[hittier] advised me to apply to the Port-Royal Com[mission] in Boston.[13] He is very desirous that I sh'ld go. I shall certainly take his advice. . . .

Boston.—Monday, Aug. 11. Left S[alem] . . . this morn. Farewell, farewell again old town! I know not when I shall see thee again. S[allie] and I . . . walked from B[oston] to Bunker Hill. Charmed our eyes with Warren's statue; exhausted ourselves with ascending the Mon[ument] were refreshed again by the magnificent view from the top, descended, went to the Public Library and the Atheneum. Saw nothing new at the latter, but some old pictures of which one never wearies. . . .

Wednesday, Aug. 13. Had gone to see some members of the P[ort] R[oyal] Com[mission] and finding them all out of town, felt somewhat discouraged, when I rec'd the kindest letter from Whittier, advising me again to apply to the Com[mission] and giving me the names of several friends of his to whom to apply, also his permission to use his name as a reference. How very kind he is. I shall go and see those whom he mentions at once.

Watertown.—Sunday, Aug. 16. Have not yet succeeded in seeing any of the Com[mission] though I have traversed this hilly city enough; but I don't despair for I have seen Dr. Howe.[14] Was disappointed in his appearance. He is not the benevolent looking genial person I expected to see. At first he even seemed cold and hard, but no wonder, he was being so persecuted with some tiresome people. When I stated my business to him, and showed him W[hittier]'s letter he was as kind and cordial as c'ld be, and entered with much interest into my wishes. He is not a member of the Com[mission] but recommended me to go to a Dr. Peck, who has been Superintendent of the schools at P[ort] R[oyal] and who has great influence with the Com[mission][15]. . . . I have been to Roxbury to see Dr. P[eck] but he was not at home will probably be on Tuesday. So I determined instead of going to W[orcester] to come to Watertown and stay . . . till Monday. Had a delightful ride out in the horse cars, through old Cambridge, past Longfellow's home, and Lowell's, the Colleges, and Mt. Auburn. . . .

Sunday, Aug. 17. My twenty-fifth birthday. Tisn't a very pleasant thought that I have lived a quarter of a century, and am so very, very ignorant. Ten years ago, I hoped for a differ-fate at twenty-five. But why complain? The accomplishments, the society, the delights of travel which I have dreamed of and longed for all my life, I am now convinced can never be mine. If I can go to Port Royal, I will try to forget all these desires. I will pray that God in his goodness will make me noble enough to find my highest happiness in doing my duty. ... Went to church this morning to hear Mr. Wiess—author of "The Horrors of San Domingo," in the Atlantic.[16] It was a beautiful earnest sermon, and I enjoyed it, but was rather disappointed that it was not on the times, as I had hoped it w'ld be. *That* is the subject which he usually chooses, I am told. It was a pleasant little church and the altar adorned with the loveliest flowers. ...

Monday, Aug. 18. Walked from W[atertown] to Mt. Auburn.[17] It was a delightful walk through the quiet, beautiful country. Spent nearly all day at Mt. A[uburn]. It was very lovely there. The beautiful chapel with its noble statues, the grand view from the Observatory, the stately monuments, the exquisite flowers—I enjoyed all perfectly. Such flowers! Geranium, heliotrope, mignonette, and everything else that is fragrant and beautiful in profusion. I sat down and *luxuriated*. The whole cemetery is like a flower garden. One or two of the monuments I liked particularly. On one—over a child's grave —was carved a cross and anchor, and, twining around them, a morning-glory vine also exquisitely carved. The inscription was —"Here in Faith and Hope, we placed our Morning Glory." On another simple white headstone, with no name upon it, were the words—"All I loved lies here." It was over the grave of a grown person. There was something very touching in those few, simple words.—

Worcester, Tuesday, Aug. 19. Saw Dr. P[eck] this morning. He was very kind, and assures me that he thinks there will be no difficulty about my going. He will speak to the Com[mission] about it, and let me know in a few days. It was very interesting to hear his account of his experiences at Port Royal. He seems deeply interested in the people there. I hope I can go. ...

Wednesday, Sept. 3. Have been anxious and disappointed at not hearing from Dr. P[eck]. ... The Com[mission] meets to-day, and then he will write immediately and let me know the final decision. Last week I heard from home that there was no doubt of my being able to go from the Phila[delphia] Com[mission]. Mr. McK[im] had spoken to them about it.[18] So if I cannot go from B[oston] I am sure of going from P[hiladelphia]; but I w'ld rather go under Boston auspices. ...

Monday, Sept. 8. No further news from B[oston]. I am determined to go to-morrow and see for myself what the trouble is. . . .

Phila. Sunday, Sept. 14. Back again in old abominable P[hiladelphia] . . . Went from W[orcester] to B[oston] on Tuesday afternoon. I got little satisfaction from the B[oston] Com[mission]. "They were not sending women at present" etc. Dr. R[ogers] promised to do all he c'ld for me, but I am resolved to apply to the Com[mission] here. . . . Remained in Boston till Friday afternoon. Had the happiness of getting a glimpse of Wendell P[hillips] before I left. W'ld not stop him to shake hands with him, and have been sorry ever since that I did not. It w'ld have been *such* a satisfaction to me, and I may never see him again. Too late now. Came to N[ew] Y[ork] on the Sound, and had a very rough night of it. On Sat[urday] Henry [Forten][19] went with me to Central Park. A delightful place it is. T'will be a perfect fairy-land when the trees are grown. H[enry] came to P[hiladelphia] with me. We got here between ten and eleven. Everybody was in bed but Aunt M[argaretta] who was astonished to see me. All well. . . .

Monday, Sept. 15. Through Mr. McK[im]'s kindness have seen the Com[mission]. They are perfectly willing for me to go. The only difficulty is that it may not be quite safe. They will write to Port Royal at once, and inquire about my going. I shall wait anxiously for a reply. . . .

Wednesday, Oct. 21. To-day rec'd a note from Mr. McK[im] asking me if I c[ou]ld possibly be ready to sail for Port Royal perhaps to-morrow. I was astonished, stupefied, and, at first thought it impossible, but on seeing Mr. McK[im] I found there was an excellent opportunity for me to go. An old Quaker gentleman is going there to keep store, accompanied by his daughter, and he is willing to take charge of me. It will probably be the only opportunity that I shall have of going this winter, so at any cost I *will* go. And so now to work. In greatest haste. . . .

At Sea. Oct. 27. Monday. Let me see. Where am I? What do I want to write? I am in a state of utter bewilderment. It was on Wed[nesday] I rec'd the note. On Thursday I said "good bye" to the friends that are so dear, and the city that is so hateful, and went to N[ew] Y[ork]. . . . The next morn did not hurry myself, having heard that the steamer "United States" w'ld not sail till twelve. . . . I went to "Lovejoy's" to meet the Hunns[20] and found there a card from Mr. H[unn] bidding me hasten to the steamer, as it was advertised to sail at nine. It was then between ten and eleven. After hurrying down and wearying ourselves, found when I got on board that it was not to sail till twelve. But I did not go ashore again. It was too bad, for I had no time to get several things that I wanted much, among them "Les Miserables," which my dear brother H[enry] had kindly given me the money for. He had not had time to get it in P[hiladelphia].

Enjoyed the sail down the harbor perfectly. The shipping is a noble sight. Had no symptoms of sea-sickness until eve when, being seated at the table an inexpressibly singular sensation caused me to make a hasty retreat to the aft deck, where, by keeping perfectly still sitting on a coil of ropes spent a very comfortable eve. and had a pleasant conversation with one of the passengers. Did not get out of sight of land until after dark. I regretted that.

Went below for the night into the close ladies' cabin with many misgivings which proved not unfounded. Was terribly sea-sick that night and all the next morning. Did not reappear on deck till noon of the next day—Saturday. What an experience! Of all doleful, dismal, desperate experiences sea-sickness is certainly the dolefulest, dismalest, and desperate-est!

T'was rather a miserable afternoon. Was half sick all the time and scarcely dared to move. There was highly pleasant talk going on around me, to which I c'ld listen in silence—that was all. My companion Lizzie Hunn was sick all the time. Poor girl, she c'ld take no pleasure in anything.

When night came, we both determined that we w'ldn't go below and have a repetition of the agonies of the night before. We heroically resolved to pass the night on deck. A nice little nook was found for us "amidships," and there enveloped in shawls and seated in arm chairs we were made as comfortable as possible, and passed the night without being sick. Two of the passengers—young men from Hilton Head, who were very gentlemanly and attentive, entertained us for some time with some fine singing; then they retired, and we passed the rest of the night in the society of Old Ocean alone. How wild and strange it seemed there on the deck in the dark night, only the dim outlines of sea and sky to be seen, only the roaring of the waves to be heard. I enjoyed it much. The thought that we were far, far, away from land was a pleasant one to me.

The next day—Sunday—was emphatically a *dismal* day. It rained nearly all the time so that we c'ld not be on deck much of the time. As soon as we established ourselves nicely outside down came the rain and we were driven into the close cabin, which was almost unendurable to me. Tried to read a little in the French Bible which H[enry] gave me, but in vain. The day

139

was mostly spent in the interesting occupation of preventing sea-sickness by keeping perfectly quiet and watching the rain drops.

Before night a storm came on. And a terrible storm it was. The steward arranged mattresses and blankets for us in the covered passage way "amidships," and we lay down, but not to rest. It was a veritable grand storm at sea. The vessel rocked and plunged, the planks creaked and groaned, the sea broke upon the bows with thunderous roars, and within one w'ld have thought that all the crockery in the establishment was going to pieces. Such a noise I never heard in my life. Such roaring and plunging, and creaking. Afterward we were told that one of the chains of the vessel broke, and indeed for a time she seemed to be at the mercy of the waves. Some one near us—one of the waiters, I think, was dreadfully frightened, and commenced praying and moaning most piteously, crying "Oh Jesus, dear Jesus," in most lamentable tones, till I began to think we must really be in danger. Then the water came into the ladies cabin, below. One lady who had a baby with her woke up in the night and c'ld not find the child. It had been rolled away from her by the tossing of the ship, the lamps were out, and after some time, and much terror on the part of the poor woman the baby was found by one of the waiters under the berth. She was very quiet, and did not seem at all alarmed at her involuntary journey. Despite all the alarm and distress and anxiety we c'ld not help being amused at this little episode. During all the storm, however, I felt no fear; and now that the danger has passed, I feel really glad that I have at last experienced a "veritable storm at sea." The most astonishing thing was that I had two or three most refreshing sleeps in the very height of the storm.

This morning the sea was still very rough, but I struggled up, and dressed with great difficulty, and with the aid of one of the waiters made my way on deck. The sky was still very much overcast, the great, white capped waves were rising to a great height and breaking against the sides of the vessel. It was a grand sight, and I enjoyed it greatly. It has quite cleared off now, and the day is most lovely. I am feeling well and *luxuriating* in the glorious beauty of sea and sky. But my poor companion is still quite sick, and while I write, sits before me on a coil of ropes, enveloped in shawls, and looking the picture of dolefulness and despair.

How grand, how glorious the sea is, to-day! It far more than realizes my highest expectations of it. The sky too is beautiful— a deep, delicious blue, with soft, white, fleecy clouds floating

140

over it. We have seen several sails today, in the distance, but still no land, whereat I am rejoiced.

There's not much to be said about the passengers on board. There are about a dozen beside ourselves, none of whom seem to me especially interesting, except perhaps our friend from Hilton Head, Mr. B[?]. He is very intelligent, and I sh'ld think even a talented young man. He has read and admires all my favorite authors, and I enjoy talking with them [him] about them. I have rarely found a *man* with so keen and delicate an appreciation of the beautiful, both in Nature and Art. There are no soldiers on board but one officer who stalks about the boat looking well pleased with himself and evidently trying to look quite grand, but *sans* success, for he was rather insignificant despite his good figure, fierce moustaches, and epaulettes.

Of the three ladies on board two go South to join their husbands, and the third accompanies hers. The first two are quite talkative, the latter very quiet. I believe that is all that can be said of them. There is a sea captain here whom I like very much. He is a Cape Cod man; has been to sea ever since he was nine years old. Has visited many lands, and I enjoy hearing him talk about them. The other gentlemen do not interest me, so I shall let them pass.

Have only been able to go to the table twice. Then there was no difficulty as I feared there might be. People were as kind and polite as possible. Indeed I have had not the least trouble since I have been on board. The waiters are as obliging and attentive as they can be, and bring us our meals out on deck every day.—

Afternoon.—I have just beheld the most glorious sight I ever saw in my life. . . . I staggered to the bow of the ship (which still rolls and pitches terribly) and there saw the sea in all its glory and grandeur. Oh, how beautiful those great waves were as they broke upon the sides of the vessel, into foam and spray, pure and white as new fallen snow. People talk of the monotony of the sea. I have not found it monotonous for a moment, since I have been well. To me there is "infinite variety," constant enjoyment in it.

I have tried to read, but in vain; there is so much to take off one's attention, besides reading makes my head dizzy. One of the most beautiful sights I have yet seen is the phosphorescence in the water at night—the long line of light in the wake of the steamer, and the stars, and sometimes balls of fire that rise so magically out of the water. It is most strange and beautiful. Had it not been for the storm we should have reached Port Royal to-day. But we shall not get there till to-morrow.

141

Tuesday, A. M. Oct. 28. How very, very lovely it was last night. Saw at last what I have so longed to see—the ocean in the moonlight. There was a beautiful young moon. Our ship rode gently along over a smooth sea leaving a path of silver behind it. There was something inexpressibly sweet and soothing and solemn in that soft moonlight. We sat on deck a long time, and the friends from H[ilton] H[ead], both of whom have very fine voices, sang beautifully. They were kind enough to change state rooms with us, and we slept up stairs very quietly.

Early this morn Mr. H[unn] came to our door to tell us that we were in sight of the blockading fleet in Charleston harbor.[21] Of course we sprang to the window eagerly, and saw the masts of the ships looking like a grove of trees in the distance. We were not near enough to see the city. It was hard to realize that we were even so near that barbarous place.—

Later— We were again in sight of land. Have passed Edisto and several other islands, and can now see Hilton Head. Shall reach it about one. Tis nearly eleven now. The S[outh] C[arolina] shore is flat and low;—a long line of trees. It does not look very inviting. We are told that the oranges will be ripe when we get to Beaufort, and that in every way this is just the loveliest season to be there, which is very encouraging.

We approach.Hilton Head. Our ship has been boarded by Health Officer and Provost Marshal. We shall soon reach the landing. All is hurry and confusion on board. I must lay thee aside, friend journal, and use my eyes for seeing all there is to be seen. When we reach our place of destination. I will give to thee, oh faithful friend, the result of my observations. So *au revoir.—*

Tuesday Night. T'was a strange sight as our boat approached the landing at Hilton Head. On the wharf was a motley assemblage,—soldiers, officers, and "contrabands" of every hue and size. They were mostly black, however, and certainly the most dismal specimens I ever saw. H[ilton] H[ead] looks like a very desolate place; just a long low, sandy point running out into the sea with no visible dwellings upon it but the soldiers' white roofed tents.

Thence, after an hour's delay, during which we signed a paper, which was virtually taking the oath of allegiance,[22] we left the "United States," most rocking of rockety propellers,— and took a steamboat for Beaufort. On board the boat was General Saxton[23] to whom we were introduced. I like his face exceedingly. And his manners were very courteous and affable. He looks like a thoroughly *good* man.—From H[ilton] H[ead] to B[eaufort] the same low long line of sandy shore bordered

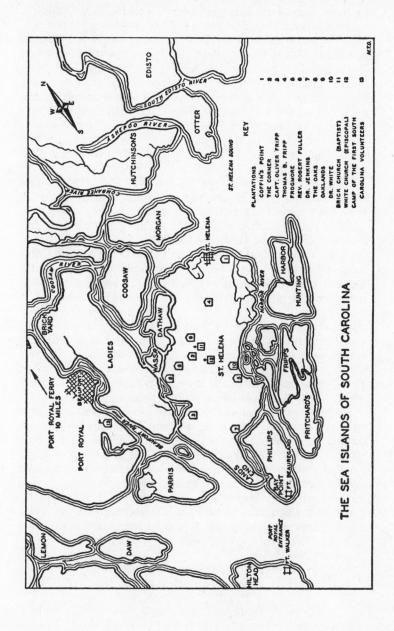

THE SEA ISLANDS OF SOUTH CAROLINA

KEY

PLANTATIONS
1. COFFIN'S POINT
2. THE CORNER
3. CAPT. OLIVER TRIPP
4. THOMAS B. FRIPP
5. FROGMORE
6. REV. ROBERT FULLER
7. DR. JENKINS
8. THE OAKS
9. OAKLANDS
10. DR. WHITE
11. BRICK CHURCH (BAPTIST)
12. WHITE CHURCH (EPISCOPAL)
13. CAMP OF THE FIRST SOUTH
    CAROLINA VOLUNTEERS

by trees. Almost the only object of interest to me were the remains of an old Huguenot Fort, built many, many years ago.

Arrived at B[eaufort] we found that we had yet not reached our home. Went to Mr. French's,[24] and saw there Reuben T[omlinson],[25] whom I was very glad to meet, and Mrs. Gage,[26] who seemed to be in a rather dismal state of mind. B[eaufort] looks like a pleasant place. The houses are large and quite handsome, built in the usual Southern style with verandahs around them, and beautiful trees. One magnolia tree in Mr. F[rench's] yard is splendid,—quite as large as some of our large shade trees, and, with the most beautiful foliage, a dark rich glossy green.

Went into the Commissary's Office to wait for the boat which was to take us to St. Helena's Island which is about six miles from B[eaufort]. T'is here that Miss Towne has her school,[27] in which I am to teach, and that Mr. Hunn will have his store. While waiting in the Office we saw several military gentlemen [sic], not very creditable specimens, I sh'ld say. The little Commissary himself . . . is a perfect little popinjay, and he and a Colonel somebody who didn't look any too sensible, talked in a very smart manner, evidently for our special benefit. The word "nigger" was plentifully used, whereupon I set them down at once as not gentlemen [sic]. Then they talked a great deal about rebel attacks and yellow fever, and other alarming things, with significant nods and looks at each other. We saw through them at once, and were not at all alarmed by any of their representations. But if they are a fair example of army officers, I sh'ld pray to see as little of them as possible.

To my great joy found that we were to be rowed by a crew of negro boatmen. Young Mr. F[rench] whom I like—accompanied us, while Mr. H[unn] went with a flat to get our baggage. The row was delightful. It was just at sunset—a grand Southern sunset; and the gorgeous clouds of crimson and gold were reflected in the waters below, which were smooth and calm as a mirror. Then, as we glided along, the rich sonorous tones of the boatmen broke upon the evening stillness. Their singing impressed me much. It was so sweet and strange and solemn, "Roll, Jordan, Roll" was grand and another

> "Jesus make de blind to see
> Jesus make de deaf to hear
> "   "   " cripple walk
> Walk in, dear Jesus,"

and the refrain

> "No man can hender me."

It was very, very impressive. I want to hear these men sing Whittier's "Song of the Negro Boatmen." I am going to see if it can't be brought about in some way.

It was nearly dark when we reached St. Helena's, where we found Miss T[own]'s carriage awaiting us, and then we three and our driver, had a long drive along the lonely roads in the dark night. How easy it w'ld have been for a band of guerillas —had any chanced that way—to seize and hang us. But we feared nothing of the kind. We were in a jubilant state of mind and sang "John Brown" with a will as we drove through the pines and palmettos. Arrived at the Superintendent's[28] house we were kindly greeted by him and the ladies and shown into a lofty *ceilinged* parlor where a cheerful wood fire glowed in the grate, and we soon began to feel quite at home in the very heart of Rebeldom; only that I do not at all realize yet that we are in S[outh] C[arolina]. It is all a strange wild dream, from which I am constantly expecting to awake. But I can write no more now. I am tired, and still feel the motion of the ship in my poor head. Good night, dear A!

Wednesday, Oct. 29. A lovely day, but rather cool, I sh'ld think, for the "sunny South." The ship still seals [*sic*] in my head, and everything is most unreal, yet I went to drive. We drove to Oaklands, our future home.[29] It is very pleasantly situated, but the house is in rather a dilapidated condition, as are most of the houses here, and the and the [*sic*] yard and garden have a neglected look, when it is cleaned up, and the house made habitable I think it will be quite a pleasant place. There are some lovely roses growing there and quantities of ivy creeping along the ground, even under the house, in wild luxuriance.—The negroes on the place are very kind and polite. I think I shall get on amicably with them.

After walking about and talking with them, and plucking some roses and ivy to send home, we left Oaklands and drove to the school. It is kept by Miss Murray[30] and Miss Towne in the little Baptist Church,[31] which is beautifully situated in a grove of live oaks. Never saw anything more beautiful than these trees. It is strange that we do not hear of them at the North. They are the first objects that attract one's attention here. They are large, noble trees with small glossy green leaves. Their great beauty consists in the long bearded moss with which every branch is heavily draped. This moss is singularly beautiful, and gives a solemn almost funereal aspect to the trees.

We went into the school, and heard the children read and spell. The teachers tell us that they have made great improve-

145

ment in a very short time, and I noticed with pleasure how bright, how eager to learn many of them seem. The singing delighted me most. They sang beautifully in their rich, sweet clear tones, and with that peculiar swaying motion which I had noticed before in the older people, and which seems to make their singing all the more effective. Besides several other tunes they sang "Marching Along" with much spirit, and then one of their own hymns "Down in the Lonesome Valley," which is sweetly solemn and most beautiful. Dear children! born in slavery, but free at last! May God preserve to you all the blessings of freedom, and may you be in every possible way fitted to enjoy them. My heart goes out to you. I shall be glad to do all that I can to help you.—

As we drove homeward I noticed that the trees are just beginning to turn; some beautiful scarlet berries were growing along the roadside; and everywhere the beautiful live oak with its moss drapery. The palmettos disappoint me much. Most of them have a very jagged appearance, and are yet stiff and ungraceful. The country is very level—as flat as that in eastern Penn[sylvania]. There are plenty of woods, but I think they have not the grandeur of our Northern woods. The cotton fields disappoint me too. They have a very straggling look, and the pods are small, not at all the great snowballs that I had imagined. Altogether the country w'ld be rather desolate looking were it not for my beautiful and evergreen live oaks.

Friday, Oct. 31. Miss T[owne] went to B[eaufort] to-day, and I taught for her. I enjoyed it much. The children are well-behaved and eager to learn. It will be a happiness to teach them.

I like Miss Murray so much. She is of English parentage, born in the Provinces. She is one of the most whole-souled warm-hearted women I ever met. I felt drawn to her from the first (before I knew she was English) and of course I like her none the less for that.

Miss Towne also is a delightful person. "A charming lady" Gen. Saxton calls her and my heart echoes the words. She is housekeeper, physician, everything, here. The most indispensable person on the place, and the people are devoted to her. . . . And indeed she is quite a remarkable young lady. She is one of the earliest comers, and has done much good in teaching and superintending the negroes. She is quite young; not more than twenty-two or three I sh'ld think, and is superintendent of two plantations. I like her energy and decision of character. Her appearance too is very interesting.

Mr. S[oule] the Superintendent is a very kind, agreeable person. I like him.

Sunday, Nov. 2. Drove to church to-day,—to the same little Baptist Church that the school is held in. The people came in slowly. They have no way of telling the time. About eleven they had all assembled; the church was full. Old and young were there assembled in their Sunday dresses. Clean gowns on, clean head handkerchiefs, bright colored, of course, I noticed that some had even reached the dignity of straw hats, with bright feathers.

The services were very interesting. The minister, Mr. P[hillips] is an earnest N[ew] E[ngland] man.[32] The singing was very beautiful. I sat there in a kind of trance and listened to it, and while I listened looked through the open windows into the beautiful grove of oaks with their moss drapery. "Ah wld that my tongue c'ld utter

The thoughts that arise in me."

But it cannot. The sermon was quite good. But I enjoyed nothing so much as the singing—the wonderful, beautiful singing. There can be no doubt that these people have a great deal of musical talent. It was a beautiful sight,—their enthusiasm. After the service two couples were married. Then the meeting was out. The various groups under the trees forming a very pretty picture.

We drove to the Episcopal Church afterwards where the aristocracy of Rebeldom used to worship. The building is much smaller than the others, but there is a fine organ there on which Miss W[?] played while some of the young Superintendents sang very finely, and then we came home.

It is all like a dream still, and will be for a long time, I suppose; a strange wild dream. When we get settled in our own house and I have fairly entered into teaching, perhaps I shall begin to realize it all. What we are to do for furniture I know not. Our sole possessions now consist of two bureaus and a bedstead. Mr. H[unn] had not time to get the mattresses in N[ew] York. So I suppose we must use blanket substitutes till we can do better. I am determined not to be discouraged at anything. I have never felt more hopeful, more cheerful than I do now—

Oaklands, Tuesday, Nov. 4. Came to our new home to-day. Felt sorry to leave the friends who have been so kind to us, but as they are only three miles distant hope to see them occasionally. But nobody here has much time for visiting.

Our house looks rather desolate; the only furniture consisting of two bureaus, three small pine tables and two chairs, one of which has a broken back. L[izzie Hunn] and I have manufactured a tolerable drugget out of some woolen stuff, red and black plaid, which will give our "parlor" a somewhat more comfortable look. I have already hung up my lovely Evangeline, and two or three other prints, and gathered some beautiful roses. This has been a busy day. A few more such and we hope that our home will begin to look homelike. I am tired, dear A. Good night, and God be with you.

Wednesday, Nov. 5. Had my first regular teaching experience, and to you and you only friend beloved, will I acknowledge that it was *not* a very pleasant one. Part of my scholars are very tiny,—babies, I call them—and it is hard to keep them quiet and interested while I am hearing the larger ones. They are too young even for the alphabet, it seems to me. I think I must write home and ask somebody to send me picture-books and toys to amuse them with. I fancied Miss T[owne] looked annoyed when, at one time the little ones were unusually restless. Perhaps it was only my fancy. Dear Miss M[urray] was kind and considerate as usual. She is very lovable. Well I *must* not be discouraged. Perhaps things will go on better to-morrow.

I am sure I enjoyed the walk to school. Through those lovely woods, just brightening to scarlet now: Met the ladies about halfway, and they gave me a drive to the church.

Lizzie H[unn] tells me that the store has been crowded all day. Her father hasn't had time to arrange his goods.[33] I foresee that his store, to which people from all the neighboring plantations come,—will be a source of considerable interest and amusement.

We've established our household on—as we hope—a firm basis. We have *Rose* for our little maid-of-all-work, *Amaretta* for cook, washer, and ironer, and *Cupid,* yes Cupid himself, for clerk, oysterman and future coachman. I must also inform you dear A., that we have made ourselves a bed, whereon we hope to rest to-night, for rest *I* certainly did not last night, despite innumerable blankets designed to conceal and render inactive the bones of the bed. But said bones did so protrude that sleep was almost an impossibility to our poor little body.

Everything is still very, very strange. I am not at all homesick. But it does seem *so* long since I saw some who are very dear, and I believe I am quite sick for want of a letter. But patience! patience! *That* is a luxury which cannot possibly be enjoyed before the last of next week.

Thursday, Nov. 6. Rained all day so that I c'ldn't go to school. Attended store part of the day. T'was crowded nearly all the time. It was quite amusing to see how eager the people are to buy. The bright handkerchiefs—imitation—Madras—are an especial attraction. I think they were very quiet and orderly considering how crowded the place was.

This afternoon made another bed; and this eve. finished a very long letter to father, the first part of which was begun last month. I wish I c'ld see them all. It w[ou]ld be such a happiness. . . .

Cut out a dress to-day for an old woman—Venus,—who thanked and blessed me enough. Poor old soul. It was a pleasure to hear her say what a happy year this has been for her. "Nobody to whip me nor dribe me, and plenty to eat. Nebber had such a happy year in my life before." Promised to make a little dress for her great-grandchild—only a few weeks old. It shall be a bright pink calico, such as will delight the little free baby's eyes, when it shall be old enough to appreciate it.

Friday, Nov. 7. Had a lovely walk to school. The trees,—a few of them—are thinning beautifully now, but they have not in general the brilliant hues of the Northern woods. The mocking birds were singing sweetly this morn. I think my "babies" were rather more manageable to-day, but they were certainly troublesome enough.

This afternoon L[izzie] and I went round to the "quarters."[34] Some of the people are really quite interesting, and all were pleasant and seemed glad to see us. One poor woman has a very sick child. The poor little thing is only a few months old, and is suffering dreadfully with whooping cough. It is pitiful to hear it moan. If our good doctor Miss T[owne] were only here. But she does not come to-day. . . .

Saturday, Nov. 8. Spent part of the morn. in the store which was more crowded than ever. So much gold and silver I've not seen for many months. These people must have been hoarding it up for a long time. They are rather unreasonable, and expect one to wait on a dozen at once. But it is not strange.

Miss T[owne] came this afternoon, and gave medicine to Tilla's baby, which seems, I think, a little better; and to all the other children. Every one of them has the whooping cough.

I've put my books and a vase of lovely roses and oleanders on our little table. The fire burns brightly, and the little room looks quite cheerful and homelike. Have done some sewing and reading.

Monday, Nov. 10. We taught—or rather commenced teaching the children "John Brown," which they entered into eagerly. I felt to the full significance of that song being sung here

149

in S[outh] C[arolina] by little negro children, by those whom he—the glorious old man—died to save. Miss T[owne] told them about him.

A poor mulatto man is in one of our people's houses, a man from the North, who assisted Mr. Phillips (a nephew of Wendell P.)[35] when he was here, in teaching school; he seems to be quite an intelligent man. He is suffering from fever. I shall be glad to take as good care of him as I can. It is so sad to be ill, helpless and poor, and so far away from home. . . .

Thursday, Nov. 13. Was there ever a lovelier road than that through which part of my way to school lies? Oh, I wish you were here to go with me, *cher ami.* It is lined with woods on both sides. On the one tall stately pines, on the other the noble live oaks with their graceful moss drapery. And the road is carpeted with those brown odorous pine leaves that I love so well. It is perfectly lovely. I forgot that I was almost ill to day, while sauntering along, listening to the birds and breathing the soft delicious air. Of the last part of the walk, through sun and sand, the less said the better.

Talked to the children a little while to-day about the noble Toussaint [L'Ouverture]. They listened very attentively. It is well that they sh'ld know what one of their own color c'ld do for his race. I long to inspire them with courage and ambition (of a noble sort,) and high purpose.

It is noticeable how very few mulattoes there are here. Indeed in our school, with one or two exceptions, the children are all black. A little mulatto child strayed into the school house yesterday—a pretty little thing, with large beautiful black eyes and lovely long lashes. But so dirty! I longed to seize and thoroughly cleanse her. The mother is a good-looking woman, but quite black. "Thereby," I doubt not, "hangs a tale."

This eve. Harry, one of the men on the place, came in for a lesson. He is most eager to learn, and is really a scholar to be proud of. He learns rapidly. I gave him his first lesson in writing to-night, and his progress was wonderful. He held the pen almost perfectly right the first time. He will very soon learn to write, I think. I must inquire if there are not more of the grown people who w'ld like to take lessons at night. Whenever I am well enough it will be a real happiness to me to teach them.

Finished translating into French Adelaide Proctor's poem "Woman's Question," which I like so much. It was an ex—, and I assure you, *mon ami,* tis a queer translation.

But it was good practice in French. Shall finish this eve. by copying some of my Journal for dear Mary S[hepard].[36]

Sunday, Nov. 16. Felt too tired to go to church to-day. Some of the grown people came in this morn. I read them the Sermon on the Mount. And then they sang some of their own beautiful hymns; among them "Down in the Lonesome Valley" which I like best of all. I want to hear it every day. This afternoon some of the children came in and sang a long time. Then I commenced teaching them the 23rd Psalm, which Miss M[urray] is teaching the children in school. Ours here are too ill with whooping cough to attend school.

I have enjoyed this day very much. For my own special benefit, have read and re-read my dear Mrs. E[lizabeth Barrett] Browning. Can anything be more exquisite than those Sonnets from the Portuguese. Is *any* man, even Browning himself, worthy of such homage from such a soul? yes, yes *he* is, I do believe. But few others are.

This eve. finished my Journal for Mary S[hepard]. Tis so voluminous, so badly written, and so stupid that I am ashamed to send it. But I suppose almost anything from this region w'ld be interesting to people at the N[orth] so it might as well go.—

Monday, Nov. 17. Had a dreadfully wearying day in school, of which the less said the better. Afterward drove with the ladies to "The Corner," a collection of negro houses, whither Miss T[owne] went on a doctoring expedition. The people there are very pleasant. Saw a little baby, just borne [*sic*] today—and another—old Venus' great grand-child for whom I made the little pink frock. These people are very gratiful [*sic*]. The least kindness that you do them they insist on repaying in some way. We have had a quantity of eggs and potatoes brought us despite our remonstrances. Today one of the women gave me some Tanias. Tania is a queer looking root. After it is boiled it looks like a potato, but is much larger. I don't like the taste.

Tuesday, Nov. 18. After school went to The Corner again. Stopped at old Susy's house to see some sick children. Old Susy is a character. Miss T[owne] asked her if she wanted her old master to come back again. Most emphatically she answered. "No *indeed*, missus, no indeed dey treat we too bad. Dey tuk ebery one of my chilen away from me. When we sick and c'ldnt work dey tuk away all our food from us; gib us nutten to eat. Dey's orful hard Missis." When Miss T[owne] told her that some of the people said they wanted their old masters to come back, a look of supreme contempt came to old Susy's withered face. "Dat's 'cause dey's got no sense den, missus,"

151

she said indignantly. Susy has any quantity of children and grandchildren, and she thanks God that she can now have some of them with her in her old age.

To-night gave Cupid a lesson in the alphabet. He is not a brilliant scholar, but he tries hard to learn, and so I am sure will succeed in time. A man from another plantation came in for a lesson. L[izzie] attended to him while I had Cupid. He knows his letters, and seems very bright.

Wednesday, Nov. 19. A steamer is in! Miss T[owne] had letters from Phila[delphia] to-day. The mail is not yet all distributed. If I don't get any I shall be *perfectly* desperate. But I surely will get some to-morrow. To-night had another pupil—Robert—brighter than Harry [Cupid]—not so bright as Harry. He will do well I think.—

Thursday, Nov. 20. . . . Wrote to-night to . . . [John Greenleaf] Whittier asking him to write a little Christmas hymn for our children to sing. I hope he will do it. . . .

Saturday, Nov. 22. Had the loveliest walk this afternoon to Mr. R[uggle]'s[37] our nearest neighbor's. The path lay partly through beautiful woods principally pines and live oaks. The air was delicious, the sunlight bright, the brown pine leaves odorous as usual, and I noticed some maple [gum] leaves that had turned a rich dark, almost copper color. Plucked some for my dear Miss M[urray] whom I heard express a wish for some a day or two ago.

Found that Miss R[uggles][38] was not at home. They have a pleasant little place, rather more civilized looking than ours. Returning, just at sunset saw a beautiful sight. In some parts of the wood the branches of the live oak formed a perfect ceiling overhead and from them depended long sprays of that exquisite moss lighted up by the sun's last rays. I c'ld think only of some fairy palace, at first, then the sight suggested the Mammoth cave as I had seen it once in an excellent Panorama. Those sprays of moss, glowing in the sunlight, were perfect stalactites, as I saw them illuminated. If they lacked the sparkling crystals they quite made up for the loss in airy grace and lightness. I wanted you my dearest A.,—and several dear friends of mine who like you have a most keen and delicate perception of the beautiful—to look upon that scene with me. And since that c'ld not be, I longed to be an artist that I might make a sketch and send it to you.

Sunday, Nov. 23. Attended church to-day. T'was even a pleasanter experience than before. Saw several new arrivals there—old ones returned, rather—among them Mr. S[amuel]

Phillips, a nephew of *the* Phillips.[39] He has not the glorious beauty of the illustrious relative, but still has somewhat the Phillips style of face. He is not at all handsome; has bright red hair, but a pleasant face, and an air *distingue.*

After the sermon an old negro prayed a touching and most effective prayer. Then the minister read Gen. Saxton's Proclamation for Thanksgiving[40]—which is grand—the very best and noblest that c'ld have been penned. I like and admire the Gen. more than ever now.

Six couples were married to-day. Some of the dresses were unique. Am sure one must have worn a cast-off dress of her mistress's. It looked like white silk covered with lace. The lace sleeves, and other trimmings were in rather a decayed state and the white cotton gloves were well ventilated. But the bride looked none the less happy for that. Only one had the slightest claim to good looks. And she was a demure little thing with a neat, plain silk dress on. T'was amusing to see some of the headdresses. One, of tattered flowers and ribbons, was very ridiculous. But no matter for that. I am *truly* glad that the poor creatures are trying to live right and virtuous lives. As usual we had some fine singing. It was very pleasant to be at church again. For two Sundays past I had not been, not feeling well.

This eve. our boys and girls with others from across the creek came in and sang a long time for us. Of course we had the old favorites "Down in the Lonesome Valley," and "Roll, Jordan, Roll," and "No man can hender me," and beside those several shouting tunes that we had not heard before; they are very wild and strange. It was impossible for me to understand many of the words although I asked them to repeat them for me. I only know that one had something about "De Nell Am Ringing." I think that was the refrain; and of another, some of the words were "Christ build the church widout no hammer nor nail." "Jehovah Halleluhiah," which is a grand thing, and "Hold the light," an especial favorite of mine—they sang with great spirit. The leader of the singing was Prince, a large black boy, from Mr. R[uggles]'s place. He was full of the shouting spirit, and c'ld not possibly keep still. It was amusing to see his gymnastic performances. They were quite in the Ethiopian Methodists' style. He has really a very fine bass voice. I enjoyed their singing so much, and sh'ld have enjoyed it so much more if some dear ones who are far away c'ld have listened it to [*sic*] with me. How delighted they would have been.

The effect of the singing has been to make me feel a little sad and lonely to-night. A yearning for congenial companionship *will* sometimes come over me in the few leisure moments I have in the house. T'is well they are so few. Kindness, most invariable,—for which I am most grateful—I meet with constantly but congeniality I find not at all in this house. But silence, foolish murmurer. He who knows all things knows that it was for no selfish motive that I came here, far from the few who are so dear to me. Therefore let me not be selfish now. Let the work to which I have solemnly pledged myself fill up my whole existence to the exclusion of all vain longings.

Tuesday, Nov. 25. . . . Miss M[urray] is teaching the children in school "Sound the Loud Timbrel." They like the words so much that I think they will soon learn them.

Saw the [Anti-Slavery] Standard to-night. Twas welcome as the face of an old friend. Read also a few numbers of "Salem Chapel," which is as intensely interesting and exciting as ever. This eve. gave Harry and Rob[ert] their lesson.

Yesterday had some visitors in school—Miss T[?] and her brother, and a Miss Merrick from Syracuse.[41] I liked the latter's face. She looks like an earnest worker. . . .

Wednesday, Nov. 26. Miss T[owne] was not at school, and Miss M[urray] and I had sole charge. After school told the children a little about the sun, stars etc., and then Miss M[urray] taught them some verses of "Sound the Loud Timbrel" which she wants them to learn for the New Year. Had a lovely walk in the woods gathering leaves and berries wherewith to decorate the church to-morrow.

Thursday, Nov. 27. Thanksgiving Day. This, according to Gen. Saxton's noble Proclamation, was observed as a day of Thanksgiving and praise." It has been a lovely day—cool, delicious air, golden, gladdening sunlight, deep blue sky, with soft white clouds floating over it. Had we no other causes the glory and beauty of the day alone make it a day for which to give thanks. But we have other causes, great and glorious, which unite to make this peculiarly a day of thanksgiving and praise. It has been a general holiday. According to Gen. Saxton's orders an animal was killed on each plantation that the people might to-day eat fresh meat, which is a great luxury to them, and indeed to all of us here.

This morning a large number—Superintendents, teachers and freed people, assembled in the little Baptist church. It was a sight that I shall not soon forget—that crowd of eager, happy black faces from which the shadow of slavery had forever passed. "Forever free!" "Forever free!" Those magical words were all the time singing themselves in my soul, and never before have I felt so truly grateful to God. The singing was, as

154

usual, very beautiful. I thought I had never heard my favorite "Down in the Lonesome Valley" so well sung.

After an appropriate prayer and sermon by Rev. Mr. Phillips, Gen. Saxton made a short but spirited speech to the people—urging the young men to enlist in the regiment now forming under Col. T. W. Higginson.[42] That was the first intimation I had had of Mr. H[igginson]'s being down here. I am greatly rejoiced thereat. He seems to me of all fighting men the one best fitted to command a regiment of colored soldiers. The mention of his [name] recalled the happy days passed last summer in Massachusetts, when day after day, in the streets of W[orcester] we used to see the indefatigable *Capt.* H[igginson] drilling his white company. I never saw him so full of life and energy—entering with his whole soul into his work —without thinking what a splendid general he w'ld make. And that too may come about. Gen. Saxton said to-day that he hoped to see him commander of an army of black men. The Gen. told the people how nobly Mr. H[igginson] had stood by Anthony Burns, in the old dark days, even suffering imprisonment for his sake;[43] and assured [them] that they might feel sure of meeting no injustice under the leadership of such a man; that he w'ld see to it that they were not wronged in any way.

Then he told them the story of Robert Small[s],[44] and added. "To-day Rob[ert] came to see me. I asked him how he was getting on in the store which he is keeping for the freed people. He said he was doing very well—making fifty dollars a week, sometimes, "But" said he "Gen. I'm going to stop keeping store. I'm going to enlist." "What," said I. "Are you going to enlist when you can make fifty doll[ar]s a week keeping store?" "Yes Sir," he replied "I'm going to enlist as a private in the black regiment. How can I expect to keep my freedom if I'm not willing to fight for it? Suppose the Secesh sh'ld get back here again? what good w'ld my fifty doll[ar]s do me then? Yes, Sir I sh'ld enlist if I were making a thousand dollars a week."

Mrs. [Frances D.] Gage then made a few beautiful and earnest remarks. She told the people about the slaves in Santa Cruz, how they rose and conquered their masters, and declared themselves free, and no one dared to oppose them. And how, soon after, the governor rode into the market-place and proclaimed emancipation to all people of the Danish W[est] I[ndies]. She then made a beautiful appeal to the mothers, urging them not to keep back their sons from the war fearing they might be killed but to send them forth willingly and gladly as she had done hers, to fight for liberty. It must have been something very novel and strange to them to hear a woman speak in public, but they listened with great attention and seemed much moved by what she said.

Then Gen. Saxton made a few more remarks. I think what he said will have much effect on the young men here. There has been a good deal of distrust about joining the regiment. The soldiers were formerly so unjustly treated by the Government. But they trust Gen. Saxton. He told them what a victory the black troops had lately won on the Georgian coast,[45] and what a great good they had done for their race in winning; they had proved to their enemies that the black man can and will fight for his freedom. After the Gen. had done speaking the people [sang] "Marching Along," with great spirit.

After church there was a wedding. This is a very common occurrence here. Of course the bridal costumes are generally very unique and comical, but the principal actors are fortunately quite unconscious of it, and look so proud and happy while enjoying this—one of the many privileges that freedom has bestowed upon them—that it is quite pleasant to see them.

Beside the Gen. and Mrs. G[age] there were several other strangers present;—ladies from the North who come down here to teach.

In Miss T[owne]'s box came my parcel—so long looked for —containing letters from my dear Mary S[hepard], [and] Aunt M[argaretta] . . . and a Liberator, the first that I have seen since leaving home. How great a pleasure it is to see it. It is familiar and delightful to look upon as the face of an old friend. It is of an old date—Oct. 31st but it is not the less welcome for that. And what a significant fact it is that one may now sit here in safety—here in the rebellious little Palmetto State and read the Liberator, and display it to one's friends, rejoicing over it in the fulness of one's heart as a very great treasure. It is fitting that we sh'ld give to this—the Pioneer Paper in the cause of human rights—a hearty welcome to the land where, until so recently, those rights have been most barbarously trampled upon. We do not forget that it is in fact directly traceable to the exertions of the editor of this paper and those who have labored so faithfully with him, that the Northern people now occupy in safety the S[outh] C[arolina] Shore; that freedom now blesses it, that it is, for the first time, a place worth living in.

This eve. commenced a long letter to Mr. [William Lloyd] Garrison, composed partly of to-day's journalism, and partly of other things that I thought w'ld interest him. He can publish it in the Liberator, if he thinks it worth printing, which I do not.[46]

Truly this has been a delightful day to me. I recal [*sic*] with pleasure the pleasant Thanksgiving Days passed in N[ew] E[ngland] in Mass[achusetts] which I believe I am in the habit of considering as *all* N[ew] E[ngland]. But this has been the happiest, the most jubilant Thanksgiving Day of my life. We hear of cold weather and heavy snowstorms up in the North land. But here roses and oleanders are blooming in the open air. Figs and oranges are ripening, the sunlight is warm and bright, and over all shines gloriously the blessed light of Freedom—Freedom forevermore!—

Friday, Nov. 28. Kept store nearly all day, and found constant sources of interest and amusement in it. I had nearly forgotten to tell you, dear A., to tell you about a very old man—Dr. Crofts, they call him—(his name is Scipio rightly) who came into the store yesterday. He was rejoicing over the new state of things here, and said to Mr. Hunn. "Don't hab me feelins hurt now. Used to hab me feelins hurt all de time. But don't hab em hurt now, no more." Poor old soul! We rejoiced with him that he and many like him no longer have their "feelins hurt," as in the old time.

This eve. finished my letter to Mr. G[arrison]. . . . Mr. H[unn] brought me a paper from the office—a Boston Transcript, sent by Sarah P[utnam].[47] It is pleasant to see a Boston paper.

Saturday, Nov. 29. Have decorated our little sitting room with ivy and autumn leaves and berries till it looks quite bright. Have hung a wreath of ivy around my lovely [picture] Eva[ngeline] which makes her, if possible, lovelier than ever. We have a clock, which is quite a treasure here. It is like the face of an old friend. . . . This eve. devoured "Aurora Leigh"[48] for the *very manyth* time. Every time I read it I discover new beauty in it.

Part 6

Life Among the Freedmen

November 30, 1862 - February 14, 1863

Sunday, Nov. 30. Farewell Autumn! It seems so very long since we came here, and yet, as they pass, the days seem short enough. But to look back upon the time seems very long.

Attended church. Mr. Thorpe, one of the young Superintendents,[1] a N[ew] E[ngland] man, was so kind as to send his wagon for us. L[izzie] did not feel well enough to go, but I went and had a very pleasant drive with old Jack—Mr. T[horpe]'s foreman, as he told me. He is a *very* polite old man, and seemed quite pleased and proud at driving a lady. It was very kind in Mr. T[horpe]. I like him much, and Mr. L. Phillips also.[2] The latter invited me to come and get some slips from his garden. And oh, dear A. he has japonicas in bloom. I shall not go, of course, but live in hourly hope that he will be moved by the spirit to bring me some japonicas.

Mr. P[hillips], the minister, is an excellent man, but certainly not an interesting preacher. To-day he was unusually dull, and I got very tired. I thought I sh'ld certainly go to sleep. Fortunately I did not. We had a bit of a Sunday School. Taught the children a hymn—"Heaven is my Home." After church three couples were married.

This eve. heard Harry read, then the children came in, and sang for us, and had a regular "shout" in the piazza, of which, of course Prince was the leader. He is the most comical creature I ever saw. Besides the old songs they sang two new ones, so singular that I must try to note down the words —some of them. But of the tune and manner of singing it is impossible to give any idea. The first is—

> "*Old elder, old elder, where hab you been*
> *When de gospel been flourishin*
> *All over dis world*
> *I have somethin fur to tell you*
> *From the secret of my heart*
> *Marry King Jesus*
> *And no more to part.*"

Then

> *Young sister, young sister where hab you been etc.*
> *   "   bruder   "   bruder   "   "   "   "*
> *   "   member " member   "   "   "   "*

Another commences

> *"My mudder's gone to glory and I want to git dere too*
> *Till dis warfare's over hallelujah*
> *   Chorus—Hallelujah, hallelujah*
> *Till dis warfare's over, hallelujah, etc.*
> *   All de members gone to glory, etc.*
> *   Then chorus.*
> *Cinda gnaw my sin, hallelujah."*
> *   Chorus*

The singular hymn that I heard them sing in school one day,
about the graveyard begins thus.—

> *"I wonder where my mudder gone,*
> *   Sing oh graveyard!*
> *Graveyard ought to know me*
> *   Sing Jerusalem!*
> *Oh carry my mudder in de graveyard*
> *   Sing etc.*
> *Oh grass grow in de graveyard*
> *   Sing etc.*
> *Lay my body in de graveyard*
> *   Sing etc."*

It is a very strange wild thing.

I am quite in love with one of the children here—little
Amaretta who is neice [*sic*] to our good old Amaretta. She is
a cunning little kittenish thing with such a gentle demure look.
She is not quite black, and has pretty close hair, but delicate
features. She is bright too. I love the child. Wish I c[ou]ld take
her for my own.

Am in a writing mood to-night, and think I will give to
you, my dearest A. a more minute description of the people
around than I've yet given to anyone. I shall write down their
names too, that I may remember them always. Don't know
them thoroughly enough yet to say much about their characters.

To begin with the older ones. First there is old Harriet. She is a very kind, pleasant old soul. Comes from Darien, G[eorgi]a. Her parents were Africans. She speaks a *very* foreign tongue. Three of her children have been sold from her. Her master's son killed somebody in a duel, and was obliged to "pay money" H[arriet] says. I suppose she means to give bail. And she and her children were sold to this place, to raise the money. Then there is her daughter Tillah. Poor creature, she has a dear little baby, Annie, who for weeks has been dangerously ill with whooping cough and fever. Our good Miss T[owne] attends it, and does all that can be done, but the baby is still very ill. For Tillah's sake I hope it will get well. She is devoted to it night and day. T[illah]'s husband is a gallant looking young soldier —a member of the black regiment.

His mother, Bella, is rather a querulous body. But who can blame her? She has had enough to try her sorely. One by one her children at a tender age have been dragged from her to work in the cotton fields. She herself has been made to work when most unfit for it. She has had to see her own children cruelly beaten. Is it strange that these things sh'ld have embittered her? But she has much of the milk of human kindness left her yet. She nurses the poor baby faithfully, and often, old as she is, sits up the entire night with it. Harry is another of her sons. I have told you, dear A. how bright, how eager to learn, he is. His wife, Tamar, is a good-natured, easy soul. She has several nice little children, and the baby—Mary Lincoln—as Mr. R[uggles] the Superintendent has named her—is a very cunning little creature, an especial pet of ours.

Celia is one of the best women on the place. She is a cripple. Her feet and limbs were so badly frozen by exposure that her legs were obliged to be amputated just above the knees. But she manages to get about almost as actively as any of the others. Her husband, Thomas, has been a soldier, and is now quite ill with pneumonia. She had several children—Rose, who is our little maid, Olivia the eldest, Dolly, a bright little thing who goes to school with me every morn. and who likes to go. Lastly Aiken, whose proper name is Thomas. He is an odd lit[tle] fellow, very much spoiled. Amaretta, Celia's sister is our laundress and cook. I like her very much.

Then there is Wilhelmina, a mulatto (the others are all black). She comes from Virginia, and speaks therefore quite intelligibly. She is a good sensible woman, and both she and her husband Rob[er]t,—who is one of my night pupils—are most anxious for their three little ones to learn.

Cupid our major-domo, is as obliging as possible. A shrewd fellow, who knows well what he is about. His wife Patience, is

Tamar's sister, and lives across the creek at Pollywana. Their children—two of them—come to our school. They are good scholars.

I do enjoy hearing Cupid and Harry tell about the time that the Secesh had to flee. The time of the "gun shoot," as they call the taking of Bay Point, which is opposite Hilton Head. It delights them greatly to recal [sic] that time. Their master had the audacity to venture back even while the Union Troops were occupying Beaufort. H[arry] says he tried to persuade him to go back with him, assuring him that the Yankees w'ld shoot them all when they came. "Bery well sur," he replied "if I go wid you I be good as dead, so if I got to dead, I might's well dead here as anywhere. So I'll stay and wait for the Yankees." He told me that he knew all the time that his master was not telling the truth. Cupid says the master told the people to get all the furniture together and take it over to Pollywana, and to stay on that side themselves. "So" says Cupid, "dey c'ld jus' swap us all up in a heap and geder us up an' put us in de boat. And he tell me to row Patience and de chilens down to a certain pint, and den I c'ld come back if I choose." "Jus' as if I was gwine to be sich a goat" adds Cupid, with a look and gesture of ineffable contempt. The *finale* of the story is that the people left the premises and hid themselves so that when the master returned not one of all his "faithful servants" was to be found to go into slavery with him, and he was obliged to return, a disappointed, but it is to be hoped, a wiser man.

Monday, Dec. 1. The first day of winter. It is hard to realize it here. Tis almost as warm as June to-day, and almost as lovely.

Tuesday, Dec. 2. After school went with the children to the Episcopal Church, where Miss M[urray] played on the organ "Sound the Loud Timbrel," while the children sang. They enjoyed it very much. Fear some of it is rather too difficult for them, but Miss M[urray] is determined they shall learn it, and I hope they will. It w'ld be so very appropriate.

The road to the church is very beautiful. It is lined with the noble live oaks, and carpeted with brown pine leaves. The woods looked particularly inviting to-day. One tree—a green tree was all a'flame in the sunlight. Every leaf looked as if it were steeped in rosy wine. Have rarely seen so beautiful a sight. Miss M[urray] and I secured as many of the leaves as we c'ld carry. I wanted to bring away the whole tree.

Found a letter awaiting me at home—a kind letter from my dear Mrs. P[utnam].[3] It was very pleasant to hear from her. But why does not Henry write? I feel very anxious at not hearing from him. Fear he must be ill. Every day I expect a letter from him, and every day, am disappointed. Has he forgotten his stupid little sister, I wonder? Or is he ill. I do wish I c'ld know. This eve. gave Harry his lesson.

Wednesday, Dec. 3. Wrote to Jane this morn—Miss T[owne] was so kind as to let me have her [Anti-Slavery] Standard of Nov. 22. It is full of interesting matter. I *devoured* Mr. Phillips' fine Music Hall speech.[4] Mr. French's account of the victory won by the blacks troops on the Georgian coast is very interesting. They did splendidly. I feel quite proud of them. See that Lucy McKim[5] has set to music some of the songs of the "contrabands" here. She has sent "Poor Rosy, poor gal" as the first of a series, to Dwight's Journal [of Music]. It is much liked.

Thursday, Dec. 4. After school went again to the Episcopal Church with the children. Miss M[urray] and I preferred walking. Gathered some more of those exquisite leaves. After the children had done singing and all had gone, stayed some time and practiced on the organ;—some of my old pieces, and one or two from the book of Church music, among them "Sound the Loud Timbrel" which I am anxious to learn so as to relieve Miss M[urray]. Tis hard for me to learn the simplest thing. Have forgotten so many of my notes. Had a good long walk home in the light rain, which I enjoyed much.

Heard to my surprise, that Wilhelmina has a little girl. Shall suggest as a name, Jessie Fremont, dear to all lovers of freedom.[6]

Friday, Dec. 5. Rained all day so that I c[ou]ldn't go to school. Has been a sad day. Heard this afternoon of the death of the young Mr. Phillips of whom I've already spoken to you.[7] It was very sudden; after only a few days' illness. Do not know when anything has made me feel so sad. He was a good young man, much loved by all the people. Saw him last Sunday at church in perfect health. And now he is dead. My heart aches for his poor mother. He was an only son. It will be a terrible shock to her. It has cast a gloom over every thing here. His people grieve for him much.

Another death—to-night. One of the old men has just come in to tell us of the death of his little grandson—Hercules—or "Harkles," as they call it. The little fellow has been ill a long time with whooping cough and fever; and now he has gone to rest.

Sunday, Dec. 7. Poor Mr. P[hillips] was buried to-day, or rather the funeral services were said at the church. The body is to be sent home. Was not well enough to go, but Mr. H[unn] says there were many people there, and that they were much affected. Everybody who knew him loved him. His poor, poor mother I can only think of her with her aching heart.

Little "Harkles" was buried, across the creek, this morn. This afternoon the people had a meeting in front of his grand-parents' cabin. There was singing—a kind of funeral chant—very sad and dismal, and then an old preacher made a prayer, and afterward a few remarks. I did not stay to hear him but went in to see poor Tillah's baby, who is worse to-day. The poor little creature looks very ill. I fear poor Tillah must lose it.

This eve. wrote a long letter to Henry. We did not have our usual singing. The children said it was too cold. And truly it has been wintry to-day. I cant get warm.

Monday, Dec. 8. Almost froze in school to-day. It was intensely cold. Grew milder at night, and the children came in. They have been singing *gloriously* all the eve. Several new hymns were sung. I will try to note them down for you dear A. I cant describe to you the effect that the singing has on me to-night. I believe I was quite *lifted out* of myself. Oh it was glorious! They all sing beautifully; but one of our girls, Grace, has the strongest voice for a child that I ever heard. And Aaron—the leader has really a magnificent voice. I want you dearest, I want everybody to hear his wonderful singing. . . .

Thursday, Dec. 11. After lessons we went again to the Epis[copal] Church and practiced the hymn with the children. The woods around seemed more beautiful than ever. I longed to explore some of those lovely paths.

Came home, and soon afterward, to my great grief, heard that poor Tillah's dear little baby was dead. It was really a shock to me; for only this morn. we thought the little creature seemed better. I hastened at once to the cabin. The baby had just died, and lay on old Nella's lap, looking as if it were sleeping sweetly. The poor mother sat by looking so very sad. My heart aches for her. During eight weeks she has been constantly devoted to this child—her only little girl—and we hoped she w'ld be rewarded by having it spared to her. But it has gone to heaven. It was one of the loveliest, most interesting babies I ever saw. We are going to bury it to-morrow, over at Polawany; I'm so sorry that William, its father, will not get to see it. It looks very lovely. Its death is a great grief to its mother and grandparents, and a sorrow to us all.

Friday, Dec. 12. This morn. Mr. R[uggles] beaming with delight, informed me that there was a large mail in by the "Star of the South." I'm afraid I answered somewhat impatiently that I was disgusted with mails, and that I wasn't going to expect

163

any more. I had been so often disappointed. Nevertheless I *did* expect, despite myself. I did hope for those letters this time. And when we heard that there were letters for us at The Oaks, we at once despatched our trusty Cupid there. With what a beating heart did I await his coming. Calm outwardly, but what a flutter of expectation within. I never sh'ld have thought that I sh'ld become so *insane* about letters.

At last Cupid came, and only *one* letter for me, and that not from home. It was entirely unexpected—from Mr. McK[im].[8] Certainly it was very kind in him to write to me. He reminds me that he expects to have a line from me. And indeed I ought to have written to him before. But I am *so* disappointed. Why do I not hear from Mary S[hepard]? I thought she w'ld certainly have written to me during her vacation. I am very much troubled at not hearing from her, and from H[enry]. Aunt M[argaretta] has probably written and put her letter in the box, which I suppose will not get here for a month. I am quite sick at heart to-night, and must go to bed. . . .

Sunday, Dec. 14. What a night last night was! A night worth telling you about, dear A. We retired early. I was very sleepy, but what with the headache, the fleas, and Miss H[unn]'s *tremendous* snoring I got very nervous, and it was a long time before I c'ld get to sleep. At last sleep came. It seemed to me that I hadn't slept more than ten minutes when I was awakened by what seemed to me terrible screams coming from the direction of the Quarters. Three or four times they were repeated, and then, with infinite difficulty I succeeded in awaking Miss Hunn. We both heard the shrieks repeated. I thought somebody was insane or dying, or that something terrible had happened. Sometimes I thought it might be that the rebels had forced a landing, and were trying to carry off the people. We were in a state of great alarm; and sleep was impossible. At last the sounds ceased. And then near day, I had a short and troubled sleep which did me no good. Consequently I felt rather wretched this morn. but the day was so beautiful [I] determined to go to church.

L[izzie Hunn] and I started, but met Mr. T[horpe]'s wagon in the lane, coming for us. How very kind he is. But I am hardly willing to be under such an obligation to a stranger. And yet we can't very well refuse. How very sad Mr. T[horpe] looked to-day. I know he must greatly miss Mr. Phillips, with whom he was so intimate. I pity him.

There were several new arrivals at church to-day. Among them Miss T[owne]'s sister—Miss Rosa T[owne]. She does not look at all like Miss Laura. Is very fair, and has light hair; an

164

English looking person, as I told her sister. A Miss Ware was also there.[9] . . . A lovely but good face. . . .

Nearly everybody was looking gay and happy; and yet I came home with the blues. Threw myself on the bed, and for the first time since I have been here, felt very lonely and pitied myself. But I have reasoned myself into a more sensible mood and am better now. Let me not forget again that I came not here for friendly sympathy or for anything else but to work, and to work hard. Let me do that faithfully and well. To-night answered Mr. McK[im]'s letter, and commenced one to my dear A[nnie][10] about whom I feel very anxious.

There, dear A, I have forgotten to tell you the cause of our fright last night. Two of the colored soldiers had come to visit their friends who live across the creek. And they blew a kind of whistle that they have so that somebody on the opposite side might send a boat over for them. That was the shrieking we heard. And it seems we were the only people who heard it on the place. And yet it was heard across the creek. They must be sound sleepers here. The rebels w'ld have a good chance to land without being discovered.

Monday, Dec. 15. Had a perfectly *immense* school to-day. 147., of whom I had 58, at least two thirds of whom were tiny A. B. C. people. Hardly knew what to do with them at first. But I like a large school. It is inspiriting. Miss Rosa T[owne] was there. Had a good long talk with her while her sister and Miss M[urray] went doctoring. Like her exceedingly. She is very social and enthusiastic. She is delighted with things down here. Never heard the children sing so well as they did to-day. There were so many of them. It was quite grand. . . .

Wednesday, Dec. 17. This eve. Mr. R[uggles] . . . spent a little time with us. I like Mr. R[uggles]. He seems to me a whole-souled kind hearted man. The negroes like him much. I asked him a little about the people on his plantations. Some are industrious, but many are not inclined to work, he says. But he thinks it is because they are so irregularly and poorly paid. He thinks if they were promptly and fully paid they w'ld work willingly. I think he is a true friend of the people; but some of the Sup[erintendent]s seem to me strongly prejudiced against them, and they have a contemptuous way of speaking of them that I do not like. It shows a lack of sympathy with them. Such people sh'ld not come here.

Miss H[unn] told me an interesting story of a man who was in the store this afternoon. He had been carried off by the rebels about a year ago and left a wife and children on this island. It was not until a short time since that he had a chance

165

to get away from Jacksonboro'—the place to which he had been taken. He and two relatives, a man and a woman, got away in the night while the family were in bed. They traveled a long distance on foot, and at last reached a stream, which they had no convenience for crossing. He made a kind of raft out of a board and some part of a ruined house, and they crossed in safety. They concealed themselves in the woods during the day, and traveled at night. They came to another stream, and again be built a raft, this time from the roof of the piazza of an old house near. On this they crossed to little Edisto, where they procured a boat from a boat-house and in this went to the blockading fleet. The captain of one of the gun-boats took them and provided them with a boat on which they came to this island. He said it was "almost like death" to his family to see him. They had feared they sh'ld never see him again. He expressed himself very grateful to the Lord for his escape. He said the Lord had been merciful to him. He was a God of mercy and Justice. He said "Put your faith in the Lord and . . . he will give you talents to do anything." They were several days making their escape, during which they lived on hominy of which they carried a peck in tin buckets.

Thursday, Dec. 18. A truly *wintry* day. I had not half as many scholars as usual. It was too cold for my "babies" to venture out. But altogether we had nearly a hundred. They were unusually bright to-day, and sang with the greatest spirit. "Sound the Loud Tim," was a grand success.

After school the children went into a little cabin near, where they had kindled a fire, and had a grand "shout." While they were performing, two officers rode up, and asked Miss M[urray] if they might look on. She assented, and they dismounted, and came to the cabin door. The children stopped at first, evidently a little alarmed at the presence of soldiers, then the latter spoke so kindly to them that at last they were reassured, and went on with their "shout" with great spirit. The visitors seemed much interested and amused. . . .

Friday, Dec. 19. Miss M[urray] and I had school to ourselves. Miss T[owne] was not able to come, on account of the illness of her sister and Miss——— [illegible]. Had 127. T'was terribly cold. Mr. Palmer,[11] one of the other teachers on the island, came in towards the close of school. He very kindly assisted us to put away our books. I was pleasantly disappointed in him. He seems much more agreeable than he looks.

Spent most of the afternoon in the store. Had a crowd. Enjoyed it very much. Felt so tired that I went to bed at seven, and consequently missed seeing Mr. and Miss Ruggles who spent the eve. here. Am sorry, for I like them.

Saturday, Dec. 20. Went round to see the people, of whom I haven't seen so much this week, being even unusually busy. Had as usual a very pleasant time talking with them all, big and little.

Came home, and worked busily. Made before school this morn. a red flannel jacket for poor old Harriet who is far from well. The good old woman and her husband seemed very grateful. I wish I c'ld do ten times as much for these people.

This afternoon a soldier, a private from the 8th Maine, came in, and we gave him some dinner.[12] The poor fellow seemed glad to get into a comfortable house, and talked about his home and his family quite confidentially, and told us how his little brothers ran out when he went to visit his home. He seemed a simple, kindly, good hearted fellow, and I was glad that we gave him a good dinner. These poor privates have rather a hard time of it, I fear. They look weary and forlorn, while the *officers* have a most prosperous, well-to-do look. . . .

Sunday, Dec. 21. Went to church, and victimized myself sitting in a cold church, and listening to the dullest of sermons, but was amply rewarded after church when Mr. Severance[13] came from B[eaufort] and I had four letters—from dear Mary S[hepard], and Hattie [Purvis] . . .[14] and, last and best of all, the kindest letter from the noble Whittier, and with it a beautiful little hymn for our children to sing at the Celebration.[15] Also his photograph—a perfect likeness. How very, very kind it was in him to write it; when he was ill too. It grieves me to hear that his dear sister is ill also. She sends me the kindest messages. I am very, very much obliged to Mr. W[hittier] for everything but his sending my letter to the Transcript,[16] as Mary S[hepard] tells me he did. He ought not to have done that. It was not worth it. How dear Miss M[urray] and I rejoiced over the hymn. With what pleasure we will teach our little ones to sing it.

Monday, Dec. 22. Commenced teaching the children Whittier's hymn. We told them who had written it; what a great friend he is to them, and that he had written it *expressly* for them, whereat they seemed greatly pleased. After school, with some of the larger children we three went into the woods in search of evergreens to decorate the church. Had a delightful ramble and got a quantity of greens. . . .

Tuesday, Dec. 23. We commenced decorating the church, and worked hard till dark. They w'ld insist upon my dressing

167

the pulpit, which I was unwilling to do, for that is the most conspicuous place. Finished it to-day. Made a drapery all around it with the lovely hanging moss, and a heading of casino berries and holly. It looks quite pretty. Came home tired but sat up till after 11 sewing on the little aprons for Christmas presents. I *cannot* realize that Christmas is so near.

Wednesday, Dec. 24. Called the children together, and let them sing for some time and then dismissed them and devoted ourselves to finishing the decorations. Miss M[urray] and Miss T[owne] made the festoons, while I made wreaths for the walls. In the afternoon Miss W[are] came, bringing evergreen letters of the words "His people are Free." . . . It was quite dark when we got through. Miss W[are] was so kind as to drive me home. Sat up till after midnight, finishing my little Christmas gifts. Saw Christmas morn. But it does not seem like Christmas to me.

Christmas Day 1862. A bright and lovely Christmas day. We were waked early by the people knocking at our window and shouting "Merry Christmas." After breakfast we went out and distributed the presents;—to each of the babies a bright red dress, and to little Jessie a white apron trimmed with crotchet braid, and to each of the other children an apron and an orange. To each of the workers a pie—an apple pie, which pleased them much.

Then we went to school. How pretty the evergreens looked in the bright light, after we had thrown open the windows. T'was a long time before the other teachers got there, and I had to keep all the children from getting restless. I kept them out of doors, and had them sing old songs and new. They sang with great spirit. After the others came, we opened school, and at once commenced distributing the presents. First Miss M[urray]'s class, then mine, then Miss T[owne]'s. Most of the children were much delighted with their gifts, and well they might be, for they were very useful ones,—principally dresses for the girls, and material for shirts and pantaloons for the boys. For the larger ones, also there were little bags, nicely fitted out with sewing utensils which Miss M[urray] and Miss T[owne] arranged. The larger children behaved well, and by great exertions I managed to keep the "babies" quiet.

After the gifts were distributed, they were addressed by Lieut. Col. Billings of the 1st reg[iment] S[outh] C[arolina] Vol[unteers].[17] He is a N[ew] E[ngland] man of very gentlemanly and pleasing manners.—A good man, and much interested in the people, I sh'ld think. I liked him. Then Mr. Fairfield [?] spoke to them about the birth of Christ. Afterward they sang; Among other things, "John Brown," Whittier's "Hymn," "Sing, oh Graveyard," and "Roll, Jordan Roll." There was no one present beside the teachers, our household, [Lt.] Col. B[illings] [,] Mr. T[horpe], Mr. F[airfield] and Miss Rosa [Towne] and Miss W[are].

I enjoyed the day very much. Was too excited and interested to feel weariness then, but am quite exhausted to-night. The children have been in, singing for us. My pet *petite* Amaretta has a sweet voice and quite strong for such a little one. She was full of music to-night. "All I want to do is sing and shout" she said to me with her pretty, dimply smile. There is something very bewitching about that child. All the children had the shouting spirit to-night. They had several grand shouts in the entry. "Look upon the Lord," which they sang to-night, seems to me the most beautiful of all their shouting tunes. There is something in it that goes to the depths of one's soul.—I am weary and must stop.

Dear friends, up North! my heart is with you to-night. What w'ld I not give for one look at your dear faces, one grasp of your kindly hands! Dear ones! I pray with my whole heart that this may have been to you a very, very happy Christmas.

Friday, Dec. 26. Kept store nearly all day. I like it occasionally. It amuses and interests me. There was one very sensible man in to-day, whose story interested me much. He had been a carpenter, and had been taken up by his master on the mainland, on "the main," as they call it, to help build houses to which the families of the rebels might retreat when the Yankees sh'ld come. His master sent him back again to this island to bring back a boat and some of the people. He was provided with a pass. On reaching the island, he found that the Union troops had come, so he determined (indeed he had determined before) to remain here with his family, as he knew his master w'ld not dare to come back after them. Some of his fellow servants whom he had left on the "main," hearing that the Union troops had come resolved to try to make their escape. They found a boat of the master's, out of which a piece about six feet square had been cut. In the night, secretly, they went to the boat which had been sunk near the edge of the creek, measured the hole, and went to the woods and, after several nights' work, made a piece large enough to fit in. With this they mended the boat, by another night's work, and then sunk it in the same position in which they had found it. The next night five of them embarked, and after passing through many perils in the shape of the enemy's boats, near which they were obliged to pass, and so making very slow progress, for they c'ld travel only at night, and in the day time, ran their boat close up to the shore, out of sight—they at last passed the enemy's lines and reached one of our gunboats in safty [sic]. They were taken on board, and their wants attended to, for their provisions had given out and they were much exhausted. After being there some time they were sent to this island, where their families, who had feared they w'ld never see them again welcomed them rejoicingly. I was much interested in the story of their escape, and give it for yr especial benefit, Dear A.

Spent the eve. in making wreaths for our windows and my lovely [picture] Eva[ngeline]. . . .

A letter from Sarah P[utnam][18] delights me much, for it tells me that my dear friend Dr. Rogers,[19] sailed last week for P[ort] R[oyal] so of course he has come in this steamer. I c'ld clap my hands and shout for joy. I am so very, very glad. This is the very place for him, and he is of all men, the man for the place. He is to be surgeon in Col. H[igginson]'s reg[iment] S[outh] C[arolina] Vol[unteers] . . . . I am most impatient to see him.

Sat. Dec. 27. A rather dreary day. So the less said about it the better. Worked quite hard. The Miss T[owne]s and Miss M[urray] paid us a brief visit. Capt. H[ooper][20] whom everybody likes, has come, and brought me a letter, which I rec'd wonderingly from Miss M[urray]'s hands. The handwriting was strange to me. It was postmarked "Boston." On opening it I found it to be from a stranger—a lady in W[est] Gloucester, who says she has read with interest my letter in the paper, and expresses her great interest in the work here. A very kind and pretty letter. Enclosed in it was a "Proclamation Song," written by a friend of hers, to be sung to the air "Glory Hallelujah," on 1st Jan. Not exquisite poetry, but a very good and appropriate song. It touched [me] receiving such a letter from a stranger. I think I must write and thank her for it. Had a lovely walk in the woods this morn. Twas almost like June.

Sunday, Dec. 28. At church had the pleasure of seeing Gen. S[axton] and his father, who has come down to visit him. The Gen[eral] presented him to me. He is a pleasant old gentleman, and spoke warmly in praise of Dr. R[ogers] who came on the same steamer with him. His nephew James R[ogers] accompanies him. Saw also the much loved Capt. Hooper, whose looks and manners I like much. He made a very good speech to the people, as also did Gen. S[axton] urging them to enlist, and inviting them all to come to the camp near B[eaufort] on N[ew] Year's Day, and join in the grand Celebration, which is to take place there. I long to go, and hope I shall.

Capt. H[ooper] handed me a letter from my dear Mary S[hepard]. It was unexpected, and so all the more delightful. I sh'ld have been very, very glad to have had letters from home and from H[enry] for Christmas gifts. But so it was not. I must try to be content.

Tuesday, Dec. 30. This eve. Mr. and Miss R[uggles] spent with us quite pleasantly. It is very rarely we have company, and so I note it down.

Wednesday, Dec. 31. Mr. T[horpe] and Mr. H[ooper] dined with us to-day. I think they are—Mr. T[horpe] especially, the most anti-slavery of the Superintendents. And they are very gentlemenly [*sic*], and I like them. This afternoon Mr. and Mrs. W[ells] called.[21] He is very agreeable, she *not* so agreeable, to me. I count the hours till to-morrow, the glorious, glorious day of freedom.[22]

Thursday, New Year's Day, 1863. The most glorious day this nation has yet seen, *I* think. I rose early—an event here—and early we started, with an old borrowed carriage and a remarkably slow horse. Whither were we going? thou wilt ask, dearest A. To the ferry; thence to Camp Saxton, to the Celebration. From the Ferry to the camp the "Flora" took us.

How pleasant it was on board! A crowd of people, whites and blacks, and a band of music—to the great delight of the negroes. Met on board Dr. and Mrs. Peck[23] and their daughters, who greeted me most kindly. Also Gen. S[axton]'s father whom I like much, and several other acquaintances whom I was glad to see. We stopped at Beaufort, and then proceeded to Camp Saxton, the camp of the 1st Reg[iment] S[outh] C[arolina] Vol[unteer]s. The "Flora" c[ou]ld not get up to the landing, so we were rowed ashore in a row boat.

Just as my foot touched the plank, on landing, a hand grasped mine and well known voice spoke my name. It was my dear and noble friend, Dr. Rogers. I cannot tell you, dear A., how delighted I was to see him; how *good* it was to see the face of a friend from the North, and *such* a friend. I think myself particularly blessed to have him for a friend. Walking on a little distance I found myself being presented to Col. Higginson, whereat I was so much overwhelmed, that I had no reply to make to the very kind and courteous little speech with which he met me. I believe I mumbled something, and grinned like a simpleton, that was all. Provoking, isn't it? that when one is most in need of sensible words, one finds them not.

I *cannot* give a regular chronicle of the day. It is impossible.

171

I was in such a state of excitement. It all seemed, and seems still, like a brilliant dream. Dr. R[ogers] and I talked all the time, I know, while he showed me the camp and all the arrangements. They have a beautiful situation, on the grounds once occupied by a very old fort, "De La Ribanchine," built in 1629 or 30. Some of the walls are still standing. Dr. R[ogers] has made quite a good hospital out of an old gin house. I went over it. There are only a few invalids in it, at present. I saw everything; the kitchens, cooking arrangements, and all. Then we took seats on the platform.

The meeting was held in a beautiful grove, a live-oak grove, adjoining the camp. It is the largest one I have yet seen; but I don't think the moss pendants are quite as beautiful as they are on St. Helena. As I sat on the stand and looked around on the various groups, I thought I had never seen a sight so beautiful. There were the black soldiers, in their blue coats and scarlet pants, the officers of this and other regiments in their handsome uniforms, and crowds of lookers-on, men, women and children, grouped in various attitudes, under the trees. The faces of all wore a happy, eager, expectant look.

The exercises commenced by a prayer from Rev. Mr. Fowler, Chaplain of the reg[iment].[24] An ode written for the occasion by Prof. Zachos,[25] originally a Greek, now Sup[erintendent] of Paris island—was read by himself, and then sung by the whites. Col. H[igginson] introduced Dr. Brisbane in a few elegant and graceful words.[26] He (Dr. B.) read the President's [Emancipation] Proclamation, which was warmly cheered. Then the beautiful flags presented by Dr. Cheever's Church [in New York] were presented to Col. H[igginson] for the Reg[iment] in an excellent and enthusiastic speech, by Rev. Mr. [Mansfield] French.[27] Immediately at the conclusion, some of the colored people—of their own accord sang "My Country Tis of Thee." It was a touching and beautiful incident, and Col. Higginson, in accepting the flags made it the occasion of some happy remarks. He said *that* tribute was far more effective than any speech he c'ld make. He spoke for some time, and all that he said was grand, glorious. He seemed inspired. Nothing c'ld have been better, more perfect. And Dr. R[ogers] told me afterward that the Col. was much affected. That tears were in his eyes. He is as Whittier says, truly a "sure man." The men all admire and love him. There is a great deal of personal magnetism about him, and his kindness is proverbial. After he had done speaking he delivered the flags to the color-bearers with a few very impressive remarks to them. They each then, Sgt. Prince Rivers and [Cpl.] Robert Sutton,[28] made very good

172

speeches indeed, and were loudly cheered. Gen. Saxton and Mrs. Gage spoke very well. The good Gen. was received with great enthusiasm, and throughout the morning—every little while it seemed to me three cheers were given for him. A Hymn written I believe, by Mr. Judd,[29] was sung, and then all the people united with the Reg[iment] in singing "John Brown." It was grand. During the exercises, it was announced that Fremont was appointed Commander-in-chief of the Army, and this was received with enthusiastic and prolonged cheering.[30] But as it is picket news, I greatly fear that is not true.

We dined with good Dr. R[ogers] at the Col's [T. W. Higginson] table, though, greatly to my regret he, (the Col.) was not there. He partook of some of the oxen, (of which ten had been roasted) with his men. I like his doing that. We had quite a sumptuous dinner. Our party consisted of Dr. R[ogers], Adjutant D[ewhurst],[31] Capt. R[ogers],[32] Mr. and Miss Ware[33] (Mrs. Winsor's brother and sister), Mr. Hall,[34] their cousin, whom I like much, and Mr. and Miss H[unn] and me. We had a merry, delightful dinner. The only part that I did not enjoy was being obliged to read Whittier's Hymn aloud at the table. I wanted Dr. R[ogers] to do it. But he w'ld insist on my doing it. So of course it was murdered. I believe the older I grow the more averse I get to doing anything in public. I have no courage to do such things.

Col. H[igginson] invited us into his tent—a very nice, almost *homelike* one. I noticed a nice secretary, with writing utensils and "Les Miserables" on it. A *wreath* of beautiful oranges hung against the wall, fronting the door. I wanted to have a good look at this tent; but we were hardly seated when the Dr. and Col. were called away for a moment, and Lieut. Col. Billings coming in w'ld insist upon our going into his tent. I did not want to go at all, but he was so *persistent* we had to. I fear he is a somewhat vain person. His tent was very comfortable too, and I noticed quite a large piece of "Secesh" furniture, something between a secretary and a bureau, and quite a collection of photographs and daguerres. But I did not examine them, for my attention was occupied by Col. H[igginson] to whom I showed Whittier's poem, letter and photo. "He looks old," he said to me sadly, as he handed back the picture.

Dr. R[ogers] introduced me to Dr. H[awks] and his wife[35]— pleasant people, and *good* anti-slavery. They mentioned having Liberators with my letters in them.[36] I am sorry they have come down here.

Col. H[igginson] asked me to go out and hear the band play, which I very gladly did. But it stopped just as we stepped outside of the tent. Just then one of the soldiers came up to the Col. and said "Do Cunnel, do ask 'em to play Dixie, just for me, for my lone self." The Col. made the request, but the leader of the band said he feared they w'ld not be able to play the whole tune as they had not the necessary pieces. "Nebber mind," said the man "jus' half a tune will do." It was found impossible to play even that but the leader promised that the next time they came they would be fully prepared to play Dixie for him.

The Dress Parade—the first I had ever seen—delighted me. It was a brilliant sight—the long line of men in their brilliant uniform, with bayonets gleaming in the sunlight. The Col. looked splendid. The Dr. said the men went through with the drill remarkably well. It seemed to me nothing c'ld be more perfect. To me it was a grand triumph—that black regiment doing itself honor in the sight of the white officers, many of whom, doubtless "came to scoff." It was typical of what the race, so long downtrodden and degraded will yet achieve on this Continent.

After the Parade, we went to the Landing, intending to take a boat for Beaufort. But the boat was too crowded, and we decided to wait for another. It was the softest, loveliest moonlight. We sat down among the ruins of the old fort. Just [as soon] as the boat had reached a favorable distance from the shore the band in it commenced playing Home, sweet Home. It was exquisitely beautiful. The lovely moonlight on the water, the perfect stillness around seemed to give new beauty to that ever beautiful old song. And then as my dear friend, Dr. R[ogers] said, "It came *very near* to us all."

Finding the night air damp we went to the tent of Mr. Fowler, the chaplain, whom I like much better in private conversation than as an orator. He is a thoroughly good, earnest man. Thither came Col. H[igginson] and Dr. H[awks]. We sat around the nice fire—the tent has *chimney* and fire place, made by Mr. F[owler]'s own skilful hands. Col. H[igginson] is a perfectly delightful person in private.—So genial, so witty, so kind. But I noticed when he was silent, a careworn almost sad expression on his earnest, noble face. My heart was full when I looked at him. I longed to say "I thank you, I thank you, for that noble glorious speech." And yet I *c'ld not*. It is always so. I do not know how to talk. Words always fail me when I want them most. The more I feel the more impossible it is for me to speak. It is very provoking. Among other things, Col. H[igginson] said how amusing it was to him—their plan of housekeeping down here. "This morning I was asked "Well,

Colonel, how many oxen shall we roast today." And I said, just as calmly as I w'ld have ordered a pound or two of beef, at home.—well I think *ten* will do. And then to be consulted as to how many gallons of molasses, and of vinegar, and how many pounds of ginger w'ld be wanted seemed very odd." I wish I c'ld reproduce for you the dry humorous tones in which this was said. We had a pleasant chat, sitting there in the firelight, and I was most unwilling to go, for besides the happiness of being in the society of the Col. and the Dr. we wanted dreadfully to see the "shout" and grand jubilee which the soldiers were going to have that night. But it was already late, and hearing that the "Flora" was coming we had to hasten to the Landing. I was sorry to say good-bye to Dr. R[ogers]. What an *unspeakable* happiness it was to see him. But I fear for his health. I fear the exposure of a camp life. Am glad to see that he has warm robes and blankets, to keep him comfortable. I wish I c'ld do something for him. He has done so much for me.

Ah, what a grand, glorious day this has been. The dawn of freedom which it heralds may not break upon us at once; but it will surely come, and sooner, I believe, than we have ever dared hope before. My soul is glad with an exceeding great gladness. But before I close, dear A., I must bring our little party safe home to Oaklands. We had a good time on the Flora. L[izzie Hunn] and I promenaded the deck, and sang John Brown, and Whittier's Hymn and "My Country Tis of Thee." And the moon shone bright above us, and the waves beneath, smooth and clear, glistened in the soft moonlight. At Beaufort we took the row boat, and the boatmen sang as they rowed us across. Mr. Hall was with us, and seemed really to appreciate and enjoy everything. I like him. Arrived at St. Helena's we separated, he to go to "Coffin's Point" (a dreadful name, as Dr. R[ogers] says) and we to come hither [Oaklands]. Can't say that I enjoyed the homeward drive very much. T'was so intensely cold, yes *intensely,* for these regions. I fear some of the hot enthusiasm with which my soul was filled got chilled a little but it was only for a short time.

Old friend, my good and dear A. a very, very happy New Year to you! Dear friends in both my Northern homes a happy, happy New Year to you, too! And to us all a year of such freedom as we have never yet known in this boasted but hitherto wicked land. The hymn, or rather one of the hymns that those boat[men] sung [*sic*] is singing itself to me now. The refrain "Religion so . . . sweet" was so sweet and touching in its solemnity.[37]

Sunday, Jan. 4. . . . To-day we had a little celebration at our church, on our own account. Gen. Saxton spoke. Gen. Seymour[38] was present. Mr. [Mansfield] French and others made very good addresses. . . . And our children sang "Sound the Loud Timbrel," and Whittier's Hymn. I thought they did not sing quite so well as usual. But the people seemed pleased. Our children wore badges of red, white and blue, which delighted them much. . . .

This afternoon Mrs. H[unn][39] arrived with the children. So of course there was great rejoicing in the household. I like her appearance. She seems a gentle, lady-like person. The little girl has a look of refinement.

Monday, Jan. 5. Went to school, but as Miss M[urray] and I were both far from well, and it was very damp and chilly, had no school. To-night wrote to Mrs. C[hew] and to Mr. Hunt.[40] I dreaded the last performance.

Wednesday, Jan. 7. Yesterday and to-day quite unwell with a bad cough, and hear that dear Miss M[urray] is quite ill. My good physician, Miss T[owne] came. How kind she is to me. She said she thought it decidedly best that we sh'ld give up school for this week. I demurred at first, but afterward agreed, seeing the prudence of the thing.

This afternoon was lying on the lounge feeling rather ill, and decidedly low-spirited, when the door opened and who sh'ld enter but my dear friend Dr. R[ogers]. Wasn't I glad to see him! It did me never [*sic*] so much good. He came on purpose to see me, but c'ld only stay a very little while. How much I enjoyed that brief visit no words can tell. He is looking well, but from what he said I fear he is *not* well. It grieves me to think it. I was so sorry to have him go.—Dear noble, kind friend! There are few as good as he is. He said he w'ld write to me often if I w'ld write to him. I shall do so gladly, for the sake of having letters from him. I don't deserve it I know. Our people here are very kind; several have been in to see me. I will not, must not be ill here.

Thursday, Jan. 8. Feel better [to]day. Went round to see the people. Then my good Miss T[owne] came and took me as far as the church, just for the sake of the drive. But she w'ld not let me go in, while she put away the books. Had a very pleasant talk with her by the way. It always does me good just to see her bright, cheerful face. Did some sewing and considerable writing to-day.

Sunday, Jan. 11. Rec'd to-day my hat, and my box of chessmen from Aunt M[argaretta] with a note;—nothing else that I wanted. I am so disappointed, for I needed the things sadly. But it c'ld not be helped. Had also a note from Hat-

[tie]⁴¹ and the box of clothing, which I am very glad to get. Drove out to The Oaks for a little while this afternoon.⁴²

Monday, Jan. 12. A bright, lovely day. Feel much better. Had school out-of doors—in the bright sunlight. T'was delightful. Imagine our school room, dear A.—the soft brown earth for a carpet; blue sky for a ceiling, and for walls, the grand old oaks with their exquisite moss drapery. I enjoyed it very much. Even the children seemed to appreciate it, and were unusually quiet.

Thursday, Jan. 15. After school drove to the Oaks, and practised for some time. Then went up-stairs and had a pleasant little chat with the ladies in their homelike room. Had a letter mailed to my good friend Whittier.⁴³ Dear Miss M[urray] is quite unwell which grieves me much. Miss T[owne] sent me the Dec[ember] Atlantic [Monthly]. Enjoyed it this eve. especially Dr. [Oliver Wendell] Holmes excellent article, wherein he speaks of our friend Charles W[?] very pleasantly.⁴⁴ It is an excellent No. *That* article is—"My Hunt after the Captain."

Saturday, Jan. 17. Spent the afternoon with Miss R[uggles]. She is a kind soul, though somewhat garrulous. Met there a new arrival, a Mrs. Clarke⁴⁵ whom I don't admire particularly, and a Mr. De la croix⁴⁶ who seems to me decidedly *lap-dogish* [*sic*]. Had a delicious tea;—which is worth recording being the first we have taken from home. Miss R[uggles] lent me "Ravenshoe," by Henry Kingsley. Some parts of it are good; others seem to me not worth reading. Don't like him as well as Charles K[ingsley]—his brother.

Sunday, Jan. 18. Had a lovely drive partly through the woods. The pines were singing "the slow song of the sea." It recalled the old Bridgewater [Massachusetts] days, when we used to lie on the brown leaves and listen dreamily to that wondrous song. We lost our way, which made it all the more delightful, of course!—

Monday, Jan. 19. Cold disagreeable day. Was too unwell to go to school. Miss T[owne] came to see me and did me good, as usual with her good medicines and her sunshiny face. Sewed in a most exemplary way. . . .

Friday, Jan. 23. Had a kind little note from my good friend, Dr. R[ogers]. His reg[iment] goes on an expedition to-day.⁴⁷ He asks me to pray for their success. And indeed I will, with my whole soul and for his safety, too—dear, kind friend that he is. I wish I c[ou]ld have seen him again before he went. How he rejoices in Gen. Hunter's coming.⁴⁸ And how I rejoice with him!

Saturday, Jan. 24. Had to-day the pleasantest visit I've had since I've been here. L[izzie] and I drove to Mr. Thorpe's plantation. . . . The gentlemen took us around to see the people of whom there are 150 on the place. 100 have come from Edisto. There were no houses to accommodate so many, and they had to find shelter in barns, outhouses and any other place they c[ou]ld get. They have constructed rude houses for themselves —many of them—which do not, however afford them much protection in bad weather. I am told that they are all excellent, industrious people.

One old woman interested me deeply. Her name is Daphne, and she is probably at least a hundred years old. She has had fifty grandchildren, sixty-five greatgrandchildren, and three great, greatgrandchild[ren]. She is entirely blind, but seems quite cheerful and happy. She told us that she was brought from Africa to this country just after the Revolution. I asked her if she was glad that all her numerous family were now and forever free. Her bright old face grew brighter as she answered. "Oh yes, yes missus." She retains her faculties remarkably well for one so old. It interested me greatly to see her. As Mr. H[?] said "it was worth coming to S[outh] C[arolina] to see that old relic of a past time."

15 of the people on this place escaped from the main land, last spring. Among them was a man named Michael. After they had gone some distance—their masters in pursuit—M[ichael]'s master overtook him in the swamp. A fierce grapple ensued— the master on horseback, the man on foot:—the former drew a pistol and shot the slave through the arm, shattering it dreadfully. Still the brave man fought desperately and at last succeeded in unhorsing the master, and beat him until he was senseless. He then with the rest of the company escaped. With them was a woman named Rina, now a cook at Mr. T[horpe]'s. She was overtaken by her master's cousin, and nearly run over by his horse. But he, having a liking for her, wheeled his horse around, when he saw who it was, without saying a word, and allowed her to escape.—A story which I record because it is a rare thing to hear anything good of a rebel. I had the pleasure of shaking hands with Rina, and congratulating her on her escape. She is a very neat, sensible looking black woman.

Mr T[horpe]'s place—which used to be the property of one of the numerous family of Fripps—Thomas by name—is most beautifully situated in the midst of noble pine trees, and on the banks of a large creek which deserves—almost—to be dignified by the name of river. Tis the pleasantest place I've seen yet. And Mr T[horpe] says it is quite healthy.

Of course we lost our way coming back, and I, in trying to turn the horse, ran up against a tree and there our *"shay"* staid. In vain did L[izzie] and I try to move the horse, and then the wheels. Both were equally immovable, till fortunately we saw a man at a little distance and called him to our aid. With his assistance we soon got righted again. All this I tell you, dear A. as a great secret. W[ou]ldn't have anybody else know of my unskilfulness. Despite this little *contretemps* we had a delightful sunset drive home.

Sunday, Jan. 25. Saw a wonderful sight to-day. 150 people were baptized in the creek near the church. They looked very picturesque—many of them in white aprons, and bright dresses and handkerchiefs. And as they, in procession, marched down to the water, they sang beautifully. The most perfect order and quiet prevailed throughout.

Monday, Jan. 26. Rec'd another kind note from Dr. R[ogers] written prior to the other. In it he gives me some account of what he is doing; and I am so glad to know. It is so good to hear from him, I fear he has not got my note. Not that t'was of much importance, but I w'ld like him to know how constantly I think of him.

Tuesday, Jan. 27. J[?] brought me from B[eaufort] to-day a package from home containing a letter from Aunt M[argaretta], some delicious candy from our good Emma, and a pair of quite nice pants, from Mrs. Chew, sent especially to Cupid. How delighted he was to get them. He c[ou]ldn't say much, but I wish Mrs. C[hew] c'ld have seen the marvelous bows and *scrapings* which he made.

Wednesday, Jan. 28. A memorable day because we had a snowstorm—in miniature. When I got up this morning some of the roofs had a white layer on them, but it did not stay on the ground. The "storm" lasted but a little while. Towards eve. there was another slight attempt at snow, which was unsuccessful. A cold, dreary day. Miss R[uggles] sent me "Say and Seal,"[49] and a bunch of lovely white flowers, which it does my soul good to see. She is very kind. . . .

Friday, Jan. 30. Finished "Say and Seal," some of which I like very much. But it is rather religious to suit me. I don't know but it seems to me the author's works have a little *cant* about them. Now Mrs. [Harriet Beecher] Stowe always has something about religion in her books, but it is so differently *administered,* that it is only pleasant and beautiful. . . .

Saturday, Jan. 31. L[izzie] and I went to Beaufort—after bread. We had a lovely row across,—at noon—in the brightest sunlight. But neither going or coming did the boatmen sing, which disappointed me much. The Sergeant said these were not singers—*That* is most surprising. I thought *everybody* sang down here. Certainly every boat crew *ought*. As we drove to the ferry, we noticed how fresh and green everything looked;—so unlike winter. The trees are nearly all evergreen. Bare branches are rarely to be seen. What a lovely morning it was!—like a May morn. up North. Birds singing on every side. Deep green in the pines and "deep delicious blue" in the sky. Why is it that green and blue together are so lovely in Nature, and so *un*lovely elsewhere?

In B[eaufort] we spent nearly all our time at Harriet Tubman's— otherwise "Moses."[50] She is a wonderful woman—a real heroine. Has helped off a large number of slaves, after taking her own freedom. She told us that she used to hide them in the woods during the day and go around to get provisions for them. Once she had with her a man named Joe, for whom a reward of $1500 was offered. Frequently, in different places she found handbills exactly describing him, but at last they reached in safety the Suspension Bridge over the Falls and found themselves in Canada. Until then, she said, Joe had been very silent. In vain had she called his attention to the glory of the Falls. He sat perfectly still—moody, it seemed, and w'ld not even glance at them. But when she said, "Now we are in Can[ada]" he sprang to his feet with a great shout, and sang and clapped his hand [*sic*] in a perfect delirium of joy. So when they got out, and he first touched *free* soil, he shouted and hurrahed "as if he were crazy"—she said.

How exciting it was to hear her tell the story. And to hear her sing the very scraps of jubilant hymns that he sang. She said the ladies crowded around them, and some laughed and some cried. My own eyes were full as I listened to her—the heroic woman! A reward of $10000 was offered for her by the Southerners, and her friends deemed it best that she sh'ld, for a time find refuge in Can[ada]. And she did so, but only for a short time. She came back and was soon at the good brave work again. She is living in B[eaufort] now; keeping an eating house. But she wants to go North, and will probably do so ere long. I am glad I saw her—*very* glad.

At her house we met one of the Superintendents from P[ort] R[oyal] I[sland], a Boston man—Mr. S[?]—who is intelligent and very agreeable. He kindly went with us to Mrs. Hawkes'—the wife of the Sur[geon] 1st Reg[iment] S[outh] C[arolina] V[olunteers] but she was at the camp with her husband who did not go with the Expedition [up the St. Mary's River]. Was sorry not to see her.

Went, afterward, to Mr. Judd's for letters, and found there one from A[nnie].[51] Am delighted to have it, and to know she is not ill. Mr. J[udd]'s house is beautifully situated. In the same street with Gen. Saxton's. On the Bay—as they call it. Saw the building which was once the Public Library. It is now a shelter for "contrabands" from Fernandino. How disgusted the rebels w'ld be. I suppose they w'ld upturn their aristocratic noses and say "To what base uses etc." It does *me* good to see how the tables are turned. The market place also we saw. Mr. S[?] said doubtless human beings had been sold there. But there is not a certainty of it, as that business was generally transacted in Charleston. The Arsenal is a fine large stone structure—fine— I sh[ou]ld say—for this region. The entrance is guarded by two handsome brass cannon, and a fierce looking sentinel. Nearly all the houses in B[eaufort] have a dismantled, desolate look. Few persons are to be seen in the streets some soldiers and "contrabands." I believe we saw only three ladies. But already Northern improvements have reached this southern town. One of them is a fine new wharf which is a convenience that one wonders how the "Secesh" c'ld have done without. They were an uncivilized people. I noticed more mulattoes there than we have on St. Hel[ena]. Some were very good-looking. Little colored children—of every hue were playing about the streets looking as merry and happy as children ought to look—now that the dark shadow of slavery hangs over them no more.

We did our few errands and were quite ready for the four o'clock boat, which was not, however, ready for us until some- time afterward. I missed the singing, in our row back.

Sunday, Feb. 1.   Quite a number of strangers at church to- day,—among them our good Gen. [Saxton]; whom it is always a pleasure to see. Reuben T[omlinson] was there.[52] I was glad to see him. It recalled the old Phila[delphia] days—the pleas- antest of them.

This afternoon went into the woods, and gathered some casino berries and beautiful magnolia leaves and exquisite ferns. How beautifully they contrast, on my table, with the daffodils and narcissus which are in full bloom now. Think of these flowers blooming out of doors in Jan[uary] and Feb[ru- ary]. Isn't it wonderful? I cant tell you how much pleasure they give me. What sunbeams they are to warm and cheer my heart.

Monday, Feb. 2.   Have just heard to-night of the return of the 1st Reg[imen]t. They came back with laurels and Secesh prisoners. Have heard no particulars, but am *glad,* emphatical- ly glad to know that they come back co:npletely successful.

That is grand, glorious! In the joy of my heart sat down and wrote a congratulatory note, to my dear friend, Dr. R[ogers]. I know how rejoiced he must be. Thank God that he and the noble Col. [T. W. Higginson] have come back safe.

Saturday, Feb. 7. One day this week Tina, an excellent woman from Palawana, came in, and told us a very interesting story about two girls, one about ten the other fifteen, who, having been taken by their master up into the country about the time of [the] "Gun Shoot," determined to try to get back to their parents who had been left on this island. They stole away at night, and travelled through woods and swamps, for two days without eating. Sometimes their strength w'ld fail and they w'ld sink down in the swamps, and think they c'ld [go] no further, but they had brave little hearts, and struggled on, till at last they reached Port Royal Ferry. There they were seen by a boat-load of people who had also made their escape. The boat was too full to take them but the people, as soon as they reached these islands, told the father of the children, who immediately hastened to the Ferry for them. The poor little creatures were almost wild with joy, despite their exhausted state, when they saw their father coming to them. When they were brought to their mother she fell down "jus' as if she was dead" as Tina expressed it. She was so overpowered with joy. Both children are living on Dalta now. They are said to be very clever. I want to see the heroic little creatures.

Another day, one of the black soldiers came in and gave us *his* account of the Expedition [up the St. Mary's River]. No words of mine, dear A can give you any account of the state of exultation and enthusiasm that he was in. He was eager for another chance at "de Secesh." I asked him what he w[ou]ld do if his master and others sh'ld come back and try to reenslave him. "I'd fight um Miss, I'd fight um till I turned to dust!" He was especially delighted at the ire which the sight of the black troops excited in the minds of certain Secesh women whom they saw. These vented their spleen by calling the men "baboons dressed in soldiers clothes," and telling them that they ought to be at work in their masters' rice swamps, and that they ought to be lashed to death. "And what did you say to them?" I asked. "Oh miss, we only tell um 'Hole your tongue, and dry up.' You see *we* wusn't feared of *dem, dey c[ou]ldn't hurt us now*. Whew! didn't we laugh . . . to see dem so mad!" The spirit of resistance to the Secesh is strong in these men.

Sunday, Feb. 8. . . . Towards night, after the others had gone, Dr. R[ogers] came. Wasn't I glad to see him. He looks none the worse for his late experience. He brought his notes of the Ex[pedition] taken on the spot, and very kindly read them to us, to-night. They are very, very interesting, more so to me even than Col. H[igginson]'s excellent Report,[53] (which the Dr. also brought) because entering more into particulars. He will not have them printed for which I am sorry. They ought to be [printed]. They, and the report also, show plainly how nobly and bravely the black soldiers can fight. I am delighted. I think the contemputuous white soldiers will cease to sneer soon. Dr. R[ogers] described beautifully the scenes through which they passed, particularly the night journey up St. Mary's River, with the grand old funereal oaks on either side. How strange and solemn it must have been.

At one place, Alberti's Mills, they went up to the plantation, and found the mistress, living in solitary splendor. She and her husband (now dead) came from the North, but have lived a long time down South, and had a large plantation and great wealth. Dr. R[ogers] describes Mad[am] A[lberti] as a very superior woman. She spent a long time in trying to convince Dr. R[ogers] that she and her husband had devoted themselves to the good of their slaves, and lamented their ingratitude in all deserting her—as they have all done except one or two petted house servants. Rob[er]t Sutton, now Corporal in the Reg[iment] was formerly her slave, and said the people were cruelly treated, and the jail on the place, where chains and handcuffs were found, bears witness to that.[54]

The soldiers brought off cattle, horses and lumber, all of great value to the Gov[ernment]. They behaved gallantly under fire from the rebels, and entered into their work with zeal. Three of them saved the life of their brave Col. H[igginson]. He, as usual, was at one time in advance, when a rebel pistol was fired at him by an officer, who immediately drew another and was about to take more fatal aim (the Col. not perceiving it) when three of the soldiers seeing his danger, fired at once, killing the rebel officer. Dr. R[ogers] says that several who were badly wounded did not report to him, fearing that they w'ld be obliged to leave their posts. The noble Rob[er]t Sutton whom Col. H[igginson] calls "the Leader of the Expedition" was wounded in three places, and still kept at his post.[55] Dr. R[ogers] speaks of him as does Col. H[igginson] —in the highest terms. He says he thinks he must be the descendant of some Nubian king. He is a grand man. My heart is filled with an exceeding great joy to-night.

I can never thank Dr. R[ogers] sufficiently for bringing me those notes. It was very kind. And it makes me so happy to see him safe back again. The kind, loving words he spoke to me to-night sank deep into my heart. "As a brother," he told me to consider him. And I will gladly do so. He read me Emerson's noble Hymn, written for the grand Jubilee Concert, on Emancipation Day in Boston.[56] Dr. R[ogers] read it to the Reg[iment] he told me, during service, this morning. I am glad. He was in full uniform to-day. Makes a splendid looking officer. I looked at him and his horse with childish admiration.

Monday, Feb. 9. Dr. R[ogers] walked part of the way to school with me, and we had a nice, long talk. He said he wished he lived nearer that he might come in and read to me sometimes. Ah! w[ou]ldn't *I* enjoy that, unspeakably! It is too bad that I can see so seldom the only old friend I have here,—and such a friend! Dear Miss T[owne] was not well enough to be at school to-day. I am very sorry. Miss M[urray] and I did the best we c'ld without her. With what eager interest and delight Miss M[urray] speaks of the success of the Reg[iment]. I believe she is as rejoiced as I am, and that's saying a great deal. It does me good to see it.

Frogmore,[57] *Wednesday, Feb. 11.* Quite unwell yesterday and to-day. This morn. the Townes—my good physician and her sister—came in and declaring that I needed change of air, forcibly bore me off to Frogmore. Well, I was glad to go, and here I am. The place is delightfully situated, on an arm of the sea, which, at high tide, comes up to within a few feet of the house. There are lovely trees around, and an almost sea air, which is most invigorating after the somewhat oppressive atmosphere farther inland. This is a very large plantation. There are nearly 200 people living on it. Ah! how pleasant this salt smell is. It recalls the dear old Marblehead days.

Thursday, Feb. 12. Have done little else but sleep. It is very quiet here. Have had most delicious rest, both for soul and body. Miss Rosa T[owne] is as kind as possible. Hers is a beautiful kindness, that does one good thoroughly. I love her. . . .

Found the first snowdrop to-day;—a lovely, pure, little darling, growing at the foot of the piazza steps. Welcome, welcome a thousand times!

Friday, Feb. 13. Miss Laura [Towne] came to-day. To-night some of the little boys came in and danced for us. It was *deliciously* comical. Miss L[aura] rewarded them by giving them belts with bright buckles, which pleased them mightily. To-night there was a bit of a shout in the "Praise House," but there were not enough to make it very enjoyable. They sang beautifully however. One song I have not heard before. Must try to get the words. "Jacob" and "w[ou]ld not let me go," are in it.

Saturday, Feb. 14. Valentine's Day *at home.* Who will send me one? A dark, gloomy, stormy day without, but cheery within. Miss W[?] and Miss M[urray] came to-day, and we have quite a large party—five ladies and two gentlemen. Stormed so much this afternoon they c'ld not go, and will be obliged to spend the night with us. That is *jolly.* I know Mr. F[?] thinks so. *Wasn't* he rejoiced to see Miss M[urray]. Ah! this love. Tis a queer thing, but very amusing—to lookers-on. Helped Miss Rosa fill bags with sewing utensils for the people —a pleasant task. We both enjoyed it.

To-night—a wild stormy night—went out on the piazza and listened to the roaring of the sea. How wild it sounded. Occasionally we c'ld hear a great wave break upon the shore. That sound of the sea is music to my ears. I c'ld not bear to come away from it. It brought N[ew] E[ngland] near to me. But the air is dangerously damp, and I had to tear myself away. Miss L[aura] T[owne] told us some delightfully horrible stories and then Mr. F[?] told us some stories from Vergil, in which he seems well read. We had a very pleasant, social evening.— Good bye, old Journal friend.

Part 7

End of a Mission

February 15, 1863 - May 15, 1864

Oaklands, Sunday, Feb. 15.   Home again! Left Frogmore this afternoon. T'was so lovely there I did not want to leave at all, and dear Miss Rosa T[owne] urged me to stay. But I c'ld not. The water was clear and beautiful, and even today we c'ld hear the sea, but rather a distant murmur, not the grand roaring of last-night. The day has been bright, lovely, and most spring-like.

Two soldiers dined at F[rogmore] with us. They are part of the patrol, which it has been found necessary to place here, on account of the depredations made by some of the soldiers, who have recently landed. They have stolen poultry, and everything else they c'ld get on the plantations, cheated the Negroes, and in some instances even burned their houses. These outrages are said to have been committed by deserters.[1] It is too bad. We are all most indignant about it, but hope now, since more vigilant measures have been taken that things will be in a better state.

Found awaiting me here letters from Mrs. Crosby, Mrs. Chew, Mr. Hunt, and Mary S[hepard][2] also a Boston Journal and two Liberators, was delighted, of course, to get them all.

Oaklands seems rather cramped and close after the larger grounds, the pleasant water view and sea breezes of Frogmore; but we have the snuggest little sitting room I've seen yet and it's pleasant to get into it again. I am much better, thanks to change of air, rest, and Miss Rosa's loving care, I feel quite ready for to-morrow's work.

Tuesday, Feb. 17.   To-night rec'd a box from Phila[delphia] containing nice little alphabet-blocks and picture cards for my little ones. They'll delight the little creature's hearts, I know. . . .

Wednesday, Feb. 18.   Too rainy this morning for school. This afternoon cleared up beautifully, and we had a lovely drive to The Oaks. . . . Read some good things in Beecher's "Eyes and Ears."[3]

Thursday, Feb. 19.   Who sh'd walk into school to-day

but my good and dear Dr. R[ogers]. *Wasn't* I glad to see him! Miss M[urray] w'ld have my children read for him, and they read remarkably well. He praised them. They sang beautifully too, which delighted him.

He came to dine with us, and then we—just he and I—had the loveliest horseback ride to Mr. Thorpe's place. It was lovely through those pines and we found the most exquisite jessamine. The ground had been burnt, and so attracted the sun's rays, and the greater heat made the flowers much larger than ours. Nothing c'ld be more perfect than the color, more delicious than the fragrance. Dr. R[ogers] broke off long sprays and twined them around me. I felt grand as a queen. How good Mr. H[unn] opened his eyes when he saw me so gloriously adorned. Mr. T[horpe] (whom Dr. R[ogers] wants to know) was not at home, so we made no stay.

Dear A. I can give you no idea of the ride homeward. I know only that it was the most delightful ride I ever had in my life. The young moon—just a silver bow—had a singular, almost violet tinge, and all around it in the heavens was a rosy glow, deepening every moment, which was wonderfully beautiful. I shall never forget how that rosy light, and the moon and stars looked to us as we caught them in glimpses, riding through the dark pines. How wild and unreal it all seemed and what happiness it was, as we rode slowly along to listen to the conversation of the dear friend who is always so kind, so full of sympathy, and of eager enthusiasm in the great work in which he is engaged. No wonder the soldiers love him so much, no wonder that, as Col. H[igginson] says, he has such a hold upon them. So that one of them said to him "Why Dr., don't you know there ain't a man in de regiment—but what *dotes his eyes on you."* There is a magnetism about him impossible to resist. I can never be thankful enough that he came here. But oh, I do not want him to be ill, or to die. Most gladly w'ld I give my life that one so noble so valuable might be preserved. He brought me a note from Col. H[igginson]. So very kind! I shall not say anything about its contents or about what Dr. R[ogers] said to me relating to it, even to you, yet my dear A. for it is a profound secret, which I must not trust to paper. But rest assured you will know all about it ere long.

After tea the Dr. read to us a grand article, in the Feb[ruary] Atlantic [Monthly] by his friend Mr. Wasson called "The law of Costs." It is in relation to the war, and is certainly the best thing I have yet seen on the subject. Full of noble truths told in the most beautiful language. He also read us Lowell's last

Biglow Paper on the same subject—a capital thing; far superior to anything he has written of late.[4]

Friday, Feb. 20. Dr. R[ogers] went this morn. I rose earlier than usual, and plucked some lovely jessamine for him and the Col. [T. W. Higginson]. I shall see him again to-morrow, for we are to go to camp Saxton. After school read the Jan[uary] Atlantic which Dr. R[ogers] very kindly brought to me. Then S[?] and I made some cakes, one large one apiece for the Col. and Mr. T[horpe] spent the night with us. He is intelligent and agreeable, and really interested in the people here. I like him.

Saturday, Feb. 21. Ah, what a day I've had! Another day "to be marked with a white stone." We—that is Mr. T[horpe], Mrs. and Miss H[unn] and I drove to the landing and at noon took a nice boat, with four oarsmen. The tide was very high, and air exhilarating, the sunshine joyous. It was a perfect row —an ideal row, through those dancing laughing waves we flew along and reached camp Saxton in half an hour. Beaufort looks really quite beautiful from the water. The sky wore its best blue. Everything smiled upon us, and the boatmen sang several singular and beautiful hymns which I have never heard before. Noted them down as well as I c'ld. C'ldn't understand the words very readily.

Had a warm welcome from the Col. and the Dr. The adjutant[5] was married last Sunday, in a hollow square. His bride is pleasant, intelligent looking, and ladylike. We dined at the Col's table, and had the happiness of listening to his always entertaining talk.

After dinner paid several visits. Am so glad the Dr. has a nice large tent, with a stove in it, and as many things to make him comfortable as one can have in a tent. The Adjutant's tent has a carpet in it—a wonderful luxury in camp,—and indeed down here, everywhere. Saw the battalion drill and the dress parade,[6] both of which were fine sights to me.

The Dr. took us to a cypress swamp about half a mile from the camp. It is a wonderful place. Never saw one before. The trunks of the trees, near the base are fluted, just as perfectly as if done by art. The branches are hung with moss, through which the sunlight was streaming. The surface of the water is covered with a plant having fine leaves of a vivid green. But the most wonderful thing about it is the variety of forms which the roots take. In many places they come up a foot or more in height and bear a striking resemblance to monks with long cloaks and shaven crowns. Others take the form of birds. But the monks are the most distinct and are most remarkable. The

Dr. got one for me and whittled off the end so as to make it more shapely. Some very fine beautiful moss is on it. I've put it in water, hoping the moss will grow. The whole swamp looks wonderfully like some old cathedral, with monks cloaked and hooded, kneeling around it. Col. H[igginson] showed us at the camp one of the finest live oaks I have ever seen. A grand old tree heavily draped with moss and with delicate little ferns growing on some of the limbs.

While in the Dr's tent Rob[ert] Sutton came in. It was very interesting to hear him talk about the expedition.[7] His manner is very simple and earnest and his words, full of eloquence and enthusiasm, flow forth with wonderful ease. It was amusing to hear him say with perfect simplicity—"Now if de Connel had done so and so, as I told him, we c'ld a taken all dem rebels right off." And the Col. bowed his noble head, and acknowledged Rob[er]t's superior wisdom. The Colonel seems to have entered into firing houses at St. Mary's with great zest.[8] We were laughing and talking about it when he turned to me with great gravity (I c'ldn't imagine what was coming) and said "Now Miss Forten, what in your opinion is the best place to begin with in setting a house on fire?" I laughingly replied that I feared I hadn't considered the subject sufficiently to venture an opinion. "Well," he said "some authorities say to the leeward, others to the windward. I've tried both and I don't see that it makes any difference—It seems to me the very best place is just under a shelf in a closet or cupboard." He talked to me, alone, for sometime, about the plan proposed in his note. How can I ever thank him for his kindness? I can only say in my heart—how noble, how splendid he is!

While the brightest day must come to a close and so mine came. I didn't want to come away at all, but come [I] must. It was nearly dark when we again stepped into "our dug out." Capt. [James S.] R[ogers] came with us. How he is improved since the old Worcester days, he seems a fine noble fellow now. The wind was high, the water quite rough to-night and our boatmen worked too hard to sing. So we had to console ourselves, by singing, as well as we c'ld ourselves. Mr. T[horpe] has quite a good voice. The moon and stars smiled down upon us. It was a wild row; and all the more delightful for that. I wished for the Dr. to enjoy it with me. Then the dark drive home—Mrs. H[unn] driving, Mr. T[horpe] and Capt. R[ogers] on horseback as escort. T'was all enjoyable.

Sunday, Feb. 22. Mr. T[horpe] and Capt. R[ogers] spent most of the day with us. Had a very pleasant time. Did a great deal of chatting. Copied several of the people's hymns for the

Col. and Dr. and gathered jessamine and ivy for them. The children came in and sang and then had some grand shouts on the piazza, which delighted the gentlemen exceedingly. Capt. R[ogers] and I had two games of chess, w[ou]ldn't that shock some people! in both of which I was most ignominiously defeated. Nevertheless I enjoyed them.

After dinner the Capt. left, and then Mr. T[horpe] and I had a good little ride on horseback, in which old Edisto, usually so slow, quite distinguished himself. He came home at a full gallop. This eve Mr. and Miss K[?] came in, bringing me letters from Mr. Hunt,[9] dear Nellie A. and the most flowery letter from a gentleman in Wash[ington] who must have read Mr. Brown's silly book,[10] I must send it home to make them laugh.

Wednesday, Feb. 25. Had no school, as the teachers went to Camp Saxton. Had a splendid ride to the Oaks, and back. Old Edisto behaved admirably. The day was delightful. Was riding nearly all the morn. This eve wrote to Mr. Hunt.

Thursday, Feb. 26. To-day several gentlemen from the 21st Mass[achusetts Regiment] came in school.[11] They listened with evident interest to the recitations and singing, and at the close expressed themselves much pleased. . . .

Saturday, Feb. 28. Had a nice long talk with some of the people this afternoon. The more one knows of them the more interested one becomes in them. I asked if there used to be people sold at auction in the market-place at Beaufort. They said "yes, often." Last night finished "Salem Chapel," which ends just as I thought it would.

Sunday, March 1. Went to church and was victimized with one of Mr. Phillips' dull sermons. Rec'd my pass. Tis necessary now that we sh'ld all have passes to show to the patrol on the island. Read some good things in the Atlantic [Monthly].

March, usually so blustering with us, comes in here soft and mild as June. These are indeed June days. Quantities of flowers are in bloom, snow drops, daffodils, narcissus, japonicas, a beautiful fine white flower whose name I do not know, and as for yellow jessamine, large-flowered and fragrant, the woods are perfectly golden with it.

On Friday, coming from school, I saw the loveliest mistletoe that ever eyes beheld. Large branches heavily laden with white berries, pure and beautiful as pearls. My children and I went busily to work. With long sticks bore down the branches so we c'ld reach them, and enriched ourselves with the treasures thereon. And each one of us marched home triumphantly, bearing long sprays of pearls. They are hanging over our broken mirror, and drooping over my little table of books now. Mr. H[unn] has brought in a large branch of jessamine, laden with exquisite blossoms, which adorns another table. So altogether our little room is made quite splendid. Plum and peach blossoms are all out now, perfuming the air, and looking most beautiful and May-like.

Wednesday, March 4. Rushing along the road from school to-day, in a shivering condition—for our stove w'ld do nothing but smoke—what sh'ld I encounter but Gen. Saxton's carriage, and, in it, himself and Mrs. [Frances D.] Gage.[12] The Gen. said "Col. Higginson wants you to go to Florida with his reg[imen]t" in his usually rather abrupt way. Now although I knew this before, for dear A. *this* is the weighty secret Dr. R[ogers] imparted to me when he was last here, the suddeness of the Gen's speech took me by surprise, and if I looked as surprised as I felt the Gen. who had of course been told that I knew all about it,—must have thought me a little hypocrite. I hardly knew what to say. Believe I stammered something about leaving my school. Mrs. Gage said I must get some one else to take it. She wants me to go to F[lorid]a. If I go, it will be to teach the soldiers. I shall like that. So much depends on these men. If I can help them in any way I shall be glad to do so. I shall be sorry to leave my dear children and Miss T[owne] and Miss M[urray] to whom I am most warmly attached; but if I can really do more good by going. I shall be content. And then I shall have the society of my dear and noble friend Dr. R[ogers], and perhaps of the good and noble Col. too, and these are very, very strong inducements. The climate also is healthier, and oh how I *crave* good health. How can one work well without it? They think it will be safer there for me, too, but of that I do not think. I have never felt the least fear since I have been here. Though not particularly brave at home, it seems as if I *cannot* know fear *here*.

To-night had letters from Dr. R[ogers] so kind, so noble. He has sent me a little friend, whose name I am not to mention. But it is a beautiful and true f[rien]d. Also a little note of Bell's full of touching and beautiful affection. Indeed it is very kind in him to let me see this little note. It somehow brings me nearer to him. The Reg[iment] will leave to-morrow, he says.[13] I shall not see him before he goes, perhaps never again, for it is an enterprise full of danger on which they go. The thought makes my heart ache. I am willing to give up my life—which is nothing—but I do not want one so good and noble as he to die yet. The world cannot afford to lose such. And yet he says "let us think how much better it is to die in this sublime struggle for universal freedom, than live to see another generation of slavery."

Rec'd also to-night a pass from Gen. Saxton, who highly approves my going [to Florida]. This permit, Dr. R[ogers] says, is equivalent to a Commission. So I shall go. I am determined now. Dr. R[ogers] tells me to be ready to join them at an early day.

Thursday, March 5. Talked over my Fl[orida] plan with Miss T[owne] and Miss M[urray]. Although they do not want me to go, they cannot help acknowledging that it would be a wider spere of usefulness than this.—

Saturday, March 7. Had a long, pleasant drive to Mr. B[ryant]'s place, near "Land's End."[14] It is a fine, stately house, beautifully situated, with much water near it. Two very fine long piazzas, one above the other were favorable for promenading. The water view from these w'ld be fine were it not for the marshes. But the air is fresher and more healthy than with us. After dinner, played euchre for the first time since I have been here.

Driving along the road noticed an oak tree, which looked very singular. One of the limbs, after growing out, bent itself back and grew into the tree again. A very strange thing. Dr. W[akefield][15] who pointed it out to us, said that he had seen only one like it on Cape Cod.

Tuesday, March 10. Was very unwell Sunday and yesterday. Felt better to-day and went with Mrs. Hunn to Beaufort, intending to do some shopping and to go to Camp Saxton and see Mrs. Dewhurst[16] to make inquiries about our going—I am to go with her and Mrs. Hawkes.[17] The Quartermaster[18] very kindly lent us his carriage and we drove off in fine spirits. Our driver Jonas, assured us that he knew where the camp was. But he mistook the place that he wanted to go to, and drove us many miles out of the way. It was the longest drive I have had yet down here. Probably between thirty and forty miles. Camp S[axton] is only four miles from Beaufort.

The weather was almost oppressively warm, the air laden with the fragrance of jasmine and fruit blossoms. At last our driver was made to understand where we wanted to go, and we reached Camp Saxton. Saw Mrs. D[ewhurst] and Mrs. H[awkes]. We may not have to go for 3 weeks. But there is no certainty about it. Returned to B[eaufort] just in time for the last boat. So no shopping was done. . . .

Friday, Mar. 13. Have been busily sewing this week, though still far from well. Miss H[unn] has taught for me.

Went to B[eaufort] again to-day, and did some shopping. Saw Gen. S[axton] who was married to Miss T[hompson] last Wed.[19] He looked quite radiant. A strange marriage, it seems to me. Coming over in the boat, the men sang one of the most beautiful hymns I have ever heard.

> "Praise believer, praise God, I praise my God until I die
> Jordan stream is a good old stream and I aint but one
> more river to cross
> I want some valiant soldier to help me bear the cross."

It is a beautiful thing.

Yesterday I had a book—A. Crummell's "Future of Africa," —from Whittier. Also a letter from him, and a precious little note from his sister;—both *very* kind and beautiful.[20] Also . . . my Tennyson, some newspapers, letters from Aunt M[argaretta], F. E. [?], Lizzie C[hurch], Hattie, and Henry.[21] The latter has rec'd and answered all my letters. Also sent me some Atlantics and the letter paper, and yet, I have rec'd nothing from him. It is very strange. I despair of ever getting them now. It is too bad!

Saturday, Mar. 14. Drove to Coffin Pt.[22] to visit Miss [Harriet] Ware—a sister of Dr. Winsor's wife. A long, dreary drive it was thro' deep Carolina sand. And we did not find Miss W[are]. But the house a large, old-fashioned one, is beautifully situated on the sea shore. There is a lovely path leading directly thro' the garden down to the beach. Oh it was *good* to stand upon that beach, feel the cool sea breezes, and listen to the gentle murmur of the waves. I was most unwilling to leave it. The sitting room was the pleasantest I [have] seen down here, with its books and pictures. And an excellent piano was there— Gilbert's of Boston—which was most refreshing to listen to after the tuneless instruments one hears generally down here. Altogether this is a place I sh'ld like to go to for a week, to rest in, thoroughly, before I go down to Florida.

The Oaks. Saturday, March 21. Miss Nellie[?] came and took me to The Oaks. Think the change will do me good. Have been unwell of late. Victimized myself in the dressmaker's hands. To-night Miss M[urray] and I had some good games of chess. Mr. E[ustis] is staying here.[23] A man of a good deal of wit. Don't think I shall like him from what I've heard of his behavior towards the people. His manners are not at all attractive to me.

Sunday, Mar. 22. Chilly, disagreeable day. Unusually small attendance at church. Some of the people sang "Glory Be to My King Immanuel." It is one of their grandest hymns. Must have the words. Mr. T[horpe] and Miss Nellie, sang beautifully for us to-night. Both have fine, rich voices.

Tuesday, Mar. 24. Miss T[owne] came from B[eaufort] to-day bringing me news that the ladies had sailed for Fl[orid]a this morn. Their letters just came to me to-day. But I am to go with Gen. Saxton day after to-morrow; which is just as well. Had a little note from Dr. R[ogers]. They are expecting me. He says "we have to keep a sharp lookout for the rebels, but I think we shall hold the town." I shall enjoy the 'spice' of danger.

With Miss T[owne] came the latest arrival—Mr. Pierce— the former *pioneer* down here.[24] His manners are exceedingly pleasant—I can't help acknowledging that, though I had a preconceived dislike for him, because I had heard that he said he "wanted no colored missionaries nor teachers down here." His conversation at table to-night was most entertaining and genial. But I shall take an early opportunity of asking an explanation of that speech. If he said that, of course there's no possibility of my liking him. Still, I must confess, it is pleasant to see somebody fresh from Boston, and full of Boston energy and spirit. It is pleasant to hear the dear, noble familiar names again; to meet one who has so lately breathed the same air and trod the same streets with such as Wendell Phillips and dear Mr. Garrison. Then Mr. Pierce himself did a great work down here, and proved himself a true friend of the people who all regard him with love and gratitude. That is a great deal in his favor. Miss T[owne] lent me some hymns to copy, which I have not.

Wednesday, Mar. 25. Went to school to-day for the last time. Said good-bye to my little ones with a full heart. Gave them each a book for a parting gift. How that delighted them. Mr. P[ierce] came in and listened to a little reciting. Some of my tiny ones "did up" the alphabet quite beautifully.[25]

Kind Miss T[owne] came to Oaklands and packed my trunks, for which I am inexpressibly thankful, for I seem to have no strength at all. Said good-bye to old Oaklands. Shall I ever see it and its inmates again, I wonder? Cupid drove me to The Oaks in the beautiful still moonlight. To-morrow we go to Beau[fort].

Thursday, Mar. 26. Just too late for the earliest boat, which was provoking. But I supposed we should have time enough, as we were not to go to Fl[orid]a till this afternoon. Had the satisfaction of seeing the boat about half-way across.

Established ourselves as well as we c'ld on the landing—Miss T[owne] on a stump and I on a basket; while Mr. P[ierce] devoted himself to our entertainment—Read a little from "Bull Run Russell's" book,[26] and talked a great deal. While we were sitting there saw The Flora pass down the stream, and by the flag, knew that the Gen.[27] was on board. I began to feel uneasy, —thinking that the hour of starting had been changed, and that the boat was off to Fl[orid]a without us. But Mr. P[ierce]—who is also going to Jacksonville—was so secure that it was not so, and so composed about it that I was reassured.

At last the ferry boat returned. On reaching B[eaufort] went at once to Capt. H[ooper]'s office, and were there told that Gen. S[axton] had just gone down to Hilton Head to see Gen. Hunter [Commanding General, Department of the South] from whom he had just rec'd a dispatch saying that he had ordered the evacuation of Jacksonville.[28] The Gen. returns at once. I waited to see him. Dined at the Judd's. Like them and Miss R[uggles] also very much. At last Gen. S[axton] came. Mr. P[ierce] saw him at once. It is true. Jacksonville is to be evacuated. Gen. Hunter needs the white troops and the gunboats to join the Ex[pedition] to Charleston, and as the rebels are gathering in great forces near the town, the black regiment alone w'ld be entirely overwhelmed. The Gen. promises to send them back when Charles[ton] is taken. But when will that be? Things move "wearily and slow" down here. I think our noble Col. will be bitterly disappointed; It is too bad, too bad. Surely with all the troops that have been raised at the North enough might be sent here to take Charleston and hold Florida too, but it is always so. Always something lacking somewhere. One can't help feeling a little discouraged sometimes.

Am back at St. H[elena] to-night. Saw exquisite orange blossoms opening—on the Gen.'s grounds, perfuming the whole atmosphere.

Friday, Mar. 27.   After school returned to Oaklands. I see it sooner than I thought to. I shall hardly hope to see Florida now.

Monday, Mar. 30.   Dreadfully raw, disagreeable day. Very unwell with the worst cold I've had. It *stupefies* me. Who sh'ld come in, all in a shiver, but Mr. Pierce. Had a good long talk with him, over the fire, during which took occasion to ask him about that speech. He emphatically denies ever having made it. Talked a long time on the subject and the result is that we are good friends. I'll allow myself to like him now;—which is very much easier than *disliking* him, *Je vous assure, ma chére* A.

Thursday, April 2.   Drearily, drearily the days drag on. Can do nothing but knit, and that grows wearisome. Have discovered a music box that was taken from a "Secesh" house in Beaufort—A remarkably fine one. Only wants a little cleaning to be perfect. The tone is exquisite. The airs are all gems and all familiar, and oh, how they recall home. This music box is the only comfort I have just now.

Had a call to-day from Mr. [Mansfield] French, Mr. and Mrs. L[?] from N[ew] Y[ork] and Miss R[uggles]. Mr. L. I like.—an exceedingly kindly and pleasant manner. His wife has much *hauteur*. To-day, news is *good*.

They say the black soldiers fought the rebels bravely;—drove them off from J[acksonville], fired the town, and returned in triumph. They marched thro' B[eaufort] this morn. How I long to see Dr. R[ogers] and hear all from his eloquent lips. I can think of nothing but this reg[iment]. How proud of it I am!

Mr. Hunt writes to L[izzie Hunn] that he has not heard from me. Strange, when I have written to him so often. Wrote to him again to-night, again enclosing my account.²⁹

On Tuesday Mr. P[ierce] paid us another visit and took dinner and tea. Had a delightful talk with him about people, literature, politics,—everything. He gave us a very interesting account of his experiences with the "contrabands" in V[irgini]a.³⁰

. . .

Friday, April 3. This morn. had a nice little note from dear Dr. R[ogers] and a very light, pretty rocking chair, from Fl[orid]a, of course. He says he will see me soon and tell me *all*. I hope it will be very soon, indeed. I do so long to see him.

Had a long talk with one of the soldiers—a connection of the Hunns. I find that the prevailing feeling among the troops is impatience at the long delay, and also a kind of discouragement caused by the want of enthusiasm on the part of the officers. It is a sad thing to hear this. He said "it's not the soldiers' fault that something isn't done,"—and I believe it. Oh, if we c'ld only have the noble [John C.] Fremont for a leader!

Mr. Pierce came in again this afternoon, and stayed to tea. We had another nice long talk; about everything, *prejudice*, among the rest. Suspect I got rather excited and talked too much, as I always do on this subject. But how can I help it? Mr. P[ierce] gave us some very pleasant reminiscences of his first acquaintance with the noble, noble, glorious [Charles] Sumner.

Saturday, April 4. Drove . . . to our new home "Seaside."³¹ Lost the way of course, taking the wrong road thro' the woods, which detained us. Reached Seaside about noon. It is delightfully situated—When the tide is in, which is was *not* while we were there. Saw not a drop of water, nothing but marsh. The house I like. It has such an old look. The parlor is painted a kind of grey, with oak panelings and white and darker wood work interspersed, and over the chimney is quite a pretty fresco painting—a landscape. The whole room has an air of taste and elegance about it that I've not seen before, down here. There is a tolerable piano, and a delightful piazza which can be enclosed with blinds at will. That looks inviting. Altogether the house is on a much finer scale than this; and—what is far more important—the situation is a very much healthier one. So we and the store will probably move this week. Had the loveliest drive home, just at sunset.

Sunday, April 5.   Lovely day. So warm, thought I might venture to go to church. But t'was so dreadfully chilly and damp inside that I was afraid to stay. Had letters from Mr. and Mrs. [Lebaron] R[ussell] and the brightest, sunshiniest little letter from dear Mary [Shepard].

Mr. Pierce came for me to go and dine with them at The Oaks. Had another long pleasant chat with him as we drove thither. He saw dear Dr. R[ogers] yesterday. I shall certainly see him this week.

Saw Dr. [William H.] Brisbane, and listened with much interest to his account of his first convictions with regards to slavery. Shall note down some of the things he said. In 1833, he thought, he, being then editor of a paper in Charleston,[32] wrote an article defending slavery from the scriptures, in reply to an anti-slavery pamphlet which had been sent him. He thought seriously on the subject of slavery though not at all considering it as morally wrong. Some time after this, in another article, he said that *Onesimus* was not a slave. For making this simple statement he was loudly abused and threatened with lynch law. Then he made up his mind that though Ones[imus] was not a slave *he* was. And he determined to live no longer in a place where he was not allowed to express his opinions. But so far was he, at that time, from being convinced of the wrongfulness of slavery that he *sold* his slaves, and removed to Cincinnatti [*sic*]. He was there a year and a half before he became converted to anti-slavery. When that happened his conscience reproached him with having sold his slaves. He returned South, bought back his slaves, brought them North and freed them. Only one man was not bought. Do not exactly understand why except that he was old and very sickly. Suppose they tho't he w'ld not live very long. The Dr. said he always felt troubled afterward, about that man. When

197

he came down here, a few months ago, this, his former slave, was one of the first men he met,—now free and still living.

Dr. B[risbane]'s friends tho't when he proposed rebuying his slaves in order to free them, that he w'ld be wronging his son by so doing. He asked his son what *he* tho't about it, and the latter nobly replied that he w'ld rather have that deed to be proud of than all the money his father c'ld leave him.

Was much interested in listening to an old man whom Mr. P[ierce], the unwearied, was questioning. This man, Don Carlos, by name, was a slave, originally from Vir[ginia] and living here in the family of the Allston's. He knew the Gov[ernor] Allston whom Aaron Burr's daughter married, and was well acquainted with her mournful story. He also knew Mr. Pierpont when he was teaching in the Gov[ernor]'s family—teaching the sons of his second wife. Carlos has been taught to read by [him] and seems to be a man of considerable intelligence.[33] He, and afterwards, Dr. B[risbane], gave us some interesting reminiscences of the Denmark Vesey Insurrection.[34] Spent the night at The Oaks—

Tuesday, April 7.   Drove with Mrs. H[unn] to call on Miss R[uggles] who gave me some of the loveliest roses I ever saw, and an exquisite flower—the petitsporum, which is a hothouse plant at home, but is blooming out of doors here. It is deliciously fragrant—almost as delicious as orange blossoms. Had a perfectly lovely drive. The air is *delicious* to-day. Surely there is healing in it.

This eve. had notes from Dr. R[ogers] and Mr. Pierce. The latter's, indeed, was quite a letter and gives me a very interesting account of his visit to the 1st [Regiment] S[outh] C[arolina Volunteers], which is now on picket duty stationed at a plantation, about seven miles from B[eaufort].[35] My good friend Dr. R[ogers] wants me to pay them a visit, and Mr. P[ierce] very kindly offers to escort me; and as I am banished from school for a time, think I shall go. Perhaps the change will do me good.—

Oaks.—Wednesday. Apr. 8.   Mr. P[ierce] came to-day, and as he will probably be obliged to go Sat[urday] on the Arago, urged me to go to The Oaks with him this eve. From there we shall go to "Head Quarters" to-morrow. He gave me a beautiful, pearl handled knife which once belonged to Charles Sumner. How I shall treasure it. He is very good to give me anything so precious. I am *unspeakably* obliged to him.

Milne's Plantation.   Thurs. Apr. 9.   Came to B[eaufort] this morn. with Mr. P[ierce]. We were met by the news that the "Washington," one of our boats lying near the Ferry had

198

been shelled by the rebels. It has got aground.[36] Of course the news created quite a sensation. And Mr. Pierce feared at first that it might not be safe for me to go to where the regiment is stationed, which is not more than a few miles from where the boat lies. But after making some inquiries he, to my great joy, concluded that I might go for the day, but not to stay all night. I demurred not, but took my carpet bag nevertheless,—believing I sh'ld stay.

We had a lovely drive along the shell road that leads to the Ferry,[37] and Mr. P[ierce] talked very entertainingly all the way. I think I never before met a stranger with whom I c'ld talk so easily. Can't generally talk to strangers at all. But there's something in his manner—such a graceful geniality—that makes it very easy to talk with him; to say whatever comes into one's head. How delightful and June-like everything looks; how fresh and beautiful! The roadsides white with Cherokee roses which contrast beautifully with the bright green leaves around them. I have rarely enjoyed a drive so much.

Arrived at the Plantation, we found the Dr. [Seth Rogers] busy attending to the wounded from the Washington. Mrs. Dr. [Esther Hawkes] was also engaged with them, so Mr. P[ierce] and I walked to a duck pond at a little distance, and amused ourselves watching some tiny ducklings. Then he entertained me with talk about our noble Sumner whom he knows well, and quoted parts of some of his finest speeches. Did it well, too.

Then we returned the the house and had a warm welcome. Am delighted to see the Dr. looking so well. The Col. [Thomas W. Higginson] appeared at dinner. It is *good* to see him and dear Dr. R[ogers] again. After dinner Mr. P[ierce] went. I was really sorry to part with him. The Arago *may not* go till Monday. If so he will come out here on Sunday, speak to the soldiers, and take me home.

Walked with the Col. and Mr. and Mrs. D[ewhurst] in the garden, which is a delightful one. Here found some exquisite roses—a species of tea rose, I think—the most beautiful I ever saw,—and the lovely, fragrant petitsporums. Arranged a basket for the Col. Then we went to the Dr.'s sunny little room;— The Dr. [Seth Rogers], the Col. [T. W. Higginson], Mrs. D[ewhurst], the Chaplain [James H. Fowler] and I,—and sat around the beautiful blazing fire talking very pleasantly. How I have enjoyed this first night here.

Friday, Apr. 10. How perfectly lovely it is to-day. This morn. walked round the grounds. There are lovely trees all around. The situation is delightful but do not like it quite so well as Camp Saxton. Miss the water. Around the house are lovely locust trees now in full bloom. The air is laden with their fragrance.

Went to ride with Dr. R[ogers] on the nicest of roans. He canters splendidly. Rode to Seabrook, where Mr. Follen is superintendent.[38] Was very glad to see him. He is very gentlemanly and agreeable, though somewhat peculiar in manner. His place is pleasantly situated. From the piazza one sees a beautiful arch formed by two trees at the end of a short avenue which leads to the water's edge. Some of the 1st Reg[iment] are on picket duty here. We rode along the water's edge to a point whence they say the rebels are frequently to be seen on the other side. But to my great regret saw not one. Visited two other plantations, and had a delightful ride home.

This afternoon went out to see the Dress Parade. There were about six companies. The others are stationed at different points on picket duty.

This eve played euchre with Mrs. D[ewhurst], Dr. R[ogers], and Dr. M[inor].[39]

Oh I must not forget to tell you, dear A. that yesterday on our way hither, we met Col. Montgomery with some of his men.[40] I've long wanted to see the Kansas hero. He is tall, muscular, with a shrewd face, browned and wrinkled. I like his look of quiet determination. Dr. R[ogers] tells me that although so full of fearless enthusiasm, he is very economical of human life,—never allowing his men rashly to throw away their lives.

In talking with the officers I find the feeling of deep disappointment general because of their being obliged to leave Florida just as they had obtained a foothold there. They are sure they c'ld have held Jacksonville with perfect security. They had driven the enemy back, and burnt the railroad for several miles. There are two gunboats constantly stationed at the mouth of the St. John's which c'ld just as well have been brought up for their protection, and that w'ld have been sufficient for their protection. I think this last order of Gen. Hunter has created universal dissatisfaction. It is too bad. As Dr. R[ogers] says "it is a sad putting off of the day of deliverance for the oppressed."

Saturday, Apr. 11. Had a perfect ride to-day with Col. H[igginson] and Dr. R[ogers]. Went to Rose's plantation, and Capers. There the Col. left us to go on board one of the gun boats. Dr. R[ogers] and I rode on to Barnwell's [Plantation], which is the most beautiful place I have yet seen. It is filled with magnificent live oaks, magnolias, and other trees. Saw there a grand old oak said to be the largest on the islands, some of its branches have been cut off, but the circumference of those remaining is more than a hundred feet. It is a wonderful tree. The grounds slope down to the water—Broad River, and here again we went to a point whence the rebels are sometimes to be seen and though we, and one of the black soldiers, strained our eyes we c'ld discover none.

How shall I tell you, dear A. about our ride home first through an avenue of beautiful trees—mostly live oaks draped with moss—and then for miles and miles through the Pine Barrens. The air was soft, Italian, only a low faint murmur c'ld be heard among the pines,—hardly "the slow song of the sea." The ground was thickly carpeted with ferns of a most delicious green, and to crown all we found Azaleas of a deep pink color and perfect fragrance. Found also sand violets, very large purple ones, and some kind of grass which bears an exquisite fine white flower, some of the petals just tinged with a delicate lilac. The flower is a little like spicea. We rode slowly through the Barrens. I think I never enjoyed anything so perfectly, I *luxuriated* in it. It was almost "too much, too much." Dr. R[ogers] and I had a long and interesting talk. How kind, how good he is! It is very pleasant to know he cared so much for me, even although I *know* he thinks far better of me than I deserve. The brightest and most delightful experiences must come to an end, and at last but too soon we emerged from the Pine Barrens and came out into the shell road. It was like leaving Paradise. Yet this is a very pleasant road, too. Noticed the finest live oak, almost the finest, I ever saw. Not quite so large as the Barnwell, but far more beautiful. Found also the most exquisite white violets I ever saw—such delicate, wonderful penciling. They were fragrant too. Had a good canter on the nice hard road.

On reaching home we were met by the news that the rebels were supposed to be bringing up pontoon bridges, were expected to make an attempt to cross [the Coosaw River] near the Ferry, at a place about two miles distant from here. The news created quite a little excitement. The Col. [T. W. Higginson] had not yet returned. A messenger was dispatched for him, and another to Gen. Saxton at B[eaufort] that gunboats and artillery may be sent up. Capt. [James S.] Rogers seems to enjoy the prospect of a fight, promises me I shall see a shell this afternoon.—The Col. has now returned. Couriers are coming in every few minutes. One of the Sup[erintenden]t's whose place is near the Ferry has been watching thro' his glass the movements opposite, and reports that the rebels are gathering in large force.[41] Meanwhile I sit composedly down taking notes; and shall now occupy myself with darning a pair of stockings for the doctor until something further occurs which is *writable*. Have no fear.

Night. Finished the stockings, then took a pleasant walk with Dr. Minor in the garden; where we discovered a lovely magnolia just opened, some perfect rosebuds, and a *strawberry* nearly ripe. At supper everybody in good spirits, gay and cheerful. We heard that the gunboats had arrived,[42] and all this eve at intervals, we hear the guns. Did not know at first which side they were on, but am incapable of fear. Can hear plainly the explosion of shells. Are sure now that the firing is from our gunboats. Being so very near us, of course it sounds heavy. The Col. has just been reading me (a magnificent reader he is) some of the ballads of the old Cavaliers. How grand, how stirring they are. And how Rob[er]t *Browning* is too. Afterward the Dr. read me a little of the "Faerie Queene" and then some letters which have just come. The battery has arrived from Beaufort. And I am told young Mr. Merriam of Boston is here.[43] He is always ready for a fight. Mrs. D[ewhurst] and I will now composedly retire. We don't fear an attack; but if it comes—why let it. Our men will fight bravely we know. As for myself, I do not fear. W'ld far rather be killed than that our noble Col. [Higginson] or the equally noble and good Dr. R[ogers] should be.

This has been an exciting day, I have enjoyed it, yes truly enjoyed it. The Arago sailed this morn. So I shall not see my good friend Mr. P[ierce] again, for which I am sorry. Regret very much that he will not be here to-morrow to speak to the soldiers. I like so much his kind genial way of speaking to these people, and Dr. R[ogers] says he does too. It gives them entire confidence in him. He has promised to call and see grandmother [in Philadelphia]. I am very glad.

Sunday, Apr. 12. Slept more soundly last night than I have before. Was only wakened once or twice by couriers coming "in hot haste." That was all. Woke quite late, to find a lovely morning.

Dr. Minor and I had a grand ride. Same programme as yesterday—Rose's Capers' and then Barnwells'; thence another perfect ride thro' the Pine Barrens. Found exquisite white azaleas this time, and the largest violets I've yet seen. T'was a lovely, dreamy kind of morning—half sunlight, half shade. How exquisite the shades of green are now. The bright, fresh green of the young oaks and plums, and gum trees contrasting most beautifully with the dark, sombre pines. I think the air to-day must be like that of Italy. Had a pleasant talk with Dr.

Minor. He is very young, full of enthusiasm and courage. I like him much. Dr. R[ogers] has a very high opinion of him. There's something so earnest, singlehearted about him. He has talent, too. Lives in Conn[ecticut] now. Was born in Ceylon he tells me. I enjoyed hearing him talk about that far away island. Rode his horse, a noble, spirited fellow, but gentle as can be. He canters splendidly; but a little more roughly than the roan I've ridden hitherto. The Col. [T. W. Higginson] has a splendid horse, Rinoldo. So has the Dr. [Seth Rogers]. They came from Florida. Had nearly four hours ride.

Got home just so as to miss seeing Gens. Hunter and Saxton, who have been paying us a visit. Wanted to see Gen. H[unter]. Found that Mr. Judd had come . . . to take me to B[eaufort]. And so unwillingly had to take my leave. How very, very much I have enjoyed this visit. Have promised the Col. that when another person can be found to take my place in school here, I will come and teach the soldiers. I shall be glad to do it. Found it hard to leave my kind friend Dr. R[ogers]. He has been very good to me.

Had a pleasant drive to B[eaufort] with Mr. J[udd] and Miss R[uggles]. Passed the fortifications which are quite complete now. There was a Negro funeral at the burying grounds. We c'ld see the crowd of people and hear them singing hymns;— not their own beautiful hymns, I am sorry to say. I do so fear these will be superseded by ours, which are poor in comparison, and which they do not sing well at all. From B[eaufort] saw Gen. Hunter in the street, but had not a good look at him.

The Oaks. Monday, morn. Apr. 13. Came hither[44] last eve., and spent the night. In the night was sure I heard some one try my door. Asked "Who's there?" No answer. The noise was repeated—the question asked again. Still no answer. Woke Miss W[are] who had the adjoining room. She lit the candle and we took our revolvers,—all ready for rebels. Waited awhile. Then as all continued quiet, put our pistols under our heads and composed ourselves to sleep. The wind or rats, I supposed afterward. At first I was sure it was some person but thought it more likely to be a robber than a rebel.

Oaklands—Night. Have had a wearisome day at school. So many little ones. And nearly all in a state of rebellion, owing to their teacher's long absence. Had some newspapers, but no letters, which disappoints me greatly. Spent the eve. in writing.

Tuesday, Apr. 14. Windy, disagreeable day. Very small school. How deliciously fragrant the air is now with orange blossoms. They've been open a week. Roses too in full bloom.

We have some superb buds in our garden. The largest I ever saw; and of an exquisite color—something between a pink and a buff.

To-night it is rumored that there are rebels—cavalry—on the island. I do not believe it. It is said they can blow brandy into their horses' noses and that will enable them to swim a long distance. And so it is tho't they may have been able to cross from Edisto over some of the little creeks. There's no probability of it. Mrs. H[unn] is somewhat alarmed. Reports are most numerous here, always. So it is better not to believe them at all.

Some rebels were nicely caught a few days ago. They were at a picket station on or near Edisto. Capt. Dutch of the King-fisher,[45] hearing that they were there from a Negro, one of their servants, went with some of his men to the house and took them all prisoners. There were nine or ten of them.— The aristocracy of the islands. Am delighted to think they were taken.

Seaside. Wednesday, Apr. 15. After school rode to "Sea-side" on my faithful horse—Edisto. Shall take up my abode here for the present. Had a delightful ride hither through the woods. Enjoyed it perfectly. House is still barely furnished, and has rather a comfortless look; but I suppose it will soon seem like home. Tis fortunate that one gets easily accustomed to these changes. Tis pleasant to have a piano, though it is a poor one.

Saturday, Apr. 18. Had a pleasant little ride to Dr. White's, a plantation a few miles from here. The grounds must once have been beautiful, but have a somewhat decayed look now. The house is rather poor looking though large. Tis painted a dull red, in which it differs from the other houses down here, most of which are white. Edisto went with great spirit to-day— quite distinguished himself—passed the other horses with as-tonishing ease.

Sunday, Apr. 19. Went to church, and afterward to Oak-lands where we dined. Mr. Tomlinson who is now Gen. Sup[er-intendent] instead of Mr. Soule (who has resigned and gone home) dined with us.[46] I enjoyed his society very much. He is so genial and happy. Makes sunshine wherever he goes. And is also deeply interested in the people here. Think he will make a splendid Sup[erintendent].

Saturday, Apr. 25. All this week have ridden to school on horseback and enjoyed it very much though Ed[isto] is rather rough.

Yesterday had a very kind letter from B. P. Hunt.

To-day went on horseback with L[izzie] and Mrs. B[?] to the village which is about eight miles from here.[47] Had a lovely ride through June woods;—the air laden with the fragrance of the locust; the birds singing merrily, the golden sunlight pouring its flood of beauty upon the delicious green of the young leaves. The village is delightfully situated on quite a large and pleasant stream of water. The ladies upon whom we went to call were not at home, but Lieut. B[?] was there, and we dined with him, then walked around under the trees and enjoyed the water.

Had a lovely ride home through the pines just at sunset. The beauty of these wonderful days sinks deep, deep, into my soul.

The people on the place have grand "shouts." They are most inspiring. Went to one Thursday night. There is an old blind man, Maurice, who has a truly wonderful voice, so strong and clear.—It rings out like a trumpet. One song—"Gabriel blow the Trumpet"—was the grandest thing I have yet heard. And with what fire and enthusiasm the old blind man led off. He seemed inspired.

Sunday, Apr. 26. After church dined at Oaklands and had another perfect ride home through the woods. Ah how I revel in these days. They are almost "too much, too much."

This eve. attended in the "Praise House," the grandest shout I have yet seen. Several of the soldiers who had come home on a visit joined in the shout with great spirit. The whole thing was quite inspiring. How thoroughly Mr. [Charles P.] W[are] enjoyed it, too. I like him exceedingly. He is such a thoroughly good abolitionist—a friend of Mr. Garrison's too—so *of course* I like him. He is very intelligent, gentlemanly and pleasant. He is Sup[erintenden]t of our plan[tation] and now lives with us.

Wednesday, Apr. 29. Last night Capt. D[utch] and one or two others called. The Capt. came to make arrangements for our accompanying him to Edisto. He is going to take every precaution for our safety. But as Lieut. B[?] says there are 5000 Union troops on the island I sh'ldn't think there'd be any danger. I am not afraid, at any rate, I think I sh'ld enjoy going very much. We are to go to the village early to-morrow morning, and thence take boats to the Kingfisher, Capt. D[utch]'s boat.

Thursday, Apr. 30. Fast Day. Started this morn. with Mrs. B[?] and L[izzie Hunn] to go to the village, but my poor horse was too sick to go. I myself felt far from well, so gave up the expedition and went to Oaklands,—thence to church, where young Mr. W[are] preached. There was but a small attendance. Am housekeeper now that the others have gone—No sinecure

—for it is not easy to get anything to eat. Barely escape starvation. Tis fortunate that we shall have our rations in a few days.[48]

Friday, May 1. A lovely May Day. Sunny and bright—not unpleasantly warm. Rode . . . this morn. to visit Mr. Sumner's school.[49] Found but a very small attendance. Just missed one class, and was too soon for the first, which comes in the afternoon. Am sorry to have missed it. Mr. S[umner] is very witty and original. Don't know half the time, however, whether he is in jest or earnest—which is provoking. . . .

Rode a nice little horse belonging to one of the men. It canters very fast—has a swift bounding motion which is most exhilarating. Her name is Linda. Shall hire her, and let my poor Jeanie have a good rest before I use her again.

This is a glorious moonlight night. From the window I can see the water in silver waves shining in the clear soft light. Sat a long time on the piazza listening to the low tones of the piano or the equally musical murmur of the wind in the tree tops, and thinking of some loved ones who are far, far away. How old memories crowd around one on such nights as these! And how dreamy, strange and unreal the present seems. Here on the piazza of this old southern house I sit and think of friends a thousand miles away—of scenes that have past, never, never to return again. Shall I ever see the dear ones "up North" I wonder? Something answers "never" but for to-night at least, I will not listen to that voice. Here the fleas interpose. Farewell to all reminiscences. Now for tortures unendurable! Oh the *fleas*!! the fleas!! The fleas!!

Sunday, May 3. Too weary and ill to go to church, which I regretted for I always like to see the people, looking so bright and cheerful in their Sunday attire, and to hear them sing. . . . The people, after "Praise" had one of their grandest shouts, and L[izzie] and I, in a dark corner of the Praise House, amused ourselves with practicing a little. It is wonderful what perfect time the people keep with hands, feet, and indeed with every part of the body. I enjoy these "shouts" very much.

Oaks, Wednesday, May 6. Miss M[urray] and I spent the day in procuring flowers and decorating the church for Miss Nellie's [?] marriage. She is to be married to-morrow. Arranged three bouquets for the pulpit and twined ivy around the little pillars supporting it; while Miss M[urray] arranged beautiful hanging baskets for each side of the pupit and another for the table. The church has been nicely cleaned by some of the people. To-night have been very busy arranging flowers for the house. Such exquisite roses! It is a real happiness to work among them. We had a tub partly filled with most exquisite flowers. I felt rich as a queen.

Thursday, May 7. Miss N[ellie] and Mr. F[?] were married to-day. The little church was quite pretty in its dress of flowers, and the bride in her pure white muslin was, of course, most lovely. Nearly all the Superintendents and teachers were there, and the bride's scholars, and the older people from the Oaks. Was sorry there were not more of the freed people there. T'was a very quiet wedding. I think it will prove a happy marriage. How beautifully Miss T[owne] decorated the table at the Oaks, to-day. All the cakes were wreathed with lovely flowers—and *the* bride cake—which came from Boston was completely imbedded in pure white roses.—Well—a day! After all a marriage is a solemn thing. The more I think of it the more I am impressed with its solemnity. Think *I* sh'ld dread a funeral much less. . . .

Sunday, May 10. Went to church. Taught Sunday School. Had letters from Aunt M[argaretta] and Mary S[hepard]. And a pamphlet from Mr. Pierce;—his speech before the Legislature. He called at our house in Phila[delphia]. Aunt M[argaretta] writes that they were delighted with him. Mr. McK[im] thinks I did him good, which is certainly absurd, to say the least.

Monday, May 11. Recommended school to-day. We had vacation last week on account of Miss N[ellie's] wedding. The church looks bright, clean and cheerful now.

Sunday, May 17. Did not attend church. This eve. had a lovely ride on horseback with Mr. [Arthur] S[umner]. How witty and entertaining he is. . . .

Monday, May 18. After school rode to Mr. T[horpe]'s with L[izzie]. . . . Returning Mr. T[horpe] . . . came with us. T'was *intensely* dark. I rode Mr. T[horpe]'s horse, a splendid, swift, high spirited creature. C'ld hardly hold him. But enjoyed the ride exceedingly. I like Mr. T[horpe]. Report says that he more than likes me. But I *know* it is not so. Have never had the least reason to think it. Although he is very good and liberal he is still an *American,* and w'ld of course never be so insane as to love one of the proscribed race. The rumor,—like many others is entirely absurd and without the shadow of a foundation. How strange it seemed riding to-night through the woods —often in such perfect darkness we c'ld see nothing—how strange and wild! I liked it.

Found, at home, to my great pleasure my friend Dr. R[ogers]. . . . Dr. R[ogers] brought me a letter from our Col. [Higginson] who thinks it best I sh'ld not join the reg[iment]

207

just now. He fears scandal. There have been of late very scandalous reports of some of the ladies down here, so of course as usual, *all* must suffer to some extent. I am very sorry, and so are the Col. and Dr. It is most annoying that one sh'ld be prevented from doing what one feels to be one's duty just because Mrs. Grundy will not mind her own affairs.

Friday, May 22. Weather still continues intensely hot. Find driving or riding to school between ten and eleven A.M. very fatiguing. Fear, sometimes, I shall not be able to stand it. Had delightful letters to-day from Mr. Pierce and dear Mary S[hepard]. . . .

Wednesday, June 3. Spent last night at The Oaks, and this morn. went, with the household to the Village. There we found Capt. D[utch] awaiting us with boats. This morn. was clear and delightful. Had a lovely row to the "Kingfisher." Tis a delightful floating palace; everything perfectly ordered and elegant. The officers were all very kind and polite; and I enjoyed listening to their explanations about the guns. Dined there; then, about three started in two row boats for Edisto. Mr. Rhoades,[50] one of the officers, accompanied us, and the boats' crews—sailors from the ship, armed with guns and cutlasses. There was no actual danger, but still, as Mr. R[hodes] said we were going into the enemy's country, so it was best to take every precaution, against surprise.[51]

Reached Edisto near sunset. Went to a part called Eddingsville, which was a favorite summer resort of the aristocracy of the island. It has a fine beach several miles long. The houses have a dismal deserted look. We walked along the lovely beach, preceded at some distance by armed sailors who explored some distance, and returned to report "all quiet, and nobody to be seen," so we walked on fearlessly. Gathered tiny and beautiful shells which were buried deep in the sands, and saw for the first time a shark's egg, which looks like an oblong piece of India rubber. The absence of stones here, as on all of these islands strikes one as very singular—especially in contrast with our stony, rocky N[ew] E[ngland] Coasts.

Night approached and we retraced our steps to make preparations for supper. As we approached the house saw one of the most singular sights I ever saw. From a very dark cloud in the sky the most vivid flashes of lightning were continually breaking. There seemed not a second's pause between the flashes. And they assumed a variety of singular forms each succeeding one being more dazzling than the other. This wonderful display lasted some time, and impressed us all very much. All around this dark cloud, the sky flushed with the loveliest, rosy sunset hues. It was a sight not soon to be forgotten.

One of the men found a table for us which was placed in a room of the deserted house in which we intended to spend the night, and was soon spread with the eatables which we had brought with us. For seats we used bureau drawers, turned up edgewise. Had a very merry supper. Afterward sat for awhile on the piazza in the lovely moonlight, then had another delightful stroll on the beach. How very, very lovely it was. I did not want to go in at all. But there was my good friend and physician Miss T[owne] to preach prudence to me, so at an unreasonably early hour—I thought—we went in to bed. We four ladies occupied one room, and the three gentlemen the other. The marines were stationed in the adjoining house, in which they had lighted a large fire, and they danced about the room and sang and shouted to their hearts' content.

Thursday, June 4. We, of course had no beds, but made ourselves as comfortable as we c'ld on the floor with boat cushions, blankets and shawls. We had no fear of rebels. There was but one road by which they c'ld get to us and on that a watch was kept. So, despite the mosquitoes, we had a good sound night's sleep.

After breakfast we explored the house, but found nothing in it except the remains of a bureau, and a bedstead. Afterward, while the others were packing up their things I went down to the shore, and sitting there alone had a long delightful communion with Old Ocean. The morning air was fresh and pure, and merrily the waves leaped and sparkled in the bright sunlight, or softly they kissed the shore with that low, sweet murmur which is the most musical of all sounds. It was very pleasant, and I was sorry enough to be summoned away.

We took our boats again, and followed the most winding little creek I ever saw. In and out, in and out, our boats went. Sometimes it seemed as if we were going into the very heart of the woods. How easy it w'ld have been for rebels secreted behind those thick bushes to fire into us! But there chanced to be none in that region. Sometimes—so narrow was the stream— we got aground, and it was hard work to pull out of the thick marsh grass. But at last we reached our journey's end—the Eddings plantation, whither some of the people had preceded us in their search for corn. This must once have been a beautiful place. The grounds were evidently laid out with great taste and are filled with beautiful trees, among which I noticed particularly the magnolia tree with its wonderful white blossoms, large, pure, dazzlingly white as they shone among the rich, dark, shining leaves. The garden was filled with lovely flowers. We explored the house, but found nothing but rubbish, and an old bedstead, and a very good bathing tub—which Lieut. R[?] graciously consented to my appropriating. It is quite a treasure in these regions. I must not forget the lovely oleanders, of which we brought away great bouquets. But when we went down to the shore to take our boats, lo! the tide had gone down so that the boats c'ld not be brought up to the landing, and between us and them was the marsh covered with water too deep for us to walk through, too shallow for the boats. What was to be done? Mr. T[horpe] rolled his pantaloons up, took off boots and stockings, and waded across. Lieut. R. and Mr. F[?] were each carried across on the back of a sailor. But what were we ladies to do? Suddenly the bathing tub suggested itself to somebody. A brilliant idea, and one eagerly acted upon. Mrs. F[?] and I, successively, seated ourselves in the tub which was raised to the shoulders of four stout sailors, and so, triumphantly, we were borne across. But through a mistake the tub was not sent back for Misses T[owne] and M[urray] and they had to be brought over on the crossed hands of some of the sailors, in the "carry a lady to London" style, where at we were all greatly amused.

Back again we rowed, through the creek, out of the creek, into the open sea—among the grand, exhilarating breakers. Well tossed we were, and Mr. T[horpe] and I both feeling just a *little* apprehensive of sea-sickness, kept exceedingly quiet. However, being very hungry we ate pound cake and drank lemonade—though in fear and trembling. We were pleasantly disappointed by finding ourselves better afterward, and so agreed that we had found, in pound cake and lemonade, the true prevention of that most dismal of all sicknesses—seasickness.

We reached the "Kingfisher" at last. Miss T[owne] and Miss M[urray] being sick, preferred returning home at once. . . . But the hospitable Capt. [Dutch] w'ld insist on Mr. T[horpe] and I staying to dine with him. While waiting for dinner, he took me over every part of the ship, into all the storerooms, in the medical department, and even into the kitchen. And throughout all the arrangements were perfect, and seemed more like those of an elegantly appointed house than of a ship. We dined with the Capt. and other officers, and were elegantly entertained. In the afternoon we bade farewell to the "Kingfisher" and its gentlemanly and hospitable officers, and were rowed across with the Capt. in his own beautiful "gig" to St. Helena. It was a lovely sunset row, which I enjoyed perfectly. Tired enough when we arrived there.

Mr. T[horpe] drove me to the Oaks, on which occasion I proved myself an exceedingly entertaining companion—going to sleep long before we reached there—having seated myself in the bottom of the buggy with my head on the seat—and sleeping most profoundly till I was waked by Mr. T[horpe] on our arrival at The Oaks.

A few more words about Edisto. It was, as everybody knows, at one time in the possession of our troops, but was afterward evacuated by them—why, I know not,—most people here think it a blunder. At the time of its evacuation the freed people were removed to the adjoining islands—many of them to St. Helena. They were very reluctant to leave their beautiful home. Only the fear of again falling into the hands of the "Secesh" induced them to do it. And they still have a warm attachment for it, and cherish the hope that they may one day return to it in safety. As we drove through the island, yesterday, on our way to the village, the people came around the carriage, and eagerly inquired "Is you gwine to Edisto?" "Shall we give your love to Edisto?" asked Miss T[owne]. "Oh yes, yes, please misses!" And when we came back they asked us "How does Edisto stan'?"

Tuesday, June 30.   Nearly a month since I have written to you, dear A. The intense heat must plead my excuse. Day after day I have driven home from school, thoroughly exhausted, and gone to bed there to remain till dark. In the evenings we have a good breeze generally. Were it not for that I think we c'ld not live through the heat. We spend our evenings on the piazza, sitting up quite late generally in fear of the fleas, which torture us so that bed, to me at least, is almost unendurable—sleep almost impossible.

This eve . . . I rode with Col. G[ilmore][52] down to see the 54th Mass[achusetts Regiment] which is encamped at Land's End.[53] We were caught in a thunder shower, which prevented the Reg[iment] from having its Dress Parade and spent the time in Major H[allowell]'s tent.[54] It was very pleasant to see my old friend J[ames] W[alton][55] again. He is a Lieut. in the 54th. But surely he is not strong enough to be a soldier. . . . Col. G[illmore] insisted on our taking tea with him. Then we must stop to play whist, so it was midnight when we got home. Had a delightful ride in the bright moonlight. Heard the mocking birds singing as we rode along. Sometimes they sing all night.

Thursday, July 2.   Col. Shaw and Major H[allowell] came

to take tea with us, and afterward stayed to the shout.[56] Lieut. W[alton] was ill, and c'ld not come. I am perfectly charmed with Col. S[haw]. He seems to me in every way one of the most delightful persons I have ever met. There is something girlish about him, and yet I never saw anyone more manly. To me he seems a thoroughly lovable person. And there is something so exquisite about him. The perfect breeding, how evident it is. Surely he must be a worthy son of such noble parents.[57] I have seen him but once, yet I cannot help feeling a really affectionate admiration for him.

We had a very pleasant talk on the moonlit piazza, and then went to the Praise House to see the shout. I was delighted to find that it was one of the very best and most spirited that we had had. The Col. [Robert Shaw] looked and listened with the deepest interest, and after it was over, expressed himself much gratified. He said, he w'ld like to have some of the hymns to send home. I shall be only too glad to copy them for him. Old Maurice surpassed himself to-night in singing "The Talles' Tree in Paradise." He got much excited and his gestures were really quite tragic. I c'ld see with what astonishment and interest our guests watched the old blind man.

Saturday, July 4. Had a very pleasant celebration to-day. The people and children all assembled in the grove around the Baptist Church. The old flag was hung across the road between two magnificent live oaks, and the children being grouped under it sang The Star-Spangled Banner—which we had taught them for that occasion. Then addresses were made by Mr. Pierce,[58] Mr. Lynch (a colored minister)[59] and other gentlemen, there was more singing by the chlidren and by the people, who made the grove resound with the grand tones of "Roll, Jordan, Roll." Then they were all treated to molasses and water—a great luxury to them—and hard tack.

Among others from Beaufort, Mrs. Lander,[60] and Mr. Page, the [New York] Tribune Correspondent were there.[61] I had met them before—they had called to see me—and Mrs. L[ander] insisted on my returning to B[eaufort] with them; promising that I sh'ld see Col. H[igginson] and Dr. R[ogers]. Of course the temptation was strong, and I went. Mrs. L[ander] seems to be a person of a great deal of character, and beneath the stage manner there is a real warmth and kindness of heart which are very attractive. Before we drove to the Ferry we— that is Mrs. L[ander], Mr. P[age], and I ensconced ourselves very comfortably under a great tree and had a charming picnic dinner. Then Mrs. L[ander] read us Buchanan Read's exquisite poem "Drifting."[62] She reads, of course, very finely.

A long drive to the ferry, made tolerable only by being in Mrs. L[ander]'s easy carriage, then a pleasant row across in the Gen's handsome "gig" and we were at B[eaufort]. Spent a delightful eve. with Dr. [Rogers] and Col. [Higginson]. We had been much disappointed in not having the Colonel at our celebration.[63] He was engaged to make an oration before a Penn [sylvania] regiment. In the eve. he came in to Mrs. L[ander]'s and we asked him what he said. "Well I don't remember everything" he said "but at the close I know I told them that we of the 1st S[outh] C[arolina Regiment] had no ill-feeling towards them, we had no prejudice against color, and like white people just as well as black—if they behaved as well! Evidently they were well pleased with these remarks as they applauded them more loudly than anything else I said." The patriotic people of Beaufort sent up three or four rockets that night—and that was all the celebration of the Fourth that I saw there. The Col. [T. W. Higginson] and I had a pleasant walk along the bank.

Sunday, July 5. Too unwell to-day for anything but lying down, and so missed the horseback ride I was to have had with Mrs. L[ander] who is a splendid horsewoman, and Mr. Page. Mrs. L[ander] took kind care of me, and in the afternoon I felt a little better. Had a visit from Mr. Pierce, whom it is always pleasant to see. Dr. R[ogers] spent the eve. with me. How very, very good and noble he is!

Monday, July 6. Came up from B[eaufort] to Land's End to-day in the "Hunter." Mr. Pierce kindly accompanied me on shore, and helped me into my most unique and ancient looking vehicle,—which the soldiers greeted with shouts of laughter, and styled the "Calathumpian." Drove hours, changed horses, and drove to school.

After school, though very tired, did not neglect my invitation to tea with the officers of the 54th. Drove down to Land's End. ... Met Col. G[illmore] who went with us.[64] Were just in time to see the Dress Parade. Tis a splendid looking reg[iment]—an honor to the race. Then we went with Col. Shaw to tea. Afterward sat outside the tent, and listened to some very fine singing from some of the privates. Their voices blended beautifully. "Jubilo" is one of the best things I've heard lately.

I am more than ever charmed with the noble little Col. [Shaw]. What purity, what nobleness of soul, what exquisite gentleness in that beautiful face! As I look at it I think "The bravest are the tenderest." I can imagine what he must be to his mother. May his life be spared to her! Yesterday at the celebration he stood, leaning against our carriage and speaking of mother, so lovingly, so tenderly. He said he wished she c'ld be there. If the reg[iment] were going to be stationed there for some time he sh'ld send for her. "But you know," he said "we might be suddenly ordered away, and then she w'ld have nobody to take care of her." I do think he is a wonderfully lovable person. To-night, he helped me on my horse, and after carefully arranging the folds of my riding skirt, said, so kindly, "Good-bye. If I don't see you again down here I hope to see you at our house." But I hope I shall have the pleasure of seeing him many times even down here. He and his men are eager to be called into active service.

Major H[allowell] rode with L[izzie] and me to Col. G[illmore]'s tent. . . . The rest of the party played whist till a very late hour but I was thoroughly exhausted. Lay down part of the time. And part of the time sat close to the water's edge, and watched the boats, and the gleaming lights over the water, and the rising moon. A deep peace was over everything—not a sound to be heard but the low, musical murmur of the waves as they kissed the shore.

Wednesday, July 8. Mr. T[omlinson] came over and drove down to Land's End for Lieut. [James] W[alton] who is still quite ill. The reg[iment] has gone.[65] Left this morning. My heart-felt prayers go with them—for the men and for their noble, noble young Colonel. God bless him! God keep him in His care, and grant that his men may do nobly and prove themselves worthy of him!

Monday, July 20. For nearly two weeks we have waited, oh how anxiously for news of our reg[iment] which went, we know to Morris Is[land] to take part in the attack on Charleston.[66] To-night comes news, oh, so sad, so heart sickening. It is too terrible, too terrible to write. We can only hope it may not all be true. That our noble, beautiful young Colonel is killed, and the reg[iment] cut to pieces! I cannot, cannot believe it. And yet I know it may be so. But oh, I am stunned, sick at heart. I can scarcely write. There was an attack on Fort Wagner. The 54th put in advance; fought bravely, desperately, but was finally overpowered and driven back after getting into the Fort. Thank Heaven! they fought bravely! And oh, I still must hope that our colonel, *ours* especially he seems to me, is not killed. But I can write no more to-night.

Beaufort, July 21. Came to town to-day hearing that nurses were sadly needed. Went to Mrs. L[ander]'s. Found Col.

H[igginson] and Dr. R[ogers] there. Mrs. L[ander] was sure I sh'ld not be able to endure the fatigues of hospital life even for a few days, but I thought differently, and the Col. and Dr. were both on my side. So at last Mrs. L[ander] consented and made arrangements for my entering one of the hospitals to-morrow.

It is sad to see the Col. [T. W. Higginson] at all feeble. He is usually so very strong and vigorous. He is going North next week. The Dr. [Seth Rogers] is looking very ill. He is quite exhausted. I shall not feel at peace until he is safe in his northern home. The attachment between these two is beautiful, both are so thoroughly good and noble. And both have the rarest charm of manner.

Wednesday, July 22. My hospital life began to-day. Went early this morning with Mrs. L[ander] and Mrs. G[?], the Surgeon's wife, saw that the Dr. had not finished dressing the wounds, and while I waited below Mrs. [Rufus] S[axton] gave me some sewing to do—mending the pantaloons and jackets of the poor fellows. (They are all of the 54th) It was with a full heart that I sewed up bullet holes and bayonet cuts. Sometimes I found a jacket that told a sad tale—so torn to pieces that it was far past mending. After awhile I went through the wards. As I passed along I thought "Many and low are the pallets, but each is the face of a friend." And I was surprised to see such cheerful faces looking up from the beds. Talked a little with some of the patients and assisted Mrs. G. in distributing medicines. Mrs. L[ander] kindly sent her carriage for me and I returned home, weary, but far more pleasantly impressed than I had thought possible, with hospital life.

Thursday, July 23. Said farewell to Col. H[igginson] who goes North in the Arago to-day. Am very sorry that Dr. R[ogers] c'ld not go with him, not having been able to get his papers. He is looking so ill. It makes me very anxious. He goes to Seaside for a few days. I hope the change, and Mrs. H[unn]'s kind care will do him good.

Took a more thorough survey of the hospital to-day. It is a large new brick building—quite close to the water,—two-storied, many windowed, and very airy—in every way well adapted for a hospital.

Yesterday I was employed part of the time in writing letters for the men. It was pleasant to see the brave, cheerful, uncomplaining spirit which they all breathed. Some of the poor fellows had come from the far west—even so far as Michigan. Talked with them much to-day. Told them that we had heard that their noble Colonel [Shaw] was not dead, but had been

215

taken prisoner by the rebels. How joyfully their wan faces lighted up! They almost started from their couches as the hope entered their souls. Their attachment to their gallant young colonel is beautiful to see. How warmly, how enthusiastically they speak of him. "He was one of the best little men in the world," they said. "No one c'ld be kinder to a set of men than he was to us." Brave grateful hearts! I hope they will ever prove worthy of such a leader. And God grant that he may indeed be living. But I fear, I greatly fear it may be but a false report.

One poor fellow here interests me greatly. He is very young, only nineteen, comes from Michigan. He is very badly wounded—in both legs, and there is a ball—in the stomach— it is thought that it cannot be extracted. This poor fellow suffers terribly. His groans are pitiful to hear. But he utters no complaint, and it is touching to see his gratitude for the least kindness that one does him. Mrs. G[?] asked him if he w'ld like her to write to his home. But he said no. He was an only son, and had come away against his mother's will. He w'ld not have her written to until he was better. Poor fellow! that will never be in this world.[67]

Another, a Sergeant, suffers great pain, being badly wounded in the leg. But he too lies perfectly patient and uncomplaining. He has such a good, honest face. It is pleasant to look at it— although it is black. He is said to be one of the best and bravest men in the regiment.

When I went in this morning and found my patients so cheerful some of them even quite merry, I tho't it c'ld not be possible that they were badly wounded. Many, indeed have only flesh wounds. But there are others—and they among the most uncomplaining—who are severely wounded;—some dangerously so. Brave fellows! I feel it a happiness, an honor, to do the slightest service for them. True they were unsuccessful in the attack on Fort Wagner. But that was no fault of theirs. It is the testimony of all that they fought bravely as man can fight, and that it was only when completely overwhelmed by superior numbers that they were driven back.

Friday, July 24. To-day the news of Col. Shaw's death is confirmed. There can no longer be any doubt. It makes me sad, sad at heart. They say he sprang upon the parapet of the fort and cried "Onward, my brave boys, onward"; then fell, pierced with wounds. I know it was a glorious death. But oh, it is hard, very hard for the young wife, so late a bride,[68] for the invalid mother, whose only and most dearly loved son he was,—that heroic mother who rejoiced in the position which he occupied as colonel of a colored regiment. My heart bleeds for her. His death is a very sad loss to us. I recall him as a much loved friend. Yet I saw him but a few times. Oh what must it be to the wife and the mother. Oh it is terrible. It seems very, very hard that the best and the noblest must be the earliest called away. Especially has it been so throughout this dreadful war.

Mr. P[ierce] who has been unremitting in his attention to the wounded—called at our building to-day, and took me to the Officers Hospital, which is but a very short distance from here. It is in one of the finest residences in Beaufort, and is surrounded by beautiful grounds. Saw Major Hallowell, who, though badly wounded—in three places—is hoped to be slowly improving. A little more than a week ago I parted with him, after an exciting horseback ride, how strong, how well, how vigorous he was then! And now how thoroughly prostrated! But he with all the other officers of the 54th, like the privates, are brave, patient—cheerful. With deep sadness he spoke of Col. Shaw and then told me something that greatly surprised me;—that the Col. before that fatal attack had told him that in case he fell he wished me to have one of his horses—He had three very fine spirited ones that he had brought from the North. How very, very kind it was! And to me, almost a perfect stranger. I shall treasure this gift most sacredly, all my life long.[69]

Home, Saturday, July 25. After my hospital duties were over came home to St. Helena, to pass Sunday. Shall return to B[eaufort] on Monday. Am delighted to find our patients, Dr. R[ogers] and Lieut. W[alton] both looking much better. Was caught in a heavy shower on my way from the Ferry, and got quite wet. Nearly every afternoon we have these sudden showers, generally accompanied by severe thunder and lightning. They last but a little while. Then the sun shines out brightly, the skies are blue, and clear again, and the trees and grass look fresh and more beautiful for the rain. But I miss our rich green grass. There is very little of it here. Nor is there a rock or the slightest approach to a hill on the island.

Sunday, July 26. Had a pleasant morning under the trees, near the water, while Dr. R[ogers] read Emerson to us. Then had a long talk with him, after which came to the very sudden determination to go North in the next steamer. It is necessary for my health, therefore, it is wiser to go. My strength has failed rapidly of late. Have become so weak that I fear I sh'ld be an easy prey to the fever which prevails here, a little later in this season.

A few weeks since I stopped going to the church finding it impossible to drive there longer through the heat of the day, and opened a small school for some of the children from Frogmore in a carriage house on our place. Most of the children are crude little specimens. I asked them once what their ears were for. One bright-eyed little girl answered promptly "To put rings in." When Mrs. H[unn] asked some of them the same question. They said "To put cotton in." One day I had been telling them about metals; how they were dug from the ground, and afterward, in review, I asked "Where is iron obtained from?" "From the ground" was the prompt reply. "And gold?" "From the sky!" shouted a little boy.

I have found it very interesting to give them a kind of object lessons with the picture cards. They listen with eager attention, and seem to understand and remember very well what I tell them. But although this has been easier for me than teaching at the church—where, in addition to driving through the hot sun to get there, I was obliged to exert my lungs far above their strength to make myself heard when more than a hundred children were reciting at the same time in the same room—yet I have found my strength steadily decreasing, and have been every day tortured by a severe head ache. I take my good Dr's advice, therefore, and shall go North on a furlough—to stay until the unhealthiest season is over.

At Sea—Friday, July 31. Said farewell to Seaside and its kind household, white and black, and very early this morn Lieut. W[alton]'s boy drove me to Land's End, whence we were to take the steamboat which was to convey us to the steamer at Hilton Head. Mr. W[illiams][70] and his son who were to be our companions were behind in another carriage. I was barely in time for the boat, and it was with great difficulty that the Capt. was prevailed upon to wait for Mr. W[illiams]. Our trunks were at least two miles behind in one of the tedious mule carts, so of course, there was no hope of getting them on board. Mr. E. W. [?] waited for them, intending to take a row boat and follow us at all speed down to Hilton Head. He was quite sanguine of getting there before the steamer left. But he did not. And here we are, homeward bound but minus our baggage. I am sorry for Mr. E. W.'s disappointment. His health is so poor, it is really important that he sh'ld go North as soon as possible.

The "Fulton" sailed from Hilton Head between eight and nine. We have quite a pleasant party on board. Several friends of mine—Mr. P[ierce], Dr. R[ogers], Mr. and Mrs. H[arrison], Mr. and Mrs. F[airfield] and Mr. Hall—all good people.[71]

We have had a perfect day. Besides our party there are two or three ladies and many gentlemen, principally officers, whom

I do not know. The waves are a rich deep green the sky a lovely blue, the sun shines brightly, it is very, very pleasant at sea. Early this afternoon we came in sight of Charleston, and stopped outside the harbor for an hour or two. Saw plainly the steeples of the hateful little rebel city. Had an excellent view of Fort Sumter, which seems to rise out of the water—bold, grim, and most formidable looking. In the distance we c'ld see the smoke from the guns on Morris Island, and through a glass caught a very indistinct view of Fort Wagner. I shudder at the thought of that place, remembering the beautiful and brave young colonel who found a grave there,[72] and his heroic men, some dead beneath the walls—some prisoners, doomed, doubtless, to a fate far, far worse than death.

Our captain is an immense man—a perfect Falstaff indeed, but wonderfully active for such a "mountain of flesh." He informs us that he is a Cape Cod man, and had been going to sea for nearly fifty years. Surely he ought to be most thoroughly *en rapport* with Old Ocean. I cannot help envying him.

Saturday, Aug. 1. How perfect last night was. Mr. P[ierce] and I sat on deck late in the lovely, lovely moonlight, talking very pleasantly. This morn. after several hours of a most doleful experience in my stateroom I at last succeeded in getting dressed, and struggled up on deck. There I literally *dropped* down upon the nearest seat feeling unspeakably woebegone. My kind friend Mr. P[ierce] secured the best seat he c'ld for me, and afterward read Dicken's Christmas Stories to me. After a time felt better. Spent the day on deck—talking, or listening to Emerson and Tennyson, very kindly read to me by Dr. R[ogers] and Mr. Hall.

Another very lovely day. The sea is unusually calm, and of the most beautiful emerald hue. Am rather sorry that nothing has occurred. Think I sh'ld like a storm if I c'ld be outside and see its full grandeur. Our captain says we shall reach N[ew] Y[ork] to-morrow. I have thought of the faithful ones who have gathered at Abington to celebrate this day in that lovely pine grove. It w'ld be very pleasant to be with them. God bless them!

N[ew] Y[ork] Sunday, Aug. 2. Came in sight of land to-day, and this afternoon had a lovely sail up the beautiful harbor, with its stately shipping and fair, green islands on every hand. We, the ladies and all, mounted to the deck from which there was a lovely view. Staten Island seemed to me particularly beautiful. Towards sunset our steamer touched the landing. There was a great crowd collected on shore, (how odd it seemed to see so many white faces!) and we c'ld not land till sometime after dark. Said good-bye to my pleasant traveling companions, and accompanied by Mr. P[ierce] came to Mrs. W[?]'s to spend the night. It seems so strange to be in a great city again. The Southern dream is over for a time. The real life of the Northland begins again—Farewell!

Phila[delphia], Monday, Aug. 3. Had the hottest and most disagreeable of rides to P[hiladelphia]. Took everybody by surprise. Eat some ice cream—How refreshing it is! What an unspeakable luxury it is! Am thoroughly exhausted, and only fit to go to bed at once. Too tired to think.

Thursday, Aug. 6. Having endured the intense heat of the city, till I c'ld bear it no longer, came with Mr. P[ierce] to Byberry to-day.[73] How delightful it is to breathe the sweet country air, to get into this quiet country home again. . . . We sat on the piazza very late talking to Mr. Pierce, who goes to-morrow morning, first to Washington, afterward to Port Royal. . . .

Tuesday, Aug. 11. Came to town to-day but found no laggard trunk awaiting me; am quite *au desespoir,* having almost literally "nothing to wear,"—certainly nothing at all presentable. . . .

Thursday, Aug. 13. In despair bought a dress . . . and this afternoon went to call on Col. (formerly Major) Hallowell.[74] Found him much improved; sitting up, and looking quite cheerful and happy. Truly theirs is worthy of having it said "the house called beautiful." It seems as if one c'ld not but get well in such a lovely place and with such tender care. Had a very pleasant chat with the Col. recalling our Southern life, but w'ld not stay long lest I sh'ld weary them. His stately mother and sisters were very gracious.

Monday, Aug. 17. This evening gladly left Phila[delphia] and Mr. P[ierce] and I whirled away to N[ew] Y[ork]. Night graciously drew her vail over the dreary fields of N[ew] J[ersey]. We had a pleasant talk. . . .

Tuesday, Aug. 18. Left for Boston this morn. Mr. Pierce and Mr. Shaw met me at the Station.[75] The latter has a good, noble face, but very sad. Said good-bye to them, and was whirled away eastward. Buried myself in "At Odds" which I read through with interest, and then had time for a good long look at the dear old hills as we glided along. Reached Salem in the eve. and went to Mrs. C[hurch]'s—Mrs. I[ves] not being at home[76]—but Mary I[ves] had not come. Spent the night there. . . .

Tuesday, Sept. 1. Went to Boston to-day and had an interview with Dr. B[?]. He examined my lungs very thoroughly, but did not give an opinion about them. Advised me to spend four or five months among the Mts. of P[ennsylvania] before returning to [the] South. It is not possible. Prescribed Fusel Oil and whiskey. He is very, very kind, I like him exceedingly.

Wednesday, Sept. 2. Mary [Shepard][77] and I had a lovely day at Amesbury. It was delightful to be with the Whittiers again. I showed them a beautiful and touching letter from Mrs. Shaw, with two excellent photographs of her noble son. I can never thank her enough for sending me these pictures. We amused ourselves with Whittier's droll parrot, walked in the garden, stood in the yard to see the returned soldiers pass; and had much pleasant quiet talk with Mr. W[hittier] and his sister in the little vine-clad porch. She is as lovely as ever, but so very, very frail. Every time I part with her I have the fear that I may not see her again. . . .

Sunday, Sept. 6. Spent most of the day with Mary [Shepard], who read me some beautiful hymns, and passages from Mrs. Kemble's book, which interested me greatly.[78] It is indeed painfully interesting, and bears the impress of truth on every line. It fills one with admiration for the noble woman whose keen sense of justice whose true humanity shrank with the utmost loathing from the terrible system whose details she saw day after day. Such a book, such a thorough exposé of slavery must do good, in this land, and in England as well.

Monday, Sept. 14. Saturday afternoon Mary [Shepard] and I went to Amesbury. Miss W[hittier] had urged our coming again, but I c'ld not resist so great a temptation. We had a perfectly delightful visit. Spent Saturday evening in pleasant talk. Sunday was rainy and gloomy without but very cheerful within. We c'ld not go to meeting as we had intended, but we had a very happy time indoors. The poet was in one of his most genial moods,—told much about his early life—a very rare thing for him to do—and was altogether as charming as he c'ld be. His drollest of parrots amused us with its astonishing performances. In the afternoon Mr. Palmer,[79] who lives only two miles from here, came in and took tea with us. It was very pleasant to see him again. I do not forget how very kind and obliging he was to us, down South. In the eve. the poet told us more about his boyhood, and showed us a venerable old book, "Davider's," being a history of David, written in rhyme by Tho[ma]s Elwood, a friend of Milton. It was the only book of *poetry,* he told us, that he had to read when a boy. And a very, very quaint book it is. We left with great reluctance this morning. Our visits there have always been delightful, but this was the best of all. It will be very, very pleasant to look back upon when I return South. If I c'ld only persuade the W[hittier]'s to come down next winter, as they w'ld like to do. It w'ld be *too* splendid.

Tuesday, Sept. 15. My last day in Salem. During all my visit have only been able to go once to my dear old hills, and not at all to the seashore. It is a great disappointment, but I had not the strength. I must be contented to do less than I used to. Made several farewell calls. . . .

Worcester, Wednesday, Sept. 16. Left Salem this morn. While in Boston, went to The Lorings, and got "Sacred and Legendary Art"[80] which Mr. P[ierce] kindly lent me. He got it from a rebel's house—in Florida, I think. It is a very fine English copy. I expect to *luxuriate* in it. In the A[nti] S[lavery] Office met Mr. Garrison, and had a very interesting conversation with him. It has done me good to see his face again. Read with great interest some of Miss Alcott's "Hospital Sketches."[81] She writes with great vivacity—somewhat in the Gail Hamilton style. Read it in the cars. Mrs. Browning's "Last Poems" which Mary S[hepard] has given me.[82] Reached W[orcester] this afternoon. . . .

Saturday, Sept. 19. Went to the old Water cure which is now only a boarding house.[83] . . . Had a long and pleasant talk with Mrs. Higginson.[84] I think I shall like her. She is an invalid, and has been so for years. She looks older than her husband. Her manners are kind and pleasant. She asked many questions about Port Royal, and says she has some thought of going down next month. She heard from the Col. [T. W. Higginson] a few days ago. His health has greatly improved, but the Major and Adjt. are both very ill; the former dangerously so. I am *very* sorry to hear it. . . .

Tuesday, Sept. 22. Had six letters to-night.—One from Mr. Pirece. He is in Boston, and I shall not see him again, I am *very* sorry. Also letters from Port Royal, which I was very glad to get.

Wednesday, Sept. 23. Left W[orcester] to-night in steamboat train.

Phila[delphia], Thursday, Sept. 24. Arrived in Phila[delphia] this afternoon, very tired. Had a kind letter from Whittier. Found our little household quite well. . . .

N[ew] Y[ork], Friday, Oct. 9. Left Phila[delphia] to-day. Arrived in New York to-night. . . .

Saturday, Oct. 10. Secured my passage on board the Fulton. She sails to-morrow (Sunday) morn.

St. Helena. Seaside, Friday, Oct. 16. Left N[ew] Y[ork] on the morn of the 11th. Did not reach Hilton Head until Thursday morning. In spite of the pleasant company with me (Dr. R[ogers] Col. H[allowell][85] and James Lee) had a rather dreary voyage being half sick nearly all the time.

On reaching Hilton Head met with a very inhospitable reception. Were told that an order had just been issued by Gen. Gillmore forbidding any lady to land unless provided with a pass from himself or the Secretary of War. One lady was taken ashore despite the guards by the surgeon of the hospital in which she was to be nurse. But Mrs. H[?] and I remained on board while the gentlemen went to Beaufort to see what c'ld be done for us, and a dreary time we had of it, with the pleasant prospect before us of being obliged to return to New York; and watched closely meanwhile by no less than three lynx-eyed guards. We stayed there until the following afternoon, when Mr. Hunn appeared with an order for our release. Came up to Land's End, where we all three squeezed into my "sulky," and reached home this eve. glad to get on terra firma again, and nearly exhausted.

Sunday, Oct. 18. Went to church. It was very pleasant to see the people gathered together again, and to receive their warm welcome.

Came home from the village to-day to find my good Col. Higginson here. How it rejoiced me to see him. But am grieved to find him so far from well. He will spend a few days with us trying to recruit. Is not really ill, but very much reduced in strength.

Our noble Col. has left us, feeling a little better. Commenced school on the Perry Place, . . . between two and three miles from here. Most of the children were former pupils of Mr. [Arthur] Sumner. Some of the older ones are quite advanced. Have forty names. Have a comparatively comfortable room with a fire in it,—much preferable to the church.

Wednesday, Nov. 25. For the past few weeks our minds have been much and sadly occupied with the dangerous illness of dear Miss Murray. For some time we feared that we sh'ld lose her. And it w'ld have been an irremediable loss. But now she is getting rapidly better; is entirely out of danger, and I, for one feel as if a great weight had been taken off my mind.

Lizzie [Hunn], Dora [?] and I, spent to-day in decorating our parlor with moss and cedar. It looks very pretty.

Lieut. Higginson,[86] a distant cousin of the Col.'s is spending a few days with us being also an invalid. He is peculiar, but very intelligent and gentlemanly. I like him.

Thursday, Nov. 26. Thanksgiving Day. We had quite a large dinner party—fifteen or sixteen,—and a very merry eve. —dancing, games. Of course Mr. Sumner was the life of the party. He is so very witty and entertaining.

Oliver Fripp Plantation, Sunday, May 15, 1864. How many months have elapsed since I last communed with thee old friend, old journal. I will sketch rapidly a few of the principal events, personal, that have occurred. Some are so painful, I cannot dwell upon them. Others are very cheerful. Early in December, 1863, I came here.[87] Our household consists of Mr. [Arthur] Sumner and Mr. [Fredrick] Williams and Miss Kellogg.[88] They are all most pleasant and congenial companions, and on the whole our winter has been passed pleasantly together.

The people on this plantation are not I think so interesting and pleasant as on many others. They have a bad reputation. Their near vicinity to Land's End and the soldiers there has not tended to improve them.

The place has an unhealthy situation so that we cannot live here in the summer. The owner used to leave in the spring, and go down to the Village. The house is comparatively new, and the best built and most comfortable one I have seen here.

On Christmas Eve, went to Beaufort, and Miss K[ellogg] and I started to go to the Heacocks' with whom we were to spend Christmas.[89] After several mishaps, such as losing our way several times and having one of our horses give out, we at last in the cold, moonlight night arrived at the H[eacock]'s house, and were ushered into a cosy little sitting-room, all aglow with the light of a blazing wood-fire. The H[eacock]'s are the pleasantest, cheeriest people, whom it does one good to meet. And A[nnie] is the veriest little sunbeam I ever saw.

Early Christmas morning we were awakened by the merry sound of children's voices shouting "Merry Christmas." Later in the day there was a Christmas tree exhibited to the wondering eyes of the children, from whose branches numerous gifts were taken down and distributed. How joyous and happy they were! At dinner beside the family and ourselves there were Miss Ireson[90] of Lynn and A. G. Brown [91] of Salem, the new Treasury Agent. Another carriage and pair came for us in the afternoon —the Gen.'s[92] orderly accompanying the driver, so we had a sufficient escort, and reached B[eaufort] without any mishaps. Had a very pleasant party at the Gen.'s in the eve;—games, charades, very good singing, etc. Miss K[ellogg] and I spent the night there. Mrs. Lander, Gen. and Mrs. S[axton] took part in the charades. They were very amusing.

[Here ends the *Journal* of Charlotte Forten. She left Port Royal in the latter part of May, 1864, and arrived in New York aboard the *Fulton* on June 3, 1864. A brief account of her later years will be found in the Introduction to this volume.]

Notes

INTRODUCTION

1. CHARLOTTE L. FORTEN: Philadelphia and Salem

[1] Accounts of James Forten's boyhood, all based largely on his own recollections, are in Lydia Maria Child, *The Freedmen's Book* (Boston, 1865), 100-102; William C. Nell, *Colored Patriots of the American Revolution* (Boston, 1855), 166-168; and Robert Purvis, *Remarks on the Life and Character of James Forten, Delivered at Bethel Church, March 30, 1842* (Philadelphia, 1942), 4-9. There is also a brief sketch in the *Dictionary of American Biography* (New York, 1928-1937), VI, 536-537.

[2] More detailed accounts of Forten's business activities and civic contributions are in Nell, *Colored Patriots,* 172-174; Child, *Freedmen's Book,* 102-103; J. Thomas Scharf and Thomas Wescott, *History of Philadelphia* (Philadelphia, 1884), I, 573-574; and William Douglas, *Annals of the First African Church in the United States of America, now styled the African Episcopal Church of St. Thomas* (Philadelphia, 1862), 107, 110.

[3] The petition, from the "free blacks" of Philadelphia, was laid before Congress on January 2, 1800, by Robert Waln, a representative from Pennsylvania. *Annals of Congress,* 6th Cong., 1st Sess., 232. Debate on the measure is in *Ibid.,* 239-246.

[4] George Thatcher, a Federalist from Massachusetts, who used the occasion to attack the "great evil" of slavery. Forten's letter is in Purvis, *Remarks on the Life and Character of James Forten,* 12-14.

[5] James Forten, *Letters from a Man of Colour, on a Late Bill before the Senate of Pennsylvania* (Philadelphia, 1813), 3-4, 7. One of the letters is reprinted in Carter G. Woodson, *Negro Orators and Their Orations* (Washington, 1925), 42-51.

[6] Nell, *Colored Patriots,* 177.

[7] A full account of the meeting, together with the text of the resolutions adopted, is in G. B. Stebbins, *Facts and Opinions Touching the Real Origin, Character, and Influence of the American Colonization Society* (Boston, 1853), 194-196. For briefer accounts see Nell, *Colored Patriots,* 177-178; William Lloyd Garrison, *Thoughts on African Colonization* (Boston, 1832), Part II, 9-10; Lewis Tappan, *Life of Arthur Tappan* (New York, 1870), 135-136; Louis R. Mehlinger, "The Attitude of the Free Negro toward African Colonization," *Journal*

of Negro History, I (June, 1916), 276-301, and John Hope Franklin, *From Slavery to Freedom* (New York, 1947), 237.

8 The meeting is described in Garrison, *Thoughts on African Colonization*, Part II, 10-13. The address is printed in Mehlinger, "Attitude of the Free Negro," *loc. cit.*, 278-279, and in Woodson, *Negro Orators*, 52-55. See also Herbert Aptheker, *The Negro in the Abolitionist Movement* (New York, 1941), 31-32.

9 *Niles' Register*, XVII (November 27, 1819), 201-202.

10 Carter G. Woodson, *The Negro in Our History* (Washington, 1941), 271-273.

11 Samuel J. May, *Some Recollections of the Antislavery Conflict* (Boston, 1869), 287.

12 Archibald H. Grimké, *William Lloyd Garrison* (New York, 1891), 144, holds that Garrison's talks with Forten helped convince Garrison that colonization was an evil, thus laying the basis for abolitionism. This is also the thesis of Clarice A. Richardson, "The Anti-Slavery Activities of Negroes in Pennsylvania" (Unpublished master's thesis, Howard University, 1937), 10-11.

13 May, *Some Recollections of the Antislavery Conflict*, 286; Carter G. Woodson, ed., *The Works of Francis J. Grimké* (Washington, 1942), IV, 96n.

14 Forten occupied a house at 92 Lombard Street during most of his lifetime. *Philadelphia Directory for 1813* (Philadelphia, 1813); *Philadelphia Directory for 1842* (Philadelphia, 1842), 88. Twenty-two persons were listed as living in the house in the census of 1830. Carter G. Woodson, *Free Negro Heads of Families in the United States in 1830* (Washington, 1925).

15 Child, *Freedmen's Book*, 103; Purvis, *Remarks on the Life and Character of James Forten*, 17.

16 The objects of the organization were described in its monthly publication, the *National Reformer*, I (February, 1829), 81. See also Nell, *Colored Patriots*, 181.

17 Nell, *Colored Patriots*, 178.

18 James Forten to William Lloyd Garrison, December 31, 1830. In Dorothy B. Porter, ed., "Early Manuscript Letters Written by Negroes," *Journal of Negro History*, XXIV (April, 1939), 199-200.

19 James Forten to William Lloyd Garrison, February 2, 1831. *Ibid.*, 200-201; *The Liberator*, March 12, 1831. See also Aptheker, *Negro in the Abolitionist Movement*, 38-39.

20 Woodson, ed., *Works of Francis J. Grimké*, IV, 96n.

21 James Forten to William Lloyd Garrison, March 21, 1831. Porter, "Early Manuscript Letters Written by Negroes," *loc. cit.*, 201-202.

22 James Forten to William Lloyd Garrison, July 28, 1832. *Ibid.*, 204-205; Booker T. Washington, *The Story of the Negro* (New York, 1909), I, 290. For an account of one of Garrison's

visits to the Forten home see Anna D. Hallowell, ed., *James and Lucretia Mott: Life and Letters* (Boston, 1884), 119.

23 May, *Some Recollections of the Antislavery Conflict,* 286; *Second Annual Report of the American Anti-Slavery Society, May 12, 1835* (New York, 1835), 12; *Fifth Annual Report of the Executive Committee of the American Anti-Slavery Society, May, 1839* (New York, 1839), 13; *The Liberator,* September 17, 1841; Woodson, ed., *Works of Francis J. Grimké,* IV, 96n.

24 *The Liberator,* May 22, 1840.

25 A typical meeting was held on April 1, 1833, at the Presbyterian Church in Philadelphia. *Ibid.,* April 13, 1833.

26 *Ibid.,* April 14, 1832; *Human Rights,* II (September 4, 1836).

27 *Proceedings of the Pennsylvania Convention at Harrisburg* (Philadelphia, 1837).

28 *The Liberator,* September 17, 1841, published Forten's letter to Garrison. Accounts of the funeral procession are in *ibid.,* March 18, 1842; and in the *National Anti-Slavery Standard,* March 24, 1842.

29 Typical accounts of the activities of James Forten's children are in *The Liberator,* April 19, 1834; *National Anti-Slavery Standard,* May 13, 1841; *Philadelphia Public Ledger,* April 25, 1844; and Nell, *Colored Patriots,* 350-351.

30 Samuel May, the abolitionist, wrote glowingly of such a visit in 1833. See May, *Some Recollections of the Antislavery Conflict,* 288.

31 Whittier wrote this poem in December, 1833, probably while visiting the Forten family during the organizational meeting of the American Anti-Slavery Society. It was discovered among Forten's effects in 1906 by his granddaughter and first published in *The Independent,* LXI (November 15, 1906), 1139.

32 *The Liberator,* March 21, 1835.

33 See pages 44 and 65 for Miss Forten's own account of her father's sentiments on this subject.

34 Forten was made a sergeant major before being assigned to recruiting service. Samuel P. Bates, *History of Pennsylvania Volunteers, 1861-1865* (Harrisburg, 1868-1871), V, 1048. The history of the regiment is also considered in Frank H. Taylor, *Philadelphia in the Civil War* (Philadelphia, 1913), 194; and George W. Williams, *A History of Negro Troops in the War of the Rebellion* (New York, 1888), 231-256.

35 *The Liberator,* May 13, 1864, has a full account of the death of Robert Forten.

36 John Greenleaf Whittier, "The Antislavery Convention of 1833," *Atlantic Monthly,* XXXIII (February, 1874), 169. May, *Some Recollections of the Antislavery Conflict,* 288-289, also recalls Purvis at the convention, calling him "an elegant, a

brilliant young gentleman, well educated and wealthy." An account of Purvis' early life is in William W. Brown, *The Black Man* (New York, 1863), 253-256; Aaron M. Powell, *Personal Reminiscences of the Antislavery and Other Reforms and Reformers* (New York, 1899), 147-149; and Henrietta Buckmaster, *Let My People Go: The Story of the Underground Railroad and the Growth of the Abolition Movement* (New York, 1941), 107-108.

[37] *National Anti-Slavery Standard,* May 17, 1848; *Annual Report of the American Anti-Slavery Society, 1855* (New York, 1855), 137, 151; *ibid., 1858 and 1859,* 194. See also Aptheker, *The Negro in the Abolitionist Movement,* 42.

[38] *National Anti-Slavery Standard,* July 30, 1846, October 16, 1851, and October 16, 1858; *Centennial Anniversary of the Pennsylvania Society for Promoting the Abolition of Slavery* (Philadelphia, 1876), 65; *Annual Report of the American Anti-Slavery Society, 1836* (New York, 1836). Harriet Purvis was also active in the Pennsylvania society. *National Anti-Slavery Standard,* October 23, 1858.

[39] His letter to the school committee was printed in *The Liberator,* December 16, 1853.

[40] Purvis served as editor of the Society's paper. See *National Reformer,* VI (February, 1839), 96.

[41] He had made an attempt to organize a Vigilance Committee in 1838 without success. William Still, *The Underground Railroad* (Philadelphia, 1872), 612.

[42] Sallie Holley, *A Life for Liberty: Anti-Slavery and Other Letters of Sallie Holley* (New York, 1899), 101.

[43] *Ibid.,* 102.

[44] Robert Purvis, Jr., after a promising career as a businessman and abolitionist, died when only twenty-eight years of age, on March 19, 1862. *The Liberator,* April 4 and April 11, 1862. Charles B. Purvis, on the other hand, was able to capitalize on his heritage. Educated at the Western Reserve Medical School, he served in the United States Army Medical Corps until the close of the Civil War, helped found the Howard University Medical School, and held an honored position on both the faculty and board of trustees of that institution. Washington, *The Story of the Negro,* I, 290-291; Woodson, ed., *Works of Francis J. Grimké,* IV, 116n.

[45] William W. Brown, *The Rising Son; or, the Antecedents and Advancement of the Colored Race* (Boston, 1874), 468-469.

[46] The *Philadelphia Directory for 1853* (Philadelphia, 1853), 135, lists her as living at 92 Lombard Street, the original home of James Forten. She was the only member of the family still in Philadelphia at that time.

[47] Remond was born in Salem in 1810, his parents having recently arrived from Curaçao and been naturalized. A con-

temporary account of his career is in Brown, *The Black Man*, 246-250. See also *Dictionary of American Biography*, XV, 499-500; Aptheker, *The Negro in the Abolitionist Movement*, 46; Carter G. Woodson, ed., *The Mind of the Negro as Reflected in Letters Written during the Crisis, 1800-1860* (Washington, 1926), 293-328; and John Daniels, *In Freedom's Birthplace: A Study of the Boston Negroes* (Boston, 1914), 99.

[48] Brown, *The Black Man*, 247; Woodson, *Negro Orators*, 126.

[49] The family lived at 9 Dean Street; the hair works was located at 18 Washington Street and was operated by C. E. Remond and C. Babcock. *The Salem Directory, 1850* (Salem, 1850), 119; *The Salem Directory, 1855* (Salem, 1855), 128.

[50] For notices of C. L. Remond's lecturing appointments see *Proceedings of the Massachusetts Anti-Slavery Society at the Annual Meetings held in 1854, 1855, and 1856* (Boston, 1856), 21, 24-26, 49-50; *Annual Reports of the American Anti-Slavery Society, by the Executive Committee, for the Years Ending May 1, 1857, and May 1, 1858* (New York, 1858), 188; *Annual Report of the American Anti-Slavery Society by the Executive Committee for the Year Ending May 1, 1859* (New York, 1859), 142. Sarah Parker Remond became a lecturing agent while Miss Forten lived at the Remond home, later (1859-1860) distinguishing herself in a well-publicized tour of England. *The Liberator*, February 4, February 18, and March 11, 1859. For a brief sketch of Miss Remond's career see Dorothy B. Porter, "Sarah Parker Remond, Abolitionist and Physician," *Journal of Negro History*, XX (July, 1935), 287-293.

[51] Brown, *The Rising Son*, 459-460.

[52] The Salem Female Anti-Slavery Society was organized in 1834. Its president during the 1850's was Mrs. William Ives, wife of the publisher of the *Salem Observer*. *The Salem Directory, 1855* (Salem, 1855), 91, 197-198.

[53] *Annual Report of the School Committee of the City of Salem, February, 1855* (Salem, 1855), 25.

[54] Brown, *The Rising Son*, 475.

[55] Brown, *The Black Man*, 190-193.

[56] Quoted in *The Liberator*, March 26, 1858.

[57] Miss Forten held the rank of assistant, at a salary of $200 a year. *Annual Report of the School Committee of the City of Salem, 1857* (Salem, 1857), 10, 40-41.

[58] Brown, *The Black Man*, 193.

[59] The hymn was printed in *The Liberator*, August 24, 1856.

[60] These poems were printed in the *National Anti-Slavery Standard*, June 19, 1858, and January 15, 1859; *The Liberator*, May 27, 1859; and Brown, *The Black Man*, 169-199.

[61] *National Anti-Slavery Standard*, February 3, 1860.

[62] Brown, *The Rising Son*, 475.

[63] *The Salem Directory, 1850* (Salem, 1850), 116. The Putnams lived at 17 South Street.

[64] *Annual Report of the School Committee of the City of Salem, January, 1859* (Salem, 1859), 17.

[65] Quoted in *The Liberator*, March 26, 1858.

[66] *National Anti-Slavery Standard*, March 20, 1858.

2. A Social Experiment: Port Royal, South Carolina

[1] Frank Moore, ed., *The Rebellion Record: A Diary of American Events with Documents, Narratives, Illustrative Incidents, Poetry* (New York, 1861-1868), I, 78, 161, prints the two presidential proclamations establishing the blockade. The reasons for the selection of Port Royal are listed in *The Union Army* (Madison, Wis., 1908), VII, 44-45, 115.

[2] Official documents dealing with preparations for the attack on Port Royal are in *The Union Army, a compilation of the Official Records of the Union and Confederate Armies* (Washington, 1889-1901), Ser. I, VI, 177; hereafter cited as *Official Records*. Other accounts are in Elizabeth W. Pearson, ed., *Letters from Port Royal Written at the Time of the Civil War* (Boston, 1906), vi-vii; and Guion G. Johnson, *A Social History of the Sea Islands with Special Reference to St. Helena Island, South Carolina* (Chapel Hill, N. C., 1930), 114.

[3] *Official Records*, Ser. 1, VI, 186-193.

[4] *Ibid.*, Ser. 1, VI, 248.

[5] General Benjamin Butler first applied the term "contrabands of war" to the slaves he captured at Hampton Roads. Their exact status was not defined until July 17, 1862, when Congress declared free all slaves whose masters were rebels and who were living within territory occupied by the Union forces. T. J. Woofter, Jr., *Black Yeomanry: Life on St. Helena Island* (New York, 1930), 38; *United States Statutes at Large*, XII, 591.

[6] In November, 1861, the Adjutant General ordered the seizure of all cotton and other property of use to the Union forces. He decreed that paid Negro workers should pick and pack the cotton preparatory to its shipment to New York. Within a short time the task of handling captured supplies was transferred to the Treasury Department, which appointed cotton agents to direct the work of the Negro laborers. *Official Records*, Ser. 1, VII, 192; Johnson, *Social History of the Sea Islands*, 155, 159-160.

[7] An excellent description of the St. Helena slaves is in Johnson, *Social History of the Sea Islands*, 120-126, 160.

[8] *Official Records*, Ser. 1, VI, 218.

[9] A. W. Stevens, ed., *Addresses and Papers by Edward L. Pierce* (Boston, 1896), 67.

[10] Henry L. Swint, *The Northern Teacher in the South, 1862-1870* (Nashville, 1941), 161.

[11] Edward L. Pierce, "The Negroes at Port Royal, S. C.: Report of the Government Agent," in Moore, ed., *Rebellion Record*, Supp. I, 308.

[12] *Official Records*, Ser. 3, II, 55.

[13] Edward L. Pierce, "Second Report," in Moore, ed., *Rebellion Record*, Supp. I, 315; Johnson, *Social History of the Sea Islands*, 166.

[14] *Ibid.*, 316; Edward L. Pierce, "The Freedmen at Port Royal," *Atlantic Monthly*, XII (September, 1863), 298.

[15] This was the opinion of J. Miller McKim, organizer of the Port Royal Relief Committee of Philadelphia, after a visit to Port Royal. J. Miller McKim, *The Freedmen of South Carolina* (Philadelphia, 1862), n.p.

[16] Pierce, "Second Report," in Moore, ed., *Rebellion Record*, Supp. I, 517.

[17] *Official Records*, Ser. 3, II, 52.

[18] *Ibid.*, Ser. 3, II, 55.

[19] *Ibid.*, Ser. 3, II, 14, 152-153.

[20] Johnson, *Social History of the Sea Islands*, 173.

[21] See Miss Forten's *Journal*, pages 119-122, for an account of her efforts to obtain a teacher's post.

[22] Congress on July 17, 1862, empowered the President to "receive into the service of the United States, for the purpose of constructing entrenchments, or performing camp service, or any other labor, or any military or naval service, for which they might be found competent, persons of African descent." *United States Statutes at Large*, XII, 599.

[23] *Official Records*, Ser. 1, XIV, 377.

[24] For a sketch of Higginson's career see *Dictionary of American Biography*, IX, 16-18; and Thomas Wentworth Higginson, *Army Life in a Black Regiment* (Boston, 1900), 2. His attitude toward the Negro troops was disclosed in his *Cheerful Yesterdays* (Boston, 1900), 235-270.

[25] Higginson, *Army Life in a Black Regiment*, 179.

[26] *Official Records*, Ser. 1. XIV, 42-43; Quincy A. Gillmore, "The Army before Charleston in 1863," *Battles and Leaders of the Civil War* (New York, 1884), IV, 52; David D. Porter, *The Naval History of the Civil War* (New York, 1886), 434.

[27] An imposing fleet that had assembled at Port Royal made the attack on April 7, only to be beaten back by the shore batteries. *The Union Army*, VII, 129; *Official Records*, Ser. 1, XIV, 240-280, 442.

[28] Luis F. Emilio, *History of the Fifty-Fourth Regiment of Massachusetts Volunteer Infantry* (Boston, 1891), 72-75; *Official Records*, Ser. 1, XXVIII, Part I, 9-10, 12, 15-16, 362, 379.

[29] *Official Records*, Ser. 1, XXVIII, Part I, 16, 21, 23, 26-27, 30, 538-539.

[30] By the close of 1863 almost seven thousand acres of former plantation land were owned by the Port Royal freedmen. *New England Freedmen's Aid Society, Annual Report, 1864* (Boston, 1864), 15; Edward L. Pierce, "The Freedman at Port Royal," *loc. cit.*, 303; Johnson, *Social History of the Sea Islands*, 180.

[31] Charlotte Forten, "Life on the Sea Islands," *Atlantic Monthly*, XIII (May, 1864), 587-596 and (June, 1864) 666-676. The articles were sent to the *Atlantic Monthly* by John Greenleaf Whittier, with an accompanying note stating: "The following graceful and picturesque description of the new condition of things on the Sea Islands of South Carolina, originally written for private perusal, seems to me to be worthy of a place in 'the Atlantic.' Its young author—herself akin to the long suffering race whose exodus she so pleasantly describes—is still engaged in her labor of love on St. Helena Island." The articles were subsequently republished in Lydia Maria Child's *The Freedmen's Book*, 251-257. Miss Child, in writing to Whittier of them, said: "To think of a mulatto girl writing such beautiful articles for the *Atlantic Monthly!* How the wheel of fortune *has* turned round." John Albree, ed., *Whittier Correspondence from the Oak Knoll Collections* (Salem, 1911), 149.

[32] Manuscript obituary notice prepared for Charlotte Forten Grimké by her husband, the Reverend Francis J. Grimké.

[33] A note by the publisher states: "Miss Charlotte L. Forten has performed the work of translation with an accuracy and spirit which will, undoubtedly, be appreciated by all acquainted with the original."

[34] Charlotte Forten Grimké, "Personal Recollections of Whittier," *New England Magazine*, VIII (June, 1893), 468-476.

[35] The early history of the Grimké brothers is in Catherine H. Birney, *Sarah and Angelina Grimké* (Boston, 1885), 289-290; and in Carter G. Woodson, ed., *Works of Francis J. Grimké* (Washington, 1942), I, viii-xxiii.

[36] Transcripts of the records of Archibald Henry Grimké and Francis James Grimké from the archives of Lincoln University. These transcripts were generously sent me by Mr. Paul Kuehner, the Registrar of the University.

[37] Manuscript minutes of the Administrative Committee of Lincoln University, August 7, 1871; *Lincoln University Biographical Catalogue* (New York, 1918). I am indebted to Mr. Paul Kuehner for both of these items.

[38] Birney, *Sarah and Angelina Grimké*, 289-295.

[39] Woodson, ed., *Works of Francis J. Grimké*, I, Introduction.

[40] *Ibid.*, I, xiii. See also Woodson, *Negro Orators*, 690-708; and D. W. Culp, *Twentieth Century Negro Literature* (Atlanta, Ga., 1902), 426-433.

[41] Manuscript obituary notice prepared for Charlotte Forten Grimké by her husband, the Reverend Francis J. Grimké.

PART 1

[1] Miss Forten was sixteen years old when she moved to Salem, seeking something more enlightened than the segregated schools of her native Philadelphia. Schools in Salem had been opened to all persons, regardless of color, in 1843. William W. Brown, *The Black Man* (New York, 1863), 191; Charles S. Osgood and H. M. Batchelder, *Historical Sketch of Salem* (Salem, 1879), 106. Miss Forten was one of the 188 students in the Higginson Grammar School for Girls. *Annual Report of the School Committee of the City of Salem, February, 1855* (Salem, 1855), 25.

[2] *The Salem Directory, 1855* (Salem, 1855) lists no Mrs. Putnam who answers the descriptions in the *Journal*. In all probability, however, Miss Forten refers to Caroline E. Putnam, a Salem Negro woman, who was a frequent contributor to antislavery societies. *The Liberator*, January 26, 1855, February 20, 1857, June 15, 1860, and February 14, 1862.

[3] A minor novel by Charles Dickens, written in 1854 and first published in the new periodical *Household Words*.

[4] Anthony Burns, an escaped slave from Richmond, Virginia, was arrested in Boston on May 24, 1854, by the United States Marshal, Edward G. Loring. His trial was set for Saturday, May 27. Excitement mounted all day Friday as crowds milled through the Boston streets demanding his release.

[5] Mary L. Shepard was principal of the Higginson Grammar School and one of Miss Forten's closest friends. *Annual Report of the School Committee of the City of Salem, 1855* (Salem, 1855), 25.

[6] The Reverend Albert Barnes, pastor of the First Presbyterian Church of Philadelphia, was an outspoken opponent of slavery.

[7] *The Liberator*, May 26, 1854, reported that a total eclipse of the sun, visible throughout the United States, would begin in Boston at 4:30 in the afternoon. The clouds that covered Salem did not obscure vision in Boston and other parts of New England. *Salem Register*, May 29, 1854.

[8] Robert Bridges Forten, of Philadelphia.

[9] A giant mass meeting to protest Anthony Burns's arrest was held in Faneuil Hall, Boston, on the night of May 26; speeches were given by Theodore Parker and Wendell Phillips. While the meeting was in progress, word arrived that a group of abolitionists, led by Lewis Hayden and Thomas Wentworth Higginson, had attempted a forceful rescue of Burns. They broke into the Court House, but were repulsed after a United States mar-

shal was killed. From that time on, both state militiamen and federal troops guarded the prisoner. *The Liberator,* June 2, 1854; Wendell P. Garrison and Francis J. Garrison, *William Lloyd Garrison, 1805-1879* (New York, 1885-1889), III, 409-410; George L. Austin, *The Life and Times of Wendell Phillips* (Boston, 1884), 173-178.

[10] The trial was postponed from Saturday until Monday to give Burns's lawyers more time to prepare their defense. *The Liberator,* June 2, 1854.

[11] Harmony Grove, Salem's principal cemetery, was famed as an arboretum, "useful in a high degree," as one orator put it, "to the student of natural history. This object alone, together with the beautiful promenades and healthful influences attending it, affording exhilarating exercise and the purest enjoyment, is of infinitely more value than its whole cost." Daniel A. White, *An Address Delivered at the Consecration of the Harmony Grove Cemetery in Salem, June 14, 1840* (Salem, 1840), 22.

[12] The New England Anti-Slavery Society held its annual meeting at the Melodeon in Boston, May 30, May 31, and June 1, 1854. *The Liberator,* June 9, 1854.

[13] Sarah Parker Remond, sister of the well-known Negro abolitionist, Charles Lenox Remond, lived with her brother at 9 Dean Street, Salem. Active in the antislavery movement herself, she later became well known as a speaker. At this time she was thirty-nine years old. Dorothy B. Porter, "Sarah Parker Remond, Abolitionist and Physician," *Journal of Negro History,* XX, (July, 1935), 287-293.

[14] Wendell Phillips, a leading radical abolitionist, was constantly in demand as a speaker at antislavery meetings. For his career see Austin, *Life and Times of Wendell Phillips, passim;* Carlos Martyn, *Wendell Phillips: the Agitator* (New York, 1890), *passim; Wendell Phillips, Speeches, Lectures, and Letters: Second Series* (Boston, 1891), *passim.*

[15] William Lloyd Garrison was the father of radical abolitionism. The standard biography is Garrison and Garrison, *William Lloyd Garrison.*

[16] Theodore Parker, Boston's noted Unitarian minister, ranked with Phillips and Garrison as a favorite of New England abolitionists. See Henry Steele Commager, *Theodore Parker* (Boston, 1936).

[17] The only important speech delivered at the New England Anti-Slavery Society meeting on May 31 was by Stephen S. Foster, an abolitionist known principally for his rugged features, ungainly appearance, vibrant voice, and insistence that the churches were allies of the slave power. Widely known as the author of *The Brotherhood of Thieves; or, A True Picture of the American Church and Clergy* (New London, 1843), he frequently invaded churches, where he interrupted the sermon to denounce slavery. His wife was Abigail Kelley Foster, an active crusader for abolition and women's rights. See *Dictionary*

of American Biography, VI, 558; and Henrietta Buckmaster, *Let My People Go: The Story of the Underground Railroad and the Growth of the Abolition Movement* (New York, 1941), 129.

[18] Helen S. Putnam, of Salem, probably the daughter of Caroline E. Putnam, was married to Jacob D. Gilliard, of Baltimore. The Reverend O. B. Frothingham, of Salem, who later became a famous clergyman in Jersey City, performed the ceremony. *The Liberator,* June, 1854; *Salem Register,* June 5, 1854.

[19] Between Monday and Wednesday, when evidence was being heard in the Anthony Burns case, Boston was in a state of great excitement. Troops patrolled the streets, and the public square before the Court House was roped off to keep back the mobs. The testimony, as was usual in such cases, was conflicting; the government maintained that Burns had escaped on March 24, but several witnesses testified that he had been working in Boston between March 4 and March 10. On June 2 the court ruled that he was an escaped slave and must be returned to his master. He was marched down State Street to a waiting Virginia-bound vessel through groaning, hissing lines of people. Federal troops, state militiamen, and the entire police force were on hand to prevent any attempt at rescue. Full accounts of the trial are in *The Liberator,* June 2, 1854; the *Salem Register,* May 29, June 1, and June 5, 1854; and the *Annual Report to the American Anti-Slavery Society by the Executive Committee, 1855* (New York, 1855), 23-40.

[20] Elizabeth Church, a student from Bridgetown, Nova Scotia, became a close friend of Miss Forten. *Catalogue of Instructors and Students in the State Normal School at Salem: for the Term Ending February, 1856* (Salem, 1856), 9.

[21] The Reverend Theodore Parker's sermon, which denounced the persecutors of Anthony Burns, was delivered at the Music Hall in Boston on May 28, 1854. *The Liberator,* June 2, 1854. Published in pamphlet form, it was advertised in *The Liberator,* September 1, 1854.

[22] The Reverend O. B. Frothingham, of Salem.

[23] John and Asa Hutchinson were well known for their fine voices and their active support of abolitionism. *The Liberator,* August 17, 1855.

[24] *Martin Merrivale: His X Mark,* a novel for children written by John T. Trowbridge under the pen name of Paul Creyton, was published in Boston in 1854. Trowbridge became a prolific writer of popular fiction and history during the Civil War era. "Moll Pitcher" was an early poem by John Greenleaf Whittier of which he was heartily ashamed. It appears in none of his published works.

[25] Charles Lenox Remond, prominent Negro abolitionist, usually spoke at conventions of both the Massachusetts Anti-Slavery Society and the American Anti-Slavery Society.

[26] The Reverend Andrew D. Foss, an agent of the Massachusetts Anti-Slavery Society, spoke on the Nebraska question. *The Liberator*, June 23, 1854.

[27] The Essex Institute, formed in 1848 by a union of the Essex Historical Society and the Essex County Natural History Society, maintained an extensive museum of historical and scientific objects. Henry F. King was curator of the Department of Natural History, and Dr. Henry Wheatland, a local physician, was secretary and treasurer of the Institute. *Salem Directory, 1857* (Salem, 1857), 217-218.

[28] The annual meeting of the Essex Anti-Slavery Society was held at Lyceum Hall, Salem, on July 8 and 9. Charles L. Remond, the president, presided; the principal speeches were given by William Lloyd Garrison and Andrew D. Foss. *The Liberator*, July 7, 1854.

[29] Louisa Hawthorne, a sister of Nathaniel Hawthorne, stayed on in Salem when her brother left there in 1850. Herbert Gorman, *Hawthorne* (New York, 1927), 103.

[30] The Reverend R. Turnbull, *The Genius of Scotland, or Sketches of Scottish Scenery, Literature and Religion* (New York, 1853).

[31] *Poems of Phyllis Wheatley Peters* (London, 1773; also later editions).

[32] New England abolitionists regularly celebrated the anniversary of British emancipation at Abington. On this occasion speeches were given by William Lloyd Garrison, Wendell Phillips, Charles Lenox Remond, Thomas Wentworth Higginson, and others. *The Liberator*. August 4, August 11, and August 18, 1854.

[33] Thomas Wentworth Higginson was a Harvard-trained Brahmin whose radical antislavery views led to his dismissal from his first pastorate. Between 1852 and 1861 he served as minister of the Free Church of Worcester, Massachusetts, a precursor of the later ethical societies. During the excitement over Anthony Burns he led one of the mobs that attempted to release the fugitive. Miss Forten met him in South Carolina during the Civil War, when he was commander of the First South Carolina Volunteers, a famous Negro regiment. *Dictionary of American Biography*, IX, 16-18; Mary P. Higginson, *Thomas Wentworth Higginson; the Story of His Life* (Boston, 1914).

[34] John C. Cluer, a radical abolitionist and agent of the Massachusetts Anti-Slavery Society, was one of the leaders of the mob that tried to release Anthony Burns from the Boston Court House on May 26. *The Liberator*, July 2, 1854.

[35] William C. Nell, of Boston, was one of New England's leading Negro abolitionists. Trained for the law, he preferred not to practice rather than to take the oath of allegiance to the Constitution necessary for admission to the bar; taking the oath, he believed, symbolized compromise with the slave power.

Instead he devoted his life to abolitionism, serving as agent of local antislavery societies. His personal crusade to open the Massachusetts schools to Negroes triumphed on April 28, 1855, when the legislature abolished separate schools for Negro children. Nell was also an author of note. *Dictionary of American Biography,* XIII, 413; William W. Brown, *The Black Man* (New York, 1863), 238-241; William W. Brown, *The Rising Son; or, The Antecedents and Advancement of the Colored Race* (Boston, 1874), 485-486.

[36] Miss Forten was seventeen years old.

[37] Thomas Ball, of Cincinnati, was a well-known Negro photographer whose patrons included the city's most prominent families. Carter G. Woodson, "The Negroes of Cincinnati Prior to the Civil War," *Journal of Negro History,* I (January, 1916), 20.

[38] A panorama depicting these objects was exhibited in Salem during early September. George F. Dow, ed., *The Holyoke Diaries, 1709-1856* (Salem, 1911), 188.

[39] The Republican Party, with Charles Sumner as a local leader, was just gaining prominence in Massachusetts during the fall of 1854.

[40] James Russell Lowell's *A Fable for Critics* was published in New York in 1848.

[41] William Wells Brown was one of several escaped slaves who were prominent in the abolition movement. Fleeing from his Missouri master in 1834, he was sheltered for a time by an Ohio Quaker whose name he adopted, then obtained work on Great Lakes steamboats. In this position he helped many other slaves to find refuge in Canada, at the same time studying so effectively that by 1843 he could become an agent of the Western New York Anti-Slavery Society and the Massachusetts Anti-Slavery Society. While visiting England as a lecturer, he learned that the passage of the Fugitive Slave Act of 1850 so imperiled his position that he dared not return to America. During the next five years he delivered more than a thousand antislavery lectures in England and on the Continent. So enthusiastic were his friends over these lectures that they raised enough money to purchase his freedom. This allowed him to return to the United States in September, 1854, where he was welcomed by a large public gathering in Tremont Temple, Boston, on the night of October 13. Brown was immediately made an agent of the American Anti-Slavery Society, with instructions to tour New England as a speaker. *The Liberator,* October 13 and October 20, 1854. Accounts of Brown's career are in the *Dictionary of American Biography,* III, 161; Buckmaster, *Let My People Go,* 119, 178; Josephine Brown, *Biography of an American Bondsman, by His Daughter* (Boston, 1856); William Wells Brown, *Narrative of William W. Brown, A Fugitive Slave, Written by Himself* (Boston, 1847); William Wells Brown, *Three Years in Europe* (London, 1852); and William

Wells Brown, *The American Fugitive in Europe: Sketches of Places and People Abroad* (Boston, 1855). Some of his letters are in Carter G. Woodson, ed., *The Mind of the Negro as Reflected in Letters Written during the Crisis, 1800-1860* (Washington, 1926), 349-383.

[42] The quarterly meeting of the Essex Anti-Slavery Society, held at the Pantheon Hall in Lawrence on October 8, was addressed by William Lloyd Garrison, Wendell Phillips, Charles Lenox Remond, and William Wells Brown. *The Liberator,* October 20, 1854.

[43] The Luca family, a group of talented Negro musicians, performed on the piano, violin and violincello. *Salem Register,* October 15, 1854. William Lloyd Garrison was so entranced with their "remarkable musical performances" that he forgot one of his speaking engagements. *The Liberator,* October 13, 1854.

[44] Mrs. William Ives, who lived on Essex Street, was president of the Salem Female Anti-Slavery Society. Her husband operated a prominent bookstore and published one of the Salem newspapers. *Salem Directory, 1855* (Salem, 1855), 189.

[45] The lecture was one of a series sponsored by the Salem Female Anti-Slavery Society, a local abolitionist organization which had functioned since 1834.

[46] Charles Lenox Remond spoke under the auspices of the Salem Female Anti-Slavery Society.

[47] This lecture was the first of the winter course sponsored by the Salem Lyceum, a venerable organization dating back to 1830. So popular were its series that two were arranged each winter, one on Tuesday nights for the town's Congregationalists and one on Wednesday nights for the Unitarians. The lecturer on this occasion was Joseph P. Thompson, who spoke on "Jerusalem and Damascus." *Historical Sketch of the Salem Lyceum, with a List of Officers and Lecturers since its Formation in 1830* (Salem, 1879), 3-7, 55.

[48] Thomas T. Stone, a Unitarian minister. James Freeman Clarke, *Anti-Slavery Days* (New York, 1884), 131.

[49] Josiah Quincy, Jr., addressed the Salem Lyceum on "Sectional Prejudices." *Historical Sketch of the Salem Lyceum,* 55.

[50] When William Wells Brown returned to the United States he left his two daughters behind, the elder to teach in England, the younger to continue her studies in France. *The Liberator,* September 22, 1854.

[51] Thomas Wentworth Higginson, of Worcester, addressed the Salem Lyceum on "The Old Puritan Clergyman." *Historical Sketch of the Salem Lyceum,* 55.

[52] Mary H. Pike, *Ida May; a Story of Things Actual and Possible* (Boston, 1854).

[53] The lecture by the Reverend Charles E. Hodges, of Watertown, was the fifth in the series sponsored by the Salem Female Anti-Slavery Society. *Salem Register,* November 23, 1854.

[54] Another in the Salem Female Anti-Slavery Society series.

[55] Louis Agassiz, the eminent Harvard scientist, spoke on "The Animal Kingdom," taking the place of Reighold Solger, who was scheduled to deliver an address on "The Present State of the Eastern Question." *Historical Sketch of the Salem Lyceum,* 55. Miss Forten's disappointment was probably due to the fact that Dr. Solger's lectures had been highly praised by William Lloyd Garrison in *The Liberator,* December 15, 1854.

[56] Another event sponsored by the Salem Female Anti-Slavery Society.

[57] James Appleton was a Massachusetts-born crusader for temperance and abolition who had been active in Maine politics. *Dictionary of American Biography,* I, 327.

[58] William C. Nell, the Negro abolitionist of Boston. Sarah was the daughter of Caroline E. Putnam, close friend of Miss Forten.

[59] The eighth lecture in the series sponsored by the Salem Female Anti-Slavery Society was given by Lucy Stone, of West Brookfield, Massachusetts. *Salem Register,* December 14, 1854. Lucy Stone, whose fame rests largely on her crusade for women's rights, was also an active abolitionist.

[60] The Anti-Slavery Bazaar was held annually in Boston to raise money for the Massachusetts Anti-Slavery Society. For months in advance, committees of women collected items from friends of abolitionism in Germany, France, Switzerland, England, Ireland, and the United States. These were sold during the week-long exhibitions, which also served as an excuse for a number of antislavery lectures. Total receipts amounted to $4800. *The Liberator,* December 15, December 22, and December 29, 1854, and January 5, 1855.

PART 2

STUDENT AND ABOLITIONIST: January 1, 1855–May 29, 1856

[1] Henry Ward Beecher, the famous Brooklyn minister, addressed the Salem Lyceum on "Patriotism." *Historical Sketch of the Salem Lyceum, with a List of Officers and Lecturers since its Formation in 1830* (Salem, 1879), 55.

[2] John Pierpont's official subject was "The Moral Influence of Physical Science." He spoke before the Salem Lyceum. *Ibid.,* 55.

[3] John Greenleaf Whittier, the poet laureate of abolitionism, was one of Miss Forten's idols. The poem is not in any of his published works.

[4] William Wells Brown, as an agent of the Massachusetts Anti-Slavery Society, was lecturing frequently in New England.

[5] The Reverend Theodore Parker, Boston's famous Unitarian

minister, addressed the Salem Lyceum on January 30 and January 31, speaking on "The Anglo Saxon" and "The Condition, Character and Prospects of America." *Historical Sketch of the Salem Lyceum,* 55.

[6] George W. Curtis, who spoke before the Salem Lyceum. *Ibid.,* 55.

[7] Asa and John Hutchinson, the prominent singers and abolitionists, were frequent visitors at the home of Charles Lenox Remond, where Miss Forten lived.

[8] R. C. Waterson, who spoke before the Salem Lyceum. *Historical Sketch of the Salem Lyceum,* 55.

[9] James Russell Lowell addressed the Salem Lyceum on "Analysis of Poetry." *Ibid.,* 55.

[10] The Salem Normal School, which opened its doors in 1854, restricted enrollment to young women sixteen years of age or more, who promised to remain in residence at least three terms and to teach in the Massachusetts public schools after graduation. No tuition was charged. The course of study included instruction in "Arithmetic, Algebra, Geometry, Geography, Projections of the Sphere, Physical Geography, Astronomy, Mechanics, Hydrostatics, Pneumatics and Optics, Anatomy and Physiology; Spelling, Reading, Etymology, Critical Study of English Authors, History of English Literature, English Grammar, Art of Reasoning, Rhetoric and Composition, Latin, Theory and Practice of Teaching." *Catalogue of the Instructors and Students in the State Normal School at Salem: for the Term Ending February, 1856* (Salem, 1856), 11-12.

[11] Miss Forten entered the Salem Normal School on March 13, 1855, as one of a class of thirty-five. The total enrollment of the school was 121. *General Catalogue of the Officers, Teachers and Students of the State Normal School, Salem, 1854-1904* (Boston, 1903), 13.

[12] The lecture on "French Character" was one of the Salem Lyceum series. *Historical Sketch of the Salem Lyceum,* 55.

[13] Richard Edwards was principal of the Salem Normal School. *Catalogue of the Instructors and Students,* 1-9.

[14] Margaretta Forten, a sister of Charlotte Forten's father, conducted a school in Philadelphia.

[15] The poem, "To W.L.G. on Reading His 'Chosen Queen,' " was published in *The Liberator,* March 16, 1855:

> A loyal subject, thou, to that bright Queen,
> To whom the homage of thy soul is paid;
> Long to her cause devoted hast thou been,
> And many a sacrifice for her hast made.
> *Thy* chosen Queen, O champion of Truth,
> Should be th' acknowledged sovereign of all;
> Her first commands should fire the heart of youth
> And graver age list heedful to her call.
> Thou, who so bravely dost her battles fight,

With truer weapons than the blood-stained sword,
And teachest us that greater is the might
Of *moral* warfare, noble thought and word,
On thee shall rest the blessing of mankind,
As one who nobly dost the Right defend;
Than thee, thy chosen Queen shall never find
A truer subject nor a firmer friend.

[16] Mr. Clark's lecture is not listed in the Lyceum series or in *The Liberator*.

[17] William C. Nell, Negro abolitionist from Boston.

[18] The New England Anti-Slavery Society held its annual convention at the Melodeon, Boston, on May 29, 30, and 31. Wendell Phillips presided. *The Liberator,* June 1, 1855.

[19] Anthony Burns returned to the North in early March. After being taken to Virginia he was sold by his owner to another purchaser, who promptly resold him to a group of abolitionists headed by the Reverend Lloyd A. Grimes, of Massachusetts. *Ibid.,* March 9, 1855.

[20] The "Panorama" was advertised in *The Liberator,* June 1, 1855, as "Ball's Mammoth Pictorial Tour of the United States." Painted by Negroes, its 23,000 square feet of canvas depicted slavery scenes in several Southern cities as well as "a voyage from Africa to America." It was exhibited in Amory Hall.

[21] Thomas Wentworth Higginson, of Worcester, was the principal speaker at the evening session. His speech was printed in *The Liberator,* June 8, 1855.

[22] Ernestine Louise Siismondi Potowski Rose had left her native Poland at the age of sixteen after rebelling against the orthodox Judaism of her rabbi father. After a career on the Continent she married William E. Rose, an Englishman, with whom she came to the United States in 1836. From that date until 1867, when she returned to England, Mrs. Rose spoke constantly in behalf of free schools, women's rights, abolitionism, and similar causes. Her brilliant mind and forceful style commanded wide audiences. For biographical sketches see *The Liberator,* May 16, 1856; and the *Dictionary of American Biography* XVI, 158.

[23] John Pierpont, a graduate of Yale University and the Harvard Divinity School, had for some years campaigned so outspokenly for abolition that he was dismissed from several Unitarian pulpits. At this time he was minister at the West Medford, Massachusetts, Unitarian Church, and constantly in demand as a speaker at antislavery meetings. *Dictionary of American Biography,* XIV, 586.

[24] Charles C. Burleigh, a reformer famed for his flowing beard and eccentric costume, had been active in the abolitionist movement since 1835, when he gave up the study of law to become a lecturer for the Middlesex Anti-Slavery Society. A close friend of Garrison, he served at one time as secretary of the American Anti-Slavery Society and as editor of the *Penn-*

sylvania Freeman. Dictionary of American Biography, III, 284–285. For a statement of his views see Charles C. Burleigh, *Slavery and the North* (New York, 1855).

[25] Samuel J. May also spoke that day. *The Liberator,* June 8, 1855.

[26] *The Liberator,* June 8, 1855, referred to Wendell Phillips' address as "a thrilling speech." His remarks and those of Theodore Parker are printed in *ibid.,* June 15, 1855.

[27] Sarah P. Remond.

[28] The Massachusetts Anti-Slavery Society held an annual celebration of Independence Day at Farmingham Grove, a wooded park some fifteen miles west of Boston.

[29] Margaretta Forten, of Philadelphia.

[30] The Abington meeting of the Massachusetts Anti-Slavery Society, celebrating the twenty-first anniversary of the freeing of England's slaves, was well attended, for the day was pleasant after a week of rain. Edmund Quincy presided, and speeches were given by the Reverend A. T. Foss, Charles L. Remond, J. B. Swasey, of Newburyport, Wendell Phillips, and the Reverend James Freeman Clarke. *The Liberator,* August 18, 1855.

[31] A meeting of the Middlesex Anti-Slavery Society was held at Reading that day, with speeches by William Lloyd Garrison, Wendell Phillips, and Charles L. Remond and songs by John and Asa Hutchinson. *Ibid.,* August 10, 1855, and August 17, 1855.

[32] A daughter of William Wells Brown who had recently arrived from abroad.

[33] William C. Nell, the Negro abolitionist from Boston.

[34] The Salem Female Anti-Slavery Society, which had conducted sewing circles and lecture series in Salem since its formation, in 1834.

[35] Garrison was attacked by a mob on October 21, 1835, while addressing the Boston Female Anti-Slavery Society. Wendell P. Garrison and Francis J. Garrison, *William Lloyd Garrison, 1805-1879* (New York, 1885-1889), II, 1-37.

[36] A meeting to commemorate the mob attack was held in Stacy Hall, Boston, the very building from which Garrison was dragged twenty years before. Speeches were given by Garrison, Henry C. Wright, Thomas Wentworth Higginson, and Wendell Phillips. *Ibid.,* III, 422-427.

[37] The lecture by the Reverend Samuel Johnson, of Lynn, inaugurated the eleventh lecture series sponsored by the Salem Female Anti-Slavery Society. *Salem Register,* October 18, 1855.

[38] Charles F. Hovey, one of Garrison's intimate friends and financial supporters. Garrison and Garrison, *William Lloyd Garrison,* III, 429.

[39] Sallie Holley, an agent of the American Anti-Slavery Society. Because she shrank from public appearances, she was less well known than most abolitionists. Sallie Holley, *A Life for Liberty: Anti-Slavery and Other Letters of Sallie Holley*

(New York, 1899), 75-76; *The Liberator,* October 19, 1855.

[40] Wendell Phillips' lecture was one of the series sponsored by the Salem Female Anti-Slavery Society. *Salem Register,* October 25, 1855.

[41] Charles Sumner addressed a meeting of the Republican Party in Mechanic Hall, Salem, that evening. *Ibid.,* November 1, 1855. The speech is printed in Charles Sumner, *Recent Speeches and Addresses by Charles Sumner* (Boston, 1856), 522-562.

[42] J. B. Swasey, of Newburyport, a lawyer and recent convert to abolitionism, spoke before the Salem Female Anti-Slavery Society. *Salem Register,* November 1, 1855.

[43] Professor Arnold H. Guyot, a Swiss geographer, came to the United States in 1848 on the invitation of Louis Agassiz. For the next six years he lectured under the auspices of the Massachusetts Board of Education in institutions and normal schools. At this time he was a member of the staff of the Salem Normal School. *Dictionary of American Biography,* VIII, 63-64; *Catalogue of Instructors and Students,* 9.

[44] Mary F. Webb, the wife of Frank B. Webb, of Philadelphia, a talented Negro woman well known for her dramatic readings. *Salem Register,* November 19, 1855. *The Liberator,* November 30, 1855, praised her performance highly: "A large and appreciative audience expressed great satisfaction with Mrs. Webb's dramatic reading. Selections were classical, sentimental and humorous. Those from Shakespeare were much admired. She introduced, for the first time, *'St. Catherine Borne by Angels,'* a recent composition by Mrs. Stowe, the reading of which secured the tribute of marked stillness. Her versatility found full scope in Irish sketches and scenes from American slave life; and she is equally at home in delivering French and German eccentricities."

[45] This lecture by the Reverend James Freeman Clarke, Unitarian pastor and prominent Boston reformer, was one of the series sponsored by the Salem Female Anti-Slavery Society. *Salem Register,* November 22, 1855.

[46] Antoinetta Louisa Brown, an Oberlin College graduate, had resigned a pastorate in the Congregational Church when unable to reconcile its teachings with her strong belief in abolitionism. She gained world-wide fame in 1853, when she was refused permission to speak at a New York World's Temperance Convention because of her sex. She spoke frequently in behalf of the crusades in which she was interested. *Dictionary of American Biography,* II, 319-320. This lecture was sponsored by the Salem Female Anti-Slavery Society. *Salem Register,* December 13, 1855.

[47] Samuel Joseph May, Boston-born pastor of a Unitarian church in Syracuse, New York, was an ardent supporter of various causes, including nonresistance, temperance, women's rights, universal education, and abolition. Active in the Ameri-

can Anti-Slavery Society from the time of its formation, his home after 1851 was a station in the Underground Railroad. His earnest efforts in behalf of his fellow men earned him Bronson Alcott's epithet: "The Lord's chore boy." *Dictionary of American Biography*, XII, 447-448; Samuel J. May, *Some Recollections of the Antislavery Conflict* (Boston, 1869); and Thomas J. Mumford, ed., *Memoirs of Samuel Joseph May* (Boston, 1873).

[48] Dr. May's lecture was entitled "Magna Charta of New York." *Historical Sketch of the Salem Lyceum,* 55-56.

[49] This lecture was one of the series sponsored by the Salem Female Anti-Slavery Society, *Salem Register,* December 20, 1855.

[50] Helen Putnam Gilliard, daughter of Mrs. Putnam, and close friend of Miss Forten.

[51] Ralph Waldo Emerson lectured on "Beauty" to the Salem Lyceum. *Historical Sketch of the Salem Lyceum,* 55-56.

[52] Wife of Charles Lenox Remond, with whom Miss Forten lived.

[53] The annual Anti-Slavery Bazaar, which opened on December 19 under the direction of Mrs. Maria Weston Chapman. *The Liberator,* November 30 and December 7, 1855.

[54] Sydney A. Storey, Jr., *Caste, A Story of Republican Equality* (Boston, 1855). The book was advertised in *The Liberator,* December 30, 1855.

[55] The Reverend O. B. Frothingham, formerly of Salem but now a pastor in Jersey City, spoke on the series arranged by the Salem Female Anti-Slavery Society. *Salem Register,* December 27, 1855.

[56] The hymn was entitled "A Parting Hymn":

> When Winter's royal robes of white
> From hill and vale are gone
> And the glad voices of the spring
> Upon the air are borne,
> Friends who have met with us before,
> Within these walls shall meet no more.
>
> Forth to a noble work they go:
> O, may their hearts keep pure,
> And hopeful zeal and strength be theirs
> To labor and endure,
> That they an earnest faith may prove
> By words of truth and deeds of love.
>
> May those, whose holy task it is,
> To guide impulsive youth,
> Fail not to cherish in their souls
> A reverence for truth;
> For teachings which the lips impart
> Must have their source within the heart.

> May all who suffer share their love—
> The poor and the oppressed;
> So shall the blessing of our God
> Upon their labors rest.
> And may we meet again where all
> Are blest and freed from every thrall.

Printed in William W. Brown, *The Black Man* (New York, 1863), 191.

[57] The Reverend Theodore Parker, of Boston, addressed the Salem Lyceum on "The Relation of Productive Industry to Social Progress." *Historical Sketch of the Salem Lyceum*, 55-56.

[58] The Reverend Charles E. Hodges, of Watertown, whose lecture was one of the series arranged by the Salem Female Anti-Slavery Society. *Salem Register*, January 24, 1856.

[59] William Lloyd Garrison was in town to give the final lecture in the series sponsored by the Salem Female Anti-Slavery Society. *Ibid.*, January 31, 1856.

[60] Nathaniel P. Banks, of Massachusetts, a Republican with outspoken antislavery views, was elected speaker of the House of Representatives over his Democratic opponent on the 133rd ballot. The election was hailed as a triumph for freedom by *The Liberator*, February 8, 1856.

[61] Mr. A. Russell, a teacher. *Salem Directory* (1850), 122.

[62] Mary Shepard, principal of the grammar school attended by Miss Forten, had been on leave for almost three months because of illness. *Annual Report of the School Committee of the City of Salem* (Salem, 1856), 16.

[63] A former pupil at the Salem Normal School.

[64] The Misses Hall, popularly known as the "Singing Sisters," gave their concert at Mechanic Hall, Salem. *Salem Register*, March 10, 1856.

[65] See page 83 for an account of the ceremony at which these compositions were presented.

[66] Richard Edwards, principal of the Salem Normal School.

[67] Robert Purvis, of Philadelphia, Miss Forten's uncle.

[68] The meeting, sponsored by the Massachusetts Anti-Slavery Society, was held on May 27, 28, and 29, 1856, at the Melodeon and Faneuil Hall, Boston, to welcome home Parker Pillsbury, who had been lecturing on abolition in England for two years. Garrison, Phillips, and others spoke, as well as Pillsbury. *The Liberator*, June 6 and June 13, 1856. Parker Pillsbury, after a brief career as a minister, had renounced the pulpit to devote all his time to abolition and women's rights. A thunderous speaker, with imposing black beard and tattered clothes, he was pictured by James Russell Lowell as

> . . . brown, broad-shouldered Pillsbury,
> Who tears up words like trees by the roots,
> A Theseus in stout cow-hide boots.

Dictionary of American Biography, XIV, 608-609; Parker Pillsbury, *Acts of the Anti-Slavery Apostles* (Concord, N. Y., 1883).

[69] Maria Weston Chapman had since 1834 been the soul of the Boston Female Anti-Slavery Society as well as one of Garrison's most valued helpers. She was with Garrison when he was mobbed in 1835, served as editor of *The Liberator* when he was ill, and after 1840 sat with him on the executive committee of the American Anti-Slavery Society. Never too effective as a speaker, she rendered yeoman service to the cause by arranging the annual antislavery bazaars and editing the *Liberty Bell*, a volume of abolitionist writings published each year in Boston. *Dictionary of American Biography*, IV, 19. For her views on slavery see Maria W. Chapman, *How Can I Help Abolish Slavery? or, Counsels to the Newly Converted* (New York, 1855).

[70] Probably Elizabeth B. Chase, of Rhode Island, who regularly attended meetings of the Massachusetts Anti-Slavery Society and contributed generously to its support. *The Liberator,* June 13, 1856.

PART 3

Teacher and Invalid: June 18, 1856–June 11, 1857

[1] Richard Edwards, principal of the Salem Normal School.

[2] Miss Forten was assigned to the Epes Grammar School, with the rank of assistant and a salary of $200 a year. The principal was L. F. Warren, who shared the teaching duties with two assistants. The Epes School, which was on Aborn Street in Salem, admitted both boys and girls. *Annual Report of the School Committee of the City of Salem, 1857* (Salem, 1857), 10, 40-41.

[3] L. F. Warren, principal of the Epes Grammar School.

[4] *The Liberator,* July 11, 1856, reported that heavy rains prevented the usual Fourth of July meeting of the Massachusetts Anti-Slavery Society in the Grove at Framingham. Instead those present took the cars to the town hall at Framingham Center, where Garrison, J. B. Swasey, and Parker Pillsbury spoke. In the afternoon, the skies having cleared, the meeting returned to the Grove, where the principal speakers were the Reverend Andrew Foss and Wendell Phillips.

[5] Graduation exercises at the Salem Normal School were held that afternoon, with the reading of a "Dissertation" by Miss S. C. Pitman, of Salem; a "Poem" by Miss C. L. Forten, of Philadelphia; and a "Valedictory Address" by Miss P. E. Church, of Bridgetown, Nova Scotia. The presentation of diplomas followed. *Order of Exercises at the Fourth Semi-Annual Examination of the State Normal School, at Salem. First Day—Monday, July 21, 1856* (Salem, 1856).

[6] The "Poem," published in *The Liberator*, August 24, 1856, was as follows:

> In the earnest path of duty,
>   With the high hopes and hearts sincere,
> We, to useful lives aspiring,
>   Daily meet to labor here.
>
> No vain dreams of earthly glory
>   Urge us onward to explore
> Far-extending realms of knowledge,
>   With their rich and varied store;
>
> But, with hope of aiding others,
>   Gladly we perform our part;
> Nor forget, the mind, while storing,
>   We must educate the heart,—
>
> Teach it hatred of oppression,
>   Truest love of God and man;
> Thus our high and holy calling
>   May accomplish His great plan.
>
> Not the great and gifted only
>   He appoints to do his will,
> But each one, however lowly,
>   Has a mission to fulfill.
>
> Knowing this, toil we unwearied,
>   With true hearts and purpose high;—
> We would win a wreath immortal
>   Whose bright flowers ne'er fade and die.

The *Salem Register*, July 24, 1856, in describing the graduation exercises, commented as follows on the student speakers: "Each was worthy of special notice, but we can not now particularize farther than to say that the poem, so skilfully written and gracefully delivered, was a production of one of that of-times oppressed race, 'guilty of a skin not colored like our own.' She presented, in her own mental endowments and propriety of demeanor, an honorable vindication of the claims of her race to the rights of mental culture and the privileges of humanity."

[7] Dr. Henry Wheatland, local doctor and secretary and treasurer of the Essex Institute.

[8] Mrs. Charles Lenox Remond.

[9] The annual celebration at Abington of the emancipation of slaves in England.

[10] Amy Matilda Remond, wife of Charles Lenox Remond, died in Salem on August 15, 1856. The daughter of the Reverend Peter Williams, of New York, she was at the time of her death forty-seven years of age. The *Salem Register*, August 18,

1856, described her as "a most estimable lady, sincerely lamented by a large circle of friends." *The Liberator,* August 22, 1856, devoted much space to an account of her labors in the cause of abolitionism. "Personally identified with an oppressed and proscribed portion of the American people," Garrison wrote, "she soared far above the meanness of an irrational prejudice, and did much for its expiration by the benignity of her temper, the goodness of her heart, and the loveliness and dignity of her person."

[11] William Wells Brown spoke in South Danvers as an agent of the Massachusetts Anti-Slavery Society. *The Liberator,* September 5, 1856.

[12] Caroline E. Putnam, Miss Forten's close friend. William C. Nell, Boston's Negro abolitionist, was a frequent visitor at the Putnam home.

[13] The lecture by Frank P. Appleton, of Lowell, inaugurated the twelfth course of abolition lectures sponsored by the Salem Female Anti-Slavery Society. *The Liberator,* October 10, 1856.

[14] Charles Lenox Remond spoke at Marblehead that evening as an agent of the American Anti-Slavery Society. *The Liberator,* October 24, 1856.

[15] "Bleeding Kansas" was much in the public eye during the autumn of 1856. Warfare had been touched off by John Brown's raid at Pottawatomie Creek in May, and had increased in intensity during the summer and fall.

[16] Probably Richard Henry Dana, who, although not an abolitionist, was actively involved in the antislavery cause as a lawyer and Republican politician.

[17] Charles Sumner, who had recently been catapulted to fame when beaten in Congress by Representative Preston S. Brooks, returned to Boston on November 3 to cast his vote in the presidential election. Sumner was escorted into the city by a cavalcade of carriages and a "vast concourse of citizens" who formed a cheering mass along the route. At the State House he was presented with flowers bearing such slogans as "No bludgeon can dim the lustre of our champion of Freedom." The reception was described in *The Liberator,* November 17, 1856; and the *Salem Register,* November 6, 1856.

[18] Miss Forten, with other abolitionists, was saddened by the triumph of James Buchanan, the Democratic presidential candidate, over John C. Frémont, who ran on the Republican ticket. *The Liberator,* November 7, 1856, was plunged into mourning.

[19] Charles Lenox Remond addressed a meeting of the Essex County Anti-Slavery Society held at Georgetown on November 15 and 16, 1856. *The Liberator,* November 21, 1856.

[20] The Reverend Sumner Ellis, of Salem, who gave the third lecture in the series arranged by the Salem Female Anti-Slavery Society. *Salem Register,* November 13, 1856.

[21] Lydia P. Chase, a member of the executive committee of the Salem Female Anti-Slavery Society. *Salem Directory, 1857* (Salem, 1857), 226.

[22] Lydia Maria Child, who wrote best-selling juvenile books during the 1820's, cast her lot with the abolitionists from the time the American Anti-Slavery Society was formed, in 1833. Applying her literary talents to the cause, she produced a veritable deluge of books, pamphlets, and articles denouncing slavery. Lydia Maria Child, *Letters of Lydia Maria Child* (Boston, 1883), Introduction. One of her best-known books, *Letters from New-York,* was published in New York in 1843.

[23] Lydia Maria Child, *Philothea: A Romance* (Boston, 1836).

[24] J. G. Hoyt lectured on "Popular Fallacies." *Historical Sketch of the Salem Lyceum, with a List of Officers and Lecturers since its Formation in 1830* (Salem, 1879), 56.

[25] Mrs. William Ives, wife of the publisher of the *Salem Observer,* and president of the Salem Female Anti-Slavery Society.

[26] John Greenleaf Whittier, the poet laureate of abolitionism.

[27] Parker Pillsbury, the abolitionist, lectured in the series sponsored by the Salem Female Anti-Slavery Society. *Salem Register,* December 18, 1856.

[28] William Elder, *Historical Sketch of the Salem Lyceum,* 56.

[29] The Annual Anti-Slavery Bazaar sponsored by the Massachusetts Anti-Slavery Society, which opened on December 23. *The Liberator,* December 19, 1856.

[30] Maria Weston Chapman, who was in charge of the fair.

[31] Eliza Lee Cabot Follen, product of an aristocratic Boston family, who devoted her life to abolitionism. She was the author of a number of tracts and poems, served on the executive committee of the American Anti-Slavery Society, and played an active part in both the Massachusetts Anti-Slavery Society and the Boston Female Anti-Slavery Society. She was particularly helpful in arranging the antislavery bazaars. *Dictionary of American Biography,* VI, 492-493.

[32] Lydia Maria Child.

[33] Francis H. Drake, of Leominster, Massachusetts, was a member of the committee in charge of the bazaar. *The Liberator,* December 19, 1856.

[34] Mrs. Follen was sixty-nine years old.

[35] Charles K. Whipple was a well-known abolitionist who served as counselor of the Massachusetts Anti-Slavery Society and on the executive committee of the American Anti-Slavery Society. *Proceedings of the Massachusetts Anti-Slavery Society at the Annual Meetings held in 1854, 1855, and 1856* (Boston, 1856), 4; *Annual Reports of the American Anti-Slavery Society, by the Executive Committee, for the Years Ending May 1, 1857, and May 1, 1858* (New York, 1858), 194.

[36] Charles F. Hovey, an outstanding abolitionist.

[37] Only two of the founders of the New England Anti-Slavery Society, which had been renamed the Massachusetts Anti-

Slavery Society, were present at the meeting: Garrison and Oliver Johnson. Both spoke. Other speakers were Samuel J. May, John A. Andrew, and Thomas Wentworth Higginson. *The Liberator,* January 2, 1857; Garrison and Garrison, *William Lloyd Garrison,* III, 448-460.

[38] *The Liberator,* January 16, 1857, endorsed the pianist Thalberg as "the greatest of all performers in his line."

[39] *The Liberator,* January 9, 1857, reprinted most of the speeches and letters presented at the Faneuil Hall meeting. The Reverend O. B. Frothingham, formerly of Salem, was at this time a pastor in Jersey City, New Jersey. Mrs. Foster, the wife of the abolitionist Stephen S. Foster, was active in the anti-slavery crusade under her maiden name, Abigail Kelley. *Dictionary of American Biography,* VI, 558.

[40] Harriet Martineau was an English writer and reformer, principally known for her widely read travel account, *Society in America* (New York, 1837).

[41] The Reverend O. B. Frothingham, of Jersey City, New Jersey.

[42] Mr. Frothingham spoke before the Salem Lyceum on "Epicurus the Philosopher of the World." *Historical Sketch of the Salem Lyceum,* 57.

[43] George S. Hillard was the author of four elementary readers—*First Class Reader, Second Class Reader, Third Class Reader,* and *Fourth Class Reader*—published in Boston between 1855 and 1858.

[44] Wendell Phillips, to whom Miss Forten wrote on January 2. The letter is not included in any of his published works.

[45] The Reverend Theodore Parker, of Boston, addressed the Salem Lyceum on "Benjamin Franklin." *Historical Sketch of the Salem Lyceum,* 57.

[46] The twenty-fifth annual meeting of the Massachusetts Anti-Slavery Society was held in Boston on January 29 and 30, 1857. Among the speakers were Garrison, Parker Pillsbury, Wendell Phillips, Theodore Parker, and Thomas Wentworth Higginson. *The Liberator,* February 6 and February 13, 1857.

[47] Abigail Kelley Foster, or Abby Foster, as she was known to her fellow abolitionists, also spoke briefly at the meeting.

[48] William C. Nell, Negro abolitionist and friend of Miss Forten.

[49] Theodore Parker's extensive library was famous. Of it the *New York Tribune* correspondent once wrote: "He buys books, of course, although his great library overflows every room in his house, and even now threatens to invade those of his neighbors, and to be complained of as a nuisance." Quoted in *The Liberator,* January 22, 1858. On his death in 1860 he left his collection of 30,000 books to the Boston Public Library. *The Liberator,* June 1, 1860.

[50] James Freeman Clarke, *Eleven Weeks in Europe, and*

What May be Seen in That Time (Boston, 1852); Mattie Griffiths, *Autobiography of a Female Slave* (New York, 1857).

[51] Julia Kavanagh, *Madeline: a Tale of Auvergne, Founded on Fact* (London, 1848).

[52] Charles Rollin, *Ancient History of the Egyptians, Carthaginians, Assyrians, Babylonians, Medes and Persians, Macedonians, and Grecians* (Boston, 12th ed., 1807-1808), 4 vols.

[53] Ralph Waldo Emerson spoke before the Salem Lyceum on "Works and Days." *Historical Sketch of the Salem Lyceum*, 57.

[54] The demonstration was given by Mrs. Ada L. Coan, a "rapping and writing medium," who displayed her alleged powers in the Lyceum Hall at twelve and a half cents a head. *Salem Register*, February 12, 1857. Miss Forten's interest in the subject can be explained partly by the fact that most radical abolitionists, including Garrison, were professed spiritualists. See *The Liberator*, August 17, 1855.

[55] The lecture was not listed among those in the Lyceum series, and it was not advertised in the local newspapers.

[56] The concert was advertised in the *Salem Register*, February 23, 1857.

[57] Charles Lenox Remond had been away for several months, speaking at antislavery meetings in New York State. *The Liberator*, March 6, 1857.

[58] James Russell Lowell spoke before the Salem Lyceum. *Historical Sketch of the Salem Lyceum*, 57.

[59] Sarah Parker Remond, with her brother and several other abolitionists, had recently completed a series of antislavery lectures in New York State. This marked Miss Remond's first appearance as an abolitionist lecturer. *The Liberator*, March 6, 1857, remarked that her dignified manner, winning appearance, and sincere earnestness won over her hearers, and that she needed only a little more practice to become an effective speaker.

[60] The first edition of Elizabeth Barrett Browning's *Aurora Leigh* was published in London in 1857.

[61] Miss Forten wrote to Harriet Martineau on January 11, 1857. The letter was forwarded to her by Maria Weston Chapman.

[62] So great was Wendell Phillips' popularity that the Reverend Theodore Parker's church was crowded with three thousand listeners even though the topic of his address had not been announced. *The Liberator*, April 3, 1857.

[63] The Reverend Thomas T. Stone delivered a series of six lectures on English literature. This was the second lecture, the first having been on "The Written Word and the Tale." Other topics treated were: "The Allegory," "The Song," "The Essay," and "The Sermon." *Salem Register*, March 30, 1857.

[64] Sarah Remond, daughter of Charles Lenox Remond.

[65] Miss Forten's motner died when she was a small girl.

[66] William H. Prescott, *History of the Reign of Philip the Second, King of Spain.* (Philadelphia, 1852-1858), 3 vols.

[67] Mrs. Kemble advertised three readings at Lyceum Hall in Salem during the week. *Salem Register,* April 16, 1857.

[68] Jones Very was a mystic poet; he was a friend of Emerson and a member of the Transcendental Club. See William I. Bartlett, *Jones Very, Emerson's Brave Saint* (Durham, N. C., 1942).

[69] *Neighbor Jackson, by the Author of "Father Brighthopes"* (Boston, 1857).

[70] Mary L. Shepard, principal of the Higginson Grammar School and one of Miss Forten's most intimate friends.

[71] Charlotte Brontë, *Jane Eyre* (London, 1847), 3 vols.

[72] The annual New England Anti-Slavery Convention was held in Boston on May 28 and 29, 1857. Speeches were delivered by Garrison, Wendell Phillips, Thomas Wentworth Higginson, William Wells Brown, Abby Kelley Foster, The Reverend Caleb Stetson, Aaron M. Powell, Parker Pillsbury, Charles Lenox Remond, and others. The meetings were apparently poorly attended; on one vote only forty-two ballots were cast.

[73] Susan Brownell Anthony, a New York Quaker, had since 1850 devoted all her time to reform. Laboring for a time in the temperance crusade, she soon developed an interest in radical abolitionism. During 1857 and 1858 she spoke throughout the North on a platform of "No Union with Slaveholders." Her militant aggressivism, which made her an effective speaker, was also used in behalf of women's rights. *Dictionary of American Biography,* I, 318-320; Rheta L. Dorr, *Susan B. Anthony* (New York, 1928); Ida H. Harper, *Life and Works of Susan B. Anthony* (Indianapolis, 1898-1908), 3 vols.

[74] Aaron M. Powell, a young man just enlisted in the antislavery crusade, gained his reputation as an abolitionist while conducting a series of meetings in New York State during the winter of 1856-1857. He later became a prominent member of the American Anti-Slavery Society. *The Liberator,* March 6, 1857; Aaron M. Powell, *Personal Reminiscences of the Anti-Slavery and Other Reforms and Reformers* (New York, 1899).

[75] Mount Auburn Cemetery, in Cambridge, Massachusetts.

[76] Harriet Beecher Stowe, *The Mayflower: or, Sketches of Scenes and Characters among the Descendants of the Pilgrims* (New York, 1843).

[77] Richard Edwards, principal of the Salem Normal School.

PART 4

[1] Mrs. Caroline E. Putnam, of Salem, a close friend of Miss Forten.

[2] At Byberry, a suburb fifteen miles from Philadelphia, was the "princely residence" of Robert Purvis, Miss Forten's uncle. Mr. Purvis was one of the nation's most prominent Negro abolitionists. For a sketch of his career see the Introduction, pages 14-15.

[3] Miss Peabody was apparently a Negro writer. A search of contemporary sources fails to reveal any mention of her.

[4] Miss Forten had read *The Autobiography of a Female Slave* (New York, 1857) six months before.

[5] Robert Purvis, Miss Forten's uncle.

[6] *Barnaby Rudge,* a story by Charles Dickens.

[7] The famous training school for boys founded by Stephen Girard, an eccentric philanthropist, who provided in his will that no clergyman should ever enter the institution. See C. A. Herrick, *Stephen Girard* (Philadelphia, 1923), 135-141, 155-158.

[8] A Philadelphia friend of the Forten family.

[9] James Miller McKim, a Presbyterian minister, had been a militant abolitionist since the formation of the American Anti-Slavery Society, in 1833. Forced to resign from the ministry because of his views, he became one of the "seventy" gathered by Theodore Dwight Weld to spread the gospel of emancipation. With his wife he aided many escaping slaves, and in addition served as secretary of the Pennsylvania Anti-Slavery Society and editor of its publication, *The Pennsylvania Freeman. Dictionary of American Biography,* XII, 103-104.

[10] The Sea Girt House and Ocean House were famous Newport hotels.

[11] A natural stairway of stone leading from the Cliff Walk to the ocean's edge. George C. Mason, *Newport Illustrated* (Newport, 1854).

[12] Fort Adams, which had been built at Newport during the War of 1812, contained a spacious parade ground where a band played every Tuesday and Friday evening. Newport's fashionable visitors usually paraded around the grounds in their carriages while the performance went on. *Ibid.,* 20-21.

[13] The first triennial convention of graduates of the Salem Normal School. The program began with ceremonies at the school in the morning, continued through a meeting at South Church in the afternoon, at which Professor C. C. Felton, of Cambridge, spoke, and concluded with a dinner and social

evening. *Order of Exercises at the First Triennial Convention of the Graduates and Pupils of the Normal School at Salem, Wednesday, August 5, 1857* (Salem, 1857).

[14] William Lloyd Garrison spoke in South Danvers on the afternoon and evening of Sunday, August 9. His subject was "The Present Religious and Political Aspects of American Slavery." *The Liberator*, August 7, 1857.

[15] Sarah Parker Remond, sister of Charles Lenox Remond, at whose home Miss Forten lived in Salem.

[16] *Jane Eyre*, by Charlotte Brontë, was published in London in 1847.

[17] Charles F. Hovey, a prominent Garrisonian abolitionist.

[18] All of Charles Lenox Remond's acquaintances noted his growing moroseness and irritability at this time, which were due partly to illness but more to his rapid eclipse by Frederick Douglass, who was becoming the country's leading Negro abolitionist. A friend, writing a few years later of Douglass' rise to fame, said: "This so soured the latter [Remond] that he never recovered from it, and even at the present time speaks disparagingly of his early friend and associate." William W. Brown, *The Rising Son* (New York, 1863), 403-404.

[19] The Reverend Thomas T. Stone, who opened the annual lecture series of the Salem Female Anti-Slavery Society.

[20] Joseph Warren, who led the American forces at the battle of Bunker Hill.

[21] Elisha K. Kane in 1853 led an expedition northward to search for the arctic exploring party of Sir John Franklin, which had been missing since 1845. Kane returned in 1855, after exploring much of the area near the North Pole. His book on the subject, *Arctic Explorations: The Second Grinnell Expedition in Search of Sir John Franklin, in the Years 1853, '54, '55* (New York, 1856), 2 vols., had an honored place on most of the parlor tables of America for a decade. *Dictionary of American Biography*, X, 256-257.

[22] William Henry Furness, a Unitarian minister from Philadelphia, who devoted his life to abolition and to a study of the life of Jesus. *Dictionary of American Biography*, VII, 80. He addressed the Salem Female Anti-Slavery Society.

[23] The new magazine was heartily endorsed by *The Liberator*, October 16, 1857.

[24] Henry W. Bellows addressed the Salem Lyceum on "Unities of Modes of Education." *Historical Sketch of the Salem Lyceum, with a List of Officers and Lecturers since its Formation in 1830* (Salem, 1879), 57.

[25] The *Atlantic Monthly*, I (November, 1857), contained an article on the Manchester Exhibition, 33-45, and Ralph Waldo Emerson's poem, "Brahma," 48.

[26] Parker Pillsbury's lecture on slavery at South Danvers was noticed in *The Liberator*, November 27, 1857.

[27] William Lloyd Garrison delivered the final lecture in the

series sponsored by the Salem Female Anti-Slavery Society. *The Liberator,* November 27, 1857.

[28] *Corinne, ou L'Italie,* by Madame de Staël, was published in Paris in numerous editions in the early nineteenth century.

[29] James Freeman Clarke addressed the Salem Lyceum on "The Yankee." *Historical Sketch of the Salem Lyceum,* 57.

[30] The change in residence to the home of Mrs. Caroline E. Putnam was made necessary by Mr. Remond's growing unpleasantness.

[31] A diligent search of contemporary sources has failed to reveal either the *Home Journal* or the story that Miss Forten mentions.

[32] Wendell Phillips spoke before the Salem Lyceum on "Toussaint L'Ouverture," the "Black Napoleon" who led the slave revolt on Santo Domingo in the late eighteenth century. *Historical Sketch of the Salem Lyceum,* 57.

[33] The annual Anti-Slavery Bazaar opened in Boston on December 17 and closed on December 26. *The Liberator,* December 11, 1857.

[34] Harriet Beecher Stowe, who, in common with other women abolitionists, arranged tables of items for sale at the bazaar.

[35] The correspondent of the *New York Tribune,* after a visit to the bazaar, noted that "Senator Sumner makes a passing visit,—a stately tower, whose outward beauty is unscathed, and whose inward defenses are, we hope, rapidly tending to restoration." Quoted in *The Liberator,* January 22, 1858. Despite this description Sumner had been in poor health since his beating by Preston Brooks. His illness forced him to leave Washington in December, 1857, for a five-month rest in Boston, New York, and Philadelphia. Edward L. Pierce, *Memoir and Letters of Charles Sumner* (Boston, 1877-1893), III, 559.

[36] Mr. and Mrs. Samuel J. May, of Syracuse, New York. May was a prominent abolitionist.

[37] Maria W. Chapman, the guiding spirit of the bazaar, whose efforts each year in its behalf won poetic tribute from James Russell Lowell:

> There was Maria Chapman, too.
> With her swift eyes of clear steel blue,
> The coiled up mainspring of the Fair,
> Originating everywhere
> The expansive force without a sound,
> That whirls a hundred wheels around;
> Herself meanwhile as calm and still,
> As the bare crown of Prospect Hill. . . .

[38] Caroline W. H. Dall, daughter of a wealthy Boston merchant and wife of the Unitarian clergyman Charles H. Dall, was one of the nation's most diligent campaigners for women's rights. *Dictionary of American Biography,* V, 35.

[39] Whittier wrote early in January, 1858, that his mother had

"passed away a few days ago, in the beautiful serenity of a Christian faith—a quiet and peaceful dismissal." Samuel T. Pickard, *Life and Letters of John Greenleaf Whittier* (Boston, 1894), II, 412.

40 Ralph Waldo Emerson addressed the Salem Lyceum on "The Finer Relations of Man to Nature." *Historical Sketch of the Salem Lyceum*, 57.

41 The lecture was not in the Lyceum series.

42 The Reverend George B. Cheever, Congregational pastor of the Church of the Puritans in New York, was a fearless champion of abolitionism and equal rights for Negroes. *Dictionary of American Biography*, IV, 48-49. He spoke before the Salem Lyceum on "Conscience of the People and the Basis of Law." *Historical Sketch of the Salem Lyceum*, 57. Miss Forten later wrote that the staid Salem audience, which would never attend an abolition lecture, was first shocked by Wendell Phillips' address on Toussaint L'Ouverture, "as admirable and thorough an anti-slavery lecture as one could possibly desire," then jarred into rebellion when Dr. Cheever returned to the same theme. "This," she recorded, "was the drop too much. The proslavery rage boiled over, and loud and bitter were the complaints." *National Anti-Slavery Standard*, June 19, 1858.

43 Mrs. William Ives, president of the Salem Female Anti-Slavery Society.

44 The parody was written by Miss Forten and William C. Nell for an antislavery celebration scheduled to be held in Boston on March 5, 1858. See below, page 115, for an account of the parody's reception.

45 The Church of the Immaculate Conception on Walnut Street, Salem, was completed early in 1858. Osgood and Batchelder, *Historical Sketch of Salem* (Salem, 1879), 96-97.

46 *The Eclectic Magazine*, XLIII (January, 1858), contained reviews of Alexander Smith's *City Poems*, 129-142, and Elizabeth Barrett Browning's *Aurora Leigh*, 10-19, as well as a sketch of Mrs. Browning, 127-128.

47 Mr. and Mrs. Frank J. Webb, of Philadelphia, had just returned to the United States after a long visit in southern France occasioned by Mrs. Webb's poor health. Mrs. Webb had been forced to abandon giving the "readings" that had won her fame. While in England Mr. Webb had, through the intervention of friends, received the appointment as postmaster at Kingston, Jamaica. *The Liberator*, March 5, 1858.

48 Miss Forten's resignation as a teacher was accepted with regret by the School Committee of Salem. "In March," the Committee reported, "Miss Charlotte L. Forten, who had served for more than a year as Assistant in the Epes school, to the entire satisfaction of the Committee, resigned, and removed from the city." *Annual Report of the School Committee of the City of Salem, January, 1859* (Salem, 1859), 17. For a more

extended account of Salem's reaction to her resignation see the Introduction, pages 26-27.

[49] The celebration, arranged by William C. Nell, commemorated the Boston Massacre of March 5, 1770, in which an American Negro, Crispus Attucks, was killed by British troops. The program in Faneuil Hall included speeches by Wendell Phillips, William Lloyd Garrison, Theodore Parker, Charles Lenox Remond, and Dr. John S. Rock, of Boston, a Negro. Interspersed among the addresses were several songs rendered by the Northern Vocalists: "Freedom's Battle," "Colored American Heroes of 1776," and a parody on "Red, White and Blue," "written for the occasion by Miss Charlotte L. Forten." The parody was rendered "in fine style." *The Liberator,* February 26, 1856.

[50] Edward G. E. Lytton Bulwer-Lytton, *Richelieu: or, the Conspiracy. A Play in Five Acts* (New York, 1857).

[51] Hattie and Robert were Harriet and Robert Purvis, Jr., the children of Robert Purvis, and Miss Forten's cousins.

[52] Elizabeth Church, Miss Forten's classmate at the Salem Normal School, was later an assistant in the Higginson Grammar School of Salem. *Annual Report of the School Committee of the City of Salem, February, 1858* (Salem, 1858), 47.

[53] Mrs. Robert Purvis.

[54] Lydia Maria Child and John Greenleaf Whittier. Whittier's poem "To the Daughters of James Forten" was many years later published in *The Independent,* LXI (November 15, 1906), 1139, by Miss Forten. See above, Introduction, page 13.

[55] Lydia Maria Child, *Letters from New-York* (New York, 1843).

[56] Hinton R. Helper, *The Impending Crisis of the South* (New York, 1857), was one of the most widely circulated antislavery books of the period.

[57] After January, 1858, Charles Sumner, who was too ill to serve in the Senate, spent most of his time in Philadelphia and Boston. Pierce, *Memoir and Letters of Charles Sumner,* III, 559-561.

[58] Lucretia Coffin Mott had gained the public eye in 1840, when she was refused admission to the World Anti-Slavery Convention in London because of her sex. Determined to right such wrongs, she launched the campaign that led to the famous Seneca Falls convention in 1848. Despite her interest in women's rights, abolitionism remained Mrs. Mott's first love. She attended the Philadelphia convention in 1833 that formed the American Anti-Slavery Society, helped organize the Philadelphia Female Anti-Slavery Society, and served as president of the latter during most of its existence. After 1850 she also aided many escaping slaves. *Dictionary of American Biography,* XIII, 288-290; Lloyd C. M. Hare, *The Greatest American Woman, Lucretia Mott* (New York, 1937).

[59] Possibly Miss Forten refers to Joseph Arthur, Comte de

Gobineau, whose four-volume work, *The Inequality of Human Races*, was published in Paris between 1853 and 1855.

⁶⁰ Israel Putnam, the husband of Caroline E. Putnam, and William C. Nell, the Negro abolitionist from Boston.

⁶¹ Lucy Larcom, poet and teacher, was a close friend of Whittier; when not teaching at the Wheaton Seminary she spent much of her time at the poet's home. She was well known at this time as the author of "The Call to Kansas," a prize-winning poem circulated by the New England Emigrant Aid Company. *Dictionary of American Biography*, X, 614.

⁶² The essay, "Glimpses of New England," was largely a description of Salem and the surrounding countryside. It was printed in the *National Anti-Slavery Standard*, June 19, 1858.

⁶³ "The day," according to *The Liberator*, August 2, 1858, "was most delightful. Nature seemed to have put on her holiday robe of beauty in honor of the auspicious event, and welcomed the friends of universal freedom with her most radiant smiles."

⁶⁴ The first message over the newly completed submarine cable between England and the United States was sent on August 16—a note of congratulations from Queen Victoria to President James Buchanan. *The Liberator*, August 20, 1858.

⁶⁵ Lucretia Mott's husband was James Mott, chairman of the executive committee of the Pennsylvania Anti-Slavery Society. *National Anti-Slavery Standard*, September 25, 1859.

⁶⁶ Howard W. Gilbert was active in the Pennsylvania Anti-Slavery Society, serving in 1855 as a member of the executive committee. *Annual Report of the American Anti-Slavery Society for 1855*, 151.

⁶⁷ *Picciola*, by X. B. Saintine, was published in numerous French editions before the first American edition was printed in New York, in 1865.

⁶⁸ Mary Grew was, with Lucretia Mott, the guiding spirit behind the Philadelphia Female Anti-Slavery Society. Serving for many years as secretary of the organization, she also found time to help J. M. McKim edit the *Pennsylvania Freeman* and to speak frequently in behalf of abolition and women's rights. Powell, *Personal Reminiscences*, 142-144.

⁶⁹ The Pennsylvania Anti-Slavery Society held its twenty-second annual meeting at West Chester, Pennsylvania, on October 6, 7, and 8, 1858. William Lloyd Garrison, Henry Grew, Mary Grew, and Lucretia Mott were among the speakers. James Mott was chosen president and Robert Purvis vice president. *National Anti-Slavery Standard*, October 16, 1858.

⁷⁰ George W. Curtis spoke on "Fair Play for Women" in a course of lectures in the Music Fund Hall, Philadelphia. *National Anti-Slavery Standard*, November 27, 1858.

⁷¹ The poem "Avis," by Oliver Wendell Holmes, was reprinted in the *National Anti-Slavery Standard*, November 27, 1858.

[72] The Pennsylvania Anti-Slavery Fair was held in Philadelphia during the Christmas season. Margaretta Forten and Harriet D. Purvis, Miss Forten's aunts, were among those on the arrangements committee. *National Anti-Slavery Standard,* October 23, 1858.

[73] The poem was published in the *National Anti-Slavery Standard,* January 15, 1859.

[74] The annual meeting of the Philadelphia Female Anti-Slavery Society was held in Philadelphia on Thursday, February 10, 1858. Mary Grew, as secretary, gave the principal report. *National Anti-Slavery Standard,* February 5, 1859.

[75] *The Liberator,* February 4, 1859, carried a full report of the Boston meeting of the Massachusetts Anti-Slavery Society held on January 27, 1859. Speeches by Parker Pillsbury, E. H. Heywood, Wendell Phillips, and William Lloyd Garrison were published.

[76] Instead of the usual bazaar, the female abolitionists of Massachusetts staged a National Anti-Slavery Subscription Anniversary at the Music Hall, Boston, on January 26, 1859. Between speeches and entertainment an opportunity was given guests to pledge financial support to the cause. Under the skilled direction of Maria W. Chapman more than $6000 was collected. *The Liberator,* February 4 and February 18, 1859.

[77] Miss Forten fails to mention another poem written at this time and published in the *National Anti-Slavery Standard,* April 2, 1859. It was entitled, "The Wind Among the Poplars."

[78] The alleged slave, Daniel Webster (or Dangerfield, as Miss Forten calls him) was arrested at Harrisburg on Saturday, April 2, charged with being a fugitive from Athensville, Virginia. Despite the willingness of numerous witnesses to swear that he had been employed in Harrisburg for nine years, he and his family were immediately sent to Philadelphia. Abolitionists there, having been informed of his coming, were ready with counsel when he arrived. When Webster was brought before United States Commissioner Cooke Longstreth that afternoon, attorneys were on hand to plead for a delay. This was granted until Monday, April 4. *The Liberator,* April 8, 1859; *National Anti-Slavery Standard,* April 9, 1859; *Annual Report of the American Anti-Slavery Society, by the Executive Committee, for the Year Ending May 1, 1859* (New York, 1860), 87-88.

[79] The trial of Daniel Webster was one of the most dramatic in Philadelphia's history. Long before the court was opened on the morning of April 4, great crowds jammed the building. Others, massed in the street, appeared so hostile that the United States Marshal felt called upon to warn the people that any attempted rescue would lead to bloodshed. When the trial began, the court was crowded with abolitionists. That day witnesses testified in behalf of the alleged owner; on April 5 so many witnesses were willing to swear that Webster had been

employed in Harrisburg for many years that the court stayed in session all that night. During this entire time Lucretia Mott and thirty other women sat constantly at Webster's side, watching every move with grim intensity. At six in the morning on April 6, with all testimony taken, the judge adjourned the session until six that evening, when the decision would be announced. At noon that day a revivalistic prayer meeting on the streets of Philadelphia offered prayers for Webster's release. Either this public sentiment or the nature of the testimony led to the unexpected verdict of acquittal from the Commissioner. The decision was celebrated throughout Philadelphia, and Daniel Webster was escorted triumphantly through the streets in a great procession. *Annual Report of the American Anti-Slavery Society . . . for . . . 1859,* 88-90; *National Anti-Slavery Standard,* April 16, 1859; *The Liberator,* April 15, 1859.

[80] The meeting was described in the *National Anti-Slavery Standard,* April 23, 1859. The editor insisted that the mob was kept from attacking by the veteran abolitionists who kept their seats, "ready to weary out their enemies, as they had often done before, by enduring patience."

[81] The Reverend William Henry Furness, pastor of a Unitarian church in Philadelphia, and an abolitionist since 1824. Of him the *National Anti-Slavery Standard* wrote on May 8, 1859: "Dr. Furness stands so near us and is so closely identified with our movement that any thing in commendation of him would seem like self-praise."

[82] Mary Shepard was principal of the Higginson Grammar School, in Salem.

[83] Charles F. Hovey, a wealthy merchant and zealous reformer, died in Boston on April 28, 1859, at the age of fifty-two. The bulk of his estate was left to the causes for which he had labored: abolitionism, women's rights, nonresistance, free trade, and temperance. *The Liberator,* May 6, 1859; *National Anti-Slavery Standard,* May 7, 1859.

[84] Miss Forten had returned to Salem, where she spent the remainder of 1859 as an assistant in the Higginson Grammar School, living, as usual, in the home of Mrs. Caroline Putnam. She kept no diary during this period.

PART 5

FROM SALEM TO ST. HELENA ISLAND:
June 22, 1862–November 29, 1862

[1] Diana M. Muloch, *Life for a Life* (New York, 1861).

[2] Miss Forten served as assistant in the Higginson Grammar School, where Mary L. Shepard was principal.

[3] Dr. Seth Rogers operated the Worcester Hydropathic Insti-

tution, in Worcester, Massachusetts, having returned from several months of observation of the water cure in Europe. His establishment was apparently favored by the abolitionists; one of them characterized him as "a very true man on the reforms." Sallie Holley, *A Life for Liberty: Anti-Slavery and Other Letters of Sallie Holley* (New York, 1899), 85; *The Liberator*, July 15, 1859.

[4] Margaretta Forten, Miss Forten's aunt, conducted a school in Philadelphia.

[5] Robert Purvis, Jr., cousin of Miss Forten and son of Robert Purvis, died on March 19, at the age of twenty-eight. A successful merchant and vigorous abolitionist, he had been ill for some time. At his funeral, remarks "appropriate to the occasion, and at considerable length" were made by Lucretia Mott, J. M. McKim, and other antislavery leaders. *The Liberator*, April 4 and April 11, 1862.

[6] Mrs. William Ives, perennial president of the Salem Female Anti-Slavery Society.

[7] The annual Fourth of July meeting of the Massachusetts Anti-Slavery Society at Framingham Grove was addressed by John S. Rock, William Wells Brown, the Reverend Daniel Foster, Andrew T. Foss, Susan B. Anthony, and E. H. Heywood. William Lloyd Garrison presided. *The Liberator*, July 18, 1862.

[8] Ezra H. Heywood, a graduate of Brown University, had abandoned the ministry to devote himself to abolitionism and women's rights. He served as agent of the Massachusetts Anti-Slavery Society until after the Civil War, then threw himself into the crusade for economic and social reform. *Dictionary of American Biography*, VIII, 609-610.

[9] Susan B. Anthony, the prominent crusader for abolition and women's rights.

[10] The library of the Boston Atheneum.

[11] Wendell Phillips delivered the principal address before the twenty-eighth meeting of the Congregational Society of Massachusetts, on July 6, 1862. *The Liberator*, July 11, 1862.

[12] Lucy Larcom, the writer and poet, was teaching at the Wheaton Seminary, in Norton, Massachusetts. She was an intimate friend of John Greenleaf Whittier and a frequent visitor at his home. *Dictionary of American Biography*, X, 614.

[13] This was the first in the chain of events that eventually took Miss Forten to Port Royal, South Carolina. The area had recently been occupied by Union troops, who freed several thousand slaves. All over the Northeast, abolitionists were forming committees to provide the freedmen with material goods and educational opportunities. The Boston Port Royal Educational Commission had been organized on February 7, 1862, to "undertake the care and education of the Negroes now in the custody and protection of the United States." *The Liberator*, March 7, 1862.

[14] Samuel Gridley Howe, early champion of Greek independence and for forty-four years director of the Perkins Institution for the Blind, was an influential intermediary between abolitionists and more conservative members of the Port Royal Commission. He had for some time been interested in abolitionism, serving during the 1840's as editor of an antislavery newspaper and in the 1850's as chairman of the Boston Vigilance Committee to prevent the return of runaway slaves. *Dictionary of American Biography*, IX, 296-297.

[15] William E. Peck, who had visited Port Royal in the spring of 1862 as an agent of the New York Freedman's Relief Commission and the Educational Commission of Boston. *The Liberator*, March 7, 1862.

[16] John Weiss, whose article on "The Horrors of San Domingo" was published in the *Atlantic Monthly*, IX (June, 1862), and later numbers.

[17] Mount Auburn Cemetery, in Cambridge, Massachusetts.

[18] James Miller McKim, the Philadelphia abolitionist, organized the Philadelphia Port Royal Relief Association in 1862. *Dictionary of American Biography*, XII, 103.

[19] Henry Forten, Miss Forten's brother, lived in New York.

[20] John A. Hunn and his daughter Lizzie were going to St. Helena Island to open a store where Negroes could purchase goods at reasonable prices. *Pennsylvania Freedmen's Relief Association, Report* (Philadelphia, 1864), 1.

[21] For an account of the naval operations about Port Royal at this time see the Introduction, pages 27-29.

[22] All newcomers at Port Royal were required to take the following pledge: "I do solemnly swear that I will support, protect, and defend the Constitution and Government of the United States against all enemies, whether domestic or foreign; that I will bear true and faithful allegiance, resolution or law of any State convention to the contrary notwithstanding. And further, that I do this with a full determination and pledge to perform it without any mental reservation whatever; and further that I will faithfully perform all the duties which may be required of me by law. So help me God." Elizabeth H. Botume, *First Days Among the Contrabands* (Boston, 1893), 30.

[23] Brigadier General Rufus Saxton, who in June, 1862, had been placed in charge of all plantations in the Department of the South, with power to "take such measures, make such rules and regulations for the cultivation of the land and protection, employment, and government of the inhabitants as circumstances might seem to require." *The Union Army, a compilation of the Official Records of the Union and Confederate Armies* (Washington, 1889-1901), Ser. 3, II, 292; hereafter cited as *Official Records*.

[24] The Reverend Mansfield French came to Beaufort from New York in January, 1862, on a government-approved mis-

sion to study the needs of the people of the Sea Islands. In March he became an agent of the New York Freedman's Relief Commission, and was later made chaplain in the Union Army, Department of the South. E. L. Price, "Second Report," in Frank Moore, ed., *The Rebellion Record: A Diary of American Events with Documents, Narratives, Illustrative Incidents, Poetry* (New York, 1861-1868), Supp. I, 314; Mrs. A. M. French, *Slavery in South Carolina and the Ex-Slaves, or, The Port Royal Mission* (New York, 1862), 25; *Official Records,* Ser. 1, XIV, 189.

[25] Reuben Tomlinson, an official of the Pennsylvania branch of the American Freedmen's Union Commission, was one of the first agents sent south by the Port Royal Relief Association of Philadelphia. Henry L. Swint, *The Northern Teacher in the South, 1862-1870* (Nashville, Tenn., 1941), 90.

[26] Mrs. Frances D. Gage, an ardent abolitionist, had written and lectured against slavery in Ohio and Missouri. She had recently come to Port Royal, without appointment or salary, to do whatever good she could among the Negroes. Mrs. Gage remained at Port Royal until 1863, when she returned to the North to lecture widely on her experiences. L. P. Brockett and Mary C. Vaughn, *Woman's Work in the Civil War: A Record of Heroism, Patriotism and Patience* (Boston, 1867), 683-690.

[27] Laura M. Towne, of Philadelphia, a teacher and physician. The school that she founded is still in existence as the Penn Normal, Industrial and Agricultural School on St. Helena Island. Swint, *Northern Teacher,* 44-45.

[28] Richard Soule, of Boston, General Superintendent of St. Helena and Ladies Island. Elizabeth W. Pearson, ed., *Letters from Port Royal Written at the Time of the Civil War* (Boston, 1906), 223.

[29] A former plantation. For its location see the map on page 143.

[30] Miss Ellen Murray, of Milton, Massachusetts, joined Miss Towne shortly after the latter arrived at St. Helena. Swint, *Northern Teacher,* 191; Guion G. Johnson, *A Social History of the Sea Islands with Special Reference to St. Helena Island, South Carolina* (Chapel Hill, N. C., 1930), 181.

[31] "Brick Church" is still used by a Negro Baptist congregation. Johnson, *Social History of the Sea Islands,* 117-118.

[32] Mr. Phillips is mentioned in Pearson, ed., *Letters from Port Royal,* 103, 115, 244, 269.

[33] John Hunn received his merchandise through the Pennsylvania Freedmen's Relief Association, the society which sponsored his store. Swint, *Northern Teacher,* 18. He probably sold clothing, pots, kettles, pans, brushes, and other household goods. These were the items in demand among the Negroes when J. M. McKim, organizer of the Philadelphia Port Royal Relief Association, visited Port Royal in June, 1862. J. Miller

McKim, *The Freedmen of South Carolina* (Philadelphia, 1862), 4.

[34] The Negro quarters resembled a camp, spreading out for a quarter of a mile back of the master's or overseer's house. Johnson, *Social History of the Sea Islands*, 89.

[35] Samuel D. Phillips, a medical student and a graduate of Harvard, who had returned north for a vacation. Edward L. Pierce, "The Freedmen at Port Royal," *Atlantic Monthly*, XII (September, 1863), 300.

[36] Miss Forten's close friend in Salem.

[37] T. Edwin Ruggles, a Yale graduate from Milton, Massachusetts, was a superintendent. Johnson, *Social History of the Sea Islands*, 167n.

[38] Miss Amanda S. Ruggles, a sister of T. Edwin Ruggles, was a teacher. Swint, *Northern Teacher*, 194.

[39] Samuel D. Phillips, a medical student, had been on vacation from his teaching duties.

[40] The proclamation set aside Thursday, November 27, as a day of public thanksgiving and praise for the blessings of the past year and "for the signal success which has attended the great experiment for freedom and the rights of oppressed humanity inaugurated in the Department of the South." It continued: "You, freemen and women, have never before had such cause for thankfulness. Your simple faith has been vindicated. 'The Lord has come' to you, and has answered your prayers. Your chains are broken. Your days of bondage and mourning are ended, and you are forever free. If you cannot yet see your way clear in the future, fear not; put your trust in the Lord, and He will vouchsafe, as He did to the Israelites of old, the cloud by day and the pillar of fire by night, to guide your footsteps 'through the wilderness,' to the promised land." *The Liberator*, December 26, 1862.

[41] Miss Chloe Merrick, a teacher at Fernandina, Florida. Swint, *Northern Teacher*, 191.

[42] Thomas Wentworth Higginson, prominent Massachusetts abolitionist who had been a captain in the Fifty-First Massachusetts Volunteers, had just been selected by General Saxton to recruit a regiment of Negro troops, the First South Carolina Volunteers, from among the freed slaves. He was given the rank of colonel. Thomas Wentworth Higginson, *Army Life in a Black Regiment* (Boston, 1900), 2. For an account of the regiment, see above, Introduction, pages 33-34.

[43] Higginson's own account of his part in the Anthony Burns case is in Thomas W. Higginson, *Cheerful Yesterdays* (Boston, 1900), 147-162.

[44] Robert Smalls was an intelligent Beaufort slave who had been a pilot on the Confederate steamer *Planter*. When the ship's officer went ashore at Charleston on the night of May 14, 1862, Smalls raised the Confederate flag and brought the

vessel out of the Charleston harbor with about forty-five slaves on board. Once at sea he hauled down the flag, raised the Union emblem, and sailed safely to Beaufort, where he surrendered the ship to Union officials. *The Union Army* (Madison, Wis., 1908), VII, 114.

[45] Twice in November, 1862, the Negro troops won victories along the coast. On November 3 and again on November 13, companies of the First South Carolina Volunteers were sent on expeditions up the rivers and lagoons between St. Simon's Island, Georgia, and Fernandina, Florida. In each case the objects were to test the Negroes' fighting ability, to destroy enemy salt works, to capture slaves, and to wipe out picket stations. Leaders reported that the men fought well, and both expeditions returned with quantities of captured stores. *Official Records*, Ser. 1, XVI, 189-194.

[46] *The Liberator*, December 19, 1862, published an "Interesting Letter from Miss Charlotte L. Forten," which consisted largely of a description of the Thanksgiving Day celebration.

[47] The daughter of Caroline Putnam, of Salem, with whom Miss Forten lived while teaching school.

[48] A poem in nine books written by Elizabeth Barrett Browning in 1856.

PART 6

LIFE AMONG THE FREEDMEN:
November 30, 1862–February 14, 1863

[1] David F. Thorpe was a Brown University student from Providence, Rhode Island. Guion G. Johnson, *A Social History of the Sea Islands with Special Reference to St. Helena Island, South Carolina* (Chapel Hill, N. C., 1930), 167n.

[2] L. D. Phillips was superintendent of Dr. Pope's plantation, The Oaks. *The Union Army, a compilation of the Official Records of the Union and Confederate Armies* (Washington, 1889-1901), Ser. 3, II, 11; hereafter cited as *Official Records*.

[3] Caroline E. Putnam, of Salem.

[4] Wendell Phillips.

[5] Lucy McKim, daughter of J. Miller McKim, visited Port Royal with her father during the summer of 1862, after he had organized the Port Royal Relief Association in Philadelphia. J. Miller McKim, *The Freedmen of South Carolina* (Philadelphia, 1862), 4.

[6] Miss Forten suggested the name of John C. Frémont, Republican candidate for President in 1856, who was commander of the Department of the West had in 1861 attempted to free all slaves in Missouri. He was adored by abolitionists.

[7] Samuel D. Phillips, the young medical student who had just returned to St. Helena after a Northern vacation. Edward

L. Pierce, "The Freedmen at Port Royal," *Atlantic Monthly,* XII (September, 1863), 229.

[8] J. Miller McKim, Pennsylvania abolitionist and organizer of the Port Royal Relief Association of P^hiladelphia.

[9] Harriet Ware, a missionary from Massachusetts, first came to St. Helena in April, 1862. She had just returned from a vacation in the North. Johnson, *Social History of the Sea Islands,* 109.

[10] Anne Forten, a sister of Miss Forten's father.

[11] James H. Palmer, a superintendent and teacher from Southampton, New Hampshire. Johnson, *Social History of the Sea Islands,* 167n.

[12] The Eighth Main Volunteers had been a part of the expeditionary force of General Thomas W. Sherman that occupied Port Royal on November 7, 1861. On May 1, 1862, the regiment was moved to Tybee Island, on the Savannah River, where it played a prominent role in the capture of Fort Pulaski, one of the defenses of Savannah. From that time on the men did guard duty at Port Royal and Jacksonville, Florida. *The Union Army* (Madison, Wis., 1908), I, 44.

[13] J. S. Severance, a superintendent from Concord, New Hampshire. *Extracts from Letters of Teachers and Superintendents of the New England Educational Commission for Freedom* (Boston, 1864), 10.

[14] Miss Forten's cousin, the daughter of Robert Purvis, of Byberry, Pennsylvania.

[15] Miss Forten had written John Greenleaf Whittier, asking for one of his poems. He replied by sending her the hymn referred to in the *Journal.* His friendly letter is printed in Samuel T. Pickard, *Life and Letters of John Greenleaf Whittier* (Boston, 1894), II, 472-473. Excerpts from the letter are also quoted in an article written some years later by Charlotte Forten Grimké, "Personal Recollections of Whittier," *New England Magazine,* VIII (June, 1893), 472.

[16] A search of the files of the *Boston Daily Transcript* fails to reveal the letter to which Miss Forten refers.

[17] Lieutenant Colonel Liberty Billings. *Official Records,* Ser. 1, XIV, 239.

[18] Sarah Putnam, of Salem.

[19] Dr. Seth Rogers, of Worcester, Massachusetts, whose water-cure establishment Miss Forten had visited some years before. Thomas Wentworth Higginson, *Army Life in a Black Regiment* (Boston, 1900), 390.

[20] Edward W. Hooper, a Bostonian and a graduate of Harvard, came to Port Royal with the first group of teachers and superintendents under Edward L. Pierce, in March, 1862. Durton's staff. Johnson, *Social History of the Sea Islands,* 167n.; Elizabeth W. Pearson, ed., *Letters from Port Royal Written at the Time of the Civil War* (Boston, 1906), 93n.

[21] Mr. and Mrs. George M. Wells, of Providence, Rhode Island. Wells was a superintendent and teacher. Johnson, *Social History of the Sea Islands,* 167*n.;* Pearson, ed., *Letters from Port Royal,* 270.

[22] The Emancipation Proclamation became effective on January 1, 1863.

[23] The Reverend Solomon Peck, of Roxbury, Massachusetts, came to St. Helena as a missionary and established the first school after the Union occupation. Frank Moore, ed., *The Rebellion Record: A Diary of American Events with Documents, Narratives, Illustrative Incidents, Poetry* (New York, 1861-1868), Supp. I, 314.

[24] James H. Fowler. Higginson, *Army Life in a Black Regiment,* 390.

[25] John C. Zachos, of Cincinnati, Ohio, was a teacher and superintendent sent to Port Royal by the New England Educational Commission. *Extracts from Letters of Teachers and Superintendents,* 15.

[26] Dr. William Henry Brisbane, a South Carolinian who had freed his slaves several years before the war. Pearson, ed., *Letters from Port Royal,* 129.

[27] The Reverend Mansfield French, who came south in January, 1862, later served as agent of the New York Freedmen's Relief Association. At this time he was chaplain in the Union Army, Department of the South. *Official Records,* Ser. 1, XIV, 189.

[28] Negro members of the First South Carolina Volunteers. Rivers was an intelligent young man who had spent much time in the North. Colonel Higginson described Sutton as "the wisest man in the ranks." Higginson, *Army Life in a Black Regiment,* 62.

[29] General superintendent of Port Royal Island and master of ceremonies at the celebration. Pearson, ed., *Letters from Port Royal,* 129, 132.

[30] Major General John C. Frémont never regained the official favor he lost when, as commander of the Department of the West, in 1861, he freed the Missouri slaves. President Abraham Lincoln annulled his proclamation, which was widely acclaimed by abolitionists. After many conflicts with his fellow officers, Frémont resigned from the army in 1862 and went to New York, where he awaited an assignment to a new command that never came. *The Union Army,* VIII, 91-92.

[31] First Lieutenant G. W. Dewhurst, adjunct of the First South Carolina Volunteers. Higginson, *Army Life in a Black Regiment,* 391.

[32] Captain James S. Rogers, of the First South Carolina Volunteers. Higginson, *Army Life in a Black Regiment,* 391.

[33] Charles P. Ware, a graduate of Harvard, was a superintendent. Johnson, *Social History of the Sea Islands,* 78.

[34] The Reverend William W. Hall, of Providence, Rhode

Island, a superintendent. *Extracts from Letters of Teachers and Superintendents,* 15.

[35] Dr. J. Milton Hawks and Esther H. Hawks, of Manchester, New Hampshire. Dr. Hawks was an assistant surgeon in the First South Carolina Volunteers; Mrs. Hawks was also a physician and was a militant advocate of women's rights. She later taught in freedmen's schools in South Carolina and Florida. Higginson, *Army Life in a Black Regiment,* 390; Henry L. Swint, *The Northern Teacher in the South, 1862-1870* (Nashville, Tenn., 1941), 186.

[36] Miss Forten wrote two letters to *The Liberator.* The first, although not mentioned in the *Journal,* was written on November 20, 1862. Describing her trip to Port Royal, her home at Oaklands, and the school in which she taught, it was published on December 12, 1862. The second letter, describing the Thanksgiving celebration of 1862, was printed in *The Liberator,* December 19, 1862.

[37] Two other descriptions of the New Year's Day celebration have been preserved. Both agree almost exactly with Miss Forten's account. One, by Harriet Ware, is in Pearson, ed., *Letters from Port Royal,* 128-134; the other was written by Colonel Thomas Wentworth Higginson, and is in his *Army Life in a Black Regiment,* 55-56.

[38] Brigadier General Truman Seymour was commanding officer of the troops stationed on Port Royal Island. *Official Records,* Ser. 1, XIV, 389.

[39] Mrs. Hannah Hunn, the wife of John A. Hunn, the storekeeper. Mrs. Hunn was a teacher. Swint, *Northern Teacher,* 187.

[40] Mrs. Chew was a Philadelphia friend; Mr. P. B. Hunt was vice president of the Pennsylvania Freedmen's Relief Association. *Pennsylvania Freedmen's Relief Association, Report* (Philadelphia, 1864), 4.

[41] Margaretta Forten was Miss Forten's aunt, Hattie Purvis her cousin.

[42] The Oaks was one of the plantations of Dr. Pope, a South Carolina planter. It was completed just before the outbreak of the war. Johnson, *Social History of the Sea Islands,* 109.

[43] The letter is mentioned in Pickard, *Life and Letters of Whittier,* II, 473.

[44] The article, "My Hunt After 'The Captain,' " was published in the *Atlantic Monthly,* X (December, 1862), 738-764. Miss Forten's friend, Charlie, is referred to only by his first name.

[45] Mrs. E. Clarke, a teacher from Boston. *New England Freedmen's Aid Society Annual Report* (Boston, 1864), 80.

[46] Jules S. De la Croix, a superintendent from Newburyport, Massachusetts. *Extracts from Letters of Teachers and Superintendents,* 15.

[47] On January 23, 1863, the First South Carolina Volunteers

were sent up the St. Mary's River to capture Confederate supplies and cripple a vessel reputedly about to run the blockade. Although repeatedly under enemy fire, the men fought bravely. The mission was a complete success, for they not only reported the vessel to be worthless, but returned with 40,000 bricks, 250 bars of railroad iron, quantities of lumber, a number of prisoners, and several Negro families. Colonel Higginson, who was in command, attributed much of the expedition's success to Corporal Robert Sutton, who had lived as a slave on the St. Mary's River and was thoroughly familiar with the region. Higginson, *Army Life in a Black Regiment,* 84-131; *Official Records,* Ser. 1, XIV, 195-198.

48 Major General David Hunter resumed command of the Department of the South on January 20, 1863, after a four-month leave of absence. *Official Records,* Ser. 1, XIV, 376, 380, 391-392.

49 Susan Warner, *Say and Seal* (Philadelphia, 1860), 2 vols.

50 Harriet Tubman had lived in Maryland as a slave. After escaping to the North before the Civil War, she frequently returned to Southern territory, helping about three hundred slaves to escape. When she heard of the capture of Port Royal by the Union forces, she visited Beaufort to work among the freed slaves. She often helped the Union cause by serving as a spy, nurse, and guerrilla fighter. *Boston Weekly Commonwealth,* July 17, 1863.

51 The only sister of Miss Forten's late mother.

52 Reuben Tomlinson, of Philadelphia, was one of the first agents sent south by the Port Royal Relief Association of Philadelphia. Swint, *Northern Teacher,* 90.

53 The report is in the *Official Records,* Ser. 1, XIV, 195-198.

54 The visit is described in Higginson, *Army Life in a Black Regiment,* 117.

55 Colonel Higginson, in his account of the expedition, quotes from Dr. Rogers' notes on the bravery of the wounded men. Higginson, *Army Life in a Black Regiment,* 104-105.

56 Ralph Waldo Emerson's hymn, "Boston Hymn," was read at the Jubilee Music Concert in Music Hall, Boston, on New Year's Day. It was printed in *The Liberator,* January 30, 1863.

57 A plantation on the east shore of St. Helena Island.

PART 7

END OF A MISSION: February 15, 1863–May 15, 1864

1 These acts of violence were committed by Union troops left free to wander about after landing on the island. Within a few days the soldiers were restricted to their camps and order re-

stored. Elizabeth W. Pearson, ed., *Letters from Port Royal Written at the Time of the Civil War* (Boston, 1906), 155.

[2] Mrs. Crosby and Mrs. Chew were friends of Miss Forten in Philadelphia; P. B. Hunt was vice president of the Pennsylvania Freedmen's Relief Association; Mary Shepard was a former teacher and friend in Salem.

[3] Henry Ward Beecher, *Eyes and Ears* (Boston, 1862).

[4] D. A. Wasson, "The Law of Costs," *Atlantic Monthly*, XI, (February, 1863), 241-251. The same number contained James Russell Lowell's "Latest Views of Mr. Bigelow," 260-265.

[5] First Lieutenant G. W. Dewhurst, adjutant in the First South Carolina Volunteers.

[6] Of the First South Carolina Volunteers.

[7] The expedition up the St. Mary's River, in which Corporal Sutton played a heroic role.

[8] After being attacked while leaving the town, Colonel Higginson and his men burned about half of St. Mary's. T¹ ere was, however, no indiscriminate pillaging or plundering. Thomas Wentworth Higginson, *Army Life in a Black Regiment* (Boston, 1900), 105, 110.

[9] P. B. Hunt, vice president of the Pennsylvania Freedmen's Relief Association.

[10] William Wells Brown, *The Black Man* (New York, 1863), contained a flattering biographical sketch of Miss Forten.

[11] The Twenty-First Massachusetts was never stationed at Port Royal; at this time it was either at Baltimore or Cincinnati. These men may have been visiting from their station, or Miss Forten may have meant the Twenty-Third or Twenty-Fourth Massachusetts regiments, which were both stationed at Port Royal. *The Union Army* (Madison, Wis., 1908), I, 177, 179-180.

[12] The Ohio abolitionist and lecturer, who was at Port Royal until the autumn of 1863.

[13] On March 5, 1863, Colonel Higginson's First South Carolina Volunteers and part of the newly formed Second South Carolina Volunteers departed on an expedition against Jacksonville, on the St. John's River in Florida. The purposes were to carry news of the Emancipation Proclamation to the Florida slaves, to occupy as much of Florida as possible, and to obtain enlistments from among the freedmen. The Negro troops occupied the city successfully, but were soon ordered to withdraw because General David Hunter needed them for his planned attack on Charleston. *The Union Army, a compilation of the Official Records of the Union and Confederate Armies* (Washington, 1889-1901), Ser. 1, XIV, 226; hereafter cited as *Official Records*. See also Higginson, *Army Life in a Black Regiment*, 132-177.

[14] Mr. Bryant was superintendent of Jenkins' plantation near "Land's End." Pearson, ed., *Letters from Port Royal*, 116.

[15] Dr. Adoniram Judson Wakefield, of Boston, a superintendent and medical attendant on St. Helena. Guion G. Johnson, *A Social History of the Sea Islands with Special Reference to St. Helena Island, South Carolina* (Chapel Hill, N. C., 1930), 167 n.

[16] Mrs. G. W. Dewhurst, wife of the adjutant of the First South Carolina Volunteers.

[17] Mrs. Esther Hawks, wife of J. Milton Hawks, an assistant surgeon with the First South Carolina Volunteers.

[18] First Lieutenant J. M. Bingham, quartermaster of the First South Carolina Volunteers.

[19] Brigadier General Rufus Saxton married Miss Matilda Gordon Thompson, of Philadelphia, on Wednesday, March 11, 1863. The ceremony was performed by the Reverend Mansfield French at the Episcopal Church in Beaufort. *New York Tribune,* March 17, 1863.

[20] The book was Alexander Crummell's *The Future of Africa, being Addresses, Sermons, etc., etc., Delivered in the Republic of Liberia* (New York, 1862). Whittier's letter, which told of the cold New England spring and of "the dreadful east winds" that "sing their harsh discords among the apple blossoms," is printed in Samuel T. Pickard, *Life and Letters of John Greenleaf Whittier* (Boston, 1894), II, 473-474.

[21] Margaretta Forten, of Philadelphia; Elizabeth Church, Miss Forten's former classmate and now a Salem teacher; Hattie Purvis, Miss Forten's cousin; and Henry Forten, her brother.

[22] A plantation on the north end of St. Helena Island.

[23] Frederick A. Eustis, a citizen of Massachusetts, had come south in 1862 to claim the estate of his mother, who had recently died on Ladies Island. The executors of the will, who were Charleston Confederates, informed him they would pay dividends only to devisees residing in rebellious states. Hence Eustis stayed on, applying for a position as superintendent of his mother's plantation on Ladies Island. Edward L. Pierce, finding him to be a man of "humane and liberal views," appointed him to that position. Frank Moore, ed., *The Rebellion Record: A Diary of American Events with Documents, Narratives, Illustrative Incidents, Poetry* (New York, 1861-1868), Supp. I, 312-313.

[24] Edward L. Pierce had been the Union agent who planned and put in operation the system of plantation control and education operating in South Carolina. After setting up the system, he returned to the North, and was only visiting at Port Royal at this time. A. W. Stevens, ed., *Addresses and Papers by Edward L. Pierce* (Boston, 1896), 107.

[25] Pierce described this visit in his article on "The Freedmen at Port Royal," *Atlantic Monthly,* XII (September, 1863), 303.

[26] "Bull Run Russell" was the popular nickname for William

Howard Russell, the correspondent of the *London Times,* whose *My Diary North and South* (Boston, 1863), had just been published.

[27] Brigadier General Rufus Saxton.

[28] The First South Carolina Volunteeis, who had occupied Jacksonville, were returned to Port Royal to strengthen the force being assembled to attack Charleston. *Official Records,* Ser. 1, XIV, 432.

[29] The teachers and superintendents regularly submitted reports to the societies that had sent them to Port Royal. Miss Forten's report was sent to B. P. Hunt, vice president of the Pennsylvania Freedmen's Relief Association. Henry L. Swint, *The Northern Teacher in the South, 1862-1870* (Nashville, Tenn., 1941), 16.

[30] At the beginning of the war, Pierce, who had enlisted as a private in the Third Massachusetts Regiment, was detailed to supervise the work of a detachment of "contrabands," or former slaves, at Port Monroe, in Virginia. Stevens, ed., *Addresses and Papers by Edward L. Pierce,* 67.

[31] A plantation.

[32] There is no record of a Charleston paper edited by Dr. Brisbane in 1833; he did, however, edit the *Southern Baptist and General Intelligencer* from January 3, 1835, to April 15, 1836. William S. Hoole, *A Checklist and Finding List of Charleston Periodicals, 1732-1864* (Durham, 1936), 36.

[33] Pierce tells the story of this conversation with Don Carlos in "The Freedmen at Port Royal," *Atlantic Monthly,* XII (September, 1863), 302.

[34] Denmark Vesey, a free Negro of Charleston, had in 1822 plotted a slave insurrection that would massacre the white people, seize the ships in the harbor, and sail away to the West Indies. One of the Negroes revealed the plan, and Vesey was seized, tried, and, with thirty-four other plotters, hanged. Albert B. Hart, *Slavery and Abolition, 1831-1841* (A. B. Hart, ed., *The American Nation: A History.* New York, 1907), 163.

[35] On April 6, 1863, Colonel Higginson's regiment was assigned to picket duty at Port Royal Ferry, on the western side of the Coosaw River. East of the river was a Confederate picket line. Higginson, *Army Life in a Black Regiment,* 179, 184.

[36] The *Washington,* together with the United States gunboat *Hale,* had been steaming up the Beaufort River toward Port Royal Ferry when the *Hale* ran aground. Seeing that the vessel could not move, the *Washington* stopped to offer assistance, and the two ships anchored opposite the brickyard on North Ladies Island. The *Hale* finally worked itself loose, but the *Washington* remained until daybreak, when she was shelled by the Confederates. Colonel Higginson, on picket duty about five miles from the scene of the shooting, hurried to the spot at once. There he found that the ship had not been aground, but "at anchor, having foolishly lingered until after daybreak."

Higginson, *Army Life in a Black Regiment,* 193-195; *Official Records,* Ser. 1, XIV, 280.

[37] The "Shell Road" was the only thoroughfare by land between Charleston and Beaufort. The road crossed the Coosaw River at the Port Royal Ferry. Just west of the river was the First South Carolina Volunteers' picket line. Higginson, *Army Life in a Black Regiment,* 184.

[38] Charles Follen, a teacher and superintendent from Boston. *New England Freedmen's Aid Society, Annual Report, 1864* (Boston, 1864), 80.

[39] Dr. Thomas D. Minor, an assistant surgeon with the First South Carolina Volunteers. Higginson, *Army Life in a Black Regiment,* 390.

[40] Colonel James Montgomery, commanding officer of the Second South Carolina Volunteers. He had been a member of the Tenth Kansas Infantry, with which he had seen service during an expedition into the Indian Territory. *The Union Army,* IV, 212; Higginson, *Army Life in a Black Regiment,* 401.

[41] On the eastern bank of the Coosaw River.

[42] At Port Royal Ferry.

[43] Second Lieutenant Eli C. Merriam, an officer in the First South Carolina Volunteers. Higginson, *Army Life in a Black Regiment,* 294.

[44] St. Helena.

[45] J. C. Dutch, captain of the bark *Kingfisher,* a vessel of the South Atlantic blockading squadron. David D. Porter, *The Naval History of the Civil War* (New York, 1886), 387, 390.

[46] Reuben Tomlinson had succeeded Richard Soule as General Superintendent of St. Helena and Ladies islands. Pearson, ed., *Letters from Port Royal,* 223n.

[47] St. Helena Village, on the eastern coast of St. Helena Island.

[48] Certain foods were furnished all inhabitants by the War Department. Pearson, ed., *Letters from Port Royal,* 10.

[49] Arthur Sumner, a teacher and superintendent from Cambridge, Massachusetts. Swint, *Northern Teacher,* 197.

[50] Acting Ensign S. W. Rhodes. Porter, *Naval History,* 390.

[51] Edisto Island had been occupied by Union troops from February to July, 1862. In July the soldiers were removed to join the attack on Fort Monroe, Virginia, and the Negroes on the island were sent to Hilton Head. Since that time Edisto Island had remained in Confederate hands. *Official Records,* Ser. 1, VI, 89, 123; Ser. 1, XIV, 363-365.

[52] Quincy A. Gilmore, who had been acting Brigadier General during June, 1863, when he temporarily relieved Major General David Hunter as commander of the Department of the South. *The Union Army,* VIII, 100-101.

[53] The Fifty-Fourth Massachusetts Volunteers was the first Negro regiment enlisted in the Northern states east of the Mississippi River. On January 26, 1863, the Secretary of War au-

thorized the governor of Massachusetts to enlist Negro troops and form them into a special corps under white officers. So great was the response from several states that by May the regiment was filled and a second, the Fifty-Fifth Massachusetts Volunteers, was organized. On June 3, 1863, the Fifty-Fourth Massachusetts reported at Hilton Head and proceeded to Beaufort. A few days later the men took part in an expedition on the Georgia coast, returning to their camp on St. Helena on June 25. Luis F. Emilio, *History of the Fifty-Fourth Regiment of Massachusetts Volunteer Infantry* (Boston, 1891), 2, 12, 24, 36, 39-46.

[54] Major Edward N. Hallowell, of Philadelphia.

[55] First Lieutenant James M. Walton, of Philadelphia.

[56] Colonel Robert Gould Shaw, of Staten Island, New York, commanding officer of the Fifty-Fourth Massachusetts Volunteers.

[57] Colonel Shaw's father, Francis G. Shaw, was prominently identified with the abolitionists; his mother possessed "rare and high traits of mind and heart." Emilio, *History of the Fifty-Fourth Regiment,* 5.

[58] Edward L. Pierce had returned to Port Royal as Supervising Agent of the Treasury Department for the Department of the South, to assist in reorganizing Florida on the basis of equal suffrage for Negroes. Actually his mission was never accomplished, for so many troops were needed for the attack on Charleston that none could be spared for the conquest of Florida. Pierce remained in the service of the Treasury Department, attending to the commercial interests of the government in the occupied portions of South Carolina, Georgia, and Florida, until September, 1863. Stevens, ed., *Addresses and Papers of Edward L. Pierce,* 132-133.

[59] The Reverend James Lynch, of Baltimore, who later became chaplain of the Fifty-Fourth Massachusetts Volunteers. Emilio, *History of the Fifty-Fourth Regiment,* 50, 232.

[60] Mrs. Jean M. Lander, a nurse, who had established a hospital for the troops. A beautiful woman and a former actress, her efforts to found hospitals elsewhere had been opposed by the national superintendent of nurses. Hence she came to Beaufort, where a sudden influx of wounded men gave General Rufus Saxton the opportunity to grant her wish. Higginson, *Cheerful Yesterdays,* 264-265.

[61] Pearson, ed., *Letters from Port Royal,* 235.

[62] The poem "Drifting" is in *The Poetical Works of Thomas Buchanan Read* (Philadelphia, 1866), II, 409-413.

[63] The Fourth of July celebration at the Baptist Church in St. Helena.

[64] Acting Brigadier General Quincy A. Gillmore, Commanding General, Department of the South.

[65] The Fifty-Fourth Massachusetts Volunteers went first to Folly Island, then to James Island, where the regiment did

picket duty until July 17. The men were then sent to Morris Island, where they led the attack on Fort Wagner on July 18. Emilio, *History of the Fifty-Fourth Regiment*, 62, 65-66, 68.

[66] For an account of the military operations about Charleston, see above, Introduction, pages 26-27.

[67] At a later date Miss Forten wrote between the lines of her *Journal:* "He has since recovered, I am surprised to hear."

[68] Colonel Shaw was married on May 2, 1863. Emilio, *History of the Fifty-Fourth Regiment*, 5.

[69] Written between the lines of the *Journal* at a later date are the words: "I afterward found this to be a mistake. He only wished me to take charge of the horse until it c'ld be sent North to his wife."

[70] Frederick J. Williams, of Brookline, Massachusetts, a teacher and superintendent. *Extracts from Letters of Teachers and Superintendents of the New England Educational Commission for Freedom* (Boston, 1864), 15.

[71] Edward L. Pierce, Dr. Seth Rogers, Mr. and Mrs. J. J. Harrison, Mr. and Mrs. J. M. Fairfield, and William W. Hall. *New York Tribune*, August 3, 1863.

[72] Robert Gould Shaw.

[73] To the home of Miss Forten's uncle, Robert Purvis.

[74] Colonel Edward N. Hallowell, of the Fifty-Fourth Massachusetts Regiment, who had returned to his Philadelphia home to recover from wounds received during the attack on Fort Wagner. When Colonel Shaw, the commanding officer, was killed at Fort Wagner, Hallowell was promoted to the rank of colonel and placed in charge of the regiment. Emilio, *History of the Fifty Fourth Regiment*, 50, 132, 328.

[75] Francis G. Shaw, the father of Robert Gould Shaw.

[76] Mrs. William Ives, an old friend and active abolitionist.

[77] Mary Shepard, principal of the Higginson Grammar School, and another old friend.

[78] Fanny Kemble, *Journal of a Residence on a Georgia Plantation in 1838 and 1839* (New York, 1863).

[79] James H. Palmer.

[80] Anna B. M. Jameson, *Sacred and Legendary Art*. (Boston, 1864), 2 vols.

[81] Louisa May Alcott, *Hospital Sketches* (Boston, 1863).

[82] Elizabeth Barrett Browning, *Last Poems* (New York, 1862).

[83] The Worcester Hydropathic Institution, on Green Street in Worcester, which had formerly been operated by Dr. Seth Rogers.

[84] The wife of Thomas Wentworth Higginson, whose home was in Worcester.

[85] Dr. Seth Rogers and Colonel Edward N. Hallowell, who were returning to Port Royal after health leaves in the North.

[86] First Lieutenant Francis Lee Higginson, of the Fifty-

Fourth Massachusetts Regiment. Emilio, *History of the Fifty-Fourth Regiment*, 504.

[87] Miss Forten's sadness was caused by the sudden death of her father, Robert Bridges Forten, in April. He had returned from abroad during the war to enlist in the Forty-Third United States Colored Infantry. Elevated to the rank of sergeant major at once, he was ordered to report to the chief mustering and recruiting officer of Maryland, where he made numerous speeches urging Negroes to enlist. After his death from erysipelas his body was taken to Philadelphia, where, for the first time in the nation's history, full military honors were paid to a Negro. *The Liberator*, May 13, 1864.

[88] Martha L. Kellogg, a teacher from Avon, Connecticut. Swint, *Northern Teacher*, 188.

[89] Misses Annie and Jessie Heacock, teachers from Jenkintown, Pennsylvania. *Ibid.*, 186.

[90] Miss Helen M. Ireson, of Lynn, Massachusetts, a teacher at Newbern, North Carolina. *Ibid.*, 188.

[91] Brown succeeded Edward L. Pierce, who left Port Royal in September, 1863. *Official Records*, Ser. 1, XXVIII, Part II, 121, 126.

[92] Brigadier General Rufus Saxton.

Index

Index

285